Broadband Bible

Broadband Bible

Desktop Edition

James E. Gaskin

WILEY

Wiley Publishing, Inc.

Broadband Bible, Desktop Edition

Published by
Wiley Publishing, Inc.
10475 Crosspoint Boulevard
Indianapolis, IN 46256
www.wiley.com

Copyright© 2004 by James Gaskin

Published by Wiley Publishing, Inc., Indianapolis, Indiana

Published simultaneously in Canada

ISBN: 0-7645-6951-1

Manufactured in the United States of America

10 9 8 7 6 5 4 3 2 1

XX/XX/XX/XX/XX

For general information on our other products and services or to obtain technical support, please contact our Customer Care Department within the U.S. at (800) 762-2974, outside the U.S. at (317) 572-3993 or fax (317) 572-4002.

Wiley also publishes its books in a variety of electronic formats. Some content that appears in print may not be available in electronic books.

Library of Congress Cataloging-in-Publication Data

Gaskin, James E.
   Broadband bible / James E. Gaskin.– Desktop ed.
      p.   cm.
   Includes index.
   ISBN 0-7645-6951-1 (paper/website)
   1. Broadband communication systems.   2. Internet service providers.   3. Digital subsriber lines.   4. Modems.   5. Artificial satellites in telecommunication.   I. Title.
   TK5103.4.G37 2004
   621.382–dc22

                                                                                          2004011593

About the Author

In 1985, **James E. Gaskin** decided he'd rather sell computers and networks than try to buy them for his father's company. So he started selling and installing Novell networks to small- and medium-sized businesses in the Dallas area. By 1988, James was on his own as an independent networking consultant to such clients as the Internal Revenue Service, First Gibraltar Bank, and Solomon Associates.

In 1989, James started contributing to *Unix Today!* magazine, and he continues to cover technology for major technology publications (such as *Network World*) today. His first book, *Integrating Unix and NetWare Networks*, was published by Novell Press in 1993, and he has continued writing books, articles, and jokes about technology and real life ever since.

His 14 (now 15) books include a best-selling series of five NetWare books for Sybex, and others on Internet technology, technology business management, and humor. James presented a series of NetWare and Internet technology tutorials for Networld+InterOp from 1994 through 1997. Media appearances include technology expert commentary for KRLD News Radio, Dallas, TX, and WGBH 89.7, National Public Radio, Boston.

An objective voice for the technology consumer, James writes a weekly column called *Small Business Technology* for *Network World*. He also presents topics such as *The Hilarious Pain of Data Security* to groups under the umbrella of GaskinGuides to Technology. Although unaffiliated with any vendor, James is biased toward cost-effective and intelligent technology products for small- and medium-sized businesses.

Credits

Acquisitions Editor
Katie Mohr

Development Editors
Sydney Jones
Jodi Jensen

Production Editor
Felicia Robinson

Technical Editor
Nadeem Muhammed

Copy Editor
Techbooks

Editorial Manager
Mary Beth Wakefield

**Vice President & Executive
Group Publisher**
Richard Swadley

**Vice President and Executive
Publisher**
Bob Ipsen

Vice President and Publisher
Joseph B. Wikert

Executive Editorial Director
Mary Bednarek

Project Coordinator
Ryan Steffen

Permissions Editor
Laura Moss

Media Development Specialist
Kit Malone

Cover Illustration
Anthony Bunyan

Interior Design
Lissa Auciello-Brogan

Layout, Proofreading and Indexing
TECHBOOKS

As always, this and everything else is for Wendy, Alex, and Laura.

Preface

Speed kills boredom on the Web. Broadband makes Web sites that were dull yesterday snap and dance today. Now that every person in the United States and Canada has at least one option for broadband service, there's no reason you can't enjoy a Web more interactive (and intelligent) than any TV show on the market.

Connecting your home or small business to a broadband service provider costs less today than ever. The tools you need are easily available, often as close as a CompUSA or Target or even Radio Shack. Why waste time waiting on the Web? Why not whip through the Web, grab what you want, and get on with your life?

Nothing in this book is beyond a typical home computer user's ability to purchase, install, or enjoy. If you have a computer, you can benefit from broadband service. If you have two computers, you benefit twice as much. If you have an office at home that you might want to connect to your business, everything you need is in here.

Jump in. Explore the Internet in ways you couldn't before. Download videos and music that you never considered in the past because of their file sizes. Finally, turn your computer into something more fun than an automated Solitaire game. Do all this easily, inexpensively, and without needing to cut a hole in your wall for wires or worry about security. Follow the directions in here, and you will connect effortlessly, protect your data in a variety of ways, and stop wondering if your computer was working for you or against you. With broadband access and the information in here, you computer will become your transport to more information and entertainment than ever before.

Who Should Read This Book?

If you have a computer in your home and are curious about broadband, this book will help you. If you have more than one computer at home and need to connect them, this book will save you time, money, and a fair amount of aggravation.

If you have a small office in your home, this book provides the data security information that will protect your most important asset, your information.

If you have a small business, this book will show you the right tools for connecting your computers with network appliances to provide storage, security, and real-time backup support. You will also build a foundation for your business on solid network design principles along with important security considerations that will help today and in the future.

What Hardware and Software Do You Need?

If your computer has a network adapter or can support one of some kind, you can use it for broadband networking. A few utilities demand Windows of some flavor (98 or above and sometimes 2000/XP), but after installation any network-able computer can play on the broadband.

Vendors provide the client software, and the operating systems for client computers have the rest of the necessary software. If you like graphics, audio, or video intensive applications, the faster your computer the better.

How This Book Is Organized

Because at least four different ways to receive broadband service at your home or business are covered in this book, I don't expect you to read it all straight through. You're welcome to, of course, but I certainly understand if you want to head to the chapters discussing the areas that most excite you.

Broadband comes in a variety of flavors, so first I explain all those flavors so you can see which may suit you the best. Then I go into some detail about how to share that broadband Internet access throughout your home or office.

If you're a home user with a computer or two who wants to figure out whether there's a difference between cable and DSL for your needs, you will get most of your information in the first half of the book. If your needs include a small business network, there's some information for you concerning ways to improve your network and increase your data security.

Part I: Determining which broadband is right for you

Part I starts out explaining why broadband access is worth the little bit of money it costs over dialup Internet access. Then you learn about the various kinds of broadband services available. Chapter 2 covers how broadband works in general, and Chapters 3, 4, and 5 cover the mainstream broadband options (cable or DSL from a telephone company), then the alternative broadband providers (wireless and satellite). Chapter 6 lists all the pros and cons for each type so you can answer the questions and learn what you really want for your connection.

Part II: Practicing safe broadband

The Internet is no longer innocent. There was a time when you could leave your metaphorical doors unlocked, but that day is long past.

Chapter 7 explains how bad people get bad things into your computers, and how you can stop them. Chapters 8 and 9 talk about how your broadband service is connected to your home, condo, office, or apartment.

Part III: Moving from stand-alone PCs to a network

Chapter 10 discusses servers and various network devices that help organize your network and protect your data. Chapters 11, 12, and 13 explain desktop networking, then TCP/IP (the protocol of the Internet) and router, then backup and disaster recovery. If you have more than one computer, these chapters will save you time, money, and grief.

Part IV: Linking your network devices

Chapters 14 and 15 jump in the world of connections, as you learn to tie your computers together in new ways. Want wires? Fine. Want no wires? That's fine too.

Chapters 16 and 17 introduce you to the world of wireless security and those who wish to deprive you of same. Keeping your wireless network private takes some planning, but it can be done.

Part V: Troubleshooting

Computers are balky, ornery devices at times. Things will not always go smoothly. But with the information in Chapters 18 and 19, you will learn how to deal with your broadband service provider when they have problems, and how to deal with your own network when the problems are on your side of the cable or DSL modem.

Appendix A

This section includes the collected Quick Hits Web site listings for music, video, games, support, and broadband speed tests. If you wonder if broadband is worth it, go to some of these sites and see if you get bored waiting for your browser screen to update. If so, get broadband.

Appendix B

Full of reference sites, this appendix provides more general technical, support, and security listings than the entertainment-heavy Appendix A. Many of these sites provided in-depth background and information for chapters in the book.

Appendix C

This appendix is the glossary. Acronyms are explained, and network terms from all chapters are defined.

Navigating This Book

Various icons are scattered throughout *Broadband Bible, Desktop Edition* for your assistance. Each chapter begins with an overview of its information and ends with a quick summary.

Icons appear in the text to indicate important or especially helpful items. Here's a list of the icons and their functions:

 Little factoids that illustrate the point under discussion but don't apply directly to understanding the topic.

 Notes offer additional advice or point out details to help you better understand the current topic.

 This icon indicates other chapters in the book where you can find more information on a particular topic.

 Cautions provide critical and often overlooked information that will help you avoid disasters.

 These notes refer you to Web sites that provide updated information or discussions of topics that go beyond the scope of this book.

The Companion Web Site

The official Web site for this book is on the Wiley site at www.wiley.com/ compbooks/gaskin. This site includes official updates, errata, and notice about new book versions. Feel free to check out other Web sites for complementary books to this one—I'm sure the other authors won't mind.

Plenty of how-to projects and information about home and small business networking that didn't fit into this book are at www.GaskinGuides.com. Some deeper digging into broadband topics can be found at www.BroadbandBible.com as well.

Further Information

I have a weekly column called "*Small Business Technology*" for *Network World* magazine that runs on the NWFusion.com Web site at: www.nwfusion.com/net .worker/columnists/gaskin.html

You can also e-mail me at

```
james@GaskinGuides.com
```

I can't promise instantaneous turnaround, but I answer all my mail. I may even send you a joke.

Acknowledgments

Many companies provided equipment for me to use and abuse during the writing of this book. Let me list some of the vendors and people who have been the most helpful and supportive:

- ✦ Linksys is now owned by Cisco but has always been represented by the wonderful Karen Sohl. Karen has been doing marketing and communications and running interference for me over the past several years. Karen is the communications professional I wish all others would emulate.

- ✦ Netgear, ably supported by Ken Hagihara and Lisa Quinn of Integrity Public Relations.

- ✦ Gary Doan and all the other smart and helpful folks at IntraDyn, Inc., the makers of the outstanding RocketVault Data Protection Appliance.

- ✦ Efficient Networks and Derek Fay's PR support.

- ✦ Mirra Personal Server

- ✦ Kanguru Solutions

- ✦ Snap Appliance

- ✦ Tritton Technologies

- ✦ Buffalo Technology

- ✦ SMC

- ✦ IOGear, Inc.

- ✦ ZyXEL Communications Corp.

- ✦ Avocent

- ✦ Microsoft Corp. provided test software operating systems and Microsoft Office.

- ✦ Last, but not least, Laura Lewin of Studio B who put me together with the folks at Wiley and made all this happen.

Contents at a Glance

Contents

● ●

Part I: Determining Which Broadband Is Right for You   1

Part II: Practicing Safe Broadband   137

Chapter 7: Understanding Computer Security 139

Chapter 8: Examining Your Home Broadband Hookup .. 161

Part V: Troubleshooting 469

Chapter 18: Troubleshooting Internet Access Problems 471

Chapter 19: Troubleshooting Your Side of the Connection 505

Determining Which Broadband Is Right for You

This is going to be great fun. I know computers all too often have the opposite effect on people, but not this time. You don't have to be serious at your computer all day, and probably the best way to have more fun with your computer is over a fast broadband connection.

But there is more than one way to get broadband to your computer. You might think you don't have a choice, but you do. Everyone in the continental United States has at least one broadband service provider available. If you live near a city, you may have a half-dozen broadband service provider options.

By the time you read this first part of the book, you'll know your options, and you'll have gone through checklists to help you decide which service provider delivers what you need. Then your new broadband connection will help you stop frowning when you sit down at the computer and start grinning.

Why You Need Broadband Internet Access

CHAPTER

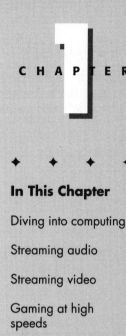

Back when sneakers were shoes kids wore to play in rather than $200 foot-borne status symbols, one company distilled its advantages into the clearest advertising slogan ever. If you wore its shoes, you could "run faster and jump higher." Doesn't that capture the dreams of every kid lacing up sneakers?

Broadband makes your computer run faster and jump higher. Doesn't that capture your desires every time you sit down at the keyboard?

To be honest, broadband Internet access doesn't make the computer sitting on your desk process bits faster or start bouncing around. Computer speed ratings are derived from a set of variables including processor speed, the amount and type of computer memory, and the access ratings of your hard disk.

Broadband does, however, make the Internet and World Wide Web run faster and jump higher for you and your computer. Web pages appear in a snap rather than at a snail's pace. E-mail's with photos or other images drop into your inbox rather than drip forever down your phone line. With broadband, you will finally realize why people get excited about Internet radio.

The world of computing will get so much faster, you may need a seatbelt for your chair. So strap yourself in and hang on tight.

Computing Without Interruption

A friend of mine helped a taskforce at Texas Instruments (TI) in the mid-1980s to study the balance between system response time and user productivity. The taskforce studied mainframe applications, but the idea remains the same. The study results showed that after a half second, the user's concentration broke, and it took mental effort and time to refocus on the task when the system finally presented the updated information on the screen.

If you're the same type of person TI studied nearly 20 years ago, after a half second of waiting for a Web page to update, you probably lose patience and your train of thought. The way everything in life has sped up during the last 20 years, the time now could be less than a half second.

Involved computing sessions demand that screens change as fast as possible. If they take longer than half a second, as far as your train of thought being disrupted they can be 4 seconds or 2 minutes. But life on the computer really runs faster and jumps higher when screens update in a half second or less.

Typical Web Page Download Speeds

An interesting note from broadband provider NTL.com in England shows how long it takes to download a typical Web page (50 Kbps in the example). Here's how they break it down:

✦ **56 Kbps modem:** 7.9 seconds

✦ **128 Kbps broadband:** 3.5 seconds

✦ **600 Kbps broadband:** 0.7 seconds

✦ **1024 Kbps broadband:** 0.4 seconds

Nice dovetail with our TI study conclusions, isn't it? If you get broadband download speeds of at least 1 Mbps, most pages update in less than a half second.

Now you can justify the cost of broadband to your spouse by saying that faster speeds mean fewer breaks in concentration, which means you'll finish on the computer faster than ever before. (Let me know if your spouse falls for that rationalization.)

Support files download in a flash

Nothing interrupts your time on the computer more than a pop-up window demanding you stop what you're doing to download a file, update, virus definition, or browser plug-in. Windows users see these computing roadblocks constantly, but Microsoft can't be blamed for all the interruptions. Here's a quick list of interruption requests on my systems recently:

✦ Windows automatic update files (okay, I can blame Microsoft for this one)

✦ QuickTime browser plug-in update (from Apple for equal time)

✦ Mozilla plug-in update for Macromedia Flash Player

✦ Real Player update

✦ Norton virus definition files

Each interruption demands that you stop and download a file or files. Sometimes, for example with a browser plug-in, it takes just a minute or two. With Microsoft and other operating system files, it can take hours to download a weekly update package. The same can happen if you download an update to your browser or one of your multimedia players.

I get more aggravated by the 3-minute interruption and download than the half-hour ones. When you know it will be 30 minutes, you can start the download and go do something else. You can take advantage of being forced from your seat at the computer by wandering around for a few minutes and grabbing a snack. But when I'm searching for something on the Web and one of those file download boxes appears and makes me slam to a stop, I curse and glare at the monitor until I can escape from the trap and go back to my search.

With broadband, however, the downloads arrive in a fraction of the time that they do with a dial-up connection. What used to be a 3-minute distraction is now a 30-second annoyance.

Of course, when downloads, such as patches for your operating system estimate they will take 30 minutes to download over a dial-up line, the broadband user can laugh. Table 1-1 lists file download times, and you can see that downloading a file that takes 30 minutes to dribble down a dial-up line takes 5 minutes over a broadband connection.

Vendors now like you to download a small (under 1MB) file that triggers an update download of the other 99MBs or whatever. The first time or two I got fooled by this it really steamed me. I downloaded the 1MB file and installed that, only to see the newly installed application begin the real work of downloading for what seemed like 24 hours. With broadband, I get up and start looking for a snack because the download and installation will probably take 15–20 minutes. With dialup, my computer is hosed for the evening and I want to threaten the computer with a baseball bat.

As more companies move toward constant updates for security and operating system patches, these interruptions will increase. Vendors want users to get broadband service because it makes it easier on them and because they can keep stuffing those large updates down the pipe to users.

If you get one of those annoying "download this update now" windows when you have broadband, it's no big deal. It will never be pleasant, but with broadband the aggravation speeds by quickly.

Applications arrive in a blink

Patches and updates arrive on their schedule and not yours, but the applications you find and download also take time. Waiting for a file you want, such as a new spam filter or digital music player, can be as frustrating as waiting for a complete virus definition file.

Unlike patch and upgrade vendors, developers offering files for download want your download experience to be quick and painless. Files are often zipped (compressed) to save time during downloading. You may not even know when you receive a compressed file because it will often have an .exe extension and decompress itself automatically when you install it.

Searching for handy utilities, such as those shown in Figure 1-1, changes from burden to delight when files download quickly. In fact, broadband connections download files so fast that most of the time you don't have to save the file and run it later because you can download and install at the same time.

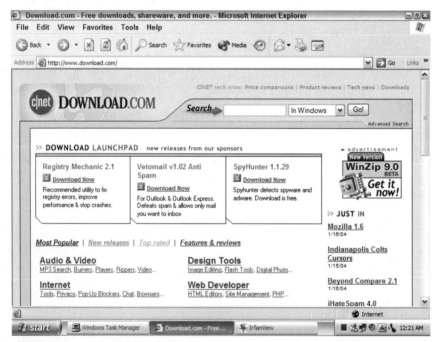

Figure 1-1: DownLoad.com is one source for new applications that you can download quickly over broadband.

Table 1-1 contrasts download times for large files using broadband and dial-up connections.

Table 1-1
Size and Download Times

Size of file	Time for dial-up (minutes)	Time for broadband (minutes)
1MB	2:40	:09
3MB	8:00	:27
5MB	13:30	:45
32MB	85:45	4:45

Do not take these numbers as absolutes or performance guarantees. Many variables across the Internet influence download times, just like congested roads influence drive times (yes, the Internet has rush hours). This table shows estimates based on real-world tests done by the nice folks at NTL.com in the United Kingdom. But now you see where broadband marketing companies get their justification for touting broadband as being up to 20 times faster than regular dialup, don't you?

The application vendors really, really want to persuade customers to download their programs rather than look for boxes on the store shelves. Offering applications online is much cheaper for the vendors because they don't need to pay for packaging and shipping, and they cut the retailer out of the equation to save even more money. The vendors say the move provides fresher programs that include the latest fixes and updates. You will soon get almost all your programs via the Internet. Transfer speeds and reliability become even more important when you're downloading a 150MB office suite.

How I Will Write Speeds

Different people use different acronyms for speeds, and it can get confusing. Just when you think you have it right, a typo will mess you up.

Here's what I will use:

✦ **Kbps:** Kilobits per second.

✦ **KBps:** Kilobytes per second

(K for Kilo isn't an even 1,000. it's 1,024 because that's what you get from 2 to the power of 10.)

✦ **Mbps:** Megabits per second

✦ **MBps:** Megabytes per second

(M for Mega isn't an even 1,000,000, but rather 1,048,576 because that's what you get from 2 to the power of 20.)

Know how you almost never use your floppy drive for anything anymore? Before long, you may use your CD-ROM drive to play music CDs rather than load new applications. That means downloading rather than installing off a local drive, and that means you need faster downloading.

Immersive Experiences

Computing without interruption enables you to get more work done. The next step, for relaxation, is to immerse yourself in some type of entertainment.

Watching a movie in a modern theater moves beyond the uninterrupted experience into an immersive experience. Sounds come from all around you. The screen takes up most of your field of sight. Darkness diminishes distractions from other audience members. When someone in the audience gets and takes a cell phone call, the movie world is destroyed and you are dropped back into the modern world where fools and their phones are never parted.

Broadband access transforms using your computer into something at least closer to an immersive experience, even though you can't duplicate a theater. The screen fills most of your vision. Lower prices make a surround speaker system affordable. And you control whether every cell phone in the area is on or off.

Modem fans may take exception to this. Wait, they cry, can't you do everything listed in the previous paragraph over dialup? Yes and no. You can get the surround sound speakers, lean close to the monitor, and turn off your cell phone.

What you can't do, however, is maintain your immersive entertainment world when the video jerks, stutters, and stops. You can't immerse yourself in music recorded at painfully low quality to enable transmission at dial-up speeds. You can't convince yourself that ground steak with ketchup is a filet mignon with béarnaise sauce.

Beyond entertainment, informational and educational programs take advantage of computer-based video regularly. Although a short video clip illustrating snake locomotion would be better on a big screen TV, it provides more valuable information moving on the computer screen than just a static picture.

Broadband performance can change your computer from something to work on to a speedy research assistant, from a maker of odd noises to a high-end music entertainment center, and from a displayer of still pictures to a streaming video treasure chest. Let me give you some examples.

Streaming audio

Today, finding and listening to interesting music outside the mainstream has become a do-it-yourself project. If you live in a rural area, you have few radio stations to choose from. If you live in or near a major city, you have more stations but not more choices because corporate radio conglomerates now own multiple stations in every metropolitan area. One owner and one program manager means mainstream radio plays the same few tunes over and over.

Internet radio and online music sites will change your world if you're a music fanatic. If you just like music, you'll find more sources for more tunes from more groups than you'll ever hear on radio. In fact, depending on your music preferences, you'll find more music online than you'll find in the largest music store in the largest cities. BeSonic, shown in Figure 1-2, will thrill music fans and particularly fans of European musicians.

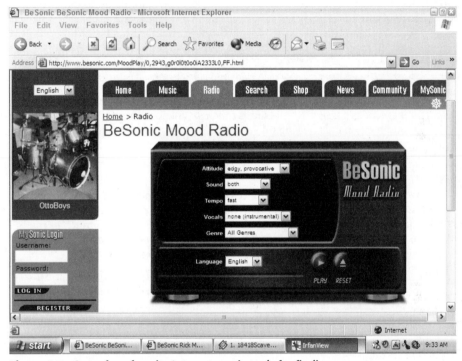

Figure 1-2: One of my favorite Internet music tools for finding new groups.

Before I talk about some of the Web sites you should visit to explore the world of music outside corporate mainstream control, let me give you an idea of what will appear in the next year or two. Computers will drive the audio entertainment for many households. This will occur whether you get a broadband connection or not, but it will be much more fun if you have the fast Internet connection broadband provides.

Consumer product companies (think Sony, Motorola, Phillips, and the like) now race to include computers inside their equipment. Computer companies (think Dell, HP, and Gateway) now race to include consumer products in their catalogs, all of which connect to their computers. Which side will win? I bet those consumers interested in linking the Internet into their stereo systems will win first; then the benefits will slow down for a couple of years until broadband speeds make downloaded video streams (as in movies) worthwhile. Although video fans have a strong push underway to liberate the TiVO and make it a broadband downloading tool rather than a second generation VCR. That will be interesting to come home to a downloaded movie you ordered from work via a Web site and had it sent to your home.

Before that happens, however, Hollywood will aggravate almost as many people as the music industry has by trying ill-considered security measures to keep honest people from enjoying their movies although doing nothing to stop large-scale pirating operations. For the next couple of years, spend your money and attention on the constantly improving world of streaming audio, and you'll have plenty of fun.

Lamented Music Site: RIP, MP3.com

The most popular Web music site for 4 years, MP3.com deserves a word of thanks and a lament for its passing. No site did as much for unknown bands than MP3.com did. I found many bands playing my favorite type of pop music (ska/punk bands with horns) by listening to play lists assembled by music fans and posted on MP3.com. Imagine good friends sitting you down and going through their favorite cuts of their favorite CDs, and you have the idea.

In 2001, Vivendi Universal, one of the world's major record companies, bought MP3.com. Fans worried, but the independent music stayed online. Mainstream artists from Vivendi and their partners blanketed the front page and much of the interior advertising, but you could still find great songs, for example: the funniest rock song I've ever heard, *"A Slut Named Rachel,"* from Skasmopolitan.

At the end of 2003, however, Vivendi sold MP3.com to CNET.com to use in some future music venture. The pleadings of fans worldwide fell on deaf ears as CNET.com shut down MP3.com and took all music offline despite the offer of several other Web sites ready to host the music files. A sad day indeed.

Quick hit: Example sites

Listing every streaming audio site on the Internet would take the rest of the book, and I would still miss some. Here are a few places to go to get started in your search for new and interesting music, or, if you prefer, old and interesting music.

Although GarageBand.com doesn't generate the most traffic of all music sites, I show it in Figure 1-3 because of Apple Computer. Apple released a new music software package in early 2004 called Garageband and I doubt they worried about overlapping the established Web site of the same name. The two have nothing to do with each other except the name confusion.

Streaming music sites with downloads

www.GarageBand.com

Figure 1-3: One of the best sites to find new groups and their music.

GarageBand.com does a good job showing the most popular tracks in each main genre with its Charts pages. For many songs, you can download an MP3 file for personal use. GarageBand also makes it easy to find CDs for sale by groups; it shows whether they have live gigs planned (although those don't seem to be up to date), and you can leave messages for the artist or group. The site also helps you find groups that sound like another band.

Music File Formats

Here's a quick rundown of the most common music file formats. The format type is usually indicated by the file extension.

✦ **.wav**: Music file format developed by Microsoft and IBM. Since Windows 95, Microsoft made .wav files the standard for all PC sounds. But the high fidelity file format requires nearly 10MBs per minute of music.

✦ **.aiff:** Audio Interchange File Format, the Apple Macintosh version of .wav files, including the high fidelity and large file size.

✦ **.mp3:** mp3 is short for MPEG version 3, from the Motion Picture Experts Group. MP3 is the third generation of a compressed file format that requires about 1MB per minute of music at nearly the same fidelity as WAV files.

Continued

Continued

- ✦ **Ogg Vorbis:** An open source, royalty free file format similar to MP3 but not as popular for downloadable music files.
- ✦ **.wma**: Windows Media Audio file format, the default to Windows Media Player. Often used by music services because of embedded digital rights controls in the file format.

www.SoundClick.com

Perhaps the most popular of the music sites after the unfortunate demise of MP3.com, SoundClick appears to be chasing that market full tilt. They promise to create play lists so people can string together their favorite tunes, like MP3.com did, and they now show the number of plays a tune has gotten.

www.CDBaby.com

Built by a working musician trying to market his own music, CD Baby now showcases nearly 55,000 CDs, all straight from the artists. You can listen to tracks CDs, search genres you like, and crank up your PC speakers.

www.IUMA.com

The Internet Underground Music Archive (IUMA) started in 1993 and was one of the first music sites on the infant WWW. It includes a streaming radio station and offers multiple tracks from every artist. It offers free MP3 downloads, streams in MP3 or Real formats, links to CD sales and the like.

www.VitaminiC.com

Connected to IUMA, VitaminiC offers much more international exposure and song protection by using Windows Media format files.

www.Ampcast.com

Another artist-oriented site, Ampcast started in 1998 and already includes play lists for gathering your favorites together. The site streams plenty of tracks, provides downloads, and sells CDs directly to you or recommends other sites.

www.AcidPlanet.com

One of many sites sponsored by music tool vendors, this Sony-owned site showcases artists using their products. In this case, Sony now owns Acid Pro and Sound Forge, among others, and the music posted has almost all been created or modified by Acid Pro or Sound Forge software.

www.BeSonic.com

Not just another music product vendor, BeSonic offers a ton of European groups. (TerraTec is a German company.) Its excellent Mood Radio page, shown in Figure 1-2, is at the beginning of this section. The site also provides a visually cool artists "cube" to help locate groups playing the type of music you want. Many artists provide a play list of their favorite BeSonic artists, offering another way to get some interesting connections to different artists.

    www.ArtistLaunch.com

This site is pretty self-explanatory, but adds some nice touches with a CD catalog that lists CDs for sale by genre. The graphics are large enough so you can actually see the CD cover, an unusual idea for many sites.

    www.DMusic.com

This artist promotion site provides an icon beside its songs so you can send a friend a link to that song. Clever marketing.

Streaming radio Web sites

Internet radio stations may be the only place left to hear interesting new music. Small groups who self-publish their own CDs or sign with one of the many small labels need distribution to reach new ears, and corporate-owned radio certainly won't give it to them. Next time you complain when hearing the pop vixen de jour again and again during the day, look to the Internet.

When I searched Google.com for "streaming radio stations," I received 2,810 listings. Internet radio stations come and go, so there's no guarantee which of the 2,810 stations will be up and running if you check them out.

However, here are a few you should give an ear to as you start your own journey:

- ✦ www.Shoutcast.com
- ✦ www.GrooveRadio.com
- ✦ www.RantRadio.com
- ✦ www.ThePavedEarth.com
- ✦ www.SomaFM.com
- ✦ www.DI.fm
- ✦ www.AccuRadio.com
- ✦ www.RadioIO.com
- ✦ www.NetRadio.com

Streaming video

Obviously you need enough bandwidth to stream the video fast enough to keep your display going at full speed. Your computer, whether running an operating system from Microsoft (Windows), Apple (OS X), or Linux needs certain minimum requirements to support streaming video. These aren't absolutes, but good guidelines.

Streaming video over the Internet suffers terribly when compared to the streaming video appliance everyone watches for several hours per day: the TV. Just about every major corporate content provider (TV networks, movie studios, music video producers, and infomercial hucksters) wants to make the Internet, and your computer, a broadcast receiver much like a television.

The world doesn't really need a new form of TV. And sitting at my desk watching a video window of maybe 4.5 inches wide by 2.5 inches high when a 37-inch Toshiba TV sits in the next room strikes me as stupid. So I hope the corporate content providers don't manage to turn the Web into more TV stations.

But the race for eyeballs will not stop for me or you. Look for new products over the next 3 years to link your computer, your broadband connection, and your HDTV set-top box. Look for appliances that act as the go-betweens for your wireless home network and your HDTV, including storing video streams for later viewing. I wonder what the TiVO developers are really up to?

The many geniuses, artists, humorists, and just plain nuts on the Internet provide enough videos to keep a person mesmerized for years. Any users with a few dollars a month for a hosting service can offer their own videos to the world. Be glad they do, because you'll see some things online you'll never see on TV, even if you have full access cable or satellite.

An example of all that's good and bad about corporate content providers is AOL. AOL broadband puts streaming video right up front for users. (Its streaming audio includes a wide range of interesting artists in 175 CD-quality radio stations as well.) Advertisements abound, of course, but music videos and movie trailers work well through AOL when you have a broadband connection. Using AOL broadband also allows multiple members of your family to be online at the same time. You can enforce parental guidelines that restrict your children's access to mature sites as long as you ensure that your children surf the Web through AOL rather than with Internet Explorer or another browser.

The faster your CPU and the larger your memory, the better. A faster hard disk always beats a slower one. Most computers built since 1998 include an Ethernet networking connection that supports 100 Mbps, so you'll be fine there. Specification minimums are shown in the following list:

 Cross-Reference Chapter 11 covers networking in depth.

✦ **CPU:** Intel Pentium III or AMD Athlon (faster is better)

✦ **RAM:** 128MB (more is better)

(The information about the previous two items can be found by clicking Control Panel ⇨ System.)

- ✦ **Video:** 800 × 600, at least 16-bit depth (more is better)
- ✦ **Sound:** Two powered speakers (the ones that came with your PC aren't worth much)
- ✦ **Broadband:** At least 200 Kbps (faster is better)

Of course, the fastest new computer in the world won't give you decent streaming video if you use a dial-up connection. Broadband service on an older computer beats the streaming audio and video performance of a newer computer without broadband every time.

Many of the Web sites offering streaming video give warnings about mature themes. Although the short films usually equate to a movie rated R, some may go further, so keep an eye on your children. Some sites with movies go much, much further.

Yes, there are adult movies and pictures on the Internet. In Part III, I'll explain how to control who in your home or office sees what, and what the legal ramifications are for business owners who provide Internet access to their employees but don't monitor those same employees when they pipe "entertainment" videos into the company network.

If you become a big fan of streaming videos on your computer, you might look for one more accessory to enhance your enjoyment. Go to the bookstore and get one of those full-page magnifying sheets or at least a big magnifying glass. You'll get tired of leaning toward the screen and squinting, I promise.

Quick hit: Example sites

There may be more streaming video sites than streaming radio stations, believe it or not. But the number includes hundreds or thousands of sites using streaming video to teach you something. Remote education often includes streaming video, and there are educational sites for every career or hobby you can imagine. Figure 1-4 shows the AOL 9.0 Enhanced video section.

In Figure 1-4, I mixed education (a National Geographic clip about volcanoes) with entertainment (AOL). Few people consider AOL an educational site, although I used it with my children to take advantage of its parental controls. Hiding Internet Explorer and forcing the kids to use AOL made it possible for me to relax when they were on the Internet.

I'm not sure how AOL does it, but the same music videos look better through AOL than on MTV.com. Perhaps there is something to all AOLs talk about broadband. And the extra speed makes it easier for my teenaged daughter to keep a dozen IM windows open while playing Solitaire, watching TV, and talking on the phone.

Mainstream and advertising supported sites

www.AtomFilms.com

Figure 1-4: Broadband greatly improves AOLs video performance.

Originally independent and pushing the Internet bubble, AtomFilms.com is now owned by Macromedia, the people who make Shockwave and Flash. Still edgy, because Macromedia appeals to many creative people, AtomFilms.com is a fun place to visit.

    www.iFilm.com

Another edgy entry, iFilm.com includes more adult short films than you may want your children to view. But the R-rated ones are often funny or thought provoking, or both. Some of the famous short films that have been e-mailed around the Internet started here.

    www.Movies.com

Not edgy, unless you think movie trailers for R-rated movies push the boundaries of good taste. But when you hear about a new movie through the grapevine, the trailer is usually here waiting for you.

    www.MTV.com

This used to be edgy, but is now alternately mainstream, corporate, tired, greedy, or historical. But there are a ton of music videos here, and few things on the Web benefit more from a broadband connection than music videos.

All major network television Web sites

ABC, CBS, NBC, CNN, and even Fox offer plenty of streaming videos, although most are from the TV rerun closet. The news sides of the major networks often include video from other parts of the world not shown on network television often.

Corporate sites

```
www.Apple.com/Quicktime
```

Apple computers didn't invent multimedia computing, but don't say that to a Macintosh fan unless you want to fight. The QuickTime player is a must-have, even when you already have Windows Media Player and Real Player on your system.

Video Players

Just like with audio players, you have some default video players (Windows Media Player and Apple's QuickTime depending on your platform) and some third-party players. Here are some of the most popular third-party players and Web sites for download:

✦ **RealPlayer (multiple versions):** `www.real.com`

✦ **Winamp:** `www.winamp.com`

✦ **Rosoft Media Player:** `www.rosoftengineering.com`

✦ **Sigma Player:** `www.ngksoft.com`

✦ **BSplayer:** `www.bsplayer.com`

```
www.Edmunds.com
```

Yes, a car magazine site. Look to the bottom of the home page for the Video section, and enjoy car videos almost never shown on TV or anywhere except a dealership. Enjoy them at home without a salesperson bugging you to sign on the line.

Odd and thrilling (and funny) independent

```
www.WebbyAwards.com
```

This group picks the best of the Web each year and shows the winners and runners-up. Not all of these are videos, obviously, but the ones they have will amaze you. They are all actual award-winning sites and the level of quality rises far above any other site collection.

```
www.Sputnik7.com
```

This site offers music videos you won't see on MTV.com, and short films you won't see on the other film sites.

www.Spongi.com

Cable access meets the Web. No clue who is behind this, or what the site hosts are thinking (or smoking). That's a joke, because some of these videos are hysterical.

www.alldaybreakfast.ca/

Sketch humor translated successfully to the Internet. Canadian humor loosed upon the world.

Communicating Over Broadband

This may seem an odd heading, because broadband is all about sending information. But information isn't always communication, and when I think "communication" I think of a two-way conversation. Many of the broadband sites listed in the previous section are as two-way as radio and TV.

Some people believe the power of broadband, that of fast communications across the public network, should be more than just "they broadcast and we watch." The beauty of getting a fast Internet connection is that it frees you to do all sorts of things you couldn't do before.

Here we hit upon one of the disruptive technologies you hear about sometimes, when a new technology disrupts established businesses and no one saw it coming. In the past, voice was analog and data was digital. The two didn't mix. But that was the old world, when all telephones had wires attached and all music played from vinyl records. (Kids, ask your parents to show you a record.)

Voice over broadband

Today, voice conversations can be turned into data streams, just like music can be turned into digital data on a CD. The process works much like capturing music for the CD, in fact, because the sounds of the voice are captured, sampled by the new Internet Protocol (IP) phone, and sent onto the network as digital data. On the receiving end, the digital data packets are converted from bits back into sound, just like your CD player does for the music it carries.

The technical term for all this is Voice over IP and the shorthand is VoIP. You pronounce it just as funny as it looks: vo-eep.

Cross-Reference Here's where things get all tangled up. As I'll explain in Chapter 3, there are two primary types of broadband services: over telephone lines owned and controlled by the telephone companies, and over cable lines owned and controlled by the cable companies. There are other broadband service options, but they don't get into the VoIP world yet.

If you're the cable company, adding VoIP services gives you a wonderful new feature to sell. Data networking companies like VoIP as well. since it gives them a wonderful new feature to sell.

Guess who doesn't like VoIP? The telephone companies. Does VoIP give them a new product? No, it replaces their most important product. The great value in Digital Subscriber Line (DSL), the broadband product sold by the telephone companies, is that it runs over existing telephone wires. The telephone companies want customers to keep using telephone services running over telephone lines, not to replace them by running VoIP over cable.

In the long term, VoIP will become more important and more common. The underlying network technology supporting VoIP makes it much cheaper to carry voice conversations across data networks than across a pair of telephone wires. VoIP quality goes up with each new product, and large companies save millions of dollars by replacing dedicated telephone circuits with VoIP over data networks for internal calls. One data network connection can carry as many telephone conversations as a hundred pair of telephone wires, and the tools used to manage the data network also manage telephone calls running over those data networks.

The telephone companies, especially the large national carriers with huge investments in data networks as well as telephone systems, are joining the VoIP bandwagon. If you can't beat 'em, join 'em, and it's better for the telephone companies to keep their customers than it is for them to keep protecting their investment in telephone wires.

Individuals and small businesses now have options to buy VoIP telephones and bypass the telephone companies if they believe the marketing from the cable companies. Quality keeps going up and the cost keeps going down.

Most small businesses won't get into VoIP for another year or two. The greatest value so far is for large companies where the majority of long-distance calling costs are generated by calls from one employee to another employee. Using VoIP over existing data networks allows such companies to avoid the long distance charges from their telecom providers and justify the new VoIP equipment.

Webcams

News flash: Webcams can be pointed at more than just friendly college girls asking for your credit card number. Some of the earliest Web entrepreneurs made a fortune with a cheap camera and a marketing list of voyeurs hiding behind their monitors. The prurient news value of those webcams overshadowed all the other ways people used a remote eye.

A few years ago, I interviewed the network manager of a check-cashing service with branches across several states. This smart guy put a webcam in every check cashing office. Whenever a security alarm went off in any office, he checked the webcam before calling the police. It saved him a bundle in false alarm charges.

Tech Bits If I remember correctly, the first networked webcam watched a coffee pot in a university in England. People got tired of walking upstairs to find an empty pot, so they rigged the camera.

Some daycare providers advertise the placement of webcams in every classroom. Parents use these cameras to check on their children during the day. Figure 1-5 shows a playpen of a different sort.

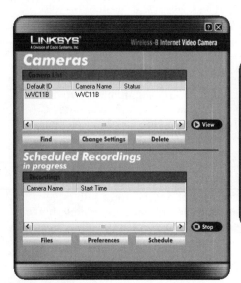

Figure 1-5: Good camera, bad subject.

Check your local TV station's news Web site and check out their traffic and weather webcams. If your local station doesn't have a good one, check out the thousands of options at www.earthcam.com/.

Anywhere you have electrical power, you can have a webcam. Every security camera you see is a webcam, but not viewable by the public. Every traffic monitoring camera you see watching your downtown streets is a webcam, but again not open to the public.

Prices for webcams are down to, well, free in some cases. I've seen major stores offer no-name webcams for $25 with a $25 rebate, which is pretty close to free.

Videophones and video IM

First shown to the public at the World's Fair in 1964, videophones captured the public's imagination (and funny faces) from the beginning. Long a staple of every futuristic movie and television show, videophones have yet to fulfill even a small portion of their exciting promise.

But once again, the availability of broadband will make videophones work much better because their big problem in the past has been the limited bandwidth over telephone lines. The only way to make a videophone at all was to keep the picture small and the frame rate low, which made no one happy.

Large companies started buying videophones and videoconferencing equipment years ago to help cut down travel costs. But the costs were high, special network protocols had to be supported, and only the executives got to play with them.

Those days when only the rich could afford small, jerky images of the person on the other end of the phone line are gone. Now normal folks can afford videophones and systems that offer better images than all but the most expensive equipment a few years ago.

Unlike most competing products, the D-Link i2eye DVC-1100 hooks to your television via standard video cables and connects to your computer wirelessly. This makes sense to me. If you want more than one person to be involved on each end, the TV offers a much better gathering point than a personal computer (especially if your desk looks like mine).

Prices for electronics like this are tricky to put in a book because prices change much faster than a book gets reprinted. But the unit shown in Figure 1-6 from

Figure 1-6: New consumer-priced videophone.

D-Link.com, one of the cost-leaders on the low end, priced this unit not much more than a video game console. For the first time, a usable videoconferencing product (I call it more than a videophone because several people can use it) costs far less than the computer it uses.

Quick hit: Example sites

For just the webcam but not the videophone feature, the Linksys folks have a nice new product, shown in Figure 1-7. It also bypasses the need for a wire to reach your network. Any place you have electrical power, you can have a webcam.

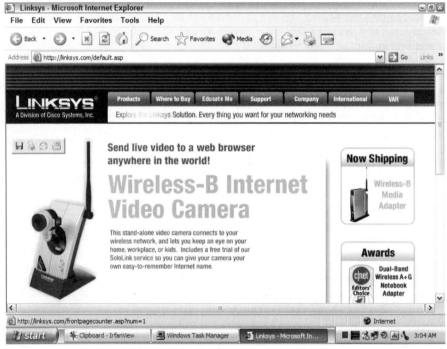

Figure 1-7: Webcam with wired and wireless network connections (used in Figure 1-5).

    www.earthcam.com

This site shows some interesting webcam sites, including an office in Tehran and antcam.com.

    www.tvweather.com/tv_cams.htm

Weather cams galore.

    www.axis.com/

This is the company that made the cameras for the check-cashing monitoring project. It also sells many of the traffic cameras and cameras used in other public places.

www.vonage.com

One of the first companies to offer VoIP products to the consumer and small business market.

Broadband Gaming

I remember Pong with great fondness. Two lines and a blip ate many of my quarters. Comparing Pong to modern games gives me the same feeling of amazement as looking at the first Volkswagen Beetle and a new Ferrari. Yes, they're the same thing, more or less, but they're a long, long way apart.

Today I no longer need to stand next to my gaming partner, each of us holding the knob on the Pong arcade game unit, to have a shared game experience. Today I can sit at home and be mercilessly slaughtered by a trigger-happy 10-year-old in Cleveland over the Internet.

If you are a gamer, or are the long-suffering parent of a gamer, you are familiar with the excitement and addiction awaiting those new to the world of modern gaming. Gamers push the boundaries of computer technology constantly and buy the newest, fastest, and most expensive hardware on the market. In a time where a complete corporate workstation costs less than $2,000, gamers might spend $3,000 and more on their systems.

Gamers love broadband connections for two primary reasons. First, downloading takes a fraction of the time it takes with a dial-up connection. Gamers download new games, new modules for older games, and demos of upcoming games constantly. Second, a faster network connection means faster interactive game playing online.

If you have a child gamer and you have broadband, you'll always know where he (perhaps a stereotype, but the gamer is usually male) is. He will be at home, playing over the Internet.

Game play requirements

Besides the most expensive PC systems on the market, what do game players need? More speed, always more speed. Latency, the technical term for the time lag between when a command is given and the results take effect, is the enemy of gamers everywhere.

The Internet, as you will learn later, consists of networks linked to networks linked to networks. It is, technically, a network of networks.

Every connection between networks is a potential bottleneck. The good thing about broadband service providers is that they tend to be the large companies and their customer networks have direct connections to other large customer networks. The *Internet backbone* is the highest level of network where all the largest networks connect.

Some service providers offer a special package for game players. This includes an extra IP network address so gamers can be online playing without blocking another family member on another computer from an Internet connection. This type of arrangement used to be special, but now many service providers automatically provide a network router for connecting more than one computer in the home or office to the Internet. But check with your service provider to ensure it supports a game console connection if that's the platform of choice for your gamer.

Using a network router between your computer and the modem provided by the service provider offers a great troubleshooting option: resetting the cable/DSL modem. When the going gets gummy, resetting the broadband modem (unplug it, wait for 60 seconds, then plug it in again) forces a new connection. Just like a telephone call sometimes has static, a network connection can get the digital equivalent of static. Resetting the broadband modem helps clear that problem, making a separate broadband modem an important piece of gear for gamers.

Cross-
Reference
More detailed information on game-specific configuration of routers, fire-walls, and proxies await you in Chapter 11. If you don't know what routers, firewalls, or proxies are, but fear you need them, don't worry, I've got your back.

Wrapping yourself in the game world

Few technologies are more engrossing and exclusionary than a good game. When I first saw the groundbreaking Wolfenstein 3D in 1992, the parts that scared me the most were the sound effects. The large steel doors that opened and closed in Castle Wolfenstein echoed with a surround sound that made it sound like they were opening behind me. That they managed that effect with the cheap PC soundcards and speakers at the time still surprises me.

Gamers spend hundreds of dollars on video cards to replace the ones you and I happily use, in order to get the highest resolution and the fastest screen-drawing times. Check out some of the game sites listed in the next section, and you will be amazed at the realism and depth of the game environment. You don't have to sign up for a paid service just to view screenshots and movies taken from actual game play, and those will be enough to show you that game effects now equal movie special effects.

Developers work with hardware designers to try and get physical impact into games. Even inexpensive handheld controllers vibrate to warn the players. Over the years, companies sold packs to strap on the players' backs with speakers inside to shake them up and special chairs with surround sound and quaking cushions to reflect driving over rough ground. These expensive options don't tend to stay on the market for long, but new ones always appear.

Parents who are afraid that their gamer children exercise only their thumbs may check into some of the new interactive game additions. A few companies are selling cameras that mount on the TV and capture physical player movements and translate those into character moves in the game. Let your child physically flail around fighting some demons and they'll get into shape again. Somehow, I doubt the chance for physical workout will attract too many gamers.

For me, ever since the first time I saw (and heard those steel doors in Castle Wolfenstein), sound provides the best immersion tool. Broadband offers higher quality music than dialup by a considerable margin. The difference in music is about the same as the difference between a cheap AM transistor radio and a modern FM home stereo.

Get a better sound card, and get better speakers. You can spend as much on surround-sound speakers for your computer as you can for your home theater. Although I don't advocate that outlay, moving up to a five-speaker system for at least $100 will make a huge sonic difference. Even the game consoles like PlayStation and X-Box support surround-sound speaker systems.

Are games intruding into everyday life? Radio@AOL has a channel with nothing but the music from the Final Fantasy game series. Even when gamers can't play, they can keep their ears in the game.

The most popular games

Warning, if you're new to the gaming world, popular online games take money. You must subscribe to play. And you thought only pornography made money on the Internet.

The choice of broadband type and other connection details will have no effect on your choice of games. Gamers play certain games for a variety of reasons, some of them innocent and some no doubt based in horrible neuroses foisted upon them by bad parenting. When your kids tell you that, explain to them all the violence in the game world has rotted their brains and they need to take up tennis to get fresh air and exercise. Don't let them tell you Topspin on the X-Box is the same as real tennis.

Your gamer will, when you hook up to broadband, begin playing multiplayer games across the Internet. These go by a variety of acronyms made from some set of the words Massive Online Player Universe and the like. Entire worlds exist for the big games, including people, places, weapons, and monsters never seen in real life (thank goodness, if you've seen some of those weapons and monsters).

There are too many games to list them all. Understand that even a relatively unpopular game may have a hundred thousand fans playing the game online now and then.

Quick hit: Example sites

ID Software, the group that started it all, comes back with another winner in its long string of winners. You've heard of Doom and Quake, its two other big hit series of games, and now you can get into Castle Wolfenstein at `http://games.activision.com/games/wolfenstein/`. I just hope you get out alive.

If you are familiar with these game worlds, you won't need the following list of sites to visit. If you're not familiar, my descriptions in two or three sentences won't begin to explain them. Go see for yourself. Most of these sites include streaming video movies of game play, so you can get a pretty good taste of what happens. Turn your speakers up to get their full impact.

- ✦ `everquest.station.sony.com/`
- ✦ `www.blizzard.com/`
- ✦ `www.unrealtournament.com/`
- ✦ `www.ubi.com/US/`
- ✦ `www.gamespot.com/index.html?reflash=1`

Ah, for a gentler set of games, you can visit `games.yahoo.com/`.

Summary

You know you want more from your computer. You know you want more from the Internet and Web. You know you want broadband, you just have to make that leap.

As I'll explain in this book, broadband is no longer outrageously expensive, and it's no longer a technical nightmare. Cheap and easy may be going a little too far, but that's the trend.

Besides, your computer will be much more fun on broadband than on dial-up connection. And don't you deserve some more fun in your life?

Getting Familiar with Broadband Technology

After reading the advantages of speedier Internet connections in the first chapter, you know that you really do want broadband—even if you're not completely sure what *broadband* means. You want to get more from the Internet and World Wide Web more quickly than you do now. Broadband gives you what you want. This chapter and the next two will eliminate the mysteries of broadband and help you justify getting the service.

No matter how fast your computer is, you want that computer to go faster. Fact of life, this urge, and an excellent example of modern man's inability to be satisfied with the status quo. You are perfectly normal if you want your computer experience to run faster and jump higher. In fact, people would only call you weird if you said your computer is too fast and you yearn for the old days when your 2,400 baud modem connected you to the world.

You want images to arrive before your finger leaves the mouse. You want music to start before you can think of what the song sounds like after you click the title. You need broadband. In this chapter, I define broadband technology and help you get a handle on how it works.

What Is Broadband?

You want an "official" definition of broadband? Good luck.

Try this definition from Webopedia.com:

> A type of data transmission in which a single medium (wire) can carry several channels at once. Cable TV, for example, uses broadband transmission.

More technically, broadband is a transmission facility having the bandwidth to carry multiple data, voice, and video channels all at once. Each of the individual channels is transmitted on a different frequency through the transmission medium (usually a wire of some type) and selected at the receiving end (such as your cable TV box). Emtpy space in the frequency range between channels ensures channels don't interfere with each other.

Digging deeper, let's call *bandwidth* the amount of data that can be sent or received in a set amount of time. Bandwidth exists as a range within a set of frequencies (for radio) or wavelengths (for light created by lasers).

Computers and other digital devices express bandwidth as bits per second (bps) most often, but sometimes they use Bytes per second (Bps). There are eight bits in a byte, so when you compare speeds make sure you check whether the ratings use Bps or bps. Marketing often decides which rating to use, so be careful.

/ **Note** Think computer people don't have a sense of humor? Four bits, (half a byte) is called a *nibble*. Really.

Let me try and explain analog and digital, two terms with specific technical meanings that are often misused. *Analog* refers to something continuous and is normally represented in a form that emphasized a range of settings. Think of a radio volume knob, hands on a watch, or a singing voice. Those all exemplify a set of points, such as volume settings, but also include all the points in between, such as the space between volume setting 5 and 6.

Digital refers to distinct measurements of values but not the steps in between. If there are only two steps, such as a computer chip with transistors able to be switched either off (0) or on (1), digital is easy to spot. Less well-defined examples of digital include items such as a radio with volume buttons for louder or a software that shows a digital display (1-11 for instance) of the volume, unlike the volume knob. On a piano, you can play C or C# but not the notes in between. Singers, being analog, can include all the different sounds from C on the way to C# (whether you and I want to hear them or not).

When talking about analog, such as voice and electricity, people talk about bandwidth in *cycles per second,* or Hertz (Hz). This can get confusing, however, because CPU speeds are expressed in Hertz (such as 2.4 GHz Pentium 4 chips) even though most of us would call a computer chip digital rather than analog. So you say 3.1415 GHz as "three point one four one five gigahertz." When you see Hertz expressed in high speeds, such as MHz (MegaHertz) or GHz, the reference usually applies to modern digital technologies such as computer chip or wireless networking speeds.

Taking the path of least resistance, let me quote Webster's definition of broadband: *operating with uniform efficiency over a wide band of frequencies.* If all this talk of frequencies makes you think of radios, you're on target.

What the Feds Call Broadband

The U.S. Government, or at least the Federal Communications Commission (FCC), at www.fcc.gov uses this definition of broadband:

> Broadband services are those that support bidirectional data transmissions of at least 200K bit/sec.

Put bluntly, if broadband is nothing more than the FCC definition, it's pretty lame. After all, the FCCs idea of broadband is only four times faster than the standard 56 Kbps modem you can buy for about $20. The broadband most of us can get today, at least in the United States, follows this Fed definition and is therefore pretty lame (like a lame leg that keeps you from running fast).

Don't believe me? How about believing some of the 300 members of the lobbying and advisory group called the Technology Network (www.technet.org/). Called TechNet for short, this group includes senior executives from many of the corporations providing broadband products, services, and network building blocks.

The TechNet group, including many of the largest companies in American technology, want to influence the FCC to change some of its rules. Check up on the rules yourself at FCC.gov, shown in Figure 2-1. It shouldn't surprise you that many of the TechNet recommendations mean new business opportunities for TechNet members, but the changes will also spread faster networks across all parts of the United States.

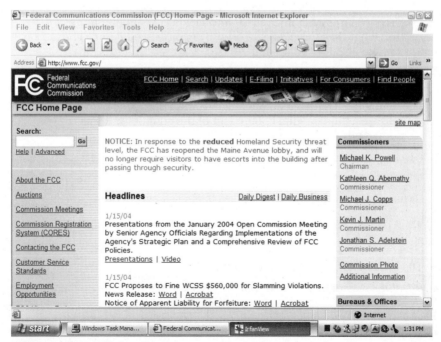

Figure 2-1: The FCC home page.

Craig Barrett, CEO of Intel, gave a keynote speech at the SuperComm convention of telecomm industry players on June 4, 2002. In that speech, he disagreed with the FCC definition of broadband and said this:

> "300 Kbps or 400 Kbps is not real broadband. When you get to five or 10 meg, going up to one hundred, that's real broadband."

Why did Barrett dis the FCC? He prefaced those remarks by saying, "I get to travel around the world and see what real broadband content looks like compared to some of the things we try to pass off for broadband in the United States." He knows real broadband, real broadband is a friend of his, and he just told the FCC they aren't real broadband.

TechNet called for a National Broadband Policy back at the beginning of 2002. What do they want? 100 Mpbs to 100 million homes and small businesses by the end of the decade. That, friends, is real broadband.

In fact, TechNet calls for the same national push to get to 100/100 by 2010 that was used to put a man on the moon. They say that for America to stay competitive, educate the workforce, and increase productivity, you must have ubiquitous broadband.

Note   Perhaps I'd feel better about this push by TechNet to improve broadband if the membership of TechNet included anyone besides executives of network and technology companies looking to make big bucks from this push. Any thoughts of adding writers, teachers, musicians, artists, and members of the public to TechNet? Seems that the push to put a man on the moon came from the government back in the 1960s, not the rocket builders and the Astronauts Union.

Groups like TechNet are pushing the FCC into making broadband more of a priority. Here's what the FCCs Web site (www.fcc.gov/broadband/) has to say about its strategic goal for broadband:

> Broadband technologies, which encompass all evolving high-speed digital technologies that provide consumers integrated access to voice, high-speed data, video-on-demand, and interactive delivery services, are a fundamental component of the communications revolution. Fully-evolved broadband will:

✦ Virtually eliminate geographic distance as an obstacle to acquiring information, and

✦ Dramatically reduce the time it takes to access information.

All will benefit as broadband's technologies are developed and deployed. Nonetheless:

✦ The infrastructure is not yet ubiquitous,

✦ Relative costs of deployment remain high compared to narrowband,

✦ Access is limited in underserved areas, and

✦ Adoption rates remain low relative to availability.

The first paragraph, and first two bullet points, certainly sound good, don't they? Reducing the time to access information sounds great because you all want the screen to update instantly when you press a button or click the mouse. Not so good are the last four bullet points. This page, when I grabbed these quotes, was last updated on 3/13/03. This means the information is more than a year old by the time this book hits the bookshelves. But nothing in the first three waffling bullet points will change soon. But the last note, adoption rates in relation to availability, are picking up, as you'll soon see. Amazing what happens when a technology becomes affordable.

Don't you love the "gov-speak" in the third bullet point? *Access is limited in underserved areas.* Correct: no one buys broadband services in areas where there are no broadband services to buy. Perhaps they could simply combine lines one and three and just say *not enough people in the United States have access to broadband* and make this clear?

Symmetrical versus Asymmetrical Connections

The two long words, *symmetrical* and *asymmetrical*, are just scientifically precise ways of describing traffic patterns in broadband service offerings. I am tempted to say *equal* and *unequal,* but that wouldn't be accurate.

Symmetrical means bandwidth throughput is equal in both directions, so as much data can come into your computer as can go out of your computer. *Asymmetrical* adopts the *not* prefix (*a*) which means that bandwidth going in one direction is greater than bandwidth going in the other direction.

Think of a highway into a city during rush hour. Many cars are going one way, and fewer cars are going the other way. You can also look at your mailbox (the physical one) where you get more mail each day than you send out. You can look at your e-mail box and see that the ratio of mail in, counting spam, may be a hundred times greater than the mail going out.

Why service providers offer both options

There are technical reasons for service providers to offer both symmetrical and asymmetrical connection options. With some providers and types of service, you don't have a choice whether you receive symmetrical or asymmetrical connections. Usually, however, you have a choice. Let me warn you now: a symmetrical connection almost always costs more.

Although the Internet developed an infrastructure based on sharing connections between networks (the Internet is really just a giant group of networks connected to each other), these high-speed data networks often don't reach out to the suburbs. The problem is the plumbing—or, in the case of data networks, the infrastructure.

Note *Infrastructure* is a fancy (and clumsy) word for the hardware and software framework that supports computing and the Internet.

Actually, if the problem really were with the *plumbing*, things would be better. Cities and towns work with developers to install physical infrastructure items such as roads, electricity, water, and sewer connections to support new homes and businesses. The idea of buying a home and then having to negotiate with Acme WaterWorks to get fresh water in and wastewater out, wouldn't even be an acceptable plot for a bad sitcom.

Housing developments include electricity and telephone service automatically. New developments often have cable TV distribution wiring built in. Fancy new developments now include digital broadband access options, such as fiber cabling, to provide high-speed Internet access.

The majority of the houses in the United States lack such expensive high-speed access, but they do have universal telephone service (by federal decree) and near-universal cable TV access. Technological restrictions on connections to you, the Internet consumer, come from the years of technology built to serve a different function, such as the telephone company. Neither the telephone system nor the cable TV distribution system was designed to do what we're asking of them now: to provide high-speed data connections.

Tech Bits Another, more technical consideration, has to do with the early chips built to support broadband connections. As is often the case with electronics, there is a finite limit to the number of actions possible within a certain timeframe. Joseph Lechlieder, an engineer at Bellcore research center in the 1980s, developed many of the algorithms establishing DSL technology. He was among the first to push an asymmetrical connection, recognizing most users would download more information than they upload.

The following section looks at why the existing structure favors downstream traffic. Then I'll share some details about upstream traffic.

Downstream details

As I mentioned in the preceding section, network plumbing hasn't yet caught up with physical plumbing for most of the homes in the world. But if you think of water pipes from the lake to your bathroom, you get the idea of how centralized the plumbing systems are and how their distribution patterns were set in stone (or actually buried in many cases) long before the Internet was even a glint in an engineer's eye.

When you turn the faucet, water comes out. That water had a long trip. First, millions of gallons of water sit in lakes and reservoirs, sometimes scores or hundreds of miles away from your city and your bathroom. Millions of gallons await your faucet's request for service. Huge pipelines carry the lake water to holding stations closer to the city. Smaller pipes carry the water to other distribution points near the suburbs and surrounding cities. Depending on the size of the area served by the reservoir, this process may repeat another time or two. Next, the water arrives in your neighborhood. Most areas still use water towers to let gravity provide water pressure to homes, but some areas use holding tanks on (or halfway into) the ground. Finally, the faucet holds back the water from the tower until you turn the handle. Then it jumps into your sink to catch you by surprise and splash onto your new pants.

Good ideas for water distribution systems turn out to be good ideas for delivering data connections to residential areas. The telephone and electrical companies use the same type of distribution scheme. You may have read about the *network tree* concept and how the data flows through the trunk, on out to the limbs, on to smaller limbs, and finally to the leaves. Our personal network connections are the leaves. But this image really should be turned upside down. It's more accurate to think of the trunk as being at the top rather than at the bottom. Our personal connections are at the bottom of this network, just like we're on the downhill side of the water pipes from the water tower.

Let's be honest here. If you chart your Internet use for a week, you'll find the vast majority of the traffic comes to you, and very little goes out from you. E-mail goes both ways; but other than mail, I'm betting that you download much more than you upload—especially when you count spam. You view (download) local weather radar to check on a coming storm. You view (download) the latest video from your favorite singer. Plenty of exceptions exist, but most people receive more content than they send.

One-to-many distribution cost advantages for providers

Centralization offers great cost benefits during a technology's development. Reservoirs, water towers, and pipes—expensive as they are—are cheaper than every house in a city drilling its own well for water. Consequently, a centralized distribution system offers substantial cost savings. The early telephone company (AT&T was The Phone Company until 1984, remember) recognized the potential cost savings of centralization when it followed the water tower-to-home concept to help contain its distribution costs.

The technology of the time demanded that AT&T create giant connection frames where the phone line from every home and office in the area terminated. Remember the old switchboard operator pictures where ladies plugged wires into a matrix of plugs in front of them? That's the way the telephone network started and still works today.

Virtual circuit, the operative word for the type of connection used by the telephone network, creates a solid wire link between the calling and receiving phone. When you call your next-door neighbor, the wire goes from your phone to the central office (the switching center with computers replacing the ladies with hair buns and wires) and back down another wire to your neighbor's house.

Some readers may politely point out that they have a cellular phone and so there is no wire involved. Correct, but the technology works the same, because the originating station (your cell phone) and the receiver (the phone you called) stay connected to each other, and only each other, during the conversation.

Besides, there are few copper wires left to carry phone calls of any distance anymore. Long distance calls go over fiber optic cable and wireless connections between transmission towers. But the virtual circuit technology remains, and we'll see that it colors the types of broadband offered by various telephone companies today.

All this virtual circuit talk may make you wonder where the *one-to-many* distribution scheme appears. The last copper wires in a telephone run between your home or office and the central office—still the hub of the local telephone network. Local telephones link to the local central office via old-fashioned copper wires inside rubber insulators, just like they did over a hundred years ago.

Each central office links to other central offices and combine lines until they connect to the national network. The phone companies concentrate their equipment in the central offices and larger switching centers connecting the central offices. Expensive equipment sits in the central offices, not inside telephones in every home. Each home links to a single central office, although businesses can link to multiple central offices for redundancy in case of a failure at one central office.

How would the telephone company connect calls using its virtual circuit method without central offices? Not well, and perhaps not at all. Your telephone, and your modem for that matter, connect your home directly to the neighborhood central office.

Everything the telephone companies do follows this pattern of a direct connection between your home or office and the central office. All the various flavors of DSL (Digital Subscriber Line) services follow the same pattern: your home by way of a wire to the central office.

When I get to the details of DSL later in this book, you will see ways in which the equipment providing DSL services make it easier to send information downstream than it does to receive information. But some of the advantages should be obvious. If the virtual circuit must handle traffic from your house, it must be able to capture the information, store the information for a fraction of a second, digest the information, and forward the information somewhere else, if necessary. These features come at a cost, but the good thing is that the cost is dropping.

 Cross-Reference You find out all about DSL in Chapter 3. Stay tuned.

The one-to-many distribution network by the telephone companies won't go away for years and years; in fact, distribution to the home will generally use this model. There is too much invested in telephone wires snaking in, around, and into our neighborhoods to abandon this system.

Centralization of resources will remain a key component of network design. The Internet philosophy calls for smart devices in the center of things (giant routers to switch traffic around the network) that support dumb devices (small routers for Internet access at homes and businesses). Which is cheaper: upgrading a thousand routers owned by service providers or a hundred million small routers and cable modems?

One-to-many distribution future developments

Since the foundation of the Internet (and therefore the Web) depends on centralized resources, will there be changes and improvements in the future? Absolutely. Many of the fun things on the Web, such as streaming Internet radio or multiplayer games, benefit from the idea of one resource providing services to many users at one time.

Yet coordinating synchronized streams across hundreds of users thousands of miles apart is tough, tough, tough. Providing multiple streaming servers scattered around the Internet is one way to improve the user experience in such a situation. This means more and smarter servers (or, more accurately, clusters of servers to provide fault-tolerant hardware and guarantee uptime) scattered around the Internet closer to more people.

Initially, expensive to deploy, once in place these extra "streaming stations" provide horsepower for a variety of new and interesting projects as yet unborn. Perhaps you remember the line from the movie *Field of Dreams:* "If you build it they will come." On the Internet, the idea is "If we have servers and bandwidth, people will use them."

The worry for the future? Increasing consolidation in major Internet providers (the cable and telephone companies) means decreased competition whereas consolidation of content providers reduces innovation and choice. Many of the same companies control both the content and method of distribution (Time Warner, for example, owns cable companies, as well as AOL, WB TV, Warner Brothers movie studio, and *Time, Fortune, Sports Illustrated* and even *MAD Magazine*), and consolidation increases daily.

Upstream details

The preceding section covered a few of the technical reasons why service providers find it easier to send content downstream rather than accept it coming upstream; but there's more to the story. There are two serious roadblocks to providing more upstream support in the short term:

- ✦ Reworking the network will cost a ton of money
- ✦ Content providers want to sell you content, not make it easy for you to upload content

The two reasons intertwine as you might expect. Since the Internet stock bubble burst in a shower of flawed stock offerings, most technology companies stopped ordering new equipment and delayed all upgrades. Things are picking up, but one way the companies hope to increase revenue, by downstreaming content, contradicts the idea of upgrading the network to encourage more upstream traffic. Companies want users to consume, not provide, content, so the downstream traffic means revenue for them, but not upstream traffic going from you to others.

I discussed the telephone network of copper lines radiating out from a central office to homes and businesses in the earlier section "*One-to-many distribution cost advantages for providers.*" Equipment for switching, routing, and processing connections from those homes and businesses all reside at the central office, as you see when you look at the various flavors of DSL in Chapter 3. Upgrading the network means upgrading equipment at each central office, an expensive proposition but in an environment they control. Telephone companies claim they are upgrading as fast as they can. Interestingly, they upgrade quickly in areas served by competitors, and slowly in areas with no competition.

Cable companies, by the very nature of cable broadband, must place quite a bit of equipment in every neighborhood they serve. You may have noticed those gray or green lumpy boxes in some yards with a wire or two hanging out? To completely upgrade the cable network, many of these boxes will require upgrading. This is on top of all the network equipment upgrades needed at the cable company's version of the central office.

Remember also that cable companies started by emulating the TV broadcast model. In other words, they send content to you and your only choice is which channel to consume, er, watch. Of course, you can also turn it off, but few off switches are overworked today.

In Dallas, the first cable franchise for the city promised a marvelous interactive system supporting upstream responses from every user. Viewers were supposed to be able to vote on programs they liked, answer surveys, register objections with a push of a button, and request that advertisers contact them. This was in the early 1980s. The company making those promises long ago disappeared, along with the grand plans.

So cable companies wanted to offer interactive, two-way systems allowing upstream data, but the technology just didn't exist during the initial cable TV deployment early on. Even if the only upstream data consists of which new product you want to buy, that technology requires considerably more investment than the strictly downstream model.

Modern cable systems may look interactive and upstream capable, but look carefully and ask your service provider what they mean by *interactive*. Choosing your channel only means that your cable box filters for a different frequency to display the right channel. All the channels flow down the cable and your set-top box chooses which to display. That's not interactive. If you can't answer a survey with a button push, the service isn't interactive.

Newer digital cable Internet access networks usually provide upstream transmission capabilities because they upgraded the network to support the higher-quality digital signals. This doesn't always mean they allow you to send much stuff upstream, but they have the capability to allow that.

Be aware that some broadband service providers choke off your ability to send content upstream. A friend of mine in the public relations business sends newsletters via e-mail to interested parties, such as writers and magazines, on a regular basis. He's been doing it for years with no problems. The local cable company got purchased (name hidden to protect the company who changed existing contract terms), and suddenly his upstream allowance dropped to nearly zero—barely suitable for an individual sending more than just a few e-mails per day. The fact that Marty had a business plan made no difference.

Always interested in redundancy, Marty called about DSL. They promised him there were no limits on upstream traffic or e-mails per day. He ordered the service, moved his network to DSL for the primary Internet connection, and sent his next newsletter.

Oops, it seems the DSL folks forgot to mention there was a little rule about upstream traffic. Marty could get out about 80 e-mails per day, but that was it. This is after the sales department assured him everything was peachy. Evidently the sales department doesn't talk to the engineering folks. Marty, last I heard, was fighting the good fight and expected resolution in his favor, one of these days.

Uploads you may not realize you make

Marty knew what he needed, and asked for a business plan to support the amount of upload traffic he generated. Some of you may be thinking you don't upload much at all, so you don't have to worry. Take a minute to examine these common Internet activities a little more closely:

✦ **E-mail:** Sure, we all send some e-mail, even if not nearly as much as we get. If you're on one or more mailing lists, you may send 20 or 30 messages a day if you have the time and are interested in your list topics. Forward a few long jokes to people? Adds up.

✦ **Photos:** Many people send digital photos via e-mail, and that's wonderful. But remember photos can be 1MB or more in size. If your upstream connection is slow, your photos will take forever to leave your e-mail program.

✦ **Music:** MP3 files, the most common for playing through your computer, include about 1MB/minute of music. If you send music via e-mail or through some type of peer-to-peer service, slow or restricted uploads will cause delays or complete disconnection.

✦ **PowerPoint:** Warning to all those tweaking your PowerPoint presentation at home: when you send it back to the office via e-mail, you may be sending multiple megabytes. Simple presentations won't get out of hand, but the more images, fades, or music clips added to your presentation the bigger (and bigger) it will grow. Of the PowerPoint files people have sent me over the last year, the average size is 1.6MB, with some as large as 8MB. Only one out of 65 is under 100KB (it's a mere 90KB).

This list doesn't count those of you hoping to run servers of some type at your home or office, or those interested in gaming. I cover those issues in the section "*Symmetrical Advantages*" in a few more pages.

If you send any of these file types on a regular basis, be careful when you choose your broadband service plan. Verify your upstream speed, even though all the salespeople want to pitch are the download speeds. Force them to talk about upstream traffic rates.

Ask if there are upload allowances. If they say there are no upload restrictions, ask them to tell you where in the service terms of agreement they say that. If they don't say there's no limit, they probably have a limit. When the service provider says there are no upload allowances, ask again. Don't think you have one now? Neither did Marty, and he asked.

Peer to peer networks

Literally everyone in positions of authority for Internet service providers and the record industry was caught by surprise by the popularity of peer-to-peer networks.

Napster and co-conspirators such as KaZaa tapped into the growing availability of broadband connections to millions of personal computers controlled by music-hungry teens and young adults. Before the Powers That Be caught on, thousands of CDs were uploaded to the world. And yes, this practice is illegal if the music is copyrighted, as all commercial CDs are.

Napster and others, however, showed the world of music fans that broadband provides new avenues for finding, getting, and listening to music. Using a broadband connection, every PC can become a real server and content provider to the rest of the Internet. This echoes the early days of the Internet, except computers are much cheaper and connection speeds are much higher these days.

Keep in mind, however, that giving away music is wrong and illegal unless you created the music or otherwise have the rights of distribution. Second, putting peer-to-peer software on your computer today opens the door for an enormous variety of viruses, worms, spyware, and computing pain of all kinds. Avoid loading a file-sharing program just to stay away from that aggravation if for no other reason.

If you're interested in the fight to make music available and affordable and in stopping the RIAA from suing kids check out the folks at www.eff.org (see Figure 2-2). They are fighting the good fight and can use your help.

Many-to-many distribution future developments

As more individuals get broadband access and start to provide content rather than just download content, peer-to-peer networks will become many-to-many networks. Napster and KaZaa and others started this trend, and it will continue.

Modern PCs (any flavor, including Windows, Macintosh, Linux, and Unix) have the horsepower and software to become content servers as well as workstations. Too much of the software available today increases your security risk rather than lessen it, but improvements are being made.

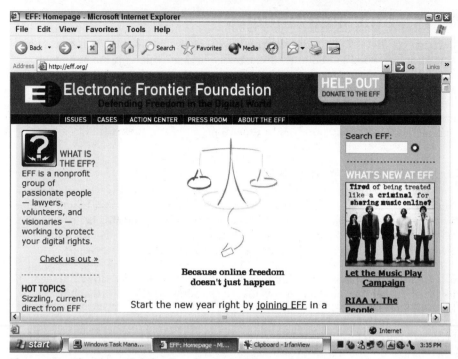

Figure 2-2: The group fighting for electronic rights and privacy.

One of the many-to-many networks up and running today are Instant Message (IM) systems. Teens, used to the immediacy of cell phones, almost always use IM to communicate with their friends over the network in place of e-mail programs. A dozen or more conversations may be running at the same time, each connection linked to another dozen conversations, but only a few will overlap. It's not truly a many-to-many network because each conversation stays between two people, but cutting and pasting and relaying of messages between conversational partners happens constantly.

The next step for these groups is the appearance of some type of personal conference room so that each participant can hear every other participant. The adult world includes products for audio and video conferencing, and the teenage world is starting to pick up on this.

Two interesting things will likely happen in this space in the short term. First, better IM tools will appear, especially for connecting multiple users at a time and supporting cameras as well. Second, users will demand the same type of constant interaction with all network connections that they get with their personal IM connections. Remote work connection support will improve, as will interactive programs based on personal software clients run by group members.

Fueling these innovations? Broadband, of course, as it moves forward by providing more speed, more speedy wireless connections for more products, and a reluctance of users to ever be out of touch.

Asymmetrical advantages

Now that you have some idea why you have a choice between symmetrical and asymmetrical broadband connections, take a look at which option suits your needs the best. Although choosing the least effective option won't ruin your broadband experience, choosing the most effective option will enhance your experience. And it may even save you some money. The following sections provide you with some things to think about when deciding between a symmetrical and an asymmetrical connection.

Common traffic patterns

"Go with the flow" works in high tech as well as everything else. The majority of users, statistically speaking, download far more than they upload. Larger groups of potential customers get more attention from vendors, and this is no exception. It's just lucky for the various broadband service providers that it's cheaper for them to handle the type of traffic their customers demand.

Although Internet packets are immune to gravity, they do head downhill most of the time. Not all the time, like water in a river rolling toward the sea, but most of the time.

If you're a *normal* Internet and Web user, an asymmetrical plan will work just fine for you. How do you know if you're a *normal* user? Unless you know why you aren't, you are.

Cost

Here you find the biggest advantage to the asymmetrical broadband option: it costs less, across the board, than symmetrical broadband. Reduced equipment needs of service providers supporting more downstream than upstream traffic results in lower costs.

The most basic and least expensive broadband option available to most users is a subset of DSL called *aDSL* (asymmetrical Digital Subscriber Line) from the local telephone company. Special offers drop the cost down to around $25–$30 per month with a year's contract. These prices almost always include all the necessary equipment for connecting one or more personal computers to the broadband connection.

Be prepared for these prices to stay steady and probably drop for three reasons:

✦ Cable has twice as many broadband subscribers as DSL in the United States.

✦ DSL equipment resides at the central office and 90 percent of users can self-install the DSL modem, saving the costs of an installer visit to the home.

✦ Phone companies want to keep their customers from switching to cable companies who offer telephone services over cable.

You will see many more cost options with DSL than with cable, for reasons made clear in Chapter 3. But as the telephone and cable companies square off against each other for broadband and telephone service, the competition will keep the price at a decent level. Actually, compared to what prices were not long ago, the bang for your broadband buck is outstanding.

As I write this, here are my service costs for aDSL and Internet cable access:

✦ **SBC Yahoo! DSL:** 384 Kbps downstream, 128 Kbps upstream for $29.95 per month. One-year contract.

✦ **Comcast cable modem:** 3 Mbps downstream, 256 Kbps upstream (minimum speeds, may be higher depending on traffic) for $42.95 per month. This is normally the price I'd pay for a cable modem with a combination cable TV/Internet plan. But I was able to take advantage of a special offer. Otherwise, I'd be paying $52.95 per month for the cable modem.

Symmetrical advantages

Just because I listed many good reasons to be happy with asymmetrical broadband service doesn't mean that's your only choice. Remember that almost all roads are built with the same number of lanes going as coming.

Earlier, I suggested that most people send more regular mail than they receive. But what if your business uses mail constantly? For example, what if you are a billing service, a direct mail company, or you send association news on a regular basis? You are one of the exceptions that prove the rule. Businesses tend to fall into this category more than individuals, but I do know people who send more mail than they receive, including some who fall into the SOHO (small office/home office) category.

If you disagreed with being called a *normal* Internet user just a few paragraphs ago, you know why you don't fit into that category. The following sections look at some of the most common reasons people feel they need the extra upstream speed they get with a symmetrical Internet connection and why they're willing to pay the increased cost of a symmetrical service plan.

Peer-to-peer file sharing

A peer-to-peer network harkens back to the early days of the Internet (before the World Wide Web) when each connected computer forwarded files, stored files, and made files available to all other systems on the network. When you're involved in a peer-to-peer network, your system often uploads as much as it downloads, or perhaps even more if you become a pseudo-server for your peers.

But let's say it straight out: peer-to-peer file sharing got more than a bad name from Napster, it gave Napster such a bad name they killed it. Now Napster has reincarnated as a pay-music site whereas the RIAA sues children and grandmothers and tries to win friends through litigation. Looks like bad times for those interested in sharing person-to-person rather than through one of the large service providers.

Perhaps the lure to set up connections between your computer and a few other computers pulls strongly. Just as you have a group of friends for social interaction, you may also have a group of friends (and their computers) for electronic interaction.

Social networking now piggybacks upon computer networking, and peer-to-peer networks facilitate this connection. One new peer-to-peer group that looks interesting is LinkedIn at www.LinkedIn.com. This freeware file-sharing community (see Figure 2-3) connects like-minded people more tightly through shared files than any e-mail list and focuses on business relationships. Not sure if these relationships work yet without a face-to-face component, but I have friends who believe it's working for them.

Figure 2-3: LinkedIn—one of the new person-to-person social networks with a business slant.

Let's take a look at a few completely legal reasons why you and some friends or family may want to user peer-to-peer connections:

✦ Photo exchange

✦ Access files at home when at work or traveling

✦ Instant message outside AOL, Yahoo!, or MSN

✦ Give (or get) computer support to a computer over the Internet

✦ Collaborate on projects of all kinds (scheduling soccer teams, organizing a family reunion, writing the great American novel with a friend)

✦ Create, send, and share your blog

✦ Back up data files to a remote computer

✦ Scan and share papers rather than fax them

✦ To ensure secure Virtual Private Network (VPN) connections between homes and offices

For every two people, there are three or more reasons to connect through a peer-to-peer network. Anything electronic can be exchanged directly between two people if they can connect in this way. Security software to guarantee the privacy of communication between peers offers great advantages to many business transactions.

 Caution Copying a commercial CD, or sharing any type of music or other media to which you do not own (or license) the copyright is illegal. Owning the physical CD gives you no rights to "share" the music.

Linking directly and securely from your home computer to the one at work, or vice versa, is another example of good use of peer-to-peer technology. Several companies, such as FolderShare shown in Figure 2-4, provide shared Web space for document storage and transfer for a fee. Some new companies offering this services are using peer-to-peer networks. Sometimes they are free, or have a basic version for free with more features available for a price.

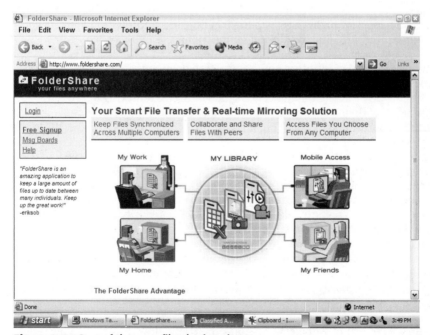

Figure 2-4: One of the new file-sharing sites.

Technically, when you get involved with peer-to-peer networks your personal computer becomes a server. Because servers, by definition, "serve" files to others, your upstream traffic will be higher than a normal Internet user. Minor and occasional peer-to-peer activity will function well enough on an asymmetrical arrangement, because upload speeds of 128 Kbps will support one other computer connection pretty well. But if your peer-to-peer network use pushes you into situations where you will be serving files to more than two people at any one time, you'll want to look at a symmetrical broadband connection.

Web and e-mail servers

When most people think of servers today, they think of Web servers and maybe e-mail servers. We all use them both constantly. If you plan to host your own Web and e-mail server(s), you should look at getting a symmetrical broadband connection.

 Most individuals and small businesses lack the expertise to secure their own Web and e-mail servers. Paying a Web-hosting company a monthly fee for service puts the security burden on them and will cost less than upgrading your broadband connection to a more expensive symmetrical connection.

Microsoft started including Web server software in its personal computer operating system several versions ago, and some third-party vendors also make server software for personal computers. On one hand, this exemplifies the "consumer and provider" of content nature of the early Internet. On the other, this created a security nightmare as people connected unprotected Web servers to their unsecured broadband Internet connections.

Security for personal computers and home users dropped even lower than dot com stock options when Microsoft configured all the networking software as "open to the world" as the default. Thousands of users, following Microsoft instructions, saw their personal computers hacked and every connected computer on their home or small business network compromised.

This isn't meant to scare you (well, maybe a little) but to emphasize the considerable security risk you run when connecting a system directly to the Internet. Each broadband equipped system on the Internet appears just as large and as tempting a target for hackers as any business site. I spend a considerable amount of time in the coming chapters closing all the security holes possible to keep you and your computer contents safe.

Now that the stern security lecture is out of the way (for now), I want to talk for a minute about why and how people use their own Web and e-mail servers. In spite of the added security considerations, running your own Web server is handy, useful, and can be just plain fun.

Again, the *server* part of Web server defines the traffic flow direction. When you have a Web server, your traffic flows more out than in; more upstream than downstream. This certainly applies to those who share photos and music from the Web sites because both create large digital files that take too long to download under the best of circumstances. Choking your upstream bandwidth connection using an asymmetrical connection just makes it worse.

Just keep in mind that every broadband service provider includes e-mail server support. So unless you feel a business need to run your own server, or you just want to have some fun with the experience, you should consider letting the experts take care of it for you.

Game networks

Game players generally blast cable because the shared network in the neighborhood causes performance fluctuations. The rule for gamers tends to be "go DSL" but that doesn't always guarantee success.

As you'll see in Chapter 3, DSL has plenty of network traffic contention issues. But these issues are in the central office and not in your neighborhood. In other words, your gaming experience will be determined by your service provider rather than by the traffic load in the network.

DSL gaming pros and cons:

- ✦ Direct, private connection to the central office
- ✦ Performance more consistent than cable
- ✦ Slower upstream speeds can mean slower response
- ✦ Slower downstream speeds can slow video response

Cable gaming pros and cons:

- ✦ Higher download speeds improve video performance
- ✦ Higher pipeline bandwidth can mean less upstream latency
- ✦ Shared neighborhood network causes performance fluctuations

Unfortunately, there is no one right answer for game fans. Checking over game forums around the Internet, I found people who loved their provider whereas the next comment would curse that same provider.

If someone in your household loves gaming, they have plenty of friends to ask for recommendations. Because an unhappy gamer generates more anguish in a household than almost anything else, you may wish to choose your broadband provider based on game requirements. After all, Web sites download pretty well on any broadband connection, but a local provider that configures its network well for games will generally serve all other content satisfactorily.

This recommendation doesn't cover those of you hosting game servers. If that's the case in your house, you need upstream bandwidth. Again, the gaming community your child uses will have valuable opinions to help define your options.

Speed comparisons

Here's a standard list of DSL speeds for symmetrical and asymmetrical broadband connections.

Typical residential aDSL speeds:

384 Kbps/128 Kbps

768 Kbps/384 Kbps

Notice you have two levels from most providers. Some DSL providers are starting to try and fight the speed advantage of cable by saying their downstream speed is "384 Kbps to 1.5 Mbps." Cable speeds fluctuate because cable is a shared medium and more traffic sharing the same bandwidth means slower speeds for all. Yet DSL touts the fact that it isn't a shared service. So where does that extra speed come from? Technically, there are ways to make that happen, but the providers aren't upfront about what they're doing.

Ask your DSL service provider before you pay extra for the increased download speed option. This could be an improvement from the marketing department rather than engineering. If the price is the same, take the higher speed option, of course, but don't be disappointed if the speed seems more like 384 Kbps than 1.5 Mbps most of the time.

Synchronous Digital Subscriber Line (SDSL) service is the symmetrical version of the DSL sold to residential and small business customers. Actually, SDSL is the "normal" DSL and aDSL is the variation, but you'd never know from the information provided by the phone companies.

The last three speeds listed in the following chart are called *IDSL* (ISDN Digital Subscriber Line), which isn't really DSL. ISDN (Integrated Services Digital Network) is a precursor to DSL from the '80s and uses technology that is a bit different from DSL. Due to prices higher than consumers were willing to bear, ISDN had little market success when it was originally introduced.

Typical business DSL speeds (SDSL and IDSL):

1.5 Mbps/384 Kbps

1.1 Mbps/1.1 Mbps

768 Kbps/768 Kbps

384 Kbps/384 Kbps

192 Kbps/192 Kbps

144 Kbps/144 Kbps

Even businesses have asymmetrical options. That makes sense, because the impact on your provider varies little if you're a household, SOHO, or (very) small business.

Larger businesses tend to host their own Web and e-mail servers and therefore need more upstream bandwidth. This means their choices tend toward DSL (or more expensive data-specific options as they need more bandwidth) rather than cable. Few cable companies allocate enough upstream bandwidth to offer businesses a symmetrical connection. But don't feel sorry for larger businesses because they have plenty of options, even though they all cost more than DSL or cable.

The technology behind ISDN, however, makes it more distance tolerant. Users out of the reach of "real" DSL often choose IDSL to grab the only broadband service they can get. At least the success of DSL and the need to reach farther means the phone companies had to break down and lower the price of ISDN to something the market would bear. The only difference for IDSL users from their aDSL counterparts is the slower IDSL speed and the (usually) higher price.

Nothing stops residential customers from ordering SDSL service, and nothing stops small businesses from ordering aDSL service. Let your needs make the decision, not the phone company salesperson trying to tell you they can't sell SDSL to a home. They can, and will, when you talk to a supervisor.

Summary

In summary, the U.S. Federal government doesn't seem to know what broadband really is, and what they define as broadband lags far behind European and Asian broadband service. In addition, there has been little government protection of consumers rights as FCC rulings routinely favor media corporation over citizen access and Fair Use access to material granted by the Constitution.

Perhaps it's not as confusing as all that. Broadband is, essentially, faster Internet access using new digital technologies (for DSL) and a large shared neighborhood bandwidth connection (cable).

Nothing bad will happen if you choose the wrong service for your needs. Your service provider will be able to reconfigure your connection if you ask. Moving from DSL to cable or vice versa will be a problem if you signed a long-term contract to grab a lower price, but you can always change when your contract expires.

When you have the choice, always get more speed. That includes upstream and downstream speed. No one's Internet response is as fast as they wish it were, so choose the fastest connections your budget will allow.

Types of Broadband Providers

There are two mainstream providers of broadband services: cable companies and telephone companies. The two alternative methods, satellite and wireless, offer advantages in some situations but have only niche markets.

 Cross-Reference Move your focus to Chapter 4 if you are out-side the range of DSL or cable broadband ser-vice, or your local provider(s) deliver such poor service you want to avoid them. Satellite ser-vice is available across the continental United States, whereas wireless broadband requires lo-cal providers.

Within the two most common broadband Internet access services, cable and DSL, lurk a range of options, speeds, and costs. Choosing the right technology for your situation requires a bit of technical background because you need to understand the options you have (or don't have) available.

Broadband from Phone Companies: Flavors of DSL

The many versions of Digital Subscriber Lines (DSL) come ultimately from one source: telephone companies. You will not always see the telephone company's name on the DSL service, but the telephone companies are the ones who own the telephone wires that reach into your home, the bulk wire connections that go to the central office, and the Internet long-distance data lines that provide access to the Internet.

Technically, each phone company is an Incumbent Local Exchange Carrier (ILEC). AT&Ts dismemberment in 1984 left seven regional Bell companies, and those are the ILECs. You may remember them being called Baby Bells, especially right after the breakup. Most commonly they fall under the label of Regional Bell Operating Company (RBOC).

The Telecommunications Act of 1996 opened the doors to the vast phone network infrastructure to competition, and hundreds (or thousands) of Competitive Local Exchange Carriers (CLEC pronounced see-leck) appeared. Many CLECs have no equipment, network, or repair personnel, so they function primarily as resellers of services they get wholesale from the larger CLECs and remaining regional ILEC (Baby Bell) companies. Some of the CLEC companies that appeared over the years had the life span of mayflies whereas others have grown and prospered.

 Note If you've ever seen the wonderful 1967 James Coburn movie *The President's Analyst* you will understand if I slip and write TPC for The Phone Company.

The important fact to remember is that all DSL companies and services stand upon the underlying telephone companies. Whether this makes you happy or nervous will depend on your experiences with various phone companies over the last few years.

You may have figured out that you'll need to have at least one telephone line connected to your home or office to support any flavor of DSL. You can call this line Plain Old Telephone System (POTS) or you may hear it referred to as a land line. Sometimes you hear it called copper because that's the metal used to make telephone wires.

Whatever you call it, you have to have an old-fashioned telephone line into your home or office. That used to be given, but today many people rely completely on their cellular phones and have no home phone. Unfortunately, cell phones don't support DSL.

Equally as important as the existing telephone lines running all over the place are the technicians who run all over the place to install, configure, and repair DSL services. Sending a technician out to a home or business to install and configure DSL for a new customer eats most of the profit for that line for the first year. The industry calls this a *truck roll* and that often sounds more like a swear word than a service description.

The expense of a truck roll for new customers kept the price too high for many consumers for years. Much research goes into designing products and creating software to enable new DSL customers to install the service themselves. After all, you can buy a new telephone and plug it into your existing jack and it works, right? The industry wants to make adding a DSL connection just that easy (and cheap), and they're getting there.

The development of DSL technology

The never-ending quest to run faster and jump higher pushes most technologies forward, and DSL follows that rule. During the 1980s, the growing cable television providers showed great promise (though most of those promises remain unfulfilled to this day) and grabbed most of the headlines. How could the dull, placid, monopolistic, and overly bureaucratic telephone industry compete?

Enter DSL and the promise of video on demand to homes everywhere. And, since everyone already had telephone lines, these fancy new digital telephone services would cost less to deploy than burying coax cable everywhere as the cable companies were doing.

Tech Bits

Copper, a handy metal for telephone lines and electricity cables, intrigued researchers with its promise as a conduit for high-speed data. Joseph Lechleider, now retired from the research facility Bellcore, first mapped out mathematically how to send broadband signals over a pair of copper wires. He also suggested most users would benefit from asymmetrical speeds to focus available bandwidth on downstream performance.

Twisted pair wiring, the kind used by the telephone company to reach your house, is exactly what it says: two physical wires twisted around each other. There is no shielding wrapped around the wires, as there is with coax used by the cable company. The twists, 12 per foot at minimum, help prevent electrical noise and interference.

T1 circuits, a symmetrical 1.5 Mbps connection, always needed expensive line-conditioning equipment. Finding a way to support those speeds without the conditioning equipment became the goal. ISDN came first, but the American public never got excited about the symmetrical low-speed (128 Kbps) data network protocol. The Europeans did, and I remember the telephone companies in America over-promising ISDN and then delaying access to the technology. No wonder consumers in the United States didn't get excited. From ISDN came HDSL, now used for most modern T1 circuits.

Cross-Reference

For a discussion of symmetrical and asymmetrical data transmissions, refer to Chapter 2.

Discreet MultiTone (DMT), hashed out largely by John Cioffi, became the standard for DSL in 1993 after comparison tests showed much better performance than other options. DMT separates the signal over a pair of copper wire into 256 subchannels to help eliminate electrical interference and line noise. Each subchannel has its own stream, starting at some frequency from 64 KHz up to 1.1 MHz, far above the 4 KHz signal used for voice telephone calls. Having separate subchannels makes it easier to provide asymmetrical data rates as well.

Tech Bits I particularly enjoy the fact that a connected group of 68 ADSL data frames is called a SuperFrame. Wonder if the SuperFrames have a little red digital cape flowing behind them on the network?

Improvements in error correction and packet framing (the way the data packets are put together) continue to increase reliability and provide better performance over distance. The goal now for researchers is to cut installation time to the point you no longer need a truck roll to install a new customer.

How DSL works for you

On one level, you can say that DSL works just like a super-charged modem. After all, you connect it directly to your computer (if you're only connecting one system), plug in a line from a phone jack to the modem, and the call goes directly to the telephone company's central office.

Just as with an old modem connection, your Internet service provider (ISP) must have a matching piece of equipment on its end to communicate with the piece of equipment at your end. Your computer is connected over a phone line to the ISPs computer. Should be nostalgic for some of you.

Note Before plugging your computer directly into your DSL modem (or more than one if your DSL modem has four ports), protect yourself. Check out Chapters 7, 11, 12, and 13 for security tools and technique to protect your computer.

You can, if you wish, skip the rest of the technical explanation and call a DSL provider and let them do the work, assuming you don't mind paying a high price for services you don't need, because the phone company is likely to add services you don't really need. This also assumes you don't mind letting some phone sales clerk at the service provider decide how fast a connection you want and that price is no object.

However, if you want to get the right service for your situation, keep reading. You don't have to know many details about DSL and cable and other Internet access technologies, but you can save yourself money and aggravation by getting an idea of what will make you happy before you place your service order.

Take some comfort in the fact that there are quite a few similarities between the way you've connected your computer to the rest of the world for years and the new, faster ways to connect. All DSL technology comes from work started inside the telephone company's research labs back in the 1980s, so they've been working on these services for quite a while. Now if they could just get a handle on that whole customer service idea, they'd be in great shape.

As you'll see in upcoming chapters, there are a number of ways to connect more than one computer to your broadband connection, so I can't say it always works like an old-fashioned modem. But the choices of your broadband provider, and your network design situation (whether two computers or a hundred) are independent of each other. After you have your decisions made, you can change your broadband access provider without changing anything except perhaps your broadband modem. Conversely, you can change just about everything inside your network and nothing will affect your broadband service.

 Cross-Reference Changing providers means changing your e-mail address and more. Check out *Keeping your old e-mail address* in Chapter 9 for your e-mail address options before signing a contract.

DSL

The term Digital Subscriber Line (DSL) has become generic and now tends to represent the family of digital data services over the telephone company's infrastructure. So referring to a "DSL connection" is like referring to a Ford. You have the right group, but you don't know if the specific item is a Mustang or an F150 pickup truck. The site shown in Figure 3-1 is one of many that can help you pick the best broadband service for your situation.

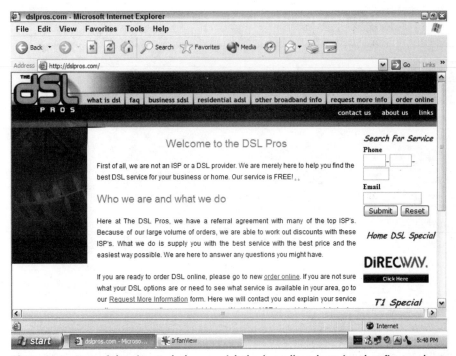

Figure 3-1: One of the sites to help you pick the broadband service that fits you best.

The Phone Company, and later the Baby Bells, lusted after a way to compete with cable television from the first day cable TV companies started digging up the streets to lay cable. One of the earliest rationalizations for research into DSL was the planned capability to download video to a consumer's TV through the person's telephone connection. I certainly call that a direct challenge to the cable industry, which at the time promised us 500 channels of quality televised entertainment.

Neither the phone or cable industries kept their word, did they? Video on demand doesn't exist from DSL providers in any sense of the word, and there's no easy way to push the video to the TV (yet). And the cable companies have only a half-way answer to their promises, with about 250 channels. They certainly missed as often as they hit that quality televised entertainment target.

If you call a service provider and ask for DSL and ask whether SDSL or G.Lite is available (definitions upcoming), you will put yourself above all the other customers who call in. This means you may get bumped up the line to talk to a supervisor, which is good because they can sometimes offer deals the first line salespeople can't. Take a look at the information provided by the DSLForum shown in Figure 3-2 for some ideas and background before calling for service.

Figure 3-2: The official Web site of the DSLForum.org.

DSL implementations have run wild throughout the United States, and even wilder in some other parts of the world. There are more total DSL broadband users in Japan than in the United States, and China added more subscribers than both in the third quarter of 2003. Table 3-1 contrasts usage in 20 countries.

Growth of DSL service made great strides outside the United States. The top three leaders in percentage increase in DSL lines in the first half of 2003 were Portugal (60 percent), China (40 percent) and the UK (32 percent). South Korea won the award for DSL penetration now that over 30 percent of the telephone

Table 3-1
Top 20 DSL Countries by Total Number of Subscribers
30 September 2003 from DSLForum.org

Ranking	Country	Total DSL Subscribers ('000)	Ranking	Country	Total DSL Subscribers ('000)
1	Japan	9,228.6	11	UK	1,414.7
2	USA	8,243.5	12	Brazil	837.7
3	China	7,817.4	11	Belgium	706.0
4	South Korea	7,069.4	11	Hong Kong	660.0
5	Germany	4,252.0	15	Netherlands	643.6
6	France	2,429.5	16	Sweden	508.0
7	Taiwan	2,374.0	17	Denmark	416.5
8	Canada	2,027.7	18	Switzerland	383.0
9	Italy	1,672.0	19	Israel	358.0
10	Spain	1,433.4	20	Australia	333.0

lines in that country support DSL. In fact, over 20 percent of DSL subscribers in South Korea have upgraded to a faster form of ADSL.

The DSLForum.org group doesn't plan to rest on these laurels. Its oft stated goal is "200 million subscribers and 20 percent of all phone lines online by the end of 2005." That's a lot of phone lines and a lot of customers surfing the Internet via broadband.

From now on, when I say "DSL" I mean that generically, and the subject at hand pertains to all the common flavors of DSL. As the big heading for this section says, think of DSL as broadband from the phone company. When the topic concerns only one type of DSL service, I'll specify that particular technology.

ADSL

When you see a phone company advertising DSL, it usually means Asymmetrical Digital Subscriber Line (ADSL). All consumer-oriented advertising, such as the TV ads and newspaper inserts, touting the low price of broadband refer to ADSL. In fact, you have to struggle sometimes to find the right department and salesperson to talk to you about faster services for business customers.

For almost all home users, including consumers and home offices, ADSL of some type will be your choice of broadband that's not cable. Many small businesses can function quite well using ADSL, especially if they are close enough to a telephone central office to get fast download speeds.

Tech Bits/ The sales literature fine print will explain that you're getting ADSL for the low price option, even though it says DSL. Remember that ADSL means you have slower upload speeds than download speeds, as explained in Chapter 2.

Standards and chipsets to put into equipment to support ADSL appeared in 1995. Officially, data rates up to 6.1 Mbps are supported. Expanded standards appeared in 2001, adding plenty of features to help the phone companies and your ISP. You can't see the improvements, but the additional network management tools may help your service provider solve a problem for you one day.

How fast is ADSL? Sorry to weasel out, but it depends. Some of the most popular downstream/upstream speeds are listed in Table 3-2.

Table 3-2
ADSL Speeds and Service Designators

Downstream	Upstream	Comment
384 Kbps	128 Kbps	Basic (and cheapest) ADSL service
608 Kbps	128 Kbps	Basic service from some providers
Up to 1.5 Mbps	128 Kbps	Basic plus
768 Kbps-1.5 Mbps	128 Kbps	Basic plus
768 Kbps-1.5 Mbps	256 Kbps	Deluxe
1.5 Mpbs-6.0 Mbps	384 Kbps	Top end ADSL

Notice your upstream speed choices: 128 Kbps, 256 Kbps, or 384 Kbps. If you need faster upstream speeds you need to look at another flavor of DSL.

Your choice of speed depends greatly on your distance from the phone company's central office. I'll cover those variables in the *Service Provider Details* section coming soon.

If you're close enough to get a choice of speeds, your provider may try to determine whether you are a business customer, a home customer, or a home office customer. This makes no difference to its equipment and network configuration, but oftentimes separate sales and marketing groups become territorial about customer bases. Use your new-found DSL lingo ability to get bumped up to a supervisor if you want a "business" connection to your home, home office, or small business.

Is ADSL the best choice for you? Check in Chapter 2 where I explained where an asymmetrical transmission speed (download fast, upload slow) makes sense and doesn't make sense. For instance, if you play interactive action games hosted by a game service provider, ADSL will work fairly well. If you plan on hosting games on your computer, the slower upload speeds will cramp your style (and your co-players will whine about your slow connection).

Most people receive more information from the Internet and Web than they send out. If that describes your Internet usage, ADSL will work for you.

Why Dial-up Speed Boosters Aren't Broadband

You may have wondered whether various speed boosters and turbo dial-up providers are worth the money versus getting broadband. Those systems work by caching information from popular Web sites at their end (the ISP) or your end (filling your computer with temporary files). If you go to popular Web sites, you will see improved speed with these systems. However, they do nothing at all to improve your download speed on e-mail, music files, applications updates, or noncached Web pages. If you can see the fine print, they will admit this, but they try hard to hide this fact.

ADSL2 and ADSL2+

Never content, ADSL vendors are working on ADSL2 and ADSL2+. ADSL2 product component developers are starting to release the building blocks necessary for equipment supporting the ADSL2 standard.

That may not mean too much for those of us in the United States, because the differences in speed and distance between ADSL2 and the current ADSL standards aren't all that great.

Where best-case ADSL speeds are now around 8 Mbps, ADSL2 promises best-case speeds of 12 Mbps. That sounds like a fair upgrade on a percentage basis, but if you're getting 6 Mbps downloads now, about the best possible, you're limited by Internet delays, not your ADSL service. ADSL2 won't make that much difference for you because it can't relieve Internet congestion between you and your favorite Web site.

ADSL2 offers increased distance, but only about 600 feet worth. Although that will make you happy if you're 400 feet beyond the limit, that doesn't mean your DSL service provider will upgrade to ADSL2 and connect you.

In fact, there are no major DSL vendors in the United States offering ADSL2 services as of early in 2004. There may be one or two who just purchased the equipment and therefore received ADSL2-compliant hardware, but I haven't found them.

A search of popular DSL discussion boards turned up reports that many ISPs in Japan are offering ADSL2 service. Finland, that hotbed of technical networking advancement, has one ISP promising to roll out ADSL early in 2004.

The big news for ADSL2 is pair-bonding. First appearing with ISDN to hook two 64 Kbps digital channels together for 128 Kbps to justify the price of ISDN over a 56 Kbps dial-up modem, pair-bonding does what it says. It takes two or more ADSL2 channels, or wire pairs, and electronically combines them into a single data conduit. Suddenly (Bam!) you have speeds approaching those offered by fiber optics over regular telephone company twisted pair wires.

ADSL2 also introduces ways to handle voice over data on ADSL connections without disturbing the existing voice connection on the underlying telephone line. Although that may seem somewhat stupid to jump through hoops to support VoIP on a phone line, the more advances companies make in handling voice over data lines will help quality increase while prices decrease.

ADSL2+ will be the newsworthy upgrade in the United States. The new standard effectively doubles the bandwidth capacity of copper wire from 1.1 MHz to 2.2 MHz of signal room. This makes it possible to offer download speeds of up to 25 Mbps as long as you're within 5,000 feet (one mile as the wire winds its way) from the telephone company's central office.

Remember those dreams of downloading movies through your telephone wires? The technology still isn't there, even with ADSL2+. Television quality (broadcast TV, not HDTV) requires 96 Mbps, but can be compressed to 6 Mbps. The compression tools still need hardware support, not just software, so the telephone lines will remain TV free for the next few years.

SDSL and T1

Symmetrical DSL (SDSL) vendors aim more toward businesses than residential customers, but make exceptions for home businesses most of the time. But they charge business rates, of course, even if they install the service at your home.

Some of the things you may get with SDSL you don't get with ADSL include the following:

✦ A fixed IP address (see Chapter 12)

✦ Multiple fixed IP addresses (ditto)

✦ Bundled service packages for long distance call discounts

✦ Support from people instead of voice response systems (no guarantees)

✦ ISPs that understand business needs

✦ Spam filtering at the ISP site

As I explained earlier in the *Development of DSL Technology* section, DSL has started to replace T1 data circuits for many situations. This helps the customers, because DSL is cheaper than any T1 offering. It also helps the service provider because DSL is cheaper for them to support.

The offerings from some service providers even call SDSL lines "Fractional T1" products. As long as they charge SDSL prices rather than T1 prices, let them call it whatever they want.

Most common SDSL speeds are 384 Kbps and 768 Kbps (upstream and downstream). These are, amazingly, two popular Fractional T1 speed options.

If your location isn't within range of a phone company central office offering DSL, you can look into a Fractional T1 connection. The T1 technology reaches farther but costs more than DSL of any flavor.

Some of the things you will get with T1 you don't get with SDSL:

✦ A Service Level Agreement (SLA) covering the provider's responsibilities

✦ Improved monitoring

✦ Improved technical support

✦ Unlimited IP addresses and network configuration options

✦ Uptime (usually 99.99 percent uptime guaranteed)

✦ Specifically filtered and conditioned telephone line

If your service provider can connect you with SDSL, it probably can also support T1 or Fractional T1 to your site. Whether it does or not is a different story. Another broadband technology, Frame Relay, is almost impossible to purchase unless your site is in a business location.

Pricing between T1 and SDSL are also two different stories. Since T1 lines can be "stretched" to reach more locations, distance strongly influences pricing. More distance and more speed always equals more expense. There are telephone company charges included because of the conditioned line, so make sure your quoted total includes that charge.

And how much is the total? Used to be horrendous ($1,500–$2,000 per month), but the prices have dropped way down. But even dropped, they're outside the range of individuals and many small businesses.

T1 cost range estimates, with common marketing labels for fractional T1 connections, for the symmetrical digital data circuits:

✦ **Full T1 (1.5 Mbps):** $600–$1,500 per month

✦ **Half (768 Kbps):** $500–$900 per month

✦ **Quarter (384 Kbps):** $400–$700 per month

✦ **Sixth (256 Kbps):** $300–$700 per month

Not all speeds are available in all areas or from all service providers. T1 is symmetrical, so you get 1.5 Mbps throughput upstream and downstream. That's one advantage of using two pairs of wires for T1.

Although conventional wisdom says homes and home offices don't "deserve" a T1 line, don't let that restrict your thinking. Some small businesses need the speed and reliability of a T1 line. If your business demands indicate a T1 or Fractional T1, get one. The prices have never been better.

IDSL and ISDN

ISDN Digital Subscriber Line (IDSL) is the poor relation of the DSL family. Integrated Services Digital Network (ISDN) is the lowest speed entry into the digital data line world. More successful in Europe than the United States, ISDN providers usually maxed out their standard offerings with dual-channel ISDN for a total of 128 Kbps over standard telephone lines.

Yes, the dial-up modem you want to get rid of does provide a third of that speed. ISDN offers digital links at longer distances than any other affordable consumer DSL option, so the phone companies are slapping a coat of DSL paint on ISDN and calling it IDSL.

IDSL can break through two big problems with DSL: distance and older repeater circuits in the telephone system. ISDN, the basis for IDSL, can use repeaters to extend signal range far beyond standard DSL connections. In addition, approximately half the homes in the United States can't yet be reached by ADSL because of an old style of telephone circuit repeater. ISDN, and therefore IDSL, can push through those circuits, as can the G.Lite technology described in the next section.

IDSL is a symmetrical connection, because it's based on ISDN and ISDN is symmetrical. For that reason the price sometimes reflects business rates rather than basic level ADSL rates. At least some IDSL service providers allow you to buy more than one circuit and bond them for better throughput.

If your service provider says you can't get ADSL or SDSL, ask about IDSL. If that doesn't do the trick, ask about ISDN. It's better than dialup. Or skip to Chapter 4 and learn about satellite and wireless networking.

G.Lite, HDSL, VDSL, and RDSL

G.Lite, a new technology that's been approved by the standards committees that hopes to eliminate or greatly reduce truck rolls. Remember that truck rolls cost the service provider a ton of money (hundreds of dollars to get a $30 per month account). Every truck roll the service providers eliminate will make that new connection profitable in less than a year.

Sometimes called Universal ADSL (by some marketing VPs, no doubt), G.Lite can handle the split between the telephone company's frequency range for voice calls and the higher frequencies used for data. Normal ADSL installations require a splitter on the line close to the customer's location, which means a truck roll. Since the DSL modem installation in the home between the computer and the DSL line has gotten so much easier, consumers can install DSL themselves, after G.Lite handles that pesky splitter problem, of course.

The other big advantage of G.Lite is its ability to go through the repeaters that block regular ADSL. This makes it possible to get connected at greater distances but drops the maximum speed to 1.5 Mbps downstream and 512 Kbps upstream in the circumstances.

If your service provider supports G.Lite, the sales representatives may not mention it unless you ask for a higher speed connection they can't provide. This is a new service and your provider may not have it yet or your sales rep may not have been trained. For your part, you don't really care whether your DSL modem connects to ADSL or G.Lite, because it will look the same to you.

The explosion of inexpensive DSL recently reflects the availability of service providers to push DSL out to about 90 percent of the U.S. residences now, thanks to G.Lite. Not to be outdone, ADSL product manufacturers are figuring out their own ways past the repeaters and truck rolls. If your service provider pitches Consumer DSL, they're pushing reworked ADSL. Rejoice in the fact there's plenty of competition trying to grab your monthly Internet access check.

The following list discusses three other DSL flavors your service provider won't mention unless your situation is unusual:

✦ High Bit-Rate DSL (HDSL), an older technology, began the development of T1 lines as DSL links. Two pairs (two phone lines) are needed for the symmetrical HDSL. HDSL-2, the new and improved version, can run over one telephone line. You won't see either of these services offered to your home or small business.

✦ Very High Data Rate DSL (VHDSL) is the dragster of the DSL family. It supports up to 55 Mbps of symmetrical traffic, but only for 1,000 feet. Large companies with a campus environment love it.

✦ Rate-Adaptive DSL (RDSL) is another improvement on ADSL. Software determines which data rates the customer can use on an RDSL line. Downstream speeds can vary between 640 Kbps to 2.2 Mbps, and upstream speeds can vary between 272 Kbps to 1.008 Mbps.

Service provider details

There are many DSL service providers other than the local telephone company. However, the telephone company will not tell you about them, even though it provides the actual lines and technology for the smaller broadband service providers. If you want options, you'll have to find them yourself.

Some broadband service providers have a national presence, and some serve a small community. Their size does not indicate their quality, but may indicate the range of services they are able to offer.

Here's a quick list of Web addresses for some of some of the major national DSL service providers in the United States:

✦ www.BellSouth.com

✦ www.Covad.com

✦ www.DSL.net

✦ www.Earthlink.com

✦ www.MCI.com

✦ www.Qwest.net

✦ SBC.Yahoo.com (notice the dot between SBC and Yahoo)

✦ www.Verizon.net

Are there other service providers offering DSL and Internet provider services in your area? Absolutely. You may have dozens or more, either located near you or including you in their service area. The previous list merely names some of the national providers so you can compare their services against those of your local companies. *Hint*: You want the smaller local companies to beat the national companies in price, service, features, or all three.

www.broadbandreports.com, shown in Figure 3-3, makes for fascinating reading, especially if you want to go through the forums and see how your fellow citizens have been treated by broadband service providers in the past. Don't try and pick out a good provider based on just this feedback, however, because the same provider will get cheers from one person and jeers from the next. But do look at the ways customers have convinced their service providers to fix their problems and try them yourself when necessary.

Figure 3-3: A site that offers reviews of broadband service providers.

One thing you must remember is that your broadband service provider becomes your ISP. If your current ISP adds broadband service, you can probably upgrade with them and change nothing about your e-mail, name servers, personal Web pages, or support contacts.

If your current ISP doesn't offer broadband service, or you're looking to go to broadband because you hate your ISP, make a note of the following details. You don't need an answer for every item before you change, but the more you plan ahead the less hair pulling you'll do later. Take a look at Table 3-3 to see what I consider important.

Table 3-3
Service Provider Feature Recommendations

Features to check	My recommendations
E-mail	Enough addresses for everyone on your network, plus a couple for future use. Web-based e-mail, virus and spam filters are nearly standard from good providers
Connection times	No limit to online connection hours
IP Addresses	Dynamic or static? One or more?
Personal Web site	Enough space for your needs, support for popular Web design tools like FrontPage, and enough allowed bandwidth for the traffic you expect
Newsgroups	Full read and write access to majority of Usenet groups
Technical Support	Online and telephone options, with either a local or toll free call. 24x7 support may come in handy one day

You may not agree with my recommendations, and that's fine. But be sure you consider your own recommendations before you sign the service provider contract. You have much more leverage before you sign than after.

Availability

Real estate agents know this joke: What are the three most important things about broadband availability? Location, location, and location.

DSL requires physical wires to connect to each client. Building out those huge bundles of twisted pair wiring took the telephone companies over a half century of constant work.

For cost saving purposes, phone companies looked for ways to support more users while building fewer central offices. They started putting extension units out in the neighborhoods and business districts called remote terminals. Sometimes these look like cabinets sitting by the side of the road. They started by using T1 connections back to the central office, but for the last couple of decades have used fiber optic cables.

Remote terminals reset the distance limit to customers out of reach of the central office. My home, for example, is over 35,000 feet away from the central office. No DSL for me for years, until SBC added a remote terminal somewhere in the area. Now I can get high bandwidth ADSL without a problem.

There is a problem with many of the older remote terminals, however. The phone companies originally used what's called a Digital Loop Carrier (DLC) to provide the signal boost. They did this before DSL development, which meant (life being the way it is) that the DLCs blocked DSL.

Tech Bits Digital Loop Carrier blocks were serious impediments to early DSL rollout efforts. At one time, over 50 percent of all U.S. homes and businesses had a DLC between them and their central office, blocking DSL for them. ISDN worked, but not ADSL.

G.Lite, as I mentioned back a few pages, figured a way around these DSL roadblocks. So have some ADSL product vendors who are claiming their networks run faster and jump higher than G.Lite. Phone companies are working to upgrade their old repeaters and put in place new DSL-friendly circuits, but the cost is high and sometimes someone (like the Federal Communications Commission on several occasions) has to nudge them to keep them moving.

Depending on which survey you believe, either 70 percent or 90 percent of all U.S. homes and businesses are now within the reach of some type of DSL service provider. The phone companies are begging off "universal" broadband service, even though they've taxed us on every phone bill for decades to support universal telephone service. Whether the phone companies will be forced to consider broadband telephone service that must be universally supported will be the subject of high political drama over the next few years.

Can you call and demand the phone company get DSL out to your location? Sure you can call, but it will have no effect. Phone companies put new remote terminals and upgrade old repeaters in areas willing to buy DSL service in large numbers. Put your name on their "call when you have DSL" list and encourage every person in the neighborhood to do the same, and maybe you'll get lucky. Location, location, location.

Distance and speed

The farther you are from a central office, or a DSL-friendly repeater in a remote terminal or other extension feature, the slower your DSL service. The closer you are, the faster your service.

Let me boil down average distance limitations in Table 3-4 and show some guidelines for what services you can get at what distances.

Table 3-4 is an estimate and average, not a guarantee. Your service provider will measure and tell you what it can do. Technical limits are as the wire winds, meaning a site physically 5,000 feet away may be 9,000 feet away following the cable. Not likely, but possible.

Table 3-4
Service Levels vs. Distance

Distance in Feet	Comment
Less than 5,000	You are golden—fast DSL easy to get
5,000–10,600	Top speeds (6 Mbps) possibly out of reach
10,600–15,000	Dicey for national providers. Service will be slower
15,000–18,000	You can get service, but minimum ADSL only
18,000–22,000	IDSL okay for you? RDSL may help when available
22,000–38,000	Cross your fingers and hope an innovative small provider in your area will make it work
22,000	Technical limit for G.Lite
9,000	Technical maximum for 8–Mbps ADSL
16,000	Technical limit for 2 Mbps ADSL

Some DSL users report that broadband service providers have a policy where a potential residential customer is just a little too far away. But, if they pony up the extra money, the business class service can reach them. The fact that the two services are functionally the same never creeps into the conversation.

 Tech Bits All speed listings for data transmissions are optimistic and theoretical rather than practical. You'll rarely if ever receive speeds as much as 80 percent of official speed.

Some Web sites can help you estimate your distance from a DSL-friendly phone company installation. One is at www.broadbandreports.com/distance, a site shown in Figure 3-3. Just about every DSL vendor includes a quick qualification test based on your telephone number and address to see what level of DSL service will reach you. Prequalification does not guarantee service, however, as SBC in 2002 said I could get DSL but later changed the story because I was just a little too far away.

Throughput

People talk about DSLs advantages since each connection runs directly from your home or office to the telephone company's central office in the area. Cable, they sneer, is a shared medium and so your neighbor sucks your bandwidth.

Yes, but let me drill down a bit more. Once your direct DSL link hits the service provider or central office, what do you think happens? Every customer connected to every line served by that service provider may try to reach the Internet through the same router. You can't see the congestion because it's upstream from you and hidden inside the service provider's walls.

Your physical street may have a direct shot to the highway, so you make great time out of your neighborhood. Yet that helps little if the highway looks like a parking lot. The same thing can happen at the broadband service provider's switch that connects its customers to the Internet.

The term for all the arrangements service providers make with each other to connect their networks is peering. Every service provider faces a bottleneck issue if all its clients attempt to reach the Internet at the same time, just like the crush at the door of a movie theater when the show's over. Making peering arrangements helps service providers ensure each data packet coming in from customers has plenty of ways to reach its Internet destination.

But nothing in DSL technology addresses this issue. After the DSL connection carries your packet to your service provider, the noncontention network design disappears.

Yes, network congestion happens in your neighborhood on broadband over cable. But network congestion happens at your service provider on broadband over DSL. So there may be a slight advantage, but only a slight one.

Of course, if your cable broadband provider has over-subscribed the cable capacity in your neighborhood, busy times on the broadband would be noticeably slower and throughput will drop. The only way to stop this is to call and complain when the "random service quality generator" kicks into overdrive. Or, convince your neighbors to stay off their broadband connections when you want access.

Reliability

Service and uptime matter, and broadband reliability does tend to favor a hub and spoke arrangement (the phone company's central office is in the middle with lines going out like bicycle wheel spokes) like that of DSL over a shared medium like that of cable. And that's not an underhanded shot at cable's reputation but the fact of a shared medium.

When your DSL line breaks, you suffer. When your neighbor's DSL line breaks, you don't know it. When your neighbor's cable breaks, and you're on that cable as well, you know it. Better you don't suffer for your neighbor's problems.

DSL connections within 10,000 feet of the central office (or service provider) may have no active components between the client and the office. Fewer active components means fewer mistakes.

Customers served by DSL via remote terminals to boost the signal for longer distances do have some active components between them and their service provider. If something happens to the remote terminal, the entire area's DSL service would be interrupted. But such a failure would ring alarm bells and send technical support folks running.

Telephone companies do a pretty good job of keeping phone lines up. Since DSL runs over the same physical wires as your home or office telephone line, the DSL service stays up as well.

One detail with ADSL you don't often see mentioned is the need for a splitter on the phone lines. The DSL signals make noise on the line that interferes with voice connections unless you put a filter on that line. Your ADSL supplier will include the filters as part of your installation kit, or you can buy them at Radio Shack. Once in place, your phone quality stays about the same even when you're listening to streaming music downloads over the Internet while talking on that same phone line.

Security

Is your computer safe on DSL? Not really, because DSL puts your computer on the Internet, and bad things can happen to computers on the Internet.

 This isn't the place to look for computer security information about viruses, hackers, and firewalls. Skip to Chapter 7 for a full examination of those topics.

However, using any flavor of DSL does not make your computer less secure than any other computer on the Internet. Some of the features increase security, such as IP addresses that change every time you connect to the Internet. Those changes make it difficult for someone to focus on your particular computer.

Technically, someone could follow your phone cable and physically tap it somewhere. Not likely, but the truly paranoid would worry about that. But if you're that level of paranoid, you shouldn't use a computer at all, because you expose all sorts of information about yourself when you traverse the Internet.

Costs

Pricing for DSL services varies from each provider, of course, but there are three levels to most price structures. Basic ADSL, the 384/128 Kbps product, gets all the promotional come-on pricing. See an ad for "High Speed Internet Access for less than a dollar a day!!!" and they're talking about 384/128 Kbps speeds to residential customers. In the spring of 2004, prices for this service level seem to be $39.95 per month with discounts and specials making the price $25 to $30 per month. Although the low prices are supposed to run out after a year, I doubt vendors will have any luck upping the price for existing customers. All you need do if they threaten to bump your price is threaten to sign up with another provider at its introductory price.

As hardware costs decrease for new generations of DSL equipment and the early adopter customers all have service, I'm betting prices will float downwards even more. Some provider will start a price war offering service at $19.95 per month before long, and that will be the new "basic" price. I've already seen $19.95 as a "Special Three Month Introductory Special Price!!!" from two providers.

Mid-tier pricing, for the downstream speeds ranging up to a guaranteed 1.5 Mbps, are at least double the retail price for the basic price. The lowest national pricing I can find now is $49.95, and most service providers run the price up to about $80 at the top end. Ask your potential provider about all service levels, because some levels only jump $5 or $10 in price but offer substantial speed increases.

Top end pricing for top speeds (6 Mbps/256 Kbps) averages around $150 per month, but that will drop as well. At least one smaller service provider has run promotions offering top speeds for $99 for a limited time. These speeds are only possible if you can throw a rock and hit your central office. (Okay, a slight exaggeration), but you can ask. Table 3-5 compares estimated pricing levels.

Table 3-5
Three DSL Pricing Levels Estimate

Speed	Price Range
384 Kbps downstream	$20–30 per month
Up to 1.5 Mbps downstream	$50–80 per month
6 Mbps downstream	$100–160 per month

Although service providers list installation charges on their Web sites, the competition today stops them from actually charging for installation. Every plan I've seen provides free installation in exchange for signing a year's contract or just to entice you to sign up. If you're situation is unusual or requires several trips to reconfigure your outside DSL connections, they still shouldn't charge for installation. If the technicians start coming into your house, especially after finishing the installation, you will almost always get charged. Keep 'em outside, and you can avoid paying because the problem will be their fault. Bring them in the house, and it will cost you, because the problem will be your fault (at least in their eyes).

Your DSL modem, at least in most cases, will cost you a few dollars per month. You can choose to buy your own DSL modem, but there's little reason to do so. If you rent the DSL modem from your service provider, they have to provide support and updates. One plan I saw asked for $3 per month, but set a price of about $200 per modem. Getting technical support is easier if you have the "standard" DSL modem. The flip side is that the service provider must repair or replace your DSL modem if there's a problem. Many of the people I know, including me, have needed a DSL or cable modem replaced. Pay the rent and you'll almost always come out ahead.

If you have a second phone line for your computer's dial-up connection, and choose the least expensive ADSL product, the two prices may actually wash out. Yes, you may be able to get ADSL and the 384 Kbps downstream speed for about the same price as your wheezing 56K modem.

Second telephone line: $22–$28 per month (including fees).

ADSL basic service: $25–$30 per month.

Looks pretty close to me.

With a financial arrangement like that, how can you not justify ordering broadband this minute? Or at least read the next section and the next chapter to see which broadband makes the most sense to you.

Broadband from the Cable Company

Over the past 30 years, the cable industry built an enormous network. This is good and bad. It has great reach, but as the phone companies found out with their digital loop carriers and other ADSL–resistant repeaters, sometimes the choices of the past complicate the future. The early cable network components often hinder introduction of new broadband services over cable.

Cable companies have different regulations and government restrictions to deal with than telephone companies do. Because of the expense in building out cable plants, (the network of cable wiring all over a city), cable companies usually get a monopoly granted from the city in question. Unlike the situation with AT&T and the Bell companies in 1984, there's been no move to break up the cable companies. Therefore, there's no move afoot to force them to support services from competitive companies and give them access to the actual cable network, as the phone companies have been forced to do.

So unlike DSL, where you usually have a choice of providers in an area, your choice of broadband from a cable company is limited. Either you want service from the cable company in your area, or you don't. A few cable companies are starting to partner with national provider such as Earthlink, America Online, and MSN, so keep an eye out for those. It will still be the same cable, of course, but you'll get a different Internet service provider brought in to provide the Internet functions like e-mail and handle technical support.

Don't think of this as wrong or right, just realize it's different. You may not have a choice of broadband service providers over cable, but you have a choice of broadband service providers reaching you through other methods such as the telephone network, satellite, and wireless. But now it's time to examine how broadband over cable works.

How broadband over cable works for you

Like the telephone company network, the cable network follows the same centralization philosophy. Although the phone companies call their collection points the central office, cable companies call theirs the head-end. Same difference, although there tend to be more central offices than head-ends because of the distance limitations of telephone wire.

Unlike the telephone company, the cable companies use a common cable with multiple homes sharing access to the same cable. For cable TV, this works fine. Your cable box filters the right frequency based on your channel selection, and your TV receives that channel. All channels are streaming by down the cable, and you pick the one you want. When your neighbor picks a different channel, there's no interaction between you and your neighbor, as shown in Figure 3-4.

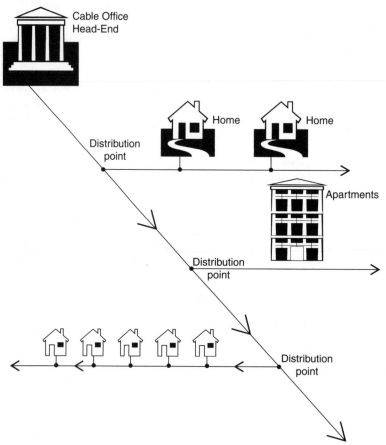

Figure 3-4: Electrically, the cable system is one long wire reaching from the distribution center to your home, and all users connect across this long wire.

Traditional cable systems replicated the broadcast TV model but transmit signals on specific radio frequencies over the cable rather than through the air. Unlike with the telephone network, there was no need to support information flowing upstream from the customer to the cable head-end. They sent the TV stations down the cable, and you chose which channel (frequency on the cable) you wanted.

Honest cable executives will admit the history of cable development includes two large mistakes:

✦ Fixating on a one-way network early on

✦ Burying their cables

Adding interactive TV tools became a hot button in the 1980s, and adoption of that feature set immediately turned existing cable company network hardware obsolete. In the 1990s, as cable companies starting offering digital cable and Internet access, most of the one-way equipment was long gone. If you live in an area where the old cable system can't support upstream communications, you have my sympathies. But don't buy broadband service from that company.

Which brings to mind the second serious problem with some cable providers: their cables are old, worn, decaying, and out of reach. Need to upgrade a cable repeater or check to see where a cable is broken? Call the heavy equipment crew to spend thousands of dollars moving the dirt and concrete off the cable so they can see it and fix it. Increased use of fiber cables to neighborhood nodes will help, because those can be easily hung off telephone poles.

The head-end station includes the Cable Modem Termination System (CMTS), the cable equivalent of the telephone switch. Your cable modem, whether for Internet or TV, communicates only with the CMTS at the head-end station providing service for your area. The back side of the CMTS connects with the signals from the TV networks, the Internet, and even the telephone system as cable companies start offering telephone services.

Your cable modem, as you'll see in Chapter 8, works more like a Local Area Network router than a modem. You will treat the cable modem just like you do your DSL modem: plug it into the broadband connection wire (telephone wire or coax cable) and plug the other end into your computer or network wiring device.

Cable bandwidth

Coax cables have a maximum bandwidth of either 330 MHz or 450 MHz of capacity, depending on the type of coax cable used. Networks with a mix of fiber and coax (sometimes called HFC for Hybrid Fiber/Coax) can support up to 750 MHz of capacity. Fiber optic transmitters and receivers increase capacity regularly, so the 750 MHz capacity limit may be long bypassed if your local cable company has new equipment.

The available bandwidth is sliced into 6 MHz section for each TV channel. Upstream and downstream channels both require 6 MHz of frequency room. Data services on early cable systems allocated two 6 MHz channels, one for downstream traffic and one for upstream traffic, separated by at least 8 MHz to keep the channels from interfering with each other.

 Tech Bits Modern cable systems use fiber optic cables from the head-end out to neighborhoods, where they connect to a *node* for distribution to homes and businesses. Nodes may be situated to support up to 4,000 homes, but cable companies design for a load of 10–25 percent for each node. This means a normal customer count for a node is 10–1,000 customers. These numbers vary according to provider, so use them as estimates rather than factoids.

Newer cable systems lean toward offering 30–38 Mbps downstream and 5–10 Mbps upstream bandwidth. Yet up to 1,000 customers can share a

30–38 Mbps upstream channel and a 5–10 Mbps channel and still receive their promised 2–3 Mbps download speeds and 128–384 Kbps upload speeds. That's because not everyone is on the network at the same time, and those who are don't all try to download Super Bowl highlight videos at the same time.

Nothing stops cable providers from adding more channels to support more customers or add more speed to downloads or uploads. That said, you as an individual will have little luck getting that channel allocated, because there is little room left on the modern cable TV network. Bandwidth, and therefore channels, is expensive because there are limits to how much is available.

This number matters because you share the cable bandwidth with all the other 999 potential people supported by your node. Remember how DSL people like to ridicule cable broadband because of local network contention? This is what they're talking about, but a properly configured and maintained cable network will still provide around 3 Mbps downstream and 256 Kbps upstream speeds.

DOCSIS

Standards turn technology ideas into products, and cable companies are not immune to that rule. Data Over Cable Service Interface Specification (DOCSIS) became an official standard in March 1998 and defined the market for cable modems and the equipment to support them at the head-end.

Now up to DOCSIS 3.0, the standard details downstream traffic rates between 27–36 Mbps and upstream traffic rates between 320 Kbps–10 Mbps. The radio frequency range for downstream is between 50–750 MHz (and up as the frequency range extends) and 5–42 MHz upstream. Notice the minimum 8 MHz space between the two ranges.

Tech Bits Do standards help? Absolutely. The reference Web site Webopedia (www.webopedia.com) says there were 1.2 million cable modems installed in the United States in 1998, with an average street price of $245. The estimate for 2004 is that 24.3 million units will be installed and they will have an average price of $50 per unit. Big improvement for consumers.

Whether you think to ask for it or not, your cable modem will be DOCSIS compliant. The trade group that designed the specification includes over 85 percent of the vendors in the market.

Service provider details

Just because you can get cable TV doesn't mean you can get cable broadband Internet access. The cable company must add some serious equipment to its head-end and often to its neighborhood network cable plant to offer Internet access.

Chances are good your cable supplier does include broadband Internet access, however. According to most research groups at the end of 2003, active cable broadband customers outnumber DSL customers by almost two to one: 10.5 million to 5.5 million.

Technical support, at least in my area near Dallas, has been good enough to not notice. They answer when I call; the techs come when they say they will, and they clear up problems when they say they will. If your cable broadband provider doesn't do the same, complain and keep notes.

Distance and Speed

When cable broadband is good, it's very, very good. When it's bad, it's still usable, but more aggravating.

DSL fans don't like to admit this, but unless you live close (within 10,000 feet) of a central office or modern remote terminal, you'll never get the downstream speed of a cable customer sitting out in the suburbs. Even congested cable during prime teenager online gaming times provides higher speeds than most of the ADSL packages customers can order. The speed may not always be consistent, but it's always there, and sometimes so fast it will astound you.

Because modern cable installations include a mix of fiber and coax cables distance from the head-end has little impact on the network speed for users. You don't need to worry about distance if you use a cable broadband supplier.

Upgrading the cable plant has the added benefit of increasing the speeds to customers. Many cable companies now advertise they guarantee (kind of) 3 Mbps rather than 2 Mbps downstream speeds. Every little bit helps. Unplug your cable modem power plug for 30 seconds, plug it in, and see if your cable system received the upgrade already.

Reliability

Write your own joke: Reliability is to cable as X is to Y. Dogs to cats? Politicians to honesty? Fish to bicycles?

A cultural touchstone, cable technical and customer service problems permeate humor because everyone can relate. When Hollywood makes a movie called *The Cable Guy* with a psycho main character, you know it's bad PR for the cable business. At least it was a comedy, so try and laugh about the stereotype.

I certainly remember the bad PR days when my AT&T (and now Comcast) broadband cable kept going out for hours every day it rained. But it went out after the rain, usually the second day of a long rain or the dry day after a rain.

Thanks to a clever technician in the area who looked at the pattern of tech support calls, I learned what the problem was. A person in my neighborhood put an electric fence in his yard to help control his dogs. Unfortunately, he put the fence down on top of the AT&T cable. Every time it got wet and the water soaked through the ground to the cable, the electrical fence leaked enough current to garble the cable signals.

Tech Bits

Only Wiley books drill deeply enough to warn you about the catastrophic mixture of electric dog fences, buried broadband cables, and rain.

To be fair and balanced, there are two reasons you can't just point to cable broadband and say it's not good. You get great bandwidth, and improvements in the physical network keep increasing uptime and reliability.

I keep a list of every cable outage I experience in the computer address book with the cable technical support contact information. When you call and say, "your service was out last Tuesday from 12:24 P.M. to 1:07 P.M." the online support person realizes standard excuses won't fly. And when you track all the service outages, you can look back and see months and months where you have no entries whatsoever.

Various reports show a wide range of reliability statistics for DSL and cable providers. You can't always be sure who paid for a survey, but you can guess it's the broadband provider who came out looking strong in comparison to the competition. Several studies seem to indicate DSL and cable have a similar amount of outages, but that cable stays offline longer than DSL. Your mileage may vary, so check out the Good, Bad, and Ugly reviews on www.broadbandreports.com/gbu.

Security

DSL fans point out that cable connections within the same node are on the same local area network (not exactly accurate technically but you get the idea.) and therefore are less secure. To a degree, that is accurate. Computers directly connected to the cable network rather than through any type of firewall can be seen by other users. If those computers have any type of hosting services on, such as file or printer sharing, others can see them. This used to be the default for Microsoft Windows operating systems, and many people had security problems because of their lack of understanding of network setup options.

Microsoft Windows 2000 and XP no longer turn on all their various hosting services by default, closing some security holes. Many users now have routers with firewalls to protect their in-house (or in-business) networks from outsiders. The ability to snoop around your neighbor's PC and find bank account numbers has declined greatly.

Speaking of bank accounts, all financial institutions with access to their services via a Web browser use a secure Web link (SSL for Secure Sockets Layer). The chance of seeing your neighbor's computer on the local cable loop has dropped, and if you could, all the stuff worth stealing would be hidden by Web page security routines guarding the data.

Costs

Most of the costs for broadband access are the same for both DSL and cable. You will need a DSL or cable modem, and they cost about the same and are often included in the service price, making it a wash. Service calls tend to be about the same, especially when dealing with national Internet service providers. Installation costs are comparable, although again, these are usually waived as part of signing up for the service.

Everyone wants to discuss the monthly bill, because that's what you see on a regular basis. And the winner there is ... <drumroll> ... DSL by a nose, thanks to aggressive ADSL pricing.

Basic ADSL, the 384/128 Kbps version, leads the broadband price parade by offering regular pricing of around $40 and introductory pricing as low as $20 to $30 per month. Cable prices bounce between $40 and $60 depending on provider and whether you have cable TV service from that same provider.

Can I argue that 1.5 Mbps/256 Kbps cable broadband at $50–$60 is a better value than 384/128 Kbps ADSL at $25? Yes, but that's a personal decision. If you're close enough to get higher speed ADSL for a few dollars, you'll usually get equal or better service when compared to a cable broadband connection during peak personal hours of 5:00 P.M. to 11:00 P.M. If you aren't close enough for faster ADSL, less absolute dollars for the ADSL broadband, but more speed per dollar for the cable broadband, make it your choice of where to spend your money.

Either way you see the situation today, keep watching. I predict prices for broadband of all types will drop even further.

Summary

The two mainstream broadband service offerings, DSL and cable, come from two different worlds. Phone companies have a long history of data transmissions over telephone lines and those companies keep pushing newer and faster broadband options out the door. Cable includes many advantages, including almost double the number of paying customers.

Both options provide broadband access suitable for many. If you live in or near a large city, you will have many provider choices. Picking the broadband service provider for your situation will be difficult with all those choices, but if you're not happy, you can choose again.

Types of Alternative Broadband Providers

T he world of broadband doesn't stop with DSL and cable, as much as the phone companies and cable providers would like you to believe that it does. You have other options.

To be honest, most casual Internet users rely on DSL or cable and make one of those mainstream choices their service provider if possible. But both technologies have service limitations, including distance and the cost of building a cable and service network to support outlying broadband clients.

Some folks just live too far from large communities to get mainstream broadband service. Some folks like to do things differently from everyone else. Some folks want an alternative broadband connection so if their cable goes out for a few days they can keep working.

Building the network necessary to reach every home with cable or DSL costs more money than providers can recoup. Satellite and wireless technologies do not need to run wires of any kind to each customer.

Niche broadband service providers, which includes satellite even though it's the most successful, remain vulnerable to market forces. Great ideas appear from companies with little money and then those companies disappear. On the other hand, most new innovations appeared in some little company first and took off and created a market. Just realize that DSL and cable broadband providers corner the majority of this market, making all others fight for customer at the fringes of the market.

That said, there are a thousand reasons to use an alternative broadband service provider. And although there aren't thousands of alternative options, there may be more out there than you think.

Satellite Broadband

Satellites provide almost all modern electronic communications now in one way or the other. Network TV signals come down to affiliates via satellite. Long distance telephone calls come down via satellite. Starting in 2003, commercial-free radio stations come down via satellite.

If you live in the suburbs as I do, near a major city, you may wonder why anyone would need satellite broadband. And according to DSL and cable companies, they have already, or will soon, reach the house of everyone in the world who wants speedy Internet access.

But according to Northern Sky Research (www.northernskyresearch.com), shown in Figure 4-1, millions of people in the United States and Western Europe will never get DSL or cable and will have only satellite as a broadband option. Thus, the need for satellite companies to push their own type of broadband access.

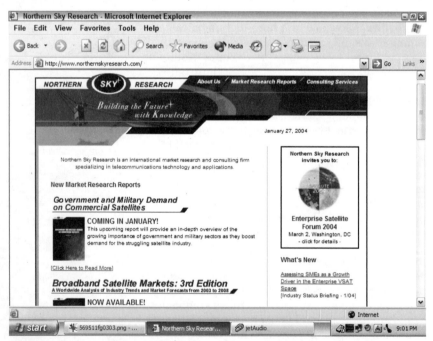

Figure 4-1: The market research firm counting potential satellite customer noses.

Studying population and census data, Northern Sky Research reported in January 2004, that approximately 9.5 million households and small offices will be forced to rely on satellite for broadband: in the United States 8.1 million and Canada 1.4 million. In Western Europe, they estimate 11.3 million households and 900,0000 small offices are in the same boat.

One satellite broadband company planning to launch a satellite by mid-2004 says up to 30 million U.S. homes won't have an option for DSL or cable during the next few years. I wish them luck, but it seems the phone and cable companies are still expanding regularly. However, with the cost of laying down new cable, the satellite company may have a few years in which people who want broadband can only look upwards.

Because of the start up expenses, there are no "regional" satellite providers. You won't have many choices for satellite service, but you do have two major choices (one-way or two-way) plus at least two vendors for each choice.

If you run a broadband company, being the only broadband supplier for a total of nearly 21 million households and small offices (or 30 million in the United States if you count those who will have DSL or cable someday but don't quite yet) will grab your attention. There are more potential satellite customers in Western Europe because there are more people and the telecommunications companies don't compete nearly as earnestly to increase DSL coverage as they do in the United States. But even the 9.5 million potential customers in the United States and Canada seem worth the effort to get a satellite up and ready to download bad jokes to users across the two countries.

Rural America and the people therein seeking broadband access should see benefits from the Federal government. The Federal Communications Commission has a variety of programs to spread advanced telecommunications throughout the countryside. They focus heavily on satellite, but wireless plays a role as well.

How satellite works

If you or your neighbor has satellite television, you know how satellite broadband works. Put a satellite dish on your roof, point toward the right satellite (installers do this quickly, do-it-yourselfers take days), and receive TV from the stars.

Channel selections, made via a set-top box that looks like the one from the cable company, are chosen via a remote control from a recliner. The selected channel's frequency is then selected and filtered and displayed on your television. Change the channel and change the frequency to display.

Where a cable TV set-top box selects the proper channel by frequency running down the cable coax, the satellite set-top box selects the proper channel by frequency running down radio signals from the satellite. The process is the same, but the transmission medium is not.

In fact, satellite TV reception technology looks quite a bit like regular broadcast TV. Signals come through the air, something at your house or office receives those signals, and you select which frequency to view. Of course, the satellite sends higher quality signals and packs more signals into a frequency range managed by the receiver, but there are more similarities than differences.

Satellite broadband works much the same way, although you don't have to tune various frequencies for various Internet and Web addresses. One frequency for the satellite company is all you need, because you're receiving a link to a single Internet service provider rather than multiple broadcast channels.

Note
Notice what hasn't been mentioned: cables or wires. Unlike DSL or cable broadband access, satellites provide service to a large section of the country while avoiding the costs of running cables to every home. That's much cheaper, if you forget about the cost of building and launching a satellite.

Yet even with the satellite cost, companies offer service to so many millions of people that the cost per subscriber (or potential subscriber) totals less than cable or DSL. Or, you can look at the economics and realize the first customer costs $500 million to connect, but the rest are free.

The dish used for broadband satellite is slightly larger than the one used for TV. Larger perhaps, but once mounted on your roof and pointing toward the south, you won't be able to tell the difference between the TV and broadband satellites. Not that it matters, but the marketing people for the slightly larger broadband dish claim extra stability through storms, wind, rain, and clouds. True, a larger dish can catch and use a degraded signal slightly better than a smaller dish.

If you have an advanced satellite receiver, you can send information to it; for example you could purchase a pay-per-view movie from the satellite provider. But didn't the box holding the satellite equipment say only "Receiver" on it, and not transmitter?

Receiver is what the box said. Satellite TV receivers are receive-only. To communicate with your satellite TV provider, you have to plug in a phone line to your satellite set-top box. Any information from you to the satellite provider goes over the telephone line.

You can get along quite well without an upstream data path when you watch satellite TV. The telephone line connection makes it easy for your children to order pay-per-view when you're not around (a good reason not to have it). I don't have an upstream telephone cable attached to my satellite set-top box, and I get along fine. (The kids may tell a different story.)

The choice to add an upstream link doesn't matter all that much for satellite TV. But if you're looking for Internet access, you must have an upstream data flow. As you can see in the next three sections, there are two ways to send data upstream.

Setup basics

Every satellite vendor requires you to install a satellite dish facing to the south. Two-way satellites, because they have transmitters, must be installed by a certified technician. You can install one-way units yourself, but professional installation will get you up and running more quickly.

Note When I ordered satellite TV, my system was installed and running in 2 hours. My next-door neighbor installed his own. I saw him on the roof five different times and noticed the satellite dish in three different places before he got it all working.

The satellite vendor will provide (or sell) you a satellite modem to connect your computer to the satellite feed. It may be internal modem or an external modem like all the DSL and cable modems. You will connect the modem to your computer via an Ethernet cable, like the DSL and cable modems. A few new systems use the USB port for connection.

If you order home satellite service, you may not get a router or other way to connect more than one computer to the satellite modem. If that's the case, you must use Windows peer-to-peer networking to share access to the satellite connection.

 Cross-Reference See Chapter 11 to get started with peer-to-peer networking software and configurations. Chapters 14 and 15 show how to connect via wires or wirelessly.

If you have a one-way satellite system, you will need to have a functioning modem and telephone line for upstream communications. You don't have to have a dedicated phone line for your Internet connection, but it helps keep peace in the family.

One-way systems

Early on, all the satellite broadband services were one way: satellite download at broadband speeds, and computer uploads through a dial-up connection at 56 Kbps maximum speed. The ratio between the two seems lopsided, with download around 400 Kbps versus upload at 56 Kbps.

Yet if you look back at the discussion about how much people upload versus how much they download, the ratio isn't terrible. Not great, perhaps, but not terrible. After all, when you send a Web address like www.broadbandbible.com, you're sending only 22 characters plus some address and formatting information. A few hundred bytes go up, 50,000 bytes come down. Not a bad ratio for most Web users.

Westband Networks, shown in Figure 4-2, makes some compelling points for the advantages of one-way satellite systems. It wasn't long ago that one-way systems were the only systems, and the vast majority of satellite users still have a one-way system.

Here's how one-way satellite works during an Internet session:

1. You connect your dial-up modem to the access number provided by your satellite broadband service.

2. You open the browser or other application that will connect to the Internet.

Figure 4-2: One of the one-way satellite vendors.

3. Your modem uploads the request to the satellite provider acting as your Internet service provider.

4. The requested Internet material is routed through the satellite by your service provider.

5. Your Internet information downloads through your satellite, your satellite modem and appears on your computer screen.

Basically, the idea is pretty simple: requests go up through your dial-up telephone connection, and come back through the satellite. Early cable Internet services worked the same way before the providers upgraded their equipment to handle two-way communications.

A normal Internet user (if there is such a thing) will surf perfectly well over a one-way satellite broadband connection. However, there are limitations to this technology.

Maximum satellite download speeds are increasing as more satellites come online and technology improves, but you shouldn't figure on much more than 400 Kbps in the short term and at the lowest price point. This speed equates to the low-end ADSL speeds discussed in Chapter 3.

Issues with one-way systems include the following:

✦ Download speeds lower than cable or higher-speed DSL

- ✦ Minimal upload speeds
- ✦ Telephone line required
- ✦ Difficulty sharing the upload telephone link with multiple computers
- ✦ Small upload bandwidth pipe to support multiple concurrent users
- ✦ Higher cost of satellite hardware over DSL and cable broadband
- ✦ Weather interference is rare but guaranteed at some point

These issues aren't killers for most people. And if satellite broadband access is your only option to upgrade beyond a dial-up telephone link, you may smile and consider these points completely irrelevant. And you'd be right, because any broadband is better than the best dial-up Internet access.

The primary advantage for a one-way satellite system is money. Two-way systems require a more complicated and expensive satellite dish that is able to throw your upstream signal 23,000 miles into the air to reach the satellite. That upgraded dish includes an upgraded price tag. If money plays an important role in your broadband satellite choice, the one-way systems will always cost less, at least for the next few years.

Two-way systems

Second generation satellite services added a transmitter to the receiver for two-way communications. Just like DSL and cable broadband, you can now download and upload information to the Internet via the same connection.

The leader in this market, DirecWay (www.direcway.com), shown in Figure 4-3), is a division of Hughes Network Systems, the giant military and industrial satellite provider. It sells direct, through retailers, and through a variety of computer and satellite TV resellers.

Advantages for the two-way systems include the ability to talk on the phone while surfing and the less complex one-step method for getting to and from the Internet.

Disadvantages for the two-way systems include the higher prices and the relatively low-speed uplink. In fact, the upstream throughput for two-way satellites only equals or slightly betters that of using a dial-up link for the upstream information. In some ways, as you'll see when we talk about latency in the next section, the two-way satellite can be slower.

One big advantage for the two-way system is the primary vendor: DirecWay. They have deep pockets behind them (Hughes) and a large dealer network helping to find new customers. DirecWay was one of the pioneers in the area, starting with one-way satellites and has moved almost completely to two-way systems.

The DirecWay DirecDuo takes advantage of its sister company DirectTV. One company provides for satellite TV and broadband Internet access. You can upgrade an existing service by adding a second dish, or you can start fresh and get TV and Internet on one dish.

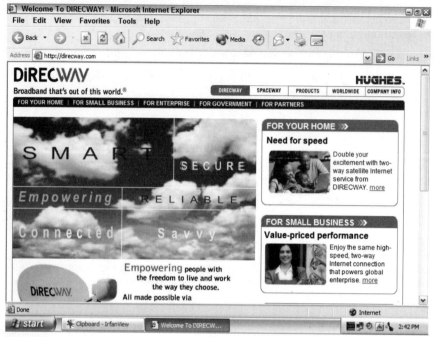

Figure 4-3: A leading two-way satellite broadband provider.

Latency

Latency is just a fancy word for delay. Even the fastest broadband connections speed-wise can have latency issues. You measure latency on a round-trip basis, so delays introduced by network equipment, such as routers, figure into the mix and are blamed for all the latency (by the vendors of cable).

For DSL and cable broadband, latency may be a slight annoyance but is rarely serious. For satellites, however, the long distances often introduce painful latency issues.

Satellites used for two-way broadband are in geosynchronous orbit 23,000 miles above the Equator. That's a long way from Cleveland. If you hit the Enter key in Cleveland to download the latest Browns football news, here's what happens:

1. Your request goes up 23,000 miles to the satellite.

2. The data packets travel 23,000 miles down to the satellite switching station to connect to the Internet router.

3. Your request goes over the Internet to your Cleveland Browns fan Web site.

4. Your information comes back from the Web site to the satellite switching station.

5. The data packets go up 23,000 miles to the satellite.

6. The data packets come down 23,000 miles to your dish.

7. The data packets arrive through your satellite modem and the requested Web site appears on your screen.

Total that up and you get over 92,000 miles of travel distance. That doesn't count the miles in Cleveland.

Each round trip to the satellite takes between 700 to 1300 milliseconds according to satellite vendors. Standard Internet Protocol (IP) Web-handling routines start to assume the page request has been lost or disconnected after about 800 milliseconds and often send a second page submission because of the behind-the-scenes timeout caused by latency. You receive the page and your browser rejects the copies of the page coming in, but delays creep in while handling all this work in the background.

The diagram in Figure 4-4 shows the long route for your football fix Web page request. Your house, your satellite provider's earth station, and the Browns Web page host may be just about anywhere, but they aren't the parts causing any serious latency.

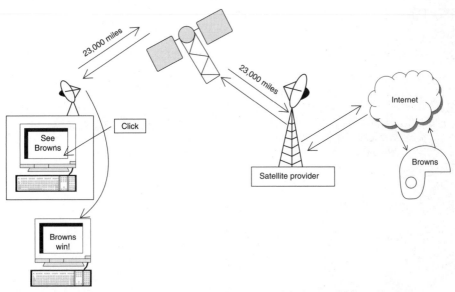

Figure 4-4: Up and down and over and back goes your Web request.

One-way satellite vendors jump on this and remind potential customers that using a telephone line for the upstream connection rather than the satellite drops the latency time down to around 400 milliseconds, providing you with your Cleveland Browns football fix in a shorter amount of time without behind-the-scenes timeouts.

Two-way satellite vendors point to their use of Internet caching to have pages waiting for you when you connect, so the chances of the page you want being ready to download increase considerably. So flip your coin and take your chances, or use another detail to help make your decision.

Tech Bits Web page caching uses special servers to hold copies of requested pages locally. When a second person asks for the same page, the provider already has it and doesn't need to fetch it from across the Internet again. This gives the second client a faster Web page update than the first client. Caching works well on sites with heavy traffic, such as major news sites and online retailers. Dynamic sites, such as auction pages, change too fast for caching to provide any benefit.

High-speed games, such as various shooter games like Quake and Doom, suffer from this latency. In fact, it can kill you, but you can click the Replay button and come back to life. Games that require less urgent trigger fingers work fine over most satellite links.

Service providers

There aren't many service providers in the satellite world because satellites are so expensive. I mentioned DirecWay, so let me show you the Web page for StarBand (www.starband.com), its primary two-way broadband competitor. (See Figure 4-5.)

Figure 4-5: Another two-way satellite broadband provider.

Because satellite broadband companies are national, you will have to deal with a national Internet service provider. You may also be offered satellite Internet by various hardware and software partners, such as PC makers or AOL, but they will be reselling one of the major satellite providers rather than starting their own satellite service.

Resellers of satellite broadband may or may not tell you they will hand you over to the national provider when you sign your contract. Going to a national provider rather than a regional reseller means that someone probably already grabbed your GreenDuck username.

Support for the Internet parts of your service will come from the satellite provider, through their national technical support centers. Your local reseller will provide the installation and physical support if needed, and intercede on your behalf if there's a problem with the satellite provider.

Availability

If you can mount a satellite dish (these are fairly small, remember) that points to the south, you can get satellite broadband service. This wide coverage provides broadband hope for the 21 million who may never get DSL or cable because they are too remote.

Satellite providers can reach the following locations:

✦ Continental United States locations (DirecWay)

✦ Continental United States plus Alaska, Hawaii, Puerto Rico, and the Virgin Islands with optional equipment (StarBand)

People often believe only the lonesome ranch house and mountain cabin are potential customers for satellite service. Not true, at least not anymore. Suburbs often lack the demographics to attract DSL and/or cable service providers. Service providers for DSL and cable may be horribly inept and the horror stories from your neighbors have scared you away. You might order satellite Internet access when you order your satellite TV service to save money on the package deals some providers offer.

Unlike with DSL and cable, you won't have to worry that your side of the street is too far away or serviced by obsolete signal repeaters. The continental United States gets excellent coverage, as does Western Europe stretching down into Africa. Anywhere a huge TV audience awaits, satellite coverage will beam them down their TV. And, in most cases, providers will also use a few transponder circuits on the satellites to sell broadband Internet access.

Every satellite vendor will say it over and over, but a southern exposure is mandatory. No clear look to the south (for those of us north of the equator) means no satellite broadband.

Speed

Early satellite broadband options topped out at 400 Kbps "burst" mode. When the marketing literature quotes burst mode speeds, you can bet dollars to donuts you'll see that speed once every few months for no more than 7 seconds.

Newer satellites, and improvements in the ground-based equipment sending and receiving signals, bump the speed up enough for basic levels. Providers claim that the standard speed for the least expensive service is 400–500 Kbps, and that's fairly accurate. Some services offer 800 Kbps and higher speeds into the Megabits per second range, but that usually means you've wandered onto a sales page for large businesses.

Satellite is a shared bandwidth system, like most Internet connections. Only so much traffic can go through each satellite channel, and it's pretty much impossible to add new channels to existing satellites. Think of this like the capacity of a highway that reaches a tunnel: you can expand the highway to support more traffic much more easily than you can expand the tunnel. The news stories you've seen about the shuttle fixing satellites were rare, and those were mostly military satellites. So the capacity the satellite had when it went into service is about all you'll ever get.

WildBlue (www.wildblue.com) is the company with plans to launch a satellite by the summer of 2004. It promises 1.5 Mbps downstream because the satellite will use new generation Ka band technology. The company Web site promises upload speeds "up to 256 Kbps" but offers no particulars. However, higher upload speeds with a new generation of equipment seem plausible.

This is a nice segue to a question that some of you are asking as you read. Is it better to get the one-way since it's cheaper, or will upload speeds for two-way increase enough to make it worth the extra money.

Satellite upstream speeds will increase, as promised by WildBlue, but dial-up speeds probably won't increase. Although the two options run neck and neck upstream today (slowly, but each about as slow as the other), the future leans more toward the two-way system taking the performance crown in another year or two.

 If you want to use a satellite link back to the office through a Virtual Private Network (VPN), you may be disappointed. Corporate VPNs encrypt each packet, and this stops the satellite broadband service from being able to batch packets together and send them in one burst. Updates in the future may change this, but be aware and alert your corporate data communications group if you plan to use a satellite for your remote access back to the office.

Reliability

The Internet service with a satellite broadband provider is always on when you ask your computer to go to a Web site. Satellites stay in orbit and won't wander away from your antenna's aim.

That said, there are a few things on the ground that will cause your satellite broadband some problems. Heavy rain, especially when thunderstorms have a frighteningly large amount of lightning, will blank out your connection for a moment or three. Heavy, wet fog and snow will cause problems. One-way satellite vendors tout the availability of their service to run over dialup as an advantage when two-way satellites are blocked by weather.

On the other hand, if your geosynchronous satellite suffers a complete failure, your personal broadband service will be gone as well. There aren't enough extra satellite slots to accept an entire service provider's client list in addition to regular customers. Failures are rare and make the news because they are so rare. Don't let this issue stop you from signing up for satellite broadband.

Security

For the truly paranoid, rejoice in the fact that no one can wiretap a radio signal stream going from you to your satellite. Attempts at intercepting your stream and rerouting that stream would cause problems on your end. Don't consider the fact that "they" could tap into your cable from the satellite on the roof to the satellite modem inside.

The more normal among us should realize that using a satellite for broadband Internet access neither helps nor hurts standard security precautions. Although you benefit from the fact that no one really can wiretap a satellite stream, your traffic on the Internet doesn't change because the first hop from your computer went up on a satellite.

Viruses and spam come down from the satellite just as easily as they come from the phone or cable company. Your satellite broadband provider may offer spam and virus filtering, but using the satellite doesn't offer any advantages over what any other broadband provider can accomplish.

 You must take the responsibility to handle your spam and viruses, and I'll tell you all about that in Chapter 7.

Costs

Satellite hardware costs extra for every satellite I checked. Sometimes the costs are high, sometimes not so high. But all satellite vendors will ask you for at least $150 for the hardware, and usually another $50–$100 for installation.

 Warning: Jokes about the costs of satellite broadband access being sky high will not be tolerated.

Okay, that's all, I promise.

One-way satellite providers charge less upfront for their equipment. Prices range from $150 to $200 from most vendors.

Two-way satellite providers charge more upfront for their newer, more complicated equipment. Look for an initial payment of at least $500 and sometimes up to $800 depending on the type of equipment and speed of broadband service. Once installed, the monthly service fees start from $50 or up. Prices are, of course, always subject to change. Some basic offers, with limited bandwidth (250 Kbps downloads) and a single e-mail account are testing the waters under $40 already.

To offset the more expensive equipment and the steeper upfront charges, the two-way companies offer plans with less money down ($100–150) along with higher monthly payments until the difference is covered. You'll lose a few dollars by paying a setup fee or initiation fee (whatever they choose to call it), but you will avoid the upfront charges.

The one-way satellite systems obviously require a working telephone line for the upstream communications. The two-way systems advertise the amount of money you save by avoiding that telephone line charge.

My guess is that satellite will always be the highest cost broadband service. The initial equipment investment for the broadband provider is too steep to drop the price down to DSL and cable levels, at least for the next few years. Besides, the primary customer for satellite broadband service is the person or small business outside the reach of DSL and cable. With no competition, prices tend to stay up.

Community Wireless

Satellite broadband providers might make a mistake watching as DSL and cable providers keep gaining on the underserved areas. Although they're looking one way, wireless broadband providers are sprouting all over the place.

You're surrounded every day by wireless data coming and going: in to your TV, out from your cellular phone, in to your radio, and out through your PDA. And wireless broadband service providers are popping up in some of the same places that lack DSL and cable that the satellite service providers hope to have all to themselves.

Radio waves have plenty of bandwidth to support broadband speeds. I'll show you how to set up a wireless network in your home in Chapter 15. With bigger antennas and special frequency tricks, the entire neighborhood (or at least the 28 square miles around an antenna) can connect through wireless broadband.

Many small wireless service providers are popping up to take advantage of new technology and lower equipment prices. Some may call themselves a Fixed Wireless Broadband (FWB) service provider, while others may call themselves a Wireless Internet Service Provider (WISP). Check listings at Yahoo and Google as well as your local advertisements to find these providers.

Unlike satellite service, wireless broadband access doesn't disappear in bad weather. The frequency ranges used by the providers cut through rain, fog, ice, and snow.

How wireless works

Wireless broadband service providers use a variety of technologies to keep the radio bits flying between them and their customers. I could put pages of explanation here about frequency hopping, frequency hopping spread spectrum, direct sequence spread spectrum, and multichannel multipoint distribution service, but instead I put the technical reference details and links at www.BroadbandBible.com, if you're interested.

Let me focus on the two technical details that determine how you place your antenna and how you determine if you can get service from a wireless broadband provider: Line of sight (LOS) and nonline of sight (NLOS).

Line-of-sight wireless networks

One provider in the Dallas area near me sums up the idea of line-of-sight wireless networks simply and clearly: "If you can see our tower, then you can get service" (www.itgbroadband.net/HowWorks.htm).

Somewhat like satellite, line-of-sight broadband service requires an antenna of some sort on the outside of your building. They tend to be not quite a foot square and flat like a pizza box. Another antenna option is about a foot high and four inches wide. Those antennas point toward a tower in the distance or a wireless hub (base station) on another roof within a couple of miles.

Officially, what some people call antennas are really transceivers because they transmit and receive radio signals. They are relatively low-powered (putting out no more power than a cell phone) and must be placed at least 12 feet above the ground. A wire from the transceiver runs into the home or office and plugs into a wireless modem with an Ethernet connection. One computer can be plugged into the modem directly, or a router may provide firewall services and allow an entire network of computers to receive wireless broadband information.

 Note Drive around your neighborhood and look at house roofs. When you see a square white box or what looks like a cricket bat, that home uses a line-of-sight wireless provider. If the provider is smart, the company name is on the antenna. If the company didn't display its name, you may have to knock on the door and ask the people which company they use for wireless broadband service.

Towers available for wireless broadband use are all over the place, mostly to support cellular telephones. It's difficult to tell the difference between an antenna for a cell phone on a tower and that for wireless broadband, but it doesn't matter. The combination of relative height, easy mounting, and electrical power exist all around you on towers, billboards, buildings, water towers, and even fake pine trees.

Frequencies used by wireless broadband providers are usually either 2.4 GHz or 5.8 GHz. Both frequencies offer strong signals and employ a variety of technologies to avoid interference with other wireless products.

Nonline of sight wireless networks

As one might guess from the name, nonline of sight networks don't need to have a clear view of the next transceiver to receive service. They do sometimes, however, need an outside antenna if the service depends on reflected signals, for example, in areas with tall buildings bouncing the signals around.

In an area covered by a nonline of sight provider, a small modem with a stubby antenna beside your computer usually gathers all the signals necessary. If you have a wireless router or access point in your home or office to provide local area network service without wires, you know what these modems look like. The new generation of wireless broadband modems is actually smaller than the wireless networking products you bought last year.

The biggest advantage for nonline of sight providers is the avoidance of sending a technician to install and configure a transceiver on your home or office. Most providers in this market send you the modem via FedEx or UPS and you plug it into your computer or existing network and turn it on. If you're in the signal range and do a couple of simple configuration steps, you're in business within about 5 minutes.

Service providers

Barriers to entry are low for wireless broadband providers, at least compared to the costs of launching a satellite or stringing wires all over the countryside. The flip side of low barriers to entry is that small companies appear and disappear with startling frequency.

Wireless broadband access is the exact opposite of satellite access. Although the technology forces satellite providers to cover entire countries, wireless technology forces those providers to cover areas neighborhood by neighborhood. The modern wireless broadband access provider is as local as a diner and includes customers from about the same area.

Wireless broadband service providers do all the same things that all other broadband providers do: provide access, connect to the Internet through multiple high-speed connections for redundancy, and provide e-mail and personal Web support. The major difference is the lack of a national wireless carrier, although many national providers advertise wireless service.

Finding a list of current, up to date wireless broadband providers is nearly impossible. Every list I located contained a huge number of dead links and references to companies now long gone. The best I can find so far is TheBoost at theboost.net/interspeed/wireless/index.htm. (See Figure 4-6.)

Most market analysts predict that sooner or later the giant national companies, especially those with cell phone networks, will start buying up successful regional wireless broadband providers. That certainly makes economic sense, since both technologies rely on multiple transceivers in service areas. Because a major regional wireless provider will have maybe 5,000 subscribers, they are susceptible to buyouts.

Availability

In the short term, before the national companies buy up the regional wireless access providers, you can take steps to help provide service to you and your neighbors. There are multiple guerilla wireless networks around the country, although most seem based in California.

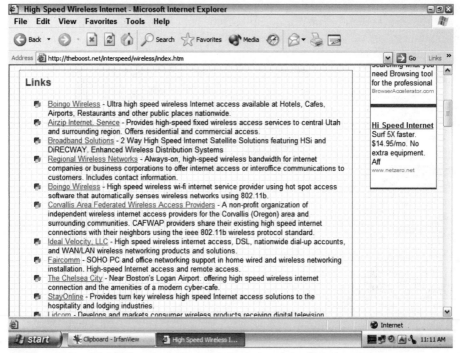

Figure 4-6: Provider listings including many wireless broadband services.

The idea is simple: a mesh network with many transceivers provides high speed and network redundancy. But the cost of putting up all the transceivers is so high that providers have trouble getting the network rolled out completely. Yet customers adding transceivers to their homes and businesses spread the network range, so people partner with their regional wireless provider.

By keeping the cost down to roll out transceivers, the wireless provider saves money. Individuals and businesses get a reduced rate because they support the network. Some groups take this so seriously they band together and have turned this into a huge movement of like-minded groups to make "wireless for the people" a reality. Check out the Association for Community Networking at www.afcn.org, shown in Figure 4-7.

Just as peer-to-peer networks changed the music industry (see Chapter 1), so has the availability of inexpensive wireless networking products changed Internet access. Why limit a hotspot of wireless access to a coffee shop when you can make your entire neighborhood a hotspot? If you think that way, you'll love the community network movement.

Distance and speed

Distances for wireless broadband providers are limited by the number of access points and transceivers. As the data packet flies, however, you must be within 4 to 6 miles of an access point to get connected.

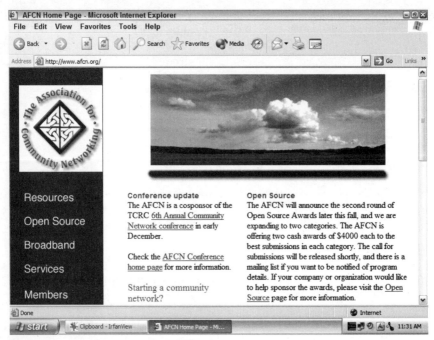

Figure 4-7: People connecting wirelessly.

Speeds are easier to list. You can go as fast as you can pay for, or slow enough to keep it within your budget. Here are some of the speeds offered by various wireless service providers, listed by downstream Kbps/upstream Kbps:

256/128 Kbps

384/128 Kbps

768/128 Kbps

768/256 Kbps

1800/384 Kbps

2500/500 Kbps

3000/1000 Kbps

3000/3000 Kbps

4500/4500 Kbps

You can see a wide range of speeds upstream and downstream are available. If you really need three times T1 speed (4500 Kbps) you can get it, depending on your provider.

Reliability

Line-of-sight systems need to keep a clear view between your location and the tower with the access point. Breaking that line for any length of time causes interruptions. Placing the transceiver on the roof or at least out of the way of any ground obstruction solves that part of the reliability issue.

Most wireless broadband providers avoid using frequencies susceptible to weather interruption. That doesn't mean that all wireless options are guaranteed to work regardless of the level of rain or snow in the area. But satellite broadband access resists all but the worst weather, and wireless broadband resists interruption even more strongly.

Nonline of sight systems have an advantage with their ability to connect and communicate with multiple access points at one time. This mesh network design, commonly used in community networks, maintains connections even when one or two transceivers go offline for any reason.

Security

You may have heard horror stories about *war driving* where people drive around with a laptop, a wireless transceiver card, and a Pringles can to intercept data communications from unprotected companies. Those problems are caused by poor wireless local area network setup, not wireless broadband. Besides, in Chapters 15 and 17 I'll tell you how to secure your wireless internal network and frustrate all the war drivers.

Since your providers supply the access points (their transceivers) and your transceivers (either attached to your building or sitting on your desk), they can securely configure communications between the two devices. Base stations, where the wireless provider connects the wireless network clients to the Internet, have authentication and authorization routines to verify that every connected client has been authorized.

Most providers encrypt all data over their wireless links. This is possible because they configure both ends. Rarely do they encrypt to such a degree that the CIA couldn't break the encryption, but they lock up data transmissions well enough that no casual eavesdropper will have a chance to decode the messages. Control over the authentication process makes it possible to lock out any other systems in the area trying to spoof your computer's details and log into the network under a false identity. Such methods won't work, because security protections include keying transceivers to the receiving antenna so only authorized client-based equipment will be authorized for access.

Don't worry about someone stealing your data because you have a wireless broadband provider. Thieves will find it easier to break into your home or office and read your filed papers than to grab your data out of the air.

Costs

Costs for wireless broadband access can range from nothing (see the community networking information in the *Availability* section) to hundreds of dollars for installation and up to hundreds of dollars per month for access fees. Between the two points there exists a wide range of speeds and fees, as you might imagine.

Low speed wireless works hard to keep the costs down in the range of DSL and cable. Many wireless vendors offer packages competitive with ADSL, such as 384/128 Kbps for $30 or so. Your numbers may vary depending on your provider and your chosen speeds. If you want T1 (1.5 Mbps) or above speeds in one or both directions, you will spend hundreds of dollars per month. But you will spend less if you ordered a physical T1 to your location, so that's an advantage.

Wi-Fi hotspots: public 802.11b

Nothing goes with a cup of expensive coffee like expensive Internet access, does it? At least that's what many coffee shops are telling us, and people seem to be buying both the coffee and the Internet access.

This type of wireless networking, although public, doesn't work the same as wireless broadband services. Yes, you can get broadband speeds in your coffee shop. Yes, you connect wirelessly. But you do all this with the same equipment and technology you use at your home or office and your personal wireless network.

Chapters 15 and 16 cover the performance and security concerns of using public Wi-Fi hotspots for Internet access. But for now, let me tell you that my paranoia pushes me to only read my e-mail from a Web page with security. This ensures that my connection to the Web e-mail server is encrypted with the same level of technology used by banks for online banking. I feel better, and you probably will too.

If you travel quite a bit and access the office constantly from the road, please, please, please use a strong password on your computer itself and an additional one on your application to connect to your home office. Otherwise, the next time you lose your laptop, you'll have to replace it and change every remote access security setting at your home network.

Summary

Satellite providers cover the world; wireless providers cover the neighborhood. That's plain but true.

If you're outside the range of DSL and cable, satellite or wireless broadband are your only real options over dialup. You can choose two-way satellite service if you're willing to pay the premium over one-way satellite service. And you can become only a customer of your wireless broadband provider, or take an active part in expanding wireless access to your neighbors.

Emerging Broadband Service Options

✦ ✦ ✦ ✦

In This Chapter

Looking for new broadband delivery methods

Deciding speed and cost issues

Streaming speedy broadband through the air

Plugging into broadband through your wall socket

✦ ✦ ✦ ✦

It's hard to run faster and jump higher when you're dragging an enormous telephone company or cable operator along for the ride. Many of the promising new ways to deliver high-speed broadband to the home bypass the telephone and cable companies. One emerging method sends broadband over wireless up to 31 miles (WiMax), one sends broadband over the high-power lines running into your neighborhood (Powerline) and another brings a fiber optic cable right to your doorstep (Fiber to the Home).

Why aren't the incumbent broadband carriers leading the charge to 100 Mbps broadband? Money.

Any economist who protects the status quo in a market will point a finger toward those with the majority market share. The mantra, "protect our investment," drowns out the call to keep pushing forward. If telephone and cable companies made a move to Fiber to the Home, they would lose billions and billions of invested dollars in copper wire strung on poles and buried in the ground. Worse, they would suddenly be on equal footing with small upstart companies determined to eliminate copper wire as a delivery mechanism.

Market transitions hurt those caught in the vise of supporting the majority market share while fighting off competitors offering new services. The companies that deliver 100 Mbps of broadband delight to our homes may well not be the ones delivering 1 Mbps to us today. That's tough on them, but the customers, meaning you and I, will finally get broadband that completely envelops us with the speed and services it delivers.

Fiber to the Home and Office

In a bizarre twist of modern electronic fate, those who want optical fiber to their home should move to the farm, or if not the farm, then to tiny Kutztown, Pennsylvania, or Huxley, Iowa. Those folks have fiber optic lines running into their houses, and the rest of us don't have even a waiting time for Fiber to the Home.

Other names for this technology include Fiber to the Premises (FTTP) and a variation called Passive Optical Networking (PON). Sometimes people throw in a "broadband" in front of Passive Optical Networking to make it BPON. Cornell University has an institute named the Advanced Fiber Networks (http://afn .johnson.cornell.edu/institute.php) so they call the process AFN.

 Note   Although I see the advantage of Fiber to the Premises to include business customers, Fiber to the People has a nice, Declaration of Independence feel to it, doesn't it? So you and I will know that FTTP has changed from Fiber to the Premises to Fiber to the People.

And the people are getting the message and pressuring their city leaders to make something happen. Provo, Utah, home of multiple computer technology companies over the past three decades staffed by students from the local universities, has its own fiber-to-the-people project underway called iProvo (see Figure 5-1).

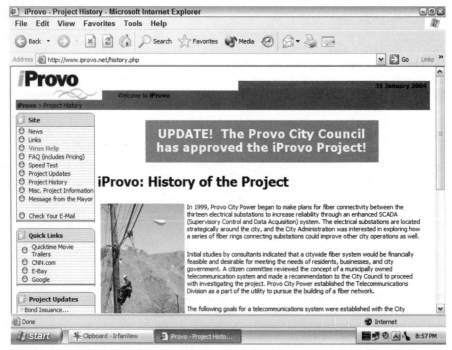

Figure 5-1: Provo makes Fiber to the Home a city service like water, electricity, gas, and sewer connections rather than an added outside service.

Many fans of the idea of pulling Fiber to the Home talk about details, such as the ease of installation and lower cost of adding fiber to the list of services provided to every home. If you build the network correctly, they say, you don't need to pull phone wires and cable wires and fiber, you just pull fiber and run all the phone, cable, and Internet access services through the one fiber connection.

Most of the data and voice services today, especially in new neighborhoods and developments, run copper wire only from homes to collecting points for each area. Remember the phone company remote terminals and the cable company nodes? Those connect upstream to their assorted central offices and head-end switches over fiber in most cases. Running new fiber to customers rather than new copper wire doesn't cost all that much extra.

The trick is to organize the ownership details of all the new fiber to the people projects correctly, according to a variety of academic and technical experts. Let the city own the actual fiber connecting to houses, but let Internet service providers and phone companies and cable companies provide services to customers over those city-owned fiber connections. Service providers pay the city a cost-plus fee based on traditional public works projects, and the people get wonderful buckets of broadband for a good price.

How fiber works

The "how" is simple: rather than running separate copper wires for the telephone and cable TV and cable broadband connections, you run a single fiber optic cable. In Figure 5-2, the Fiber to the Home Council (www.ftthcouncil.org) lists some of the new projects underway.

Figure 5-2: This page lists new developments, but you should also check Case Studies under the FTTH information button.

Any service provider that would ordinarily run copper wires to a home or residence can choose to run fiber instead. The upstream network must support fiber connections all the way to the central office or head-end or Internet Service Provider, but most systems run fiber from collection points anyway. The difference is running Fiber to the Home or office building to support more bandwidth and offer more services.

Coordination between service providers often gums up the works of a deal for Fiber to the Home. Rather than the phone company and cable company running two different types of copper wires out to your house, they must work together at the central office or head-end to connect their service to the fiber network running out to the homes. Large entrenched monopolies tend not to play well with others, which brings us to the real items gumming up the works: lawyers and politicians.

Tech Bits One research report counts over 400,000 Fiber to the Home connections with paying customers worldwide, but only 50,000 are in the United States.

There are four types of Fiber to the Home wiring options. Each leans toward one feature or another, such as less fiber cable needed or easy access for competitive service providers.

✦ **Home Run Fiber, also known as Point-to-Point or Single Star Architecture:** Each fiber connection for each customer runs all the way back the central office. This requires the most fiber cable and the most optical termination equipment at the central office, but also offers the most flexibility for service providers located at the central office.

✦ **Active Star:** Remote nodes with active electronics support from four to 1,000 customers and link via a shared feeder fiber optic cable back to the central office. This option offers less bandwidth and flexibility for each user.

✦ **Passive Optical Network (PON):** Similar to the Active Star but with only a passive splitter at the remote node rather than an active switch. Saves the setup fiber cable runs and is less expensive due to lack of switches at the remote node collection points.

✦ **Wavelength Division Multiplexing Passive Optical Network (WDM-PON):** Similar to the Passive Optical Network described previously, but with more wavelengths on each fiber cable to increase bandwidth and provide more service provider flexibility. However, this raises the cost of the fiber used and the electronics needed to light those fibers for data communications.

Building the network with home-runs from each central office to each customer would cost too much to be palatable in the near term. Because municipal fiber network projects for customer broadband access piggyback off municipal needs for fiber connections around the city, the local government will dictate the network architecture. Cities or public utilities build a fiber network backbone around the area to connect and control services, such as the electric utility, water and sewer controls, or traffic signals.

Once the fiber gets back to the central office (or head-end if you prefer), different providers can offer their services. Each provider has its own services to offer, but all go to the customer over the one fiber to each customer. Think of this like one road leads to your house, and you choose whether FedEx or UPS brings special packages to you.

Politics

More American fortunes have come from some form of public media than any other source, if I remember one of the economic experts correctly. It doesn't take a stretch of the imagination to believe that statement when you look around at all the television and radio stations. See any going broke? The companies leveraging those publicly allocated monopolies (frequencies) for their own products, like record companies, advertising agencies, television production studios, and major sports leagues seem to gather money like dryers gather lint. Count the telephone companies in as a publicly allocated monopoly as well, even though they get right of way for their wires rather than a frequency for their TV stations.

Whenever large piles of money gather, large companies, lawyers, and the government regulators gather as well. Fiber to the Home exacerbates confusion because one tiny fiber cable can carry all the television, radio, and telephone connections in the city to the customer.

Do you regulate Fiber to the Home as cable TV? As a telephone company? Is it still regulated as cable TV if the cable company offers telephone service over that link? This can get messy.

The push for municipalities and public utility districts to lay the foundation for Fiber to the Home ran smack into the lawyers and lobbyists for phone companies and television conglomerates.

Four cases so far have been bumped up to the Supreme Court. Three cases resulted in favor of letting municipalities run the fiber network and sell retail services, directly or wholesale, the bandwidth required to let third-party service providers sell the services over the municipal network. One case went against the rights of municipalities to provide retail or wholesale telecommunications services.

According to *Lightwave Magazine* (www.lw.pennnet.com), as of December 2003, the following organizations were delivering Fiber to the Home:

Competitive local exchanges (45.3 percent)

Municipalities (20.4 percent)

Developers (16.7 percent)

Public utility districts (11.6 percent)

Incumbent local exchange carriers (5.6 percent)

Regional Bell operating companies (0.4 percent)

Frankly, I'm a bit surprised at the high number of customers serviced by Competitive Local Exchange Carriers (new telephone companies) and developers. I'm not at all surprised at the nearly nonexistent fraction of the market served by old-line telephone companies (Bell spin-offs). They're the ones with all the copper wire in place. The fact that DSL, and sometimes only slow DSL, is the only broadband that wiring network supports is our tough luck. Telephone companies won't write off their huge investment in all their installed wiring until they're forced to do so. That won't happen anytime soon.

Laws regarding municipalities offering fiber to home

The role of the status quo is to maintain itself, meaning it must squash competitors before they become a threat. Such is the rule of the economic jungle, and the world of Fiber to the Home is no exception. Municipalities getting into the Fiber to the Home business, even when it makes great sense, steps on the market toes of the incumbent telephone and cable companies.

Nine states have laws restricting municipalities from providing retail or wholesales services on a telecommunications network they build, including Fiber to the Home:

Arkansas

Florida

Minnesota

Nevada

South Carolina

Tennessee

Texas

Utah

Washington

Three states have overturned laws restricting municipalities from building a fiber network to allow pilot projects to proceed:

Missouri

Nebraska

Virginia

Individuals can do little in this fight. If you have a chance to make your voice heard by writing a letter or e-mail to a local, state, or federal official, please do so. The earlier list in the politics section tells you how much Fiber to the Home you and I will get if the big telephone companies get their way and they block cities from building out fiber networks and renting bandwidth to service providers: 0.4 percent. Enough to say they are rolling out a pilot project, but never enough to give us, the customers, real broadband at high speeds.

Coverage areas

Physically, the coverage area of Fiber to the Home includes any location within 33,000 feet from a central office (30,000 from the central office to a passive remote node, then 3.000 feet more to the home or office). Although you may not be within 6.25 miles of a central office or remote node, I bet some type of city or public utility service is closer than that to you. Power lines come right to your house, so fiber can piggyback on them.

In essence, every home or business with any connection to municipal services or a public utility device can be within a broadband coverage area. That's assuming the world works in favor of the little guy, the one sitting at home waiting for real broadband. In real life, unfortunately, the little guy better be sitting on a street where a fiber to the home pilot test is underway if he wants to be connected.

Developers, especially in high-end neighborhoods, now regularly run fiber to each home they build. When done during construction, the incremental cost of adding fiber to the home adds little to the price, and provides a great selling point. But connecting to service providers able to take advantage of that fiber connection depends on your location. If there's no trial project close by, you are out of luck.

Trials in progress

Many cities jump into the fiber to the home movement because the city leaders realized something critical: bandwidth for homes and office, the kind of bandwidth fiber cable connections provide, is becoming a necessity. Companies looking to move in or expand look carefully at the telecommunications support in place. Because the traditional broadband providers, telephone and cable companies, are playing hard to get (and trying to block the municipal fiber networks in court), the only entity large enough, and able to benefit from such improvements, is the local municipal government.

Tacoma, Washington, has 65,000 people who can get fiber connections today out of the planned 184,000 when the rollout is complete. Only about 10 percent of those homes eligible have so far opted to pay for broadband cable service from one of four different service providers or one of the two cable TV providers.

One of the largest trials in the United States is the Zipp Network in central Washington state. The Grant County Public Utility District formed more than 50 years ago and installed fiber cables first to manage its own electrical service.

The iProvo project mentioned earlier passed the bond election to fund broadband buildout. 32,000 homes and businesses should benefit before too long.

Back in California, the city of Palo Alto plans to deliver video, voice, and data over a Fiber to the Home network to 26,000 residents (see Figure 5-3). Part of the incentive is to replace much of the city's legacy network and communications facilities.

I can't go on without mentioning the exciting, but poorly named, UTOPIA project in Utah. 18 cities, anchored by Salt Lake City, are planning to build an ultra-high speed network, using municipal fiber. The Utah Telecommunication Open Infrastructure Agency estimates it will cost around $470 million and cover

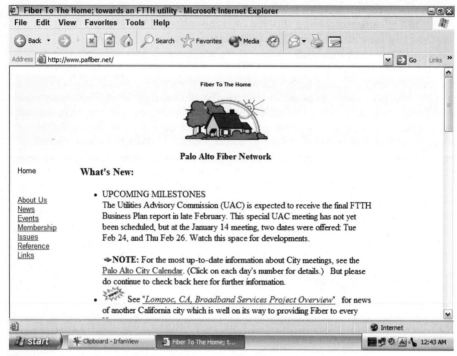

Figure 5-3: Another large trial getting to work, this one in Palo Alto, CA.

75percent of the population of the state of Utah. The following list shows the figures for Utopia:

Total population: 723,933

Total households: 248,791

Total businesses: 34,580

The details about UTOPIA (the one in Utah, not the idyllic land) can be seen at www.utopianet.org. They may claim the prize as largest project by far, if the numbers all check out and the plan doesn't crash and burn.

Cities are finding they must offer modern communications links, just as they must offer good schools, fair taxes, and a low crime rate. Developers must not show potential, say, warehouse clients only a site with easy access to highways and rail roads, but also high-speed communications networks. Fiber to the Home isn't quite a commodity everyone expects to have, but it may reach that point in this decade.

A good trend for Fiber to the Home is that some of the major telephone companies are deciding to join them rather always than fight them (in court). BellSouth, SBC, and Verizon adopted a set of common technical requirements for implementing Fiber to the Home. Only 10 percent of all business in the United States currently have access to a fiber-based Internet service provider.

And those little farm towns that had fiber back when your cable picture was still fuzzy? They're rocking along. Kutztown, Pennsylvania, has over 5,000 people, and supports the Kutztown University. Huxley, Iowa, is gradually replacing the copper pairs from the phone company to with fiber connections for each of the 600 customers in town.

The Fiber to the Home Council counts 94 communities in 16 states up and running toward Fiber to the Home. Size ranges obviously swing to both extremes and cover from a few hundred to nearly a million customers.

Speed

Fast.

How fast? Faster than you imagined the first time.

Speed estimates run from 10 Mbps (like old-fashioned Ethernet coax cable supported) to gigabits per second. Which do you believe? Yeah, me too. Early project customers will be lucky to get 10 Mbps connections at all. There may be a time when you and I have a choice between 100 Mbps and 1 Gbps (GigaBit), but I doubt either of us will have a chance for even 100 Mbps during these next few years.

In fairness to the Fiber to the Home proponents, the choice between 10 Mbps and 1 Gbps means an enormous increase in costs. Higher speeds force the use of more expensive equipment up and down the network. Realistically, putting all the foundation equipment in place for 10 Mbps will cost a fortune for high-end optical cards, memory, and network switches. Our best hope for Fiber to the Home is to eagerly buy 10 Mbps connections to get the project rolling and profitable, and let the providers upgrade components over time to higher speeds.

Everything, as always, depends on the service providers and how fast they want to take their customers down the broadband road. But if they want to open the throttles and let people have super broadband, I'm all for that.

Reliability

Once installed, fiber cable doesn't suffer from electromagnetic interference no matter how many other cables are around it. And, if your electric dog fence shorts out when wet, the broadband over fiber services will stay up despite the rain.

Fiber to the Home won't cause any reliability problems and in fact will prevent quite a few. Any problems will be at the remote node point or more rarely in the central office where the various service providers make their connections. Problems there may affect many customers, lending urgency to troubleshooting.

Although tiny and thin, a single strand of fiber optic cable can withstand a fair amount of torture by being wrapped in strong insulation. Conduits are great and probably necessary for protection, and you can stuff in all the other wires for a home, such as electrical and telephone (at least until the fiber replaces the home phone telephone wires in a few more years.).

Security

Fiber optic cables can't be tapped easily, and eavesdropping will be nearly impossible. The security from your home to the central office will be as good as anyone can hope for. Electronic switches or optical transceivers at the remote terminal can be intercepted, true, but it would take some real work and quite a bit of time.

Normal caveats apply here. After your computer(s) are on the Internet, typical security procedures must be followed (antivirus software, firewall, and so on) or you will be sorry.

WiMax

The quickest way to describe WiMax is "wireless broadband." Sporting data speeds much higher than the normal wireless options detailed in the previous chapter, WiMax connects Wi-Fi hotspots to the Internet over a range up to 31 miles of linear service area range. A shared data rate up to 70 Mbps, as well as nonline of sight installation options, makes WiMax an interesting new technology. Figure 5-4 shows the official site for the WiMax standards development team.

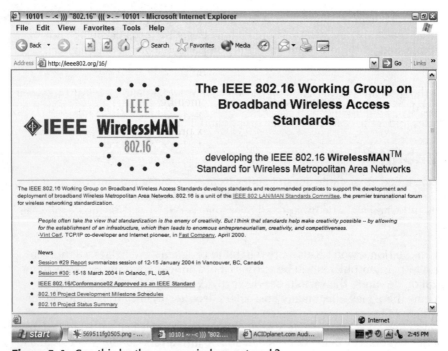

Figure 5-4: Can this be the super-wireless network?

Ratified by the appropriate standards committee in early 2003, the official name for WiMax is IEEE 802.16. (IEEE is the Institute of Electrical and Electronics Engineers.) Defined as a wireless Metropolitan Area Network, WiMax has the strong support of Intel, Nokia, and Proxim as its primary proponents along with a large group of other wireless vendors. By collecting various Wi-Fi hotspots, WiMax can cover an entire city without requiring too many transceivers and towers. Some feel (or at least hope) that WiMax will offer inexpensive high-speed wireless to entire communities.

You may see some reference to 802.20, and think it's WiMax as well. Not exactly. That's the standards label for mobile broadband wireless access, a group trying to develop ways to deliver broadband to moving users, such as those in cars and trains. 802.16, WiMax, is a fixed wireless technology.

How WiMax works

Designed to be a do-everything fixed broadband wireless access (sometimes called BWA) system, WiMax started with a frequency range between 10 GHz and 66 GHz. An improvement already in the works will include frequencies between 2 GHz and 11 GHz. That's a lot of frequency with plenty of room to avoid interference and support multiple high-speed channels at one time. In other words, it is enough wireless bandwidth to provide broadband. Some reports already reference WiMax as 802.16a up to 802.16e for added frequencies and improvements.

Plans are grand. Pop open your laptop or PDA 30 miles from the base station and get a minimum 2 Mbps broadband connection. Connect wirelessly at high speed everywhere in the city, not just at the coffee shop.

That's the plan, at least. For the next few years WiMax users will have to connect a wireless transceiver (the pizza box on the building) and wire that to an internal Ethernet network. Power requirements for WiMax transceivers remain too high for laptop and PDA use, but remember the primary backers of WiMax: companies selling chips and other hardware to support wireless communications. A generation or two of WiMax products will bring size and power requirements to a range comparable to today's Wi-Fi levels.

Coverage area

Big. Thousands of users over a wide area can be supported by a single base station.

The long reach (30 miles) from the fixed wireless base station offers great advantages for developing areas. One of the primary WiMax backer, Nokia, obviously knows some tricks in voice communications. With the bandwidth available from WiMax equipment, there's plenty of room for voice channels as well as data. One base station, configured properly, can instantly become the telephone switch for an entire small city.

"Last mile" problems to connect homes to broadband service providers can be solved by WiMax. Although Wi-Fi (802.11b) can transmit at speeds up to 11 Mbps (best case) up to 1,000 feet, blanketing a neighborhood with Wi-Fi will require far more access points in the area than providers want to pay for. However, a single base station per large neighborhood can be a good value for delivering broadband.

Wireless options for the last mile don't require two critical components: physical wires to the home or office, and a truck roll to connect them. Just as with some wireless broadband providers today, a WiMax customer in the future may be able to buy a home transceiver at the store, plug it into their computer or home network, and get WiMax service. That level of installation service from the broadband provider (basically nothing) makes the provider happy. It also keeps the price down, because the service providers don't have to amortize hundreds of dollars of installation costs over your monthly contract.

Trials in progress

Unless you're British, you're not going to see WiMax anytime soon. There have been a few trials scattered around the United Kingdom, including ways to use WiMax to let train passengers maintain their wireless Internet connections through their entire journey.

One planned test in central Georgia will get started sometime in 2004 if all goes well. What must go well includes someone putting up about $2 million for the necessary WiMax towers and transceivers. Keep an eye on what people are saying about WiMax at the official standards site: www.ieee802.org/16/pub/buzz.html.

Speed

Total bandwidth for WiMax could be up in the 70 Mbps range. Whether that figure will be reached per base station or for a total area remains unproven.

The few vague plans for service rollouts mention just enough speeds to beat ADSL but not much more. Business early adopters would see about 2 Mbps, while consumer pioneers will be allocated about 400 Kbps. If you think that sounds suspiciously like the numbers of ADSL and cable broadband access, the two primary competitors for jumping across the last mile to the customer, I agree.

Reliability

There's nothing to judge WiMax on yet except very early trials and vendor tests. However, if we accept the fact that wireless systems using many of the same technologies as WiMax have good reliability records, we can convince ourselves WiMax will be just as reliable, if not more.

The long reach of every base station makes WiMax less expensive to deploy, but more vulnerable to an outage. If all customers within 30 miles in any direction of the base station lose their connections because of a problem with the tower transceiver, every customer will be out of luck. The likelihood, especially early on, to add redundant WiMax towers and base stations will be low. In a few years, areas served by WiMax will have multiple base stations and the ability to move customers if their primary contact drops. So if you have WiMax today and your signal stops, it won't take more than two or three years to rollout more WiMax base stations in your area.

Security

Wireless systems always make some people (okay, me) nervous when speaking of security. After all, every wireless systems broadcasts, by definition, everything you're doing on the network to the world or at least the part of the world within range.

Nothing special is decided about WiMax security. It makes sense to extend the Wi-Fi security technology to include WiMax, but logic doesn't always rule in these areas. We'll have to wait and see what we get, but my money's on the Wi-Fi security model.

Powerline Broadband

What copper wires come into every home and business? Telephone and electrical lines. What hasn't been exploited for broadband yet? Electrical lines.

Running data over home electrical lines has developed into a strong, viable option for wiring home and office networks. Chapter 14 will cover that option in depth.

"Power Grid" broadband points to another option of data over electrical lines, such as using the electricity distribution network to distribute data. Sometimes called Digital Powerline Technology, sometimes Power Line Communications, and sometimes Powerline Communications, the goal is the same: piggyback data on the high-power electrical transmission network.

Electrical companies have been using narrowband signals over their power grid for control purposes for years. Although reliable and well tested, the narrowband technology used by the power companies themselves offers too little bandwidth to help consumers.

As a proof of concept idea, however, their own narrowband control technology gives the power companies a leg up on some of their competitors. And because power grids are ubiquitous, the last mile problem disappears.

How Powerline broadband works

Voltages across the power grid run up to 35 kV, far above the 120 volts in the normal U.S. home. Lower voltages for home use are created by step-down transformers located near the line endpoints. Powerline developments focus on the middle voltage range because that's what feeds the transformers for home and business voltage delivery. The transformers come within 100 yards of most of the homes and businesses in the United States.

There are two ways to encode data packets to travel across the modern Powerline network:

> Digital Spread Spectrum (DSS) passes through line equipment such as transformers and is therefore less expensive to deploy.

> Orthogonal Frequency-Division Multiplexing (OFDM) does not pass through line equipment, but works better through noisy electrical sources, impedance changes, and the multipath loop problems created by the Powerline network.

Most likely, third-party broadband service providers will administer the service across the platform supplied by the power companies. That's already the case in Manassas, Virginia, which introduced the service early in 2004.

Trials in progress

Manassas Virginia offers "real" Powerline service, although it just started late in January of 2004. Cities in Georgia and Colorado have signed up for the service, but are not yet installed as I write this. Figure 5-5 shows one of the private companies helping to test powerline networks with real customers.

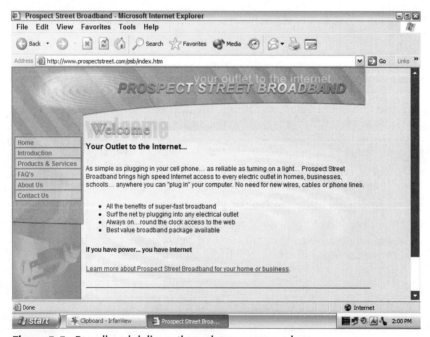

Figure 5-5: Broadband delivery through your power plugs.

Several projects are underway, but just barely. Look for news coming out of Colorado and Missouri. There has been quite a bit of work in Brazil as well. Developing areas benefit greatly when technology allows them to acquire more than one service at a time, and broadband over power lines does that. After all, every country trying to grow out of the "developing" tag needs power, so power line availability is a safe assumption.

Speed

A combination of data transmission technologies, such as the OFDM mentioned in the *How powerline broadband works* section along with Ethernet methods used to determine successful packet delivery, add up to some decent speeds across the Powerline network. Inside the home or office, a maximum speed of 14 Mbps is standard. The Powerline grid itself supports speeds up to 45 Mbps, and that may increase to 100 Mbps as the technology gets fine tuned over time.

Consumer options to this point are limited to around 1 Mbps. This puts Powerline broadband into the same area as DSL and cable, plus or minus a little depending on your supplier.

Another nice point is the performance upstream from Powerline broadband customers. Speeds upstream are the same as the speeds downstream. Companies, large and small, with their own Web and e-mail servers can relax knowing their upstream information flow to customers is as fast as their downstream flow.

Reliability

Every service in the world of computing wants to compare itself to the electrical service in the United States. Whenever you hit a switch, you expect lights, and are almost never disappointed.

Just because the broadband signals go over power lines doesn't mean that broadband service will be as reliable as the power itself. Extra equipment and different technologies are at work to provide broadband, making it different enough from electrical power to take away all guarantees.

However, I doubt anyone with Powerline broadband will have less service uptime than those on cable broadband. Even DSL has more outages than the electrical company.

Security

Security details are sketchy, probably because the Powerline broadband technology hasn't been around long. Several documents outlining planned trials and reports from Manassas mention security but give no details.

HomePlug network devices, the ones inside your home or office running data over power lines, do offer some security options that I'll detail in Chapter 14.

Whether the Powerline broadband groups pick up on that security technology or not hasn't been decided.

If you're lucky enough to get a connection in one of these trials or early adopter programs, assume you have no security on the line. At least assume you have the same security concerns as you do on a shared cable broadband installation.

Summary

Broadband isn't standing still. New ways to deliver the high-speed broadband experience you deserve to your home or office are cooking at this very moment. And the good news is that you don't have to rely on the telephone or cable companies, those hotbeds of crawling pseudo-innovation, to be the ones to bring you faster and better service.

Where will you get your broadband in a few years? I'm guessing a combination of Fiber to the Home when you're stationary and WiMax when you're traveling. But I'm an optimistic guy, so it may be more than just a few years.

Pros and Cons: Choosing Your Best Broadband Option

Many people have multiple broadband service provider choices. With that good fortune comes a nagging worry: what if you make the wrong choice?

First, like the old joke says when updated for new network technology, bad broadband service is a lot better than no broadband service.

Second, if you don't make the best choice, you'll still make a good choice. Every broadband service option described so far in this book will make your Internet access better than ever before.

Finally, no decision you make here is binding forever. In fact, technology will improve so much over the next few years that you will need to rethink your broadband service option in two years no matter what you choose today.

Get your pencil, get ready to make some decisions, and by the end of this chapter you will have a good idea of the best choice for your broadband service needs. And if that service isn't available in your area, you'll still get a good broadband experience. Then update your decision in a year or two as new options become available to you.

There is no hidden agenda in the fact that cable starts the list for your broadband service options checklist. Something had to start, and cable comes earlier in the alphabet than DSL, satellite, or wireless. Feel free to go through the DSL checklist first, and if DSL gives you the comfort level you need, sign up for DSL and don't look back. But if you want to check around just a little, just to be sure, this is the place to do so.

Decision Points for Your Comparisons

Cable and DSL broadband vendors all ask for your address to verify that they can deliver service to you. The screens always include plenty of marketing and sales excitement, but that's to be expected. Figure 6-1 shows the search screen for EarthLink, a national service provider of all types of broadband service.

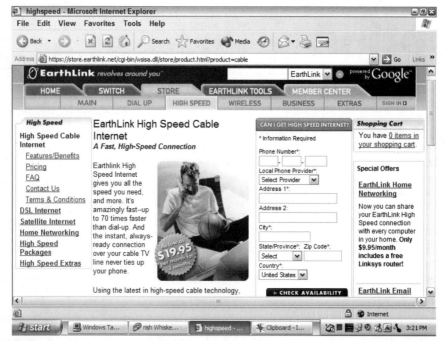

Figure 6-1: Type in your address to see if you win the "broadband available" prize.

Interestingly, EarthLink told me I couldn't get cable broadband access at my location, even though I received the information over my Comcast Cable Broadband service. This only means that Comcast handles its own service provider chores and doesn't feel the need to allow EarthLink to share its customers. EarthLink did offer me DSL and satellite wireless broadband access, however.

How do you know where to check for broadband access? The best search Web site I know for this, www.broadbandreports.com, not only shows you the names of local broadband providers, it gives you the feedback from your neighbors using those services. (See Figure 6-2.)

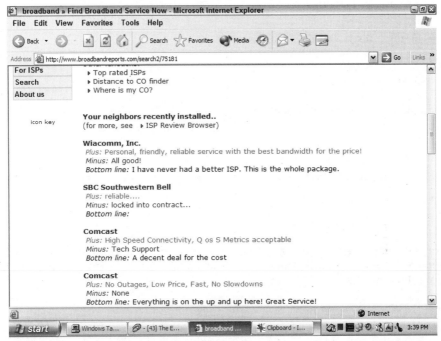

Figure 6-2: I scrolled partway down the window to show service providers and user comments.

If you're interested primarily in cable, the National Cable and Telecommunications Association (www.ncta.com mentioned earlier) includes a service locator based on your address. It correctly found the Comcast service listing for my address.

How to compare service features

You not only choose a way to connect your home or office to the Internet via broadband, you also choose your service provider. Make sure you feel comfortable with access speeds, service provider features, and restrictions before you sign on the virtual dotted line.

First, you must verify you can get some type of broadband service at your location. There will be a few poor souls unable to connect to anything due to a collision of bad luck factors such as distance, southern exposure, and no local wireless service provider. All I can suggest for those folks is to learn the joys of patience.

Figures 6-1 and 6-2 show two methods of finding names of service providers in your area. Check the business pages and the inserts in your phone bills for broadband service provider advertising.

You must prioritize your broadband service requirements. List, in order, your three or four most important broadband service qualifications, as in the following example:

✦ Speed

✦ Spam and virus e-mail controls

✦ Reliability

✦ Free phone support

Don't feel bad if your list differs. What's important to you may not be as important to me and vice versa. Your list might just as easily say:

✦ Cost

✦ Web mail application to read e-mail via a browser when traveling

✦ Dial-up number for backup

✦ Personal Web pages included free

There is no "right" list, period. Whatever you feel is most important is most important for you. But prioritizing before you make your decision will help narrow your choices.

When doing product reviews for magazines, I have to assign a score in five or six areas of product evaluation. Those areas are weighted, so that a 9 rating in performance counts more toward the overall score than a 10 in installation. This thinking assigns more weight to the features assumed to be more critical and important.

If one service provider offers the world's greatest features in an area you care nothing about, don't let that outweigh another service provider with good scores in areas you do care about.

Look at the opening screen of www.broadbandreports.com/gbu for their "Good, Bad, and Ugly" list of broadband provider reviews. If a local provider consistently appears in the Horror Story column, you may want to keep looking.

Pros and Cons for Cable

Cable broadband access subscribers outnumbered DSL subscribers about two to one at the end of 2003, but those numbers vary, depending on who tallied the numbers. Surprisingly, the numbers reported by the cable industry don't exactly match those provided by the DSL industry. One might be tempted to think the statistics reflect a wee bit of bias.

Cable companies have had longer to install the huge network of cables to reach homes and businesses in the United States, which you would think gives them an advantage. But many of the early cable systems didn't support two-way

Internet access until upgrades added that functionality. Similarly, the telephone companies have wires to every home and business, but also had to overcome earlier technical difficulties that restricted broadband service to many customers.

Placing your cable modem at the termination point of your interior cable wiring may not be the best place for your computer. Cables terminate in great locations for televisions, not computers.

Competition for broadband access between the cable and telephone companies gets more pointed every day. Add local telephone service over cable networks, and you raise the competitive stakes even higher. This is a good time to be a broadband customer looking for a service provider.

Current coverage areas

Typical suburban homes, cable's prime grazing area, are almost guaranteed to have a ready cable connection. According to numbers from the National Cable and Telecommunication Association (www.ncta.com) and from research company InStat/MDR (www.instat.com), here's how cable coverage areas work out (numbers are rounded):

- ✦ **108 million:** Total U.S. households
- ✦ **103 million:** Occupied households passed by a functioning cable
- ✦ **73.5 million:** Basic cable (or above) subscribers
- ✦ **12 million plus:** Cable broadband subscribers
- ✦ **60 million:** Total number of cable-ready homes that can get broadband from their cable provider

Looking at the numbers, it appears that about half the homes capable of getting cable TV can get broadband access through their cable provider. It appears the cable companies still have a serious number of network upgrades left to complete. It also appears 5 million customers will never get cable broadband or cable TV, making them prime candidates for satellite service.

If your housing development sprouted less than 20 years ago, you will almost certainly have cable access. If it sprouted less than a decade ago, you may have extra features above and beyond cable, such as Fiber to the Home options.

Decision checklist

When evaluating your cable service provider, use this list when going through their sales material and check off the items they meet or don't meet. After you're done, go through and see which of these are dealbreakers for you. If none are, you can then decide the cable service provider will give you the broadband service you need, or you can run through checklists for your other options for comparison.

✦ Can you get cable broadband Internet access service at your location?

    ❑ Yes

    ❑ No

       If not, skip to the next sections on DSL, satellite, and community wireless.

✦ Does the broadband service provider meet your most important criteria?

    ❑ Yes

    ❑ No

       If not, skip to the next sections on DSL, satellite, and community wireless. Return to the cable service provider checklist only if all other options are closed to you, or meet fewer of your requirements than cable Internet access from your local provider.

✦ Does the provider offer enough e-mail addresses?

    ❑ Yes

    ❑ No

✦ All broadband service providers offer Post Office Protocol version 3 (POP3) for incoming e-mail and Simple Message Transfer Protocol (SMTP) for outgoing e-mail. Do the service provider offer Web e-mail you can read via a browser from anywhere on the Internet?

    ❑ Yes

    ❑ No

✦ Do the service provider offer virus filtering on incoming and outgoing e-mails?

    ❑ Yes

    ❑ No

✦ Does the service provider offer spam filtering?

    ❑ Yes

    ❑ No

✦ Do e-mail attachments count against your total storage allocation?

    ❑ Yes

    ❑ No

✦ Does your broadband provider limit the number of hours per month you can use its service?

    ❑ Yes

    ❑ No

✦ Does your broadband service provider include a personal Web site?

❑ Yes

❑ No

✦ Does the personal Web site include enough storage space so you can create the site you want?

❑ Yes

❑ No

✦ Does the personal Web site support design tools you use, such as Microsoft FrontPage?

❑ Yes

❑ No

✦ Does the personal Web site include enough bandwidth allowance to support the traffic you expect?

❑ Yes

❑ No

✦ Can you read the broadband service providers Acceptable Use Policy and Terms of Service before signing up?

❑ Yes

❑ No

✦ Are those policy documents readable by normal humans without a law degree?

❑ Yes

❑ No

✦ Does your broadband service provider offer free technical support, at least during installation?

❑ Yes

❑ No

✦ Does your broadband service provider offer 24-hour technical support?

❑ Yes

❑ No

✦ Can you speak to a real live person on the phone when you call technical support?

❑ Yes

❑ No

✦ Does your broadband service provider include the newsgroups you want?

❑ Yes

❑ No

✦ Can everyone on your home or office network use the Internet access service concurrently?

❑ Yes

❑ No

✦ Have you gotten good referrals or testimonials from people you trust about this broadband service provider?

❑ Yes

❑ No

Total up your answers. If this doesn't seem to be a slam dunk choice for your situation, check the number of good, acceptable, and bad answers against other service provider categories. Remember to give more weight to the answers related to the features you feel are most critical.

Pros and Cons for DSL

Most DSL industry reports admit cable broadband access providers have more total subscribers than the DSL broadband providers. However, they claim (and provide research numbers to back them up) that their DSL subscriber base grows faster than the cable subscriber base. In other words, new broadband users pick DSL over cable.

Jupiter Research (www.jupiterresearch.com) covers broadband from a variety of angles and lists a big reason that DSL growth now outpaces cable broadband subscriber growth: money. Interviewed dial-up customers were asked about moving to broadband. At $29.99 per month, nearly half (47 percent) said they would be somewhat or very likely to get broadband within a year. As prices rose, broadband interest dropped. By the time Jupiter asked about a price of $44.99, around the cost for many cable broadband providers, only 22 percent of dial-up customers felt broadband would be a good fit for them.

The two major broadband service providers never make life easy on you. At $30, you get the slowest ADSL broadband service, generally 384 kbps downstream and 128 Kbps upstream. Better than dialup, but slower than cable. Is four to seven times the download speed, which cable broadband provides, worth 50 percent more ($30 up to $45)? Only you can determine whether the speed difference is worth the cost difference for you.

One good thing about DSL is your flexibility inside your home or office. When the cable technician comes to install a broadband cable connection, you're likely to be stuck with a less than optimal connection location. After all, the cable will terminate where the television (or home theater focus point) belongs, not where your computer belongs.

DSL service works on every telephone outlet in your home or office connected to the number hosting DSL. Most homes have telephone outlets all over the place, but certainly in great places for computers like dens, offices, bedrooms, and even living rooms. Although there's no reason to move your DSL modem and router (if you have one) after installation, placing it anywhere there's a phone jack can make initial installation arrangements much easier.

Current coverage areas

Market research reported that at the end of 2003, the four major telephone companies could offer DSL of some type on nearly 152 million telephone lines. The largest two carriers, Verizon and SBC, claimed 37 percent and 36.4 percent of those lines, respectively.

Because there are now over 280 million men, women, and children in the United States, the telephone companies have one DSL-capable line for every two of us. But they continue to face competition from cable, satellite, and wireless broadband service providers.

Businesses hopped on the DSL bandwagon, with a 40 percent jump in DSL lines to businesses between the end of 2002 and 2003. That adds up to over 3.7 million DSL business connections. DSL-friendly prognosticators estimate the number of DSL business lines will grow to around 6.3 million by the end of 2007.

Here's a breakdown showing DSL coverage in the United States. There appear to be millions more homes supported by DSL than are supported by cable, but I'm not sure that I believe these numbers. In my experience and those of people I contacted, the telephone lines may be ready according to the phone company but the word hasn't gotten over to the DSL sales department. However, the phone companies are running to convert every line possible, so the 152 million number may not be a lie, it just may be a future truth.

 108 million: Total U.S. households

 152 million: Telephone lines able to support DSL

 8.2 million: DSL customers in the United States

This all means that if you don't have DSL coverage now, you should very soon. Remember, there are 108 million households in the United States at the start of 2004, and nearly 152 million DSL lines to serve them.

Just like cable broadband providers, various DSL providers offer Web sites where you can put in your phone number and address and see if you can get DSL service, and which speed of DSL. The screen in Figure 6-3 is typical of DSL providers.

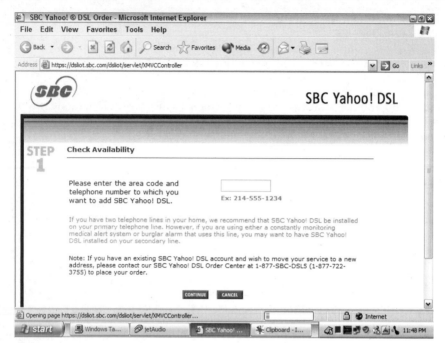

Figure 6-3: Type your address to see if you win the "broadband available" prize, this time with DSL.

In my case, I can get DSL but only the slowest ADSL variety. But I can get SDSL at 384 kbps/384 kbps upstream and downstream. That's fast enough to support a mid-level Web and e-mail server for a business.

How to compare service features

Unlike with cable, assuming you're close enough to the central office or a remote terminal to take advantage of such speeds, DSL gives you multiple options for download speeds, along with multiple options for the monthly fee.

The speed options for the locationally lucky make your priority listings more interesting. If speed is your first option, fast (close to the central office) DSL may be your best choice.

Cross-Reference Refer to Chapter 3. Table 3-4 shows how longer distances cut DSL speeds.

Remember the opening screen of www.broadbandreports.com and its list of broadband provider reviews? If a local DSL provider consistently appears in the Horror Story column, you may want to keep looking for another provider.

Various smaller companies will piggyback on your local telephone company and provide DSL service, often competing with the telephone company they rely on completely. Odd situation, but thank the government for at least allowing some competition over the telephone network we taxpayers bought and paid for several times over.

With this competitor/supplier relationship, the DSL lines into your home or office may support half-dozen different service providers. If that's the case in your area, pay close attention to their Internet service provider information. If the underlying cable and DSL are the same, you would use the service provider details to help you make your decision.

Decision checklist

Most cable-based broadband service providers enjoy a monopoly, but you almost always have multiple choices for a DSL service provider. The competing providers will probably all rely on the same local telephone company for installation and support, but at least the Internet Service Provider part of their DSL offerings will be different.

You may want to use two or three different colored pencils if you're comparing multiple DSL providers. Or, you may get lucky and all are roughly equal and you can pick the one with the lowest service charges.

✦ Can you get some type of DSL broadband Internet access service at your location?

❑ Yes

❑ No

If not, skip to the next sections on satellite and community wireless or back up to the section on cable broadband.

✦ Does the broadband service provider meet your most important criteria?

❑ Yes

❑ No

If not, skip to the next sections on satellite and community wireless or back to the section on cable broadband. Return to the DSL service provider checklist only if all other options are closed to you, or meet fewer of your requirements than DSL Internet access from your local provider.

✦ Does the provider provide enough e-mail addresses?

❑ Yes

❑ No

✦ All broadband service providers offer Post Office Protocol version 3 (POP3) for incoming e-mail and Simple Message Transfer Protocol (SMTP) for outgoing e-mail. Do the provider offer Web e-mail you can read via a browser from anywhere on the Internet?

❑ Yes

❑ No

✦ Does the provider offer virus filtering on incoming and outgoing e-mails?

❑ Yes

❑ No

✦ Does the provider offer spam filtering?

❑ Yes

❑ No

✦ Do e-mail attachments count against your total storage allocation?

❑ Yes

❑ No

✦ Does your broadband provider limit the number of hours per month you can use its service?

❑ Yes

❑ No

✦ Does your broadband service provider include a personal Web site?

❑ Yes

❑ No

✦ Does the personal Web site include enough storage space so you can create the site you want?

❑ Yes

❑ No

✦ Does the personal Web site support the design tools that you use, such as Microsoft FrontPage?

❑ Yes

❑ No

✦ Does the personal Web site include enough bandwidth allowance to support the traffic you expect?

❑ Yes

❑ No

✦ Can you read the broadband service providers Acceptable Use Policy and Terms of Service before signing up?

❑ Yes

❑ No

✦ Are those policy documents readable by normal humans without law degrees?

❑ Yes

❑ No

✦ Does your broadband service provider offer free technical support, at least during installation?

❑ Yes

❑ No

✦ Does your broadband service provider offer 24-hour technical support?

❑ Yes

❑ No

✦ Can you speak to a real live person on the phone when you call technical support?

❑ Yes

❑ No

✦ Does your broadband service provider include the newsgroups you want?

❑ Yes

❑ No

✦ Can everyone on your home or office network use the Internet access service concurrently?

❑ Yes

❑ No

✦ Have you gotten good referrals or testimonials from people you trust about this broadband service provider?

❑ Yes

❑ No

Total up your answers. If this broadband service doesn't seem to be a slam-dunk great choice for your situation, check the number of good, acceptable, and bad answers against other service provider categories. Remember to give more weight to the answers related to the features you feel are most critical.

Pros and Cons for Satellite Broadband

Distance from the central office or head-end doesn't apply when examining satellite service. The node point that gathers customer information for routing to the Internet is about 23,000 miles away from all of us.

Realistically, the majority of satellite customers are beyond the reach of DSL and cable broadband service providers, and have no community wireless options. They turn to satellite as a last resort.

Yes, you can order and receive satellite service even if your home or office sits only a hundred yards from a telephone company central office and right beside a brand new cable distribution box. But people do this so rarely it's not worth discussing.

Satellite providers do a good job, and new technology and new vendors getting into the market will continue to improve the technology. Yet the advantages of DSL and cable for speed and convenience outweigh the cool factor of satellite Internet access, especially if the satellite provider still charges $150-$400 for equipment installation.

Current coverage areas

Good news: If you're in the continental United States, and can see the southern sky at about a 45 degree angle, you can get satellite access.

Your coverage checklist is short and simple:

✦ Are you in the huge coverage area for satellite service?

❏ Yes

❏ No

✦ Do you have a clear view to the south?

❏ Yes

❏ No

If both of those Yes check boxes are filled, you can get satellite broadband service.

How to compare service features

You have less choice with satellite when comparing service features than you do any other service. When there is little competition there is little reason for the vendors in that market to push to provide new and improved features. With satellite, you pretty much have to take what you can get.

This is not meant to insult the few satellite vendors and their Internet service provider features. But most people looking at satellite service have no other way to get broadband service. When your choices are broadband satellite or dialup, you will probably find getting broadband outweighs a missing service provider feature or two.

Speeds for downloads will not pass the 500 Kbps level for standard satellite broadband service. If you buy faster satellite service, such as for a business, you will pay substantially more money for the extra speed. For home and small business users, figure the best download speed you'll ever see is 500 Kbps. Compare this to 384 Kbps and up for DSL and between 1.5 Mbps and 3 Mbps for most cable providers.

Pay attention to the Terms of Service agreement for satellite vendors if you have more than one computer. Some basic satellite packages are strictly one-computer plans. You may have to pay extra or upgrade your access plan if you have a network of users wanting Internet broadband access through the satellite.

Downlink and uplink details

You have one choice to make: one-way satellite or two-way satellite? If you choose one-way, you must use a dial-up connection to upload Internet commands and requests. If you use two-way, the satellite dish includes a transmitter to allow upstream communications. One-way upstream is tough to configure for more than one computer at a time.

Upstream speed compares equally, at least for standard residential satellite service with the generation of equipment in place. Newer providers, such as WildBlue (www.wildblue.com), promise high-speed upstream connections, but they are not yet ready to demonstrate that service.

You have to answer the following questions about upstream:

✦ Should you pay more upfront for two-way satellite?

✦ Should you save money upfront and keep using dialup for upstream?

Simple question, isn't it? Again, there is no right answer; there is just the answer that you prefer.

Decision checklist

There aren't many satellite-specific decisions to make. Many customers who use satellite have no other options.

✦ Do you have a clear view to the south for the satellite dish to aim up about 45 degrees at the satellite?

❑ Yes

❑ No

If not, skip to the next section on community wireless or back up to the section on cable and DSL.

✦ Does the broadband service provider meet your most important criteria?

❑ Yes

❑ No

If so, and you're checking satellite providers as your last hope for broadband access, none of the rest of the issues matter. Service-poor broadband Internet access beats service-rich dial-up access anytime.

Pros and Cons for Community Wireless Broadband

Some picky wireless reporters claim only WiMax can be considered "community" wireless because it serves an entire community at once. I call all local wireless service providers community providers because they are the most local service providers possible. Community wireless providers are tied to the local community by the short reach of most wireless technologies in use today.

The local nature of wireless service providers works against community wireless providers when they are providing services and technical support. Large regional or national providers can easily amortize support costs over all their customers, but a local wireless provider may have only a few hundred or few thousand customers. Such a small installed base won't sustain 24-hour support manned by real people, although coordination between wireless providers into associations helps give them the "big provider" look for many services. Talk to your local wireless provider and see how it can help you.

Small companies or not, one of the major research groups (InStat) expects the wireless market to more than double over the next 4 years. By 2007, they expect the market to hit over $1.2 billion. That's a pretty big community.

WiMax will jumpstart consumer awareness of community wireless in a big way with the high speeds and wide coverage area. Even with a 30-mile reach from the base station, however, wireless remains rooted in the community and is the most "local" of all broadband access technologies.

Current coverage areas

Local community wireless providers are generally small, local, and not able to spend marketing dollars like their broadband service provider competitors. Finding them may be tougher than getting installed and running.

A listing service Web site run by *Broadband Wireless Exchange Magazine* (www.bbwexchange.com) does a good job collecting wireless provider's names and contact information. In Figure 6-4 I've scrolled down to show the map BBW Exchange provides to drill down and find a local wireless service provider.

If you're interested in getting into the Internet business in some way (outside the spam offers you get every day), community wireless may be the place for you. Small businesses with a building to serve as a base station are welcomed by the wireless community. You can not only make some money but feel good by providing a service as valuable to others as to yourself.

Security concerns

Some people believe community wireless cannot be as secure as DSL or cable. Those people are working from incorrect information. (I'm politely saying

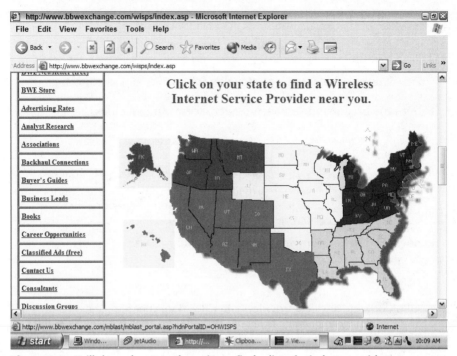

Figure 6-4: Drill down by state then city to find a list of wireless providers.

they're wrong.) Wireless access of every kind requires different security procedures than wired connections, but they can be extremely safe and secure.

 Cross-Reference Chapter 12 dives into firewalls and other security issues.

Your location's wireless modem that connects you to the wireless service will be keyed to that service. Only authorized serial numbers of authorized user modems will get access to the wireless service. Data between your location and the wireless provider will be encrypted to a level similar to secure Web browser connections.

Far be it for me to tell people not to worry about security, but a properly configured wireless community network provides as much protection as a DSL or cable connection. Careless users will always have trouble.

Decision checklist

Fixed wireless broadband service providers vary greatly in the range of standard service provider amenities they include. A few national service provider firms, such as EarthLink, work with community wireless providers, but most of the service providers in this market provide all services themselves. The good news is that most wireless providers are local, friendly, and willing to answer questions.

✦ Can you get wireless broadband Internet access service at your location?

❑ Yes

❑ No

If not, go back to the sections on DSL, cable, and satellite.

✦ Does the broadband service provider meet your most important criteria?

❑ Yes

❑ No

If not, go back to the next sections on DSL, cable, and satellite. Return to this service provider checklist only if all other options are closed to you, or meet fewer of your requirements than cable Internet access from your local provider.

✦ Does the provider provide enough e-mail addresses?

❑ Yes

❑ No

✦ All broadband service providers offer POP3 for incoming e-mail and SMTP for outgoing e-mail. Does the provider you are considering offer Web e-mail you can read via a browser from anywhere on the Internet?

❑ Yes

❑ No

✦ Does the provider offer virus filtering on incoming and outgoing e-mails?

❑ Yes

❑ No

✦ Does the provider offer spam filtering?

❑ Yes

❑ No

✦ Do e-mail attachments count against your total storage allocation?

❑ Yes

❑ No

✦ Does your broadband provider limit the number of hours per month you can use its service?

❑ Yes

❑ No

✦ Does your broadband service provider include a personal Web site?

❑ Yes

❑ No

✦ Does the personal Web site include enough storage space for you to create the site you want?

❑ Yes

❑ No

✦ Does the personal Web site support any design tools that you use, such as Microsoft FrontPage?

❑ Yes

❑ No

✦ Does the personal Web site include enough bandwidth to support the traffic you expect?

❑ Yes

❑ No

✦ Can you read the broadband service providers Acceptable Use Policy and Terms of Service before signing up?

❑ Yes

❑ No

✦ Are those policy documents readable by normal humans without law degrees?

❑ Yes

❑ No

✦ Does your broadband service provider offer free technical support, at least during installation?

❑ Yes

❑ No

✦ Does your broadband service provider offer 24-hour technical support?

❑ Yes

❑ No

✦ Can you speak to a real live person on the phone when you call technical support?

❑ Yes

❑ No

✦ Does your broadband service provider include the newsgroups you want?

❑ Yes

❑ No

✦ Can everyone on your home or office network use the Internet access service concurrently?

❑ Yes

❑ No

    ✦ Have you gotten good referrals or testimonials from people you trust about this broadband service provider?

        ❑ Yes

        ❑ No

Total up your answers. If this doesn't seem to be a slam dunk great choice for your situation, check the number of good, acceptable, and bad answers against other service provider categories. Remember to give more weight to the answers on questions you decided were more critical than others.

Service Provider Restrictions

Every Internet service provider includes rules and regulations for its clients, normally called their AUP or Acceptable Use Policy. Usually the terms of service list what is and is not acceptable to do while using the system. Providers sometimes call this Terms of Service (TOS), Terms and Conditions, or Members Agreement. They can (and do) change these terms at any time.

You will rarely find a large headline called "Things You Can't Do Here" on the marketing Web sites of broadband service providers. After all, the job of marketing is to convince you to buy the service, not run you off.

The place to find these restrictions is down deep in the service or support sections of their Web site. Often providers detail some restrictions in their Frequently Asked Questions (FAQ) pages. Sometimes they will be hidden on the support page, and every now and then you can find them on the System Requirements page.

If you don't find the restrictions early on, keep looking. Every broadband service provider has restrictions, and the one you're about to sign on with is no different. Better to find out onerous details about service restrictions before you agree to a year-long service contract.

After you find the restrictions, you may find they're just as impenetrable as the End User License Agreement (EULA) on software products. If you can't read the restrictions because the legalese can't be interpreted by a normal person, you might want to rethink your choice of service provider. When two providers are about equal but one offers a common-sense set of restrictions, and the other looks like a law-school contracts test, sign with the common sense provider. It will be easier to work with when issues come up later.

Acceptable use policies

If you carefully read the acceptable use policies of most service providers, you may believe the only thing you can do on the Internet is turn it off. Taking advantage of the small personal Web page many providers offer adds an entire new list of things you can't do.

Here are some standard boilerplate restrictions that come from several national providers I checked. They clearly state YOU WILL NOT do any of the following:

✦ Upload, post, e-mail, or transmit in any way any content that is unlawful, harmful, threatening, abusive, harassing, defamatory, vulgar, obscene, libelous, invasive of privacy, hateful, or racially or ethnically objectionable

✦ Harm minors in any way

✦ Upload, post, e-mail, or transmit in any way any content that you do not have a right to make available under law or under contract from the copyright holder

✦ Upload, post, e-mail, or transmit in any way any content that infringes any patent, trademark, trade secret, copyright, or other proprietary rights

✦ Upload, post, e-mail, or transmit in any way any content that can be considered spam or junk e-mail in any way, but you can post solicitations in shopping areas, such as eBay

✦ Upload, post, e-mail, or transmit in any way any content with viruses or any other program that causes problems for any computer hardware or software or any telecommunications equipment

✦ Stalk or harass someone else through the service

✦ Collect personal data about other users

 Note   There goes almost every forwarded joke on the Internet. According to this, they're all against the Terms of Service in one way or another.

This is not an exhaustive list by any stretch. Most policies I checked were almost three times this long.

Every one of us agrees to play by these rules when signing up for Internet access. If you sign up to host a Web page, the restrictions become more involved because hosting companies don't want to be slammed for holding pornographic or other illegal material on their servers because you provide those types of files on your Web site.

You have no control over how your service provider administers and enforces these guidelines. Users can, and do, get cut off from their service provider for breaking the terms of service. Rarely does this happen unless someone, or some law enforcement agency, asks the service to throw the users off.

However, it is legal for law enforcement to "tap" your connection to your Internet provider without informing you of the action. Recent laws, such as the Patriot Act, make it possible for authorities to tap your communications without a court order.

The vast majority of service providers and their customers never have a problem, regardless of how many tasteless jokes are sent. But service providers must put all these restrictions in there to protect themselves in case someone gets out of control.

Rules on connection sharing

Different service providers have different rules about connection sharing. Sometimes they put these rules in their terms of service or acceptable use policies, but sometimes they list those rule separately.

If you have only a single computer that will connect to the Internet through your broadband service provider, this section won't matter to you. If you have more than one computer and you expect them to connect to the Internet at the same time, you need to check your broadband service provider's rules on connection sharing.

There are several ways to "share" your broadband service connection. Linking a home network to the cable or DSL modem obviously falls into that area. But service providers set rules on the following:

✦ How many user names you can establish

✦ How many users can be connected concurrently

✦ Whether you can connect via broadband and dialup at the same time

✦ Whether premium services (extra access to content) purchased by one user name can be used by another user name

The trend for service providers is to allow multiple computers on the home or small office network to connect to the Internet concurrently. One reason, especially for home users, is that service providers want to sell home networking equipment. And realistically, two or three normal Internet users at one home generate far less traffic than any type of Web server hosted at the customer site.

Satellite vendors, however, get stickier about concurrent connections. Check your satellite terms of service if you plan to have multiple computers online at the same time. At least one vendor charges extra to connect three users through the satellite link.

Bandwidth hogs

Warning: In a quirk of language, "unlimited" Internet access may not really mean you can stay connected and upload and download all day and all night. Many Internet service providers now set a high number of access hours, such as 150 hours per month total (a quarter of the total number of hours in a normal month) and charge you if you go over that limit. "Always on" service on your end doesn't mean providers allow "always using service resources" on their end.

Admittedly, these are primarily restrictions leftover from dial-up providers. Each connection at a dial-up provider requires a modem at its end to communicate with the modem at your end. The rule of thumb for service providers used to be seven users for every modem. You can see that if you stay connected 24 hours per day there will be six angry customers. At least they won't be able to send you rude e-mails (that's a joke, son, a joke I say).

Offering the MP3 files from your CD collection free to anyone who asks? That's illegal for one (unless you have written permission from the copyright holders) and an easy call to make from the broadband service provider's point of view. You will be labeled a bandwidth hog and may be restricted in terms of service hours or uploads allowed.

Offering family photos to relatives and close friends? Should be no problem. Offering photos not of family nature? Filters can actually check image contents to see how prevalent flesh tones are in the files. Read the section on acceptable use policies if you think you can get away with this. (You won't for long.)

If MP3 files flow upstream from your residential, noncommercial Internet access account all day, the service provider will cut your connection. Actually, the provider will most likely inform you of your transgression beyond the limits of your residential customer terms of service, and force you to upgrade to a commercial account. It will impose service restrictions only if you don't upgrade and pay more money.

Running your computer as a multiplayer game server all day will get the same reaction from your service provider. That also is against some fine print somewhere, and your service will be cut unless you upgrade to a commercial account.

Summary

Use these checklists and your broadband choice will provide the type of service you want based on your situation. But even if you make a mistake, you can change your mind and try again.

Practicing Safe Broadband

Computer security becomes even more important when you use a broadband service provider because your systems are on the Internet all the time, not just when you dial up. New precautions are necessary.

There are several ways to keep your systems safe, even while surfing at high speed over your new broadband connection. The equipment used to connect to your service provider will help, as will free or inexpensive software.

Broadband connections at a private residence have certain responsibilities shared by the owner and the service provider. Connections in multitenant locations, such as apartments and office buildings, have equal, but different, responsibilities. Whichever group you fall into, the tools and guidelines you need are in this section.

Understanding Computer Security

On one hand, having to protect their personal computers against attacks from strangers aggravates people to no end. People who don't even know you want to trash your computer and steal your data.

On the other hand, you regularly lock your home, office, and car, and you store your valuable papers in a fireproof vault or in a bank safety deposit box. Why should you believe the virtual world of computing is safer and nicer than the real world?

Computer security, and the time and expense users must go through to protect their computers and data, really stinks. But we spend even more time and money protecting ourselves from similar things in the real world. If you keep in mind that computer hackers are no more personally motivated than pickpockets, you may be able to deal with all this less emotionally.

In many cases, computer attacks are crimes of opportunity. Just like car thieves who find the keys inside an unlocked car, hackers find easy targets whenever possible. So when you look like an easy target and don't do the computer equivalent of locking your car and arming your car alarm, hackers will gleefully ruin your day. But when you have your computers locked and protected, hackers go to the next victim.

If I could just find a way to be calm and less annoyed about spam, I'd be in great shape.

How Miscreants Get into Your Computer

Before you get to how, think about why someone would like to gather the information on your computer. If you're like most people, you have credit card numbers, bank account numbers, and perhaps even passwords to your office network on your computer. That means, at the least, burglars, identity thieves, and corporate spies would love to dive in to your data.

Some people like to destroy things and paint graffiti on walls. Their computer equivalents are making viruses, worms, and other destructive programs. Aggravating but not deadly, at least not if you take the proper precautions, these destructive people cause more grief in the computer world than almost anyone.

Distinguishing a virus from a worm can be tough and the different attack methods used today overlap quite a bit. A virus is any program that inhabits your computer without your permission. These applications sometimes wreak havoc by displaying taunting messages or destroying data, but they often hide and launch attacks against other computers.

The term worm describes the method of transport more than the payload and action. A worm often attacks computers across a network by looking for openings in the operating system software. When holes are found, the worms move into your computer and become a virus.

A Trojan Horse program (usually referred to just as a Trojan) refers to the Greek story of the Trojan horse where Odysseus snuck into Troy disguised inside a wooden horse. The gates open, the Trojans dragged the huge horse into the city, and later the soldiers inside snuck out and wreaked havoc. Notice the repetition of havoc wreaking? That's what happens.

Sometimes, security experts and writers get tired of trying to separate what's a worm from a virus from a Trojan. That's where the term *malware* came from. Malware is good shorthand for malicious software and covers various incarnations of evil programs.

The worst part of all this is that almost every time you hear about a huge virus outbreak, users have only themselves to blame for their troubles. Viruses, worms, and Trojan developers attack computers on several fronts, but the most successful front, by far, is to trick users into opening the door and letting the virus walk right in.

The following list describes some of the most common ways computers are infected:

- ✦ Opening an e-mail attachment from an unknown sender
- ✦ Opening a Microsoft Word document with malicious macros
- ✦ Downloading from unsafe Internet sources

✦ Sharing disks and CD-ROMs (including some from big-name software vendors)

✦ Contacting infected files on a file server

✦ Contacting infected files in a peer-to-peer network

✦ Visiting malicious Web pages

Can you stop exposing your computer to viruses if you're careful? No, but the smarter you surf around the Internet, the less trouble you will have. You can certainly refuse to open e-mail attachments from people you don't know. You can refuse to download files when a pop-up window in your Web browser tries to convince you to download some wonderful file you never heard of and didn't request. You can refuse to put disks and CDs of unknown origin into your computer.

However, you can't avoid worms and viruses just by being careful. You need tools to help you avoid infection. You need several layers of tools to help you avoid infection when you have a broadband connection that's always on, keeping your computers always connected to the Internet.

E-Mail

E-mail is the giant hole in your home or business through which almost all worms, viruses, Trojan horse files, general malware, and, of course, spam pour. Spam and malware go hand in hand.

When users open file attachments from e-mail without checking the file for a virus first, they run the risk of infection. Yes, I know that you shouldn't blame the victim and that the virus writers are to blame often fail to teach users to protect themselves. Users who open attachments from people they don't know pay the price.

Making the situation worse, many viruses spread by sending e-mails (with infected attachment) to every address in the infected machine's Microsoft Outlook or Outlook Express address book database. So trusting users who may never open an e-mail from an unknown person open e-mails from someone they do know. Bam! They're infected, because the e-mail really wasn't from someone they know; it came from the virus stealing the addresses from someone they know.

Be careful

E-mail (and spam) senders trick you into loading a virus in the following ways:

✦ Pretend to be from someone you know and trust

✦ Hide the fact that an attachment is executable

✦ Offer help handling virus infections

✦ Include HTML code to activate programs located on Web sites

When you get an attachment you don't expect, verify the sender and ask that person about the file you received. If the person sent it on purpose, you'll have no problem. If that person has no idea that an e-mail with an attachment came bearing their address, both of you need to disinfect your systems.

Don't open attachments if they are executable files. You can tell this by checking their file extension (the letters to the right of the dot at the end of the file name). Unless you are positive the sender and files are trustworthy, do not click the attached files. Files with the following extensions can cause problems by executing when you open them:

```
.bat
.com
.exe
.pif
.reg
.vb
.vbs
```

When you look at the files on your computer, you will notice many of your files have these extensions and the files are trustworthy. Your operating system and all your applications rely on these file types. However, when you click an unexpected file in an e-mail message, the application will begin working so quickly your system will be compromised before you can react.

Protecting yourself

Microsoft Windows hides the extensions from you by default. This setting makes it easier for virus attachments to get by users. Change this setting immediately. Go to Start; then open the Control Panel and choose Folder Options ➪ View, to see the selection options shown in Figure 7-1.

The check box is named Hide Extensions for known file types and that's what it does. If Windows believes it knows what type of file the extension describes, you'll never see the extension.

Devious virus writers try and fool users by hiding the file extension of an executable program. Windows, in all recent versions, lets you have periods in the filename. If your Windows settings hide extensions (by default) the virus may come inside a program named Jokes.txt.exe. The file extension, the letters after the last period, remains hidden by Windows, so users think a text file of jokes can't cause them any harm. After you clear the check box shown in Figure 7-1, you'll see the entire filename and realize the trick. Any program with a file extension from the list before Figure 7-1 might wreak havoc and even go so far as to erase all your data and reformat your hard disk if allowed to run.

Many attackers aim at Microsoft's Outlook and Outlook Express e-mail applications for the following reasons:

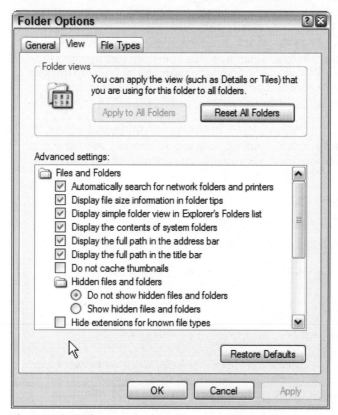

Figure 7-1: Make sure the box the arrow points to is unchecked.

✦ The majority of personal computer users rely on them.

✦ Microsoft opens application interfaces so one program can change data for other programs.

You can't blame Microsoft's problems on lack of market penetration and dominance. The minute Microsoft included an e-mail and Web browser application in its operating systems, it took over the market share lead. If you're a hacker or virus monger, you want to attack the leading programs to make more of a splash.

You can blame Microsoft for building in all types of programming hooks between their e-mail client (Outlook and Outlook Express), browser (Internet Explorer), address book, and execution support for Visual Basic. Any code in any program within the Windows operating systems and the Office application suite can trigger actions in other programs without requiring security checks or authentication. The handy way you can send someone an e-mail and have it show up on their calendar. Viruses use the same tricks to read your address book and launch malware-laden e-mails with your name as sender and return address.

Microsoft turns on HTML (formatted) e-mail display by default. Links in HTML messages can connect to Web sites and download programs or start other mischief. Some users (yours truly included) read e-mails only in text format to avoid triggering a connection to an unknown Web site. Even just opening the e-mail message with an HTML reader can tell the spammer or hacker who sent the message details about your system for future attacks, and even open connections making further infection possible. Reading the URL in a text-only reader eliminates that possibility.

If you're interested in alternative e-mail applications to prevent another virus attack sending e-mail malware with your name attached, check out these free options:

✦ **Netscape:** channels.netscape.com/ns/browsers/download.jsp

✦ **Mozilla:** www.mozilla.org/

✦ **Other choices:** www.download.com/ and other download sites.

The following options aren't free forever. They offer a free trial option, and a good reputation:

✦ **Eudora:** www.eudora.com/

✦ **The Bat:** www.ritlabs.com/en/products/thebat/

Using non-Microsoft e-mail applications breaks the coordination between your e-mail, your calendar, and your task list. If you need those connections and enjoy the automated connections between the applications, stay with Microsoft Outlook or Outlook Express. If you prefer to gain more virus protection, try another e-mail client application. If you prefer to stay with Outlook, pay your protection money for the security applications like spam control, virus checking, and personal firewall software.

Downloaded files

Your mother used to tell you, "put that down, you don't know where it's been." That same advice stands for users tempted to download files they find here and there.

Sometimes the file you download causes problems directly, and sometimes the problem comes from a stowaway program attached and unnoticed in the process. Either way, you can invite worms and viruses in the front door of your computer when you download the wrong file from the wrong place.

Rule of thumb: If you go to a Web site looking for files, such as drivers from a software vendor or the downloads section from the Web portion of technical magazines, you will be fine. If an e-mail comes out of the ether offering some wonderful screensaver or the like, delete it quickly.

Be careful

Don't download programs you don't ask for. Some Trojan programs get downloaded from a spam message pretending to be a legitimate service update request from some company like Microsoft. Download that program and pay the price, because either that program will cause problems directly or will download other programs that will cause problems.

Don't download programs from friends unless you're expecting a file from that person. One of the primary ways viruses spread is by spoofing the name and address of the sender. After all, would you download an attachment from an e-mail from "Scumbag Scammer" with a subject "Pain in a pretend application patch?"

Spoofing and Phishing

When a virus program reads the Outlook address book on an infected computer and sends messages to every listing, it almost always uses the address of the PC's owner. That's spoofing.

When an e-mail arrives unbidden from some type of financial firm, such as a request from eBay or PayPal to click a special link and "verify your account information" or provide passwords, that's phishing. Even major national banks have been victimized by phishing, but not as victimized as the users who fell for the trick and provided their account numbers and passwords to thieves.

Protecting yourself

Download support files only from sites you went to directly, hosted by vendors you trust. When an e-mail says it's from a vendor and wants you to download something, don't click the link included in the e-mail message. Go to the vendor's Web site directly and download what you need.

The major Web sites for file downloads carefully virus-check all the files they offer. Vendors will also virus-check, although in rare instances viruses hide inside major vendor software. That's why you must have virus protection yourself rather than trust your good fortune.

If you own a small company, tell users never to download files themselves. Let you or the IT person download patches and apply them properly.

 Note Peer-to-peer networks, especially those used for exchanging pirated music, are full to overflowing with viruses, worms, and other malware hiding in some of the files.

Whether you are a home user or small business owner, keep an active virus-protection application running at all times. At least that way, if you download a malicious file by accident, your application may catch it as it downloads or when it tries to execute.

Web sites

I didn't put Web sites in with downloaded files because some jerkwad/con artists now build fake Web sites to trick people. They do this do this grab your bank account passwords or credit card numbers; the trick is called *phishing*. Usually invited by a fake e-mail built to look like a notice from some trustworthy company, users go to the faux Web site and try to login or put in their credit card numbers for verification.

These phishing Web sites often copy the real company Web site so closely you couldn't tell the difference unless you looked at the code behind the façade. By the time you realize nothing happened after you put in your login name and password or credit card number, it's too late to erase the information from the Web site. And some of the phishers send a polite thank you for providing the information, just as the spoofed Web site would, to keep you from suspecting you've been had.

 Note   Don't provide any critical information to a Web site reached by clicking a link in an e-mail you didn't request.

Why does this work? Users click the Web site link within their e-mail message without thinking. And the phishers hide the real Web site name within a long, convoluted Web site address so it's hard to see.

Be careful

As bad as phishing is, that's not the only Web site problem waiting to trap the unwary. Two of the most serious viruses in the last few years, Code Red and the Nimda worm, often spread to unprotected computers when the Web browser application (Microsoft's Internet Explorer) visited Web sites.

Yes, just visiting the wrong Web site can clobber your computer with viruses, worms, and even the electronic hives. (Okay, I made that one up.) Web sites run by known retailers, major vendors, and other reputable companies with a real-world reputation tend to be pretty close to worry free. Web sites run by unknown groups with no real-world counterpart vary greatly in quality and safety.

Web sites mentioned in spam messages may not be actively trying to infect your computer, but cross your fingers. Any Web site referred by a spam message offering cheap software, free music downloads, or passes to pornographic sites does not have your best interests in mind.

Protecting yourself

Even if you don't plan to go to questionable Web sites, you will by accident now and then. Many unscrupulous Web site developers register "typo" sites, placing pornography or worse on a Web site with a URL that differs by one letter from that of a major site.

There are no absolute guidelines to distinguish a "good" Web site from a site full of hackers, virus mongers, and thieves ready to pounce. However, here's a list of suspicious details, each of which should make you slightly more wary and nervous. When enough details add up, bail out. So hit the eject button on a site that

   ✦ Has no contact information listed

   ✦ Reads like a direct mail advertisement

✦ Offers the traditional "too good to be true" products or services

✦ Pushes obviously illegal products, such as new hit songs or current released movies for download

✦ Bombards you with pop-up ads

✦ Contains a high number of typos, misspellings, and syntax errors (because those of us married to English teachers find that wrong in several ways)

✦ Feels odd, even if you can't say exactly why

If you don't want to suffer through the security holes (well-documented in virus circles) of Microsoft's Internet Explorer that allows Visual Basic programs to make changes in other Microsoft applications, you can try a different Web browser. Netscape and Mozilla were mentioned a bit earlier because they include excellent e-mail applications. The best other third-party Web browser, according to many sources, is the Opera Web Browser for Windows (www.opera.com), which offers a free version with ads in the upper-right corner of the application, or a paid (ad-free) version.

Keep a good real-time virus scanning program loaded if you surf into odd and seedy Web neighborhoods on a regular basis. Just as some bad parts of town strongly suggest the need for a bodyguard, so do some parts of the Web.

Physical Security Details

Early viruses (starting back to 1982 or so for Apple II and 1986 for the IBM PC) spread by infecting disks used to boot the personal computers of the time. No one could afford a hard disk then, particularly because the IBM XT had yet to burst on the scene with the unheard-of extravagance of a personal hard drive with its 10MB (yes, MegaByte) hard disk.

Few people (maybe none) boot their computers with floppies today. Some new computers don't even ship with a floppy drive, but all modern computers can boot from the CD-ROM or DVD drive. So you can get a boot virus (one that loads during the boot-up process), or some other type, from a dirty CD-ROM. This makes great sense when you realize that booting from a CD-ROM bypasses your typical startup procedures, especially the step loading your virus protection software.

Home users won't have to worry about physical security too much. After all, if your home gets burgled you're more likely to have no computer than a computer with a virus or Trojan program installed on it surreptitiously.

Business users have slightly more worries, especially if the business invites the public inside the doors regularly. Frankly, however, the chances of someone slipping one of your computers a virus is low. That doesn't mean there aren't physical security details to watch.

Keep servers far away from employees, much less visitors. Why would people need to hack your company from outside if they could physically reach your server? Someone copying files onto a floppy or USB mini-drive can walk away with your entire accounting database on a keyring.

Every security checklist for companies, whether a one-person startup based in the garage or a multinational conglomerate, always demands the server(s) be kept out of physical reach of everyone. If outsiders can reach your physical servers, you have no security. If employees can reach your physical server, you have only slight security.

Traveling laptops

Laptops create multiple security problems, as I'll cover in upcoming chapters about security, wireless connections in public, and data backups. Just as a person who travels picks up interesting souvenirs, traveling laptops often pickup interesting things as well.

If your business has people come in and plug their laptops onto your production network, you will soon have virus and worm problems. Try and stop these laptops from becoming the transportation of choice for viruses if possible.

If your laptop travels around, verify the status of your virus protection software. Make sure your operating system and your virus protection software are up to date. Do the same for laptops of employees who take their systems home.

Laptop Paranoia is Good for You

Although not quite in the spirit of this chapter, let me digress for a moment and strongly encourage some extra precautions for your laptop. First of all, backups for laptops get ignored regularly. Chapter 13 will cover that.

Second, laptops often carry valuable information, yet are stolen on a regular basis. Even if your laptop carries personal information rather than international commerce secrets for a conglomerate, giving that information to a thief won't make your life easier. Check into software to lock your laptop or encryption for the hard disk. A little bit of trouble and expense, but far less trouble and expense than having someone in possession of your complete banking history and account numbers.

Disks from outside

Floppy disks floated around, free for grabbing, for years. Programs, tightly written and cheap, could fit onto a floppy or two, making it inviting to try the application.

Now the concern comes from CD-ROMs filling your physical mailbox, magazines, and books. Personally, I trust CDs inside books without question. (I've done two books with CD inserts myself.) Magazine CD inserts rate pretty high trust as well, especially name brand magazines with good reputations in the market. CDs that appear in the mail should be virus checked if possible, or at least run on a nonnetworked computer with virus protection software loaded and up to date.

Be wary of employees bringing CDs or floppies from home. You have no idea where those disks have been or under who's protection. Even trustworthy employees can accidentally bring viruses to work.

Wired network security

When wires connect your computer to the other computers in your home or office, security for data transmissions remains high. After all, you would probably notice another computer plugged into your wiring hub.

There are other ways to breach physical security, unfortunately. Are you getting the idea that protecting your data takes more time and effort than you ever imagined?

Note   Some early cable broadband access service providers and equipment didn't properly handle the barrier between the private network inside your home or office and the rest of your neighbors on the cable segment. Users would jump onto their broadband connection and see the disks and printers of other users all over neighborhood. That problem no longer exists, luckily, thanks to improved security from Microsoft Windows and the cable broadband service providers getting up to speed.

Popular remote control programs like GoToMyPC (.com) and PC Anywhere (www.Symantec.com) allow a remote computer to effectively reach across the telephone wire and completely control the PC running the client software. Many people leave this type of program running on their work computer so they can dial in from home or on the road to retrieve documents and look up information.

If you run the reverse scenario and leave the remote control client running on your home computer, someone else could dial in and gain full access to your computer and everything else on your network. Security holes exist wherever the remote control software runs, because individuals rarely pick adequate passwords. If someone finds the number of the modem, especially someone who knows you, guessing your password may not be too hard.

Making Passwords

Great passwords look like this: a*RD!▷,m7+d, but are impossible to remember. The old joke about passwords on sticky notes attached to the monitor. Still happens in every big company today, and that's no joke.

Mix upper and lower case letters, numbers, and symbols into a password you can remember. Do it intelligently. Your name and birthday isn't a proper mix like

Continued

Continued

this: james0903 but is better like this: j0a9m0e3s. Better would be J0a9m0e3s to gain a capital letter, or better yet J0a9*m0e3!s. See the distortion of an easily remembered pattern? The name and birthday are there, but mixed up to confuse guessers.

Dictionary attacks, where hackers try every word in a dictionary to break your password, which means you can't use a "real" word in your password. But you can use words that mean something and are therefore easier to remember as you scramble them all up

Speaking of modems, many companies have modems they have forgotten existed connected to computers and other devices scattered around their networks. Not many small companies have this problem, because finding a stray phone line on small company's bill takes less effort than in a big company. But if you have an outside company handle networking installations, there may be modems attached to some of your equipment to allow remote management sessions. Check to be sure.

Wireless network security

Unlike the wired network with excellent security based on physical wires, wireless networks actually eliminate all those secure wires (duh). With those wires go many people's last comfortable thought about a secure network.

Chapter 16 covers wireless security in considerable depth, but here are a few things to chew on before you get that far back in the book.

✦ Standard Wi-Fi signals go through only two walls, at least according to the "rule of thumb" for network experts. However, you can't count apartment walls as a "real" wall, can you? The signals also go through windows much easier than through walls.

✦ Almost every vendor ships its wireless products with security disabled. This helps get new users up and running, but many never go back and add security. You wouldn't forget that, would you?

✦ The vendor defaults for name brand wireless networking equipment are well known to people interested in eavesdropping on your wireless communications. Change the defaults.

✦ Place wireless access points near the center of your home and business if at all possible. The pictures of wireless access by the pool look wonderful, but they aren't trying to sell security. Dropping your laptop into the water ruins your entire day and ruins the relaxation.

 Cross-Reference This is only a quick overview of wireless security. Look to Chapter 16 for details.

Remember that a curious neighbor or determined business competitor will not knock on your door to tell you how leaky your wireless signals are. They will not mention how lame your passwords are, if you even have any passwords at all.

Keeping Things Out (Viruses, Worms, Trojans, Hackers)

You must approach computer data security, and keeping your systems and files safe from worms, viruses, and other malware much like you approach the physical security of your home. The doors all have locks, and you remember to use them. An alarm alerts the authorities in case of an intrusion. Valuables hide inside a safe, or at least out of sight in drawers. Insurance doesn't act exactly like a backup, but does offer a way to replace items in case of loss.

Once connected to a broadband service provider, your computer(s) can be seen on the Internet anytime by anyone. This is the flip side of the "always-on" feature of a broadband connection. Always on means, always visible, but so are your house and car.

The layered approach works best in security. I describe, sometimes in painful detail, how to construct layers for security in upcoming chapters (12, 13, 15, 16, and 17).

Tech Bits

Security experts follow trends like everyone else. Lately most of them seem to prefer a Medieval layer description. The King must be guarded, so he sits inside the castle along with his army. More troops sit between the castle residence building and the walls of the castle. Outside the wall swims alligators in the moat. Outside the moat is the village, which slows attackers down. And putting the castle on high ground forces attackers to climb up toward the castle in full view of the lookouts. That's layered security, although the idea of your money inside a bank vault inside a bank building wired with electronic alarms has appeal, but not as picturesque as a castle.

But if you're new to broadband access, you want to play with the Internet, and I don't blame you. So I just want to drop in a few security details before you get too carried away.

Update your operating system

Examine the circle of computer life:

1. Hacker or virus writers find hole in operating system
2. Developer patches operating system
3. Users apply patches to their machines with that operating system
4. Hackers and virus writers find new hole in operating system

5. Developer patches operating system

6. Users apply patches to their machines with that operating system

7. Hackers and virus writers find new hole in operating system (repeat and repeat and repeat)

The part that often trips up users is the users apply patch part. Many don't, making their life more exciting if you consider viruses, worms, and hacker attacks exciting. Many people class those as giant pains in the rear, and do everything necessary to avoid that type of excitement.

When a new virus or worm hits, the news reports makes a point that many of the users hit at the beginning have yet to patch some operating system flaw that's been well documented. In other words, these people left their front door open. Don't be one of those people.

Microsoft greatly improved its update technology with Windows XP. Figure 7-2 shows the update screen in Windows XP Home.

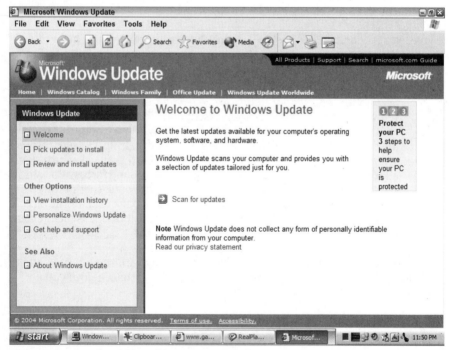

Figure 7-2: You should see this screen regularly.

You can reach the Windows Update screen in Windows XP by choosing Windows Update from the Start Menu and clicking Programs or by looking in the left-side menu from Control Panel. On Windows 2000 you just look on the Start menu. If you have automatic updates turned on, your system does the downloading and installing of patches for you. If you haven't checked out the options, let me show you where to enable automatic updates.

If you're nervous about letting your computer do such things when you're asleep, you can turn off automatic updates. Do I trust Microsoft to make this work properly every time? No. But I believe Microsoft is causing less harm with the automatic updates than they used to, and the potential harm from attack is a greater worry. But be sure and read Chapter 13 about backing up your data.

Figure 7-3 shows you have three options for updates. You can be notified before any downloads start and give permission at your leisure. You can download the update files automatically and apply them at your leisure, or you can have Windows download and install them automatically.

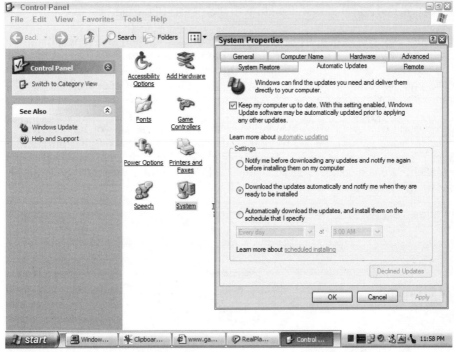

Figure 7-3: Make your choice for automatic updates.

You reach the screen in Figure 7-3 by opening the Control Panel, and clicking the System icon. The Automatic Updates page tab is in the middle of the System Properties box that opens. On the left you can see the menu listing Windows Update just under the See Also heading. Clicking that opens the screen shown in Figure 7-2. You can also click Windows Update on the left-side menu in Control Panel.

Caution   Microsoft encourages you to use automatic updates. So do most security experts. Other computer experts feel that mistakes in automatic updates will cause more problems than they solve. If you don't want to use automatic updates, at least run a backup and then manual updates on a regular basis.

If you have only one or two computers, this process takes little or no time. If your business has a dozen or more computers, along with a server or three, time will become more of an issue. However, not updating operating systems might cause you to loose much more time sometime in the future. A dozen computers that need patching will make the investment in a management suite that pushed patches out without your intervention worthwhile.

Update your virus protection

Most modern antivirus software works by matching patterns in the virus program, called signatures, to a database of known viruses. Every time a new virus appears, the antivirus companies grab it, scan it for a recognizable signature, and add that new signature to their virus database.

The only way you benefit from ongoing virus protection and installing a defense against new viruses is to keep your virus database up to date. It does no good to buy a virus program and never update the signature database. After a short time, you'll have no protection against the new viruses that appeared in the computer world after your purchase.

If you don't trust your virus protection software, or are afraid you have a virus your software vendor has yet to figure out, take a look at HouseCall from Trend Micro (www.trendmicro.com). For personal use, Trend Micro provides an excellent virus-checking program, HouseCall, free for the downloading. Figure 7-4 shows the Trend Micro personal page. HouseCall is in the upper-right corner.

Figure 7-4: Free is always good.

The program downloads a small client application but that won't take long. Running HouseCall gives you peace of mind and a quick way to double-check other virus protection routines you have in place.

HouseCall does not leave a resident application running to watch all file activity, such as when you download a new file from the Internet. This is a nice service from Trend Micro, but it doesn't eliminate the need for a real-time virus monitoring application running on your PC at all times (and, of course, Trend Micro wants you to consider its products, and you should).

If you don't have virus protection, get some. If you do have virus protection, check that you're still able to update your virus definition database. Sometimes people miss or ignore the virus vendor's offers to extend licensing to get necessary updates. Those users think they're still safe because they see their virus application running. The software could well be running yet allow a virus access to your hard disk because the outdated database didn't recognize the new virus signature.

Verify that your antivirus software includes e-mail application protection and use it to scan all incoming and outgoing e-mail. Because most viruses spread via e-mail, the more eyes watching for miscreant software the better. Do not rely on your ISPs e-mail scanning software alone unless you enjoy cleaning up virus-ridden computers.

Update your personal firewall

Not every computer has a personal firewall. In fact, few do, but more should have them. A firewall emulates the physical firewall, like the one in your car that keeps your engine compartment and your passenger compartment separate. Mixing the engine and passengers never makes for a happy ending. A personal firewall runs only on your computer, and closes the software port addresses worms use to infiltrate systems across a network. When the worm comes knocking, your firewall keeps the door shut.

Sometimes firewall programs are included in a security suite of products from one of the big vendors. Sometimes you can get individual firewall programs for free or cheap. One of the long-time free personal firewalls, Zone Alarm, can be downloaded from the Zone Labs Company at www.zonelabs.com. See the Zone Alarm family of products in Figure 7-5.

 Tech Bits Internet devices talk about ports, which are software addresses used to communicate between programs. Hackers look for unprotected ports, which open the software to outsiders like an unlocked house door opens to burglars. Firewalls block ports and examine packets to see if they're allowed through the open ports.

Routers have firewalls, but if your broadband connection goes directly to your computer, you will need a personal firewall. If your router has a firewall built in, or you have a separate firewall appliance, individual computers won't need personal firewalls.

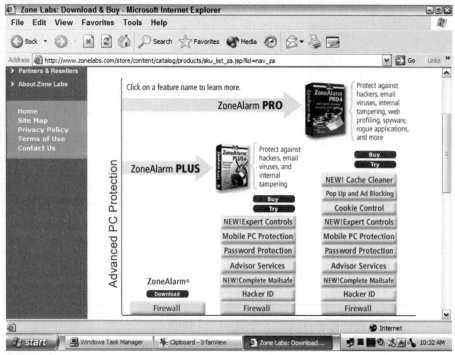

Figure 7-5: Free is still always good, and you can see your upgrade options.

If you have a personal firewall, keep the software updated. The same goes for the firewall in your router, as discussed in the next section.

Keeping Things In (Your Information)

Protecting your data should be your top security concern. Worms, viruses, Trojan horse programs, and hackers can be tolerated barely, but patience disappears when your files disappear.

Although many settings in Microsoft Windows XP do a better job of protecting your system by default, Microsoft sets the software to make some networking tasks simple. Unfortunately, in the world of security, simple generally means porous. Not good.

Chapter 11 will go through the details of configuring your computers to close the security door. If you can't wait, go to your computer file settings now and turn off file sharing of any type. That will make it harder for any hackers to see your computer on the Internet, and keep them from adding, modifying, or deleting any of your files.

For a quick concealment with Microsoft Windows XP, follow these directions:

1. Click Start ⇨ My Computer. Then click the C drive (or main hard disk if not C).

2. If contents are hidden, find System Tasks in the menu on the left and click Show the Contents of This Drive.

3. Open Documents and Settings to find your User folder.

4. Right-click the folder to keep it hidden, and click Properties; then click Sharing.

5. Check the Make This Folder Private box (see Figure 7-6).

6. If you don't have a password for your username, the system will nag you to add one. If you care about security, add the password.

7. Click OK to save and exit.

Figure 7-6 shows the screen on my PC. Notice the Network and sharing security blurb says that the files on this computer are not being shared. That's what you want to see, at least until you read Chapter 11 and understand more about the risks and benefits of sharing across the network.

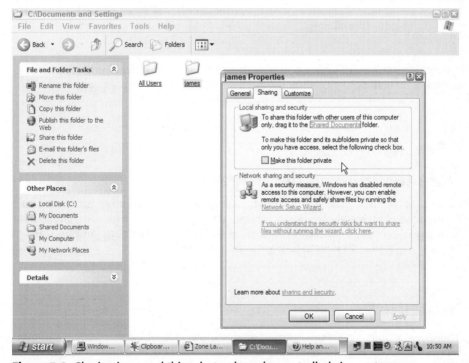

Figure 7-6: Sharing is a good thing, but only under controlled circumstances.

Router firewall settings

If you have a router with a firewall, configure the firewall so that it ignores Internet Control Message Protocol (ICMP) messages, which are pings from outside. This is covered in Chapter 11, but setting your router to ignore these queries makes it harder for hackers to find you.

Second, block or at least monitor any outgoing messages. If you have a program sending information out through some TCP/IP port address, it may be a Trojan program left by a virus. The outgoing information could contain system information that provides easy entrance to hackers, or spam e-mailers. Some spam now comes from machines that are hijacked in this manner. If the spammers are nice, they hide the sending address. If they leave the address, it looks like you just offered the world a new low-cost mortgage or something even more embarrassing, depending on the spam messages.

In short, set your router firewall to block outgoing messages unless they're authorized. Also, update your router firewall software regularly.

Desktop firewall settings

Personal firewalls vary as much as those on routers, but they tend to offer more help in configuration. If you have one, check out the settings to monitor outgoing messages. Individual computers on broadband services rate high as targets for viruses, worms, and hackers because so few people properly protect their systems.

Protect yourself by blocking outgoing messages unless they're authorized. Your personal firewall software should have a setting to block or filter outgoing traffic. Set that; then test it to make sure you can still send e-mail.

Nag, nag, nag: update your firewall software regularly.

Note to online game players

Game players must make extra security allowances for outgoing traffic, because multiplayer games sometimes get treated like hacker activity by some firewalls. Your game support information should tell you how to configure your firewalls to allow game play to pass safely through the firewall.

Summary

There are people out on the Internet who want to ruin or exploit your computer. Some of them do it as some bizarre idea of fun, whereas others do it for profit. I'm more worried about the ones doing it for profit.

You take precautions in the real world, such as locking your doors, having alarms, paying attention to where you are, and generally making yourself less of a target. The same approach works in the Internet world. Keep your doors locked, your alarms set, and watch where you go. You can go where you want on the Internet and Web, just as you can in the real world, but take the proper precautions.

Examining Your Home Broadband Hookup

Intersections cause tension. This is true when driving or on TV shows. When driving, intersections allow other vehicles to come at you from all directions. On TV dramas, whenever the good guys and bad guys run into each other, something happens (or at least there are threats of future happenings).

The same goes for your broadband connection. Outside your walls, the service provider must take care of all the details. Inside your walls, you are responsible for your computer or the computers connected to each other and the broadband connection.

Where your network meets the broadband service provider network is a true intersection and therefore a potential conflict. You are responsible for all broadband access problems starting at any of the following intersections:

✦ Where the broadband service provider wire hits your house

✦ Where the broadband connection plug is inside your house

✦ At the plug where you connect your computer or network to the broadband modem

✦ At the router plug where you connect your computer or network to the broadband access router

Where you take responsibility, and where your broadband service provider stops being responsible, depends on your service and the equipment involved. The focus here is the link between your service provider broadband cable or modem and your router or computer.

Cable and DSL "Modems"

When you get a broadband connection, the provider will send or deliver what they call a broadband modem. Depending on where the broadband access line comes into your home and whether the service provider installed the connection, you will be responsible for everything beyond the cable modem.

The Phone Company used to, and often still does, call this type of equipment CPE for Customer Premises Equipment. In other words, it is an equipment the phone company controlled yet placed at your site. It might be less confusing if cable and DSL modems were called Customer Premises Connection Equipment to make it clearer to people what they really mean by cable and DSL modem. Of course, normal people (those not in the computer or networking business) understand *modem* perfectly well.

Your broadband service provider will do one of the following:

✦ Provide your cable/DSL modem for free

✦ Provide your cable/DSL modem for a small fee each month

✦ Sell you the cable/DSL modem for a retail price

✦ Tell you which cable/DSL modem to purchase separately

One way or another, you need a cable/DSL modem to make the connection to your broadband service provider. These units are typically external, small boxes with at least two plugs: one for the line from the service provider and one for your computer or network connection. Internal modems fit inside a computer (almost always a PC running Windows and almost never a Macintosh or Linux system) but they have a small and dwindling percentage of the market.

You will almost always have an external unit for the following reasons:

✦ Many customers don't like opening their computers.

✦ Service providers don't like opening customer computers when they do the installation.

✦ Replacing the customer computer hardware requires a new installation, as do many software updates.

✦ Access to the broadband connection for multiple computers is much simpler with an external unit.

Early on, cable and (particularly) DSL providers used the internal PC card more often because of cost. The internal system didn't need a housing or power supply, so it cost less to manufacture. Every installation required a truck roll, because the installing technician usually installed the card into the computer for the customer. But the provider had to roll a truck anyway to bring the wiring into the home, so that extra expense existed already.

This practice gave way, thankfully, to the use of external units for almost every installation. External unit prices dropped and the installation software improved. This makes it possible for customers to install the client side of the broadband connection hardware and software themselves, eliminating the truck roll. No truck roll means the service provider saves big money.

Using the external cable/DSL modem also makes networking simpler. Yes, you can configure the single PC with an internal cable/DSL modem to be a router for all other computers in the home or office, but if you do, you would have to rely on Microsoft networking software. The networking software can be tricky at times, and software updates often require network reconfiguration.

Worse, with an internal cable/DSL modem you have to rely on Microsoft's security software to protect all the systems from hackers and viruses. External units released recently include the cable/DSL modems, routers for networking, and firewalls for security.

Cable/DSL modems have gotten more reliable, faster, and easier to configure for the service providers over the past few years. Now the race continues to add features and increase the ability of modems from different manufacturers to work together.

Modem/not modem

I keep referring to cable and DSL "modems" because everyone tends to call them modems. They are not modems, at least by any technical definitions of the word. I don't mean they should be called customer premises connection equipment, but the term "modem" has a specific meaning, and cable/DSL modems do not, according to some experts, fit that meaning.

Modem is a truncated word from the awkward phrase *modulator-demodulator* and originated early in the world of telecommunications. Digital signals from computers were modulated into analog sound wave forms for travel over voice telephone lines. At the receiving end, the analog sound wave forms were demodulated back into a digital signal.

You can hear this for yourself when you pay attention to your dial-up modem connection sequence. That chrchrchrchr noise you hear right before the modem connects to your dial-up site is the sound of digital signals being turned into noise. Coherent and reproducible noise, but noise nonetheless. The modems cut off the speaker when connections succeed so you won't hear that noise.

Purists maintain only a dial-up modem can be called a modem because you must connect a digital computer to a voice telephone line. Nonpurists say that a modem encodes signals from one type of carrier signal to another, such as digital to voice-line analog or digital computer to cable frequency, and so that cable/DSL modems use the name correctly. You can argue back and forth if you want, but the common usage does not obscure the original definition, and I think most people define a modem as something connecting a computer to a service. Although you may be able to throw network interface cards into that definition, I don't have any serious objection to calling these boxes modems.

But if you get chastised by people who claims a cable/DSL modem isn't really a modem, don't get nervous. Just ask them to call it a Customer Premises Connection Equipment node, no acronyms or truncated words allowed, and watch how fast they go back to calling it a modem.

Cable modem information

You may not need a single bit of cable modem information. Your cable broadband service provider will give you (or sell or lease you) a cable modem as part of your service agreement.

External units vary from the size of a paperback book up to the size of a decent hardback book. Wonder how many varieties of cable modems there are? Figure 8-1 shows a gallery of photos. There are more than I ever imagined.

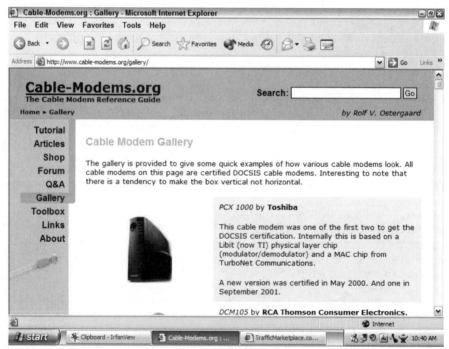

Figure 8-1: Not sure it's art, but it's an interesting gallery.

Notice that Rolf at `www.cable-modems.org` references the term DOCSIS. This acronym stands for Data Over Cable Service Interface Specifications. The DOCSIS standard was created and is maintained by Cable Television Laboratories, Inc., at `www.CableLabs.com`. This group was founded by cooperating cable television companies back in 1988 and started testing cable modems for compliance to standards that enable any cable modem to connect to any cable provider head-end equipment.

Even if you want to buy your own cable modem, your choices remain severely restricted. At the other end of the cable line, at the Head-End office, the equipment must communicate sync with your cable modem. If they don't communicate exactly, you don't have service.

DOCSIS standards aim for mixing and matching of equipment; but your cable broadband provider may not have upgraded its head-end equipment to the latest models. It may have a mix of open standard and proprietary head-end equipment. It may have proprietary management tools that work only with a certain model of client cable modem. It may have a distribution contract with one of the cable modem vendors and make a few bucks extra off each one installed.

If your cable broadband service provider allows you to purchase your own cable modem, and you can save money by doing so, it still may not be a great idea. Who handles the warranty in that situation? If it's the cable modem manufacturer, you would have to send the cable modem back and wait several weeks for any repairs. You would lose your cable broadband service for that length of time because you have no cable modem to connect your computer(s) to the cable. Bummer.

When your cable company upgrades or changes its service configuration, it has no responsibility to update your privately owned cable modem. Any type of upgrade may disable your cable modem, or at least force you to scramble around and upgrade your cable modem yourself.

If your cable broadband service provider allows you to purchase your own cable modem and you wish to do so, there are many places in the real world where you can comparison shop online. Check your favorite computer retailer, and don't forget the more general suppliers, such as Best Buy, Circuit City, Office Depot, Office Max, and Staples among others. Prices range far under a hundred dollars for a wide variety of cable modems.

When the new 2.0 DOCSIS compatibility specification becomes widespread, the equation may change in favor of buying your own cable modem. Until then, however, you may want to look at Table 8-1 and see if the upside is worth the potential downside for your purchase.

Table 8-1
Pros and Cons of Buying Your Own Cable Modem

Pros	Cons
Save money on your monthly cable broadband bill	Cable provider responsible for warranty and maintenance on modem
Get the features you want, such as wireless support or an included router and firewall	If you buy a non-DOCSIS complaint modem, cable provider may upgrade to DOCSIS making your modem obsolete

Continued

Table 8-1 (continued)	
Pros	**Cons**
Get the size and form you want	You may move and your new cable broadband service doesn't support your old cable modem
All-in-one unit convenience	Separate units make repairs or upgrades possible without replacing everything

Choosing whether to supply your own modem is one of those situations in which what I think, and experts recommend, matters far less than what you think. It's your modem, your service, and you can make your own choice. The new DOCSIS 2.0 standard may change the equation a bit, but probably not until 2006 or so.

I let my cable provider supply my cable modem. (I lease it, officially.) That came in handy when Comcast replaced my fading old unit with a nice new unit. My cost for that replacement and service call? Zero.

DSL modem information

Much of the information concerning cable modems applies to DSL modems. Service providers offer them free as part of the installation package even more often, it seems, than cable broadband service providers do. After all, phone companies coined the idea of customer premises equipment.

But a wide variety of DSL modems are on the market. Like the cable modems, DSL modems are incorporating more and more features. For example, several vendors (Netopia, 2Wire, and ZyXel among the leaders in this market) incorporate wireless routers into ADSL modems. Other features added include router software, firewall software, and Ethernet connections to support the local network.

The size and shape of the DSL modems match those of cable modems. The wireless units have antenna, obviously, but otherwise they look the same. Pricing for DSL modems runs about the same as the cable modems, but may lean slightly toward the higher end of the average cable modem.

Although cable modems hit the market first, the standards work in the DSL community may make owning a DSL modem safer than owning a cable modem. Almost all the DSL service providers support ADSL for the best speeds possible based on distance from the central office or remote terminal. DSL modems from different vendors work better than cable modems when trying to connect to equipment from other vendors at the central office. Because standards change or at least get new features added to them, make sure any modem you buy includes the ability to upgrade its firmware to keep pace with updates.

Note For pedantic sticklers, complaining about the term DSL modem may be even more of a stretch than complaining about the term cable modem. After all, the idea behind DSL in general and ADSL in particular is the ability to support high-bandwidth digital service over a standard telephone line. Doesn't modem seem like the right term to describe connecting your computer to the Internet over a plain old telephone line?

Demarcation point

You are not responsible for upkeep on your broadband access media (cable or telephone line) out of your house, over the physical wiring across the neighborhood, and up into the phone company's central office or cable company's head-end equipment Conversely, the service provider is not responsible for its telephone or cable wiring all the way to the computer in your bedroom. Somewhere, a split must take place, and responsibility for the wire and the signal therein pass from one party to the other.

This spot is called a *demarcation point*. First used by the phone company, the "demarc" as it's sometimes called occurs where the provider's wiring ends and your wiring begins.

For your telephone lines, that point is usually on the wall outside your home closest to the telephone line service entrance point. If your home has a basement, you may find the box there.

If your telephone line is buried, look for a box (gray, beige, or some other boring color) that's not very big (deck of cards, slice of bread, VHS tape) with one wire coming in from the ground and another wire going up the wall and entering your house. If your telephone line comes through the air from a pole, you can find the box easily. The box is where the telephone line attaches to your house.

This box is the Network Interface Device (NID) and is the official demarcation point for your regular telephone connection. The phone company likes to call its voice lines "the network," which is where that first "N" of the acronym comes from. My network interface box can be opened on one side so I can look the connections or test the system. The other side of the network interface, where the telephone wires connect, has a lock that uses a key carried by the phone technicians that keeps me locked out.

In my case, the phone company ran a wire from the network interface box through the garage wall from outside and then through the wall into my office. They mounted a jack on my office wall, which they labeled as "their" plug. I laugh at the label because it was done three DSL providers ago (bankruptcy of one carrier, discontinued service, new service). Although the phone companies consider the network interface the end of their responsibility, I count that plug as the demarcation point for my DSL service because the phone company installed the wiring and the plug.

Your cable connections do not terminate at a network interface box, but there will be a demarcation point somewhere. In my situation, the cable tech put a hole through the wall of the garage from outside, and another hole in the garage wall into the office, about four inches from the hole used by the telephone company.

A cable plug plate sits where the cable comes into the office from the garage. From there, a patch cable goes to my Speedstream (designed and made originally by Efficient Networks, which is now owned by Siemens) model 5100 cable modem. I don't count the cable plug on the wall of my office as the demarcation point for my cable broadband. I count the internal network connection plug on the Speedstream cable modem as my demarcation point, because Comcast installed and configured the cable modem.

Satellite and wireless broadband service providers follow similar rules for demarcation points and future responsibility. Of course, the wiring heading to the demarcation point usually comes from a satellite dish or wireless antenna.

In this case, everything said about cable or DSL broadband access applies to satellite and wireless service providers as well. However, I can speak only in generalities. The fine print of your service agreement with your provider will be the final arbitrator of service responsibility.

The provider's responsibility

The company that installed your broadband service must take responsibility for proper cable integrity and service function up to the demarcation point in your home or office. If you have cable broadband service, the cable company almost certainly provides the physical wiring connection and the Internet service portions. One provider, one contact.

DSL installations become much more confused at times. If the primary telephone company in your area provided your DSL service, like my situation with SBC Yahoo providing cabling and Internet services, the situation looks much like the typical cable broadband situation. One provider, one contact.

But the courts forced regional Bell companies like SBC (Southwestern Bell Telephone Company renamed) to support third-party DSL providers. This means another DSL service company, such as Darrell's DSL, relies on SBC to connect the physical wires; then Darrell's DSL takes care of the Internet service provider functions. Who do you call when there's a problem? Call Darrell, but he may have to call SBC to get your problem fixed.

Where do broadband service providers have problems they must fix? Let me count the ways (and places) in Table 8-2.

Table 8-2
Potential Trouble Spots in Broadband Service

Problem	Location	How Common	Responsibility
E-mail server down	Central office	Minutes per month	Service provider
Hosted Web servers down	Central office	Minutes per month	Service provider

Problem	Location	How Common	Responsibility
Router down between service and Internet	Central office	Rare	Service provider
Node to central office disconnected	Node to central office	Rare	Physical cable install company
Spotty service between node and home	Neighborhood	Rare to constant	Physical cable install company
Cable/DSL modem	Your home	Rare	Owner of modem
Network Interface Device failure	Wall of your house	Rare	Physical cable install company

Your job, when you have a service problem, is not to diagnose and explain exactly which piece of the network connection needs replacing or upgrading. Your job is to explain, clearly, logically, and politely, exactly what problems you are having. Take notes, with times and dates if problems are intermittent.

Providers advertising their Service Level Agreements strive for uptime. Telephone companies getting into the Internet service provider business have a great advantage because they already have a large technical support staff in place to handle physical wiring problems anywhere in the network.

Service providers may detail their demarcation point in the service contract somewhere, or they may not. A good rule of thumb is that if they installed it as part of your service, they are responsible for it.

Your responsibility

Because the rule of thumb for service providers says they are responsible for everything they install, that means you are responsible for everything they didn't install. This works out fairly cleanly regarding physical network components, but can get messy inside the computer when considering added software.

If your broadband access connection looks like mine, with the termination point from the service provider right next to the cable and DSL modem, you won't have many trouble spots to check. In my case, one connecting cable goes from the cable and DSL modem to the routers supporting my internal network. You probably won't have two broadband access points and two internal networks, but having both makes it easy for me to see how similar they are in many respects.

If your broadband access connection runs over your home telephone wiring to reach your router or computer, you have many more potential trouble spots. Phone wires that work fine with voice signals can have trouble carrying DSL. Wall jacks that have been painted over may have paint on the connections that weaken or stop the signal on one or more of the telephone wires. Phone cords receive an amazing amount of abuse as they are often stepped on, rolled over with wheeled office chairs, and serve as puppy teething rings. If the phone cord connecting your router to the telephone jack can be stepped on, it will be stepped on.

The links between your router and your computer(s) offers another group of potential problems, all of which you must fix on your own. After all, even if the phone or cable company sold you the home or small business networking equipment, they aren't responsible for how you're using the products.

Ethernet Unshielded Twisted Pair (UTP) wires look much like phone cords but are almost always thicker and have a larger connector on the end (the connector is an RJ45 with eight wires for Ethernet versus an RJ11 with four wires for telephones, if you're curious). But as with wire, repeated stomping, mashing, rolling over, or bending will eventually break it down. Even if the wire doesn't break completely, the damage will cause network problems.

After your wiring physically reaches your computer, potential problems remain. Network interface cards rarely break, but it can happen. Much more often, some software configuration in a computer changes and makes it appear the network card quit. Never start yelling at your Internet service provider about problems until you take a careful look at what's changed in your computer. Any software installation or reconfiguration can impact network functionality. It doesn't always make sense, but computers are only logical, not sensible. Table 8-3 gathers together some problems and the responsible party.

Table 8-3
More Potential Trouble Spots in Broadband Service

Problem	Location	How Common?	Responsibility
Cable/DSL modem	Your home	Rare	Owner of modem
Substandard wiring	Inside your walls	More common as wiring ages	You
Wiring damage	Patch cables between devices	Somewhat rare to often	You
Router problems	Your network router	Rare, but increases with each change	Owner of router
Computer hardware	Your computer(s)	Rare	You
Computer software	Your computer(s)	Every change increases chance	You and operating system vendor

You can see that the demarcation point sits in the middle of multiple potential problems. Looking at lists like these, I sometimes feel it's amazing anything ever works.

Why should you care which party holds responsibility for each potential trouble spot? Because when you call your service provider to fix something that's your responsibility, you must pay for the repair. Sometimes the provider charges far more than you expect, but after the work is done you're stuck paying the bill. That's when knowing your responsibilities hits home and sticks.

Routers for Access Sharing

Routers connect at least two networks and send data packets from one network to another. They can be stand-alone hardware devices or software within a separate appliance or computer. Most routers used by homes and small businesses to connect to the Internet are stand-alone hardware units. Figure 8-2 shows one of the early successes in the consumer router market.

Figure 8-2: An early Linksys router that helped solidify the consumer broadband router market.

Internet service providers, including cable and DSL broadband providers, use large routers capable of processing millions of packets per second. Routers look at the header information in each data packet, decide the best path for that packet across the Internet to the proper destination, and communicate with other routers along that path to ensure delivery.

Check your service agreement with your provider to make sure you are allowed to have more than one computer accessing the broadband service. Some service providers now demand you pay extra if you have a home network and use a router to connect more than one local computer to their service.

One good thing comes from paying extra for the ability to network multiple computers to your Internet connection: you get a static IP address from your service provider. Using a static IP address makes it possible to have servers at your site, such as your own e-mail or Web server. Some service providers offer a static IP address for a just a few dollars per month.

If you feel you need a static IP address (a unique number in all the world in the form of 123.123.123.123 that identifies a particular network device across the Internet), check out Chapter 12 to learn about home and small business servers that require that address.

Wireless vendors talk about access points quite a bit. A wireless router is an access point (linking the wireless clients directly to the wired network), but not all access points are wireless routers that include directional capabilities to send packets to different networks. You can save money installing access points only for connecting wireless clients to the existing wired network rather than getting routers for every location supporting wireless client connection.

Router features

Simply put, routers route traffic between two or more networks. They can be hardware or software. Routers are extremely specific in their job description, and in the following list you can see how many things routers don't do in your network.

✦ Routers don't filter packets going through them.

✦ Routers don't stop viruses going through them.

✦ Routers don't examine packets going through them.

✦ Routers don't stop hackers from penetrating your network.

✦ Routers don't hide your internal computers from outsiders.

✦ Routers don't connect multiple computers, they only connect networks.

✦ Routers don't report on Trojans sending packets out of your network.

Luckily, the hardware stand-alone routers often include firewall software and other security software to provide a full service connection device. In this current market, the hardware devices sold as routers almost always include the following features:

✦ Either a wiring hub to support more than one computer or a switch to support multiple connected local networks

✦ Some level of firewall or other security tools

✦ Network Address Translation to hide internal IP addresses from outsiders so hackers can't find and attack your computers

✦ Dynamic Host Control Protocol software to allocate IP addresses to computers on the network when they join the network for easier administration

Some router devices include quite a few more features, but the previous list should be your minimum acceptable feature set. Pure routers with the minimum features listed can be bought for around $50 or less, which is why many service now include them for free. The increasing sophistication of network device manufacturers make for interesting combinations of features packed in a small box along with routers today. Paying extra will get you Web filtering software (keep children from going to adult sites), time and date controls to block Internet access after bedtime for some users, and more sophisticated security controls against hackers.

Ethernet connections

Every router provided by a broadband service provider, or recommended by one, must have at least one Ethernet network connection along with the connection for the broadband service. After all, if you don't have at least two networks you don't have a router.

Early routers included a single Ethernet connection, and some routers still follow that model. The market demands inexpensive options, and a user with a single computer (almost always a PC for this to work) can use the single-port Ethernet to cable/DSL router to connect to an Ethernet port on the PC.

Connections between a PC and a router need a different cable configuration than connections between a network wiring device and a router. The first option needs a cross-over cable to match the right outgoing pins in the PC Ethernet port to the incoming pins on the router's Ethernet port (Ethernet hubs provide the cross-over function, but a direct connection doesn't use a hub). Some router vendors include the special cross-over cable in the box, and other vendors add a switch on the router to change the router port's configuration. I prefer the switch on the router, because vendors of cross-over cable don't use a special color or differentiate it from the other, straight-through cables used all over the network.

The Linksys router in Figure 8-2 was an early model that included an Ethernet wiring hub as part of the router itself. This worked great because people with two, three, or four PCs could plug them all into the router and get broadband service. If you already have a network in place, just connect one port on your existing wiring hub to the router, and all computers will get broadband access.

Wireless connections

Some vendors now sneer at Ethernet twisted pair wiring because wires are so passé. They use wireless connections, which have gotten better and faster than I thought possible.

Figure 8-3 shows a Linksys WRV54G, a new member of the router family boasting support for the fast new wireless standard. This case style appeared after the formerly independent Linksys company was grabbed up by the giant network vendor Cisco. Notice how much more businesslike the new router looks.

Just like the friendly blue router in Figure 8-2, the new corporate-looking Linksys router includes four Ethernet ports for connecting more computers or an existing network to the router. But the antenna sticking up gives away the fact that this router also handles wireless connections.

Wireless connections on cable/DSL routers have been available for years and will continue to be the "hot new thing" for a while longer. Some models don't

Figure 8-3: An updated Linksys router with Ethernet and advanced wireless networking options

have the antenna sticking up, as you can see in Figure 8-4 of the Buffalo AirStation G54 (www.buffalotech.com).

The Buffalo router includes all the features of the Linksys router in Figure 8-3, including advanced firewall services and high-speed wireless networking. You decide if you prefer the friendly rounded look of the Buffalo and early Linksys routers or the more business-like appearance of the newer Linksys router.

To be fair, the newer Buffalo wireless routers with support for the higher speeds also look more businesslike. The design is midway between the Buffalo router pictured in Figure 8-4 and the Linksys router pictured in Figure 8-3. I guess vendors can't bring themselves to add the high-speed wireless access without making the box look more serious.

Figure 8-4: Wireless but no antenna sticking up.

Router security

The term heading this section misleads you about the ability of routers to provide security. Routers don't do security; they send data packets as efficiently as possible across a network. But now every router must have some substantial security to make sales in this market.

Good news: Router security gets more sophisticated but easier to use with each new version. Instead of feeling helpless when looking at security configuration pages, normal nontechnical users can make their routers reasonably safe without sweating.

I strongly recommend a router with security tools enabled between your computer(s) and the Internet. Even if you have a single computer, a router will pay for itself with increased security. Default settings now protect you better than before, and far better than the default settings of Microsoft Windows software.

Firewall software

Several legends account for the origin of the term *firewall* as applied to the Internet. My favorite is the firewall in your automobile. It sits between the engine and the passenger compartment and makes sure that never the twain shall meet.

Firewalls can be software only, such as when you find a firewall in a router, or they can be a hardware appliance. The hardware appliance really uses software for the firewall control functions, but putting it in a hardware unit helps isolate networks all the more. It gives the users a nice, secure feeling, because they have something tangible to plug into their network.

Firewalls keep things out (like your engine should stay out of your lap while you drive). Private networks (that's you) set firewalls to block unauthorized access by hackers. Figure 8-5 shows some default firewall settings.

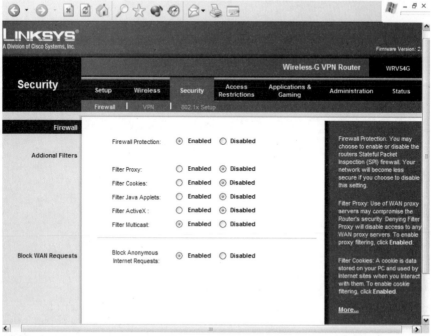

Figure 8-5: Default firewall settings for the Linksys WRV54G.

The four types of firewalls, defined in the following list, have their own strengths and weaknesses. The more public and critical your network, the more firewall options you throw in front of your network.

✦ **Packet filter**: Uses predefined rules to accept or reject every packet that comes through the firewall. Difficult to configure and can bog down under heavy load.

✦ **Application gateway**: Works with specific applications, usually File Transfer Protocol (FTP) and terminal emulation connections (Telnet). Special gateways for Web services are used by some large companies. The extra level of packet inspection can slow performance.

✦ **Circuit level gateway**: Verifies established two-way connections using TCP and UDP protocols and allows packets to flow freely after the connections are configured.

✦ **Proxy server**: Hides the true network IP addresses of internal users by looking like the server is doing the work. Used to provide cache services for Web sites as well.

Firewall software provides good security, but not complete security. Okay, there's no such thing as a completely secure network, because people are involved. But having a good firewall covers up many of the mistakes people make.

The more advanced firewalls advertise Stateful Packet Inspection (SPI). This feature tracks the state of each transaction so it can match incoming packets to earlier outgoing packets.

You want to keep the bad guys, and their bad packets, out of your network. What some people don't understand is that you also want to keep bad packets inside your network from getting out. Trojan programs, delivered by worms, often gather and send information out so the virus writer can exploit the weak networks found. A firewall should block those packets (and you can learn how to configure a router to do this in Chapter 12).

Web content filters

One of the features many routers now include is a way to block access to Web sites. You can also block certain services, such as Instant Messaging and games, if you don't want anyone playing those on your network.

Businesses need to take care with Internet access because one bad apple leaving obscene Web sites on screen can cause a real employee nightmare. Whether businesses handle this with software blocks or education is up to them.

Parents, especially those with young children, often think site blocks are the way to handle objectionable content. I have found that is shortsighted and prone to mistakes, even with the best content blocking software.

Here's the quick method of controlling your children's use of inappropriate Web content:

 ✦ Put the PC in the family room, not in a child's room.
 ✦ Put a good password on the system so children can't use it while you're not there.

Sure, you can jump through the rest of the hoops, but children with the computer in the family room behave themselves better. When people walk through constantly, children can't easily hide what they're doing.

On the other hand, I am pleased with the job AOLs parental control blocks do. Hide the icon for Internet Explorer or any other browser, and make your kids go through the AOL browser so the parental controls are in force across the Internet. That works for me.

At least playing with the Web content controls can be fun. Here is what my teenage daughter is dying to get when she can drive: a Toyota Tacoma. Figure 8-6 shows the object of her desires.

But I'm not ready to buy her a truck because she's not yet old enough to drive. So I blocked www.Toyota.com and the keyword Tacoma as a joke.

Figure 8-7 shows what Laura saw when she looked for a truck the next day.

The tool for blocking Web sites with any router firewall is crude and far too unintelligent to use. Linksys has a nice screen for adding Web site names and

Figure 8-6: When my daughter Laura looks for a truck.

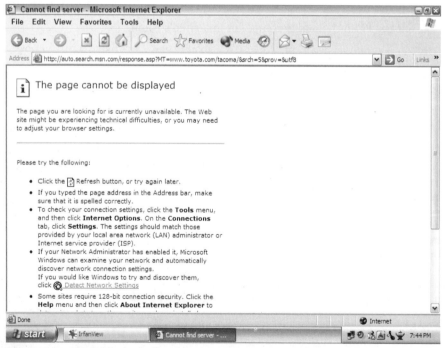

Figure 8-7: After I block my daughter Laura from looking for a truck.

keywords, but you can never manually put in enough keywords to block Web sites effectively. If you want to use Web content blocking software, talk with your service provider or look for one of the software options you can install on your computer.

You can, however, turn off Internet access after certain hours. Linksys' Access Restrictions page includes a good time control setting. If you have problems with children (of all ages) staying up too late playing on the Internet, you can turn the router connection off at whatever time you prefer. Figure 8-8 shows that screen. The time settings are at the top of the page, whereas the Web site and keyword restrictions are at the bottom.

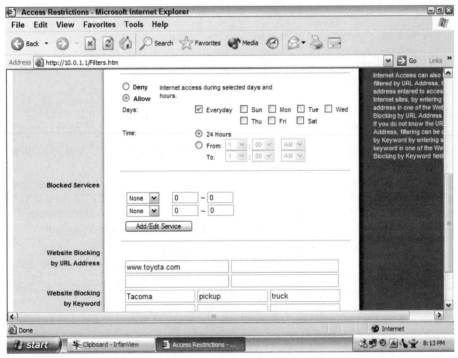

Figure 8-8: Time lock settings for the Linksys router/firewall software.

Don't use your router firewall to block access to Web sites, and you won't be disappointed. Keep the computer in the family room and look over shoulders, and you'll block all the objectionable Web sites, not just the ones you can remember.

Wireless Broadband Routers

Plenty of noise recently about wireless everything, isn't there? Coffee shops with free wireless Internet, PDAs full of wireless e-mail, and every company promising more speeds and more distance with every new press release.

Let me outline the basic wireless data communications standards used by home and small business networks in the next section. If I can explain this clearly enough now, you'll have an easier time keeping the standards straight.

Wi-Fi speeds and more

Wi-Fi makes plenty of noise today, especially for a family of radio waves. Truncated from Wireless Fidelity (a bit of a stretch for the name I think), Wi-Fi is the new umbrella name for the standards-based wireless local area network communications protocols. If you talk about wireless data connections, you're almost always talking about Wi-Fi today.

There are four current standards now called Wi-Fi:

✦ **802.11**: The original standard, and the foundation for the others. Released in 1997, 802.11 specifies frequencies in the 2.4 GHz range and a maximum bandwidth of 2 Mbps. Any more questions why you can't buy 802.11 products?

✦ **802.11a**: One of two standards delivered in 1999 that upped the speed to something exciting. In the case of 802.11a, the speeds jumped up to 54 Mbps but used frequencies in the 5 GHz range, a regulated frequency. The higher frequency shortened the distance but added other complications. Vendors focused on the sibling standard, 802.11b.

✦ **802.11b**: Uses the same unregulated frequencies around 2.4 GHz but ups the speed to 11 Mbps. This speed matches standard 802.3 Ethernet, which runs at 10 Mbps. Practical throughput for both is about half the rated speeds, but that's still far faster then the original 802.11 specification.

✦ **802.11g**: Released in mid-2003, although many vendors prereleased products based on the pending standard. 802.11g ratchets the speed up to 54 Mbps while retaining the 2.4 GHz frequency range. 802.11b and 802.11g products work together, so existing 802.11b networks can add 802.11g gear and gain bandwidth as new access points and clients are added.

Originally, Wi-Fi referred to the 802.11b products. Chasing ever-better speeds and marketing opportunities, Wi-Fi folks have spread the name to include all 802.11 technologies.

But don't let that label fool you. Just because it says "Wi-Fi" doesn't mean you get the fastest, newest speeds and products. Intel's Centrino systems, a nice chipset for mobile computers, uses only 802.11b. Of course, most laptop hard disk controllers won't handle sustained speeds of 5 Mbps anyway. Plus, do you remember any broadband services from cable or DSL providers that guaranteed 5 Mbps throughput? Only ADSL if you lived next door to the central office, and not always then.

Figure 8-9 shows the Linksys Basic Wireless Settings screen for the new WRV54G 802.11g cable/DSL wireless router. Notice the range of frequencies available and how each channel uses a slightly different frequency.

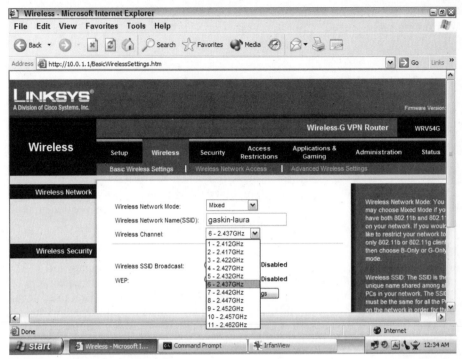

Figure 8-9: Wireless basic settings.

The top pull-down menu, Wireless Network Mode, has four settings:

✦ **Disable**: Turn wireless support off

✦ **B-only**: 11 Mbps networking only

✦ **Mixed**: 11 Mbps and 54 Mbps networking

✦ **G-only**: 54 Mbps networking only

This illustrates my earlier point about mixing and matching 802.11b and 802.11g products in one network. Linksys makes it easy to include both standards by selecting the Mixed mode, as I did. However, 802.11b (11 Mbps) transmissions monopolize the channel and force 802.11g (54 Mbps) to slow down. When only 802.11g devices are communicating, the speed remains high.

Interference

Business, and especially technology, requires constant decisions. The same goes for Wi-Fi. 802.11, 802.11b, and 802.11g all use frequencies right around 2.4 GHz. That frequency range is unregulated, meaning any vendor can make products using frequencies in that range. And so many did, and not just wireless networking vendors, either.

The following common items create interference for 802.11b and 802.11g products:

✦ Microwave ovens

✦ Cordless phones

✦ New Bluetooth short-range wireless devices

Most interference issues can be overcome by moving the wireless access point or adding an antenna extender. That, or hope people making popcorn in the microwave finish soon.

802.11b network devices use Complementary Code Keying (CCK) modulation, relying on a single-frequency waveform. Interference on the same frequency as your network really clobbers the data throughput.

802.11a and 802.11g network devices use Orthogonal Frequency Division Multiplexing (OFDM), which splits data over multiple small subsignals and transmits them at different frequencies. This lessens the interference problem for 802.11g, but 802.11a uses a regulated frequency different from that used by microwaves and cordless phones. The 802.11g standards group was smart to grab the technical advantages of 802.11a and make them work with the 802.11b products already out in the field.

Interference doesn't kill a Wi-Fi network connection; it just slows it way down as the connection fights through the competing radio waves. The intermittent nature of interference in the home or workplace makes it tough to track down the offending products. But focus on cordless phones and microwaves.

Distances

Again you must take these numbers with a bit of skepticism, because distance figures rival bandwidth numbers for "creative accounting." Anything that blocks a radio signal degrades the signal and shortens the distance. That *anything* includes interference, walls, corners, and smoke. (Okay, the last two may be a little harsh, but moving a metal file cabinet will change the radio wave pattern in an office.)

In the best case (outdoors) at low speeds (1 Mbps), 802.11b and 802.11g can go over 500 meters. In the worst case, you won't get the high-speed connection, 54 Mbps, through even one thin interior wall.

Signals go through glass better than through walls. Mounting access points higher in the room seems to increase distance. The upcoming *Antennas* section will provide ways to increase range.

Here is a list of speeds and approximate indoor distances for 802.11g:

✦ **54 Mbps**: 20 meters (65 feet)

✦ **18 Mbps**: 60 meters (195 feet)

✦ **11 Mbps**: 75 meters (245 feet)

✦ **1 Mbps**: 125 meters (410 feet)

Does this mean the distance and speed ratings in the marketing literature are fraudulent? Absolutely not, although they are optimistic, perhaps, but not exactly fraudulent. You can cover a pretty large room at 54 Mbps if you put the access point in the center of the room and place all computers within 65 feet in any direction. Nearly 250 feet in any direction covers a pretty big warehouse at a pretty good (11 Mbps) speed rating.

Mixing vendors

Standards, when followed, make it possible to mix and match products from different vendors into a working network. Let me tell you how it really works.

The newer the standard, the less likely it is that products from different vendors will work together. Why? Because all the vendors start designing their products before the standards are official. If they waited until every standards committee member gave thumbs up, their products would take another six months to reach the market, and the market would be full of their competitors.

This standards jumping behavior infected just about every single wireless vendor in the 802.11b market as they anticipated 802.11g. It didn't make any sense to see a full shelf of 802.11g products from different vendors, all claiming to be "standards based" before the 802.11g standard was ratified, but there they were.

Can you take two first-generation 802.11g products from different vendors and guarantee they will work together? Absolutely not.

But by the time vendors put out their second-generation products based on standards, working together becomes easier. The first generation of 802.11b products didn't work well outside their own vendor family, but the second generation works pretty well. The second generation of 802.11g products will work the same way.

Buying all your wireless network products from a single vendor isn't a bad idea, but it's hard to maintain. Your dealer runs out of stock when you need some additional equipment. The vendor changes the model line, so you no longer have the same products available. Your company buys another company, or your company is bought.

Whatever the reason, you must start mixing products. Do it the smart way:

✦ Don't mix products from the first generation of a standard.

✦ Keep products from the same vendor in the same area.

✦ Try connections at lower data rates.

✦ Get products talking before adding security settings.

✦ Look for Wi-Fi certification on all products.

The Wi-Fi Alliance now includes over 200 companies selling over 1,000 products (as of early 2004). Not every firm keeps in step with the increasing certification demands, but you'll have better luck with certified products than with uncertified ones. Plus, if they're certified to work together and they don't, you stand a better chance of getting your money back.

Be flexible in your installation and testing. If a wireless laptop card doesn't work in one laptop, try it in another. If a card and access point can't connect, try a different card and then a different access point.

Improving distances

People are never satisfied, and you're no exception. You always want the wireless link to reach a little bit farther and the speeds to be a little bit higher.

Vendors are never satisfied either. They always want you to buy more products. Luckily, they sometimes make it easy to justify buying more. If more distance drives you in your search, vendors have been listening.

Antennas

As you can see in Figures 8-3 and 8-4, some wireless routers have external antennas and some don't. External antennas can be made to stand higher and include more usable projection area than most internal antennas, at least according to those selling external antennas.

The older Linksys cable/DSL modem model shares a case with the wireless routers. Some Linksys routers have one antenna, like the one shown earlier this chapter, and some have two antennas. Double the antennas, increase your range.

To retrofit some earlier wireless routers, Linksys released a signal booster built to fit on top of its routers. Figure 8-10 shows the unit on the Linksys Web page.

The housing holds the electronics and extra-strength transmitter and receiver. Cables run from the old antenna connections on the lower unit to the new booster.

Sometimes industrial strength antennas make the difference. SMC (www.smc.com) makes a variety of wireless products that compete across the board with Linksys and Netgear, and they have a couple of interesting antennas.

The antenna in Figure 8-11 looks the most sinister in some ways, but also pumps out some serious power. Pushing 802.11b out to 7 miles takes some work, and SMC says this antenna can do it.

SMC makes other antennas for shorter distances. They also make some odd looking ones to place on office ceilings to cover large areas and push the signal through cubicle walls.

More power

Besides an antenna, another way to get more distance is to use more power. Most wireless PC cards top out at 100 milliwatts (mW) and many use only

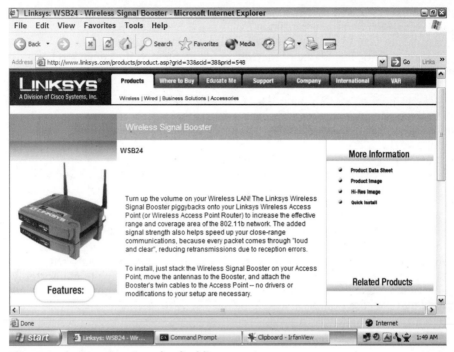

Figure 8-10: Boosting range by doubling your antennas.

Figure 8-11: Industrial strength add-on antenna.

around 50mW. The SMC EliteConnect 802.11b High Power Wireless PC card doubles the high end by using 200mW.

In real-world tests, I used one of the SMC cards and tested the signal strength with a standard 802.11b card and then added the SMC High Power card.

I checked signal strength in four places: the same office as the wireless access point, the next room (20 feet and a wall away), at the top of the stairs (50 feet and a wall and a floor away), and in the kid's playroom (75 feet and two walls and a floor away).

The normal 802.11b card could barely make a connection in the kid's room: 10 percent to 15 percent signal strength and 1M to 2 Mbps throughput. Not great, and in fact, I could never use a wireless link up to the kid's playroom

Using the SMC High Power card along with the same Linksys Wireless Access point in the office as before, results were surprisingly improved. In the kid's room, I have 50–70 percent signal strength at a full 11 Mbps. Suddenly, with the purchase of a different card, the connection went from not viable to comfortably usable. A more expensive card, to be sure, but it was cheaper than adding several more access points.

Summary

Your broadband service provider will either supply (most likely) or identify a cable or DSL modem for your installation. Basic routers to link a computer or network to your broadband connection have given way to routers full of firewalls, security features, and wireless services.

Routers have dropped in price while increasing features, a happy situation for consumers. Always use a router between your computer(s) and your cable/DSL modem. Using a wireless router/access point cuts the cord and supports wireless networking directly to your broadband connection and on to the Internet. And increasing speeds arriving with newer standards (802.11g at 54 Mbps for wireless connections) in routers will make broadband networking inside your home as easy as Web browsers have made the Internet.

Examining the Multitenant Broadband Hookup

Chapter 8 covered what you do with broadband after you get it into your home. In the case of a traditional single family dwelling in the suburbs with a white picket fence and nice flowerbed, you control all the access rights from the broadband service provider to your internal connection. But what if you don't control that access? What if someone else owns the building?

When more parties get involved, things generally get messier, but not in this case. Service providers love finding a dense population, which reduces their costs because they can place a node of some type at the location to service all the clients in the immediate area. In some cases, service providers actually put central office equipment at the site and use fiber optic cables to link to the real central office.

The good news is that any modern apartment, condo, executive suite, or office park you move into should have excellent broadband access and perhaps a dedicated service provider. The bad news is that sometimes you don't have a choice about your service provider and are stuck with the company holding the contract from the landlord or property manager.

If your apartment management allows primary broadband access providers to connect to individual apartments, ignore this chapter. This chapter is important only when the management of your site controls the access and forces you to use a service provider of their choice.

Broadband When You Don't Control Access

Large groups of people look like a herd of customers to most large service providers. In fact, American cities are an interesting mix of services chasing customers (like public transportation near huge apartments) and customers chasing services (like development around a new highway).

Often, especially today when serious money is at stake, developers and service providers get together and strike a deal long before individual customers have a chance to mess up their plans by choosing a different service provider. Governments get in on the act as well, choosing cable TV franchises for communities, and, of course, there used to be a single phone company for everyone.

You can get upset about the lack of control you have over your broadband access when you move into a multitenant situation if you want, but you won't suffer. When cable TV came out, and satellite TV afterwards, apartments and other multitenant properties received service long before surrounding residential areas. After all, if you were starting a service, wouldn't you want to hook up as many customers as possible with the least expense? That means multitenant customers got connected first to generate cash flow for further expansion.

The building local exchange carrier

Yikes! Another confusing acronym! Building Local Exchange Carrier (BLEC) now tries to force its way into conversation, but honestly the sound of BLEC doesn't bode well for wide acceptance.

However, a service provider resident at your apartment or condo can make life much easier. Apartment managers don't get any training on broadband network management and sometimes struggle just to keep the elevators and washing machines running. Farming out broadband service to a specialized third party makes great sense for those managers and residents.

Office buildings were the first targets of BLECs (say that out loud although keeping a pleasant image in mind), especially those buildings outside the easy reach of the telephone company central office or cable node. Although many newer buildings include fiber optic cable connections to central services, this feature doesn't cover anywhere near the majority of buildings needing service.

The equipment developed by service providers to reach out to office buildings works perfectly well in apartments and condos today. In fact, a building local exchange carrier almost always provides faster broadband access and speedier service connections than either telephone companies with DSL or cable operators.

How is this possible? When developing access equipment for remote sites, often called "edge connections" (as in the edge of the network), vendors added remote management tools to avoid having to send a technician out to each building for each change. After a building has the wiring required to connect each client location to the site of the edge connection hardware (usually a basement wall beside the incoming trunk lines for the telephone connections), service can be added, modified, or deleted for any client office or apartment through management software from a remote office.

That's exactly how these companies can connect you with broadband access in as little as an hour. (Vendors make this exact promise to building owners.) Here's what happens (best case):

1. You arrange for service.
2. The service provider activates the port on the access hardware at that location that connects to your apartment or office.
3. You plug in your computer to the provided wall plug or broadband modem.
4. High speed Internet broadband access zooms you to the Internet.

Well-managed buildings make these arrangements before you arrive, just as they do with other services. Some details must be arranged, such as username, password, and network authentication details, but this is exactly the way you get telephone service. When you move to a new apartment, you don't have to beg the phone company to run a wire to your apartment, because it's already there. Broadband service providers hope you soon assume the same level of readiness for broadband access in new apartments.

Connection speeds from your building to the central office or other access provider office vary. Less populated locations will generally have at least a T1 connection, meaning a 1.5 Mbps connection to share among all residents. A bigger client population almost always means faster backhaul speeds from the building to the access provider's Internet connection location.

Not all third-party providers at a multitenant site are full-fledged local exchange carriers. Often the developer farms out management, up to and including billing, to a service provider. You call your provider for service details and for technical support.

Physical connection options

A service provider's dream, apartments, condos, office buildings, and executive suites (and hotels, but that's a different book) put hundreds or thousands of broadband customers in one location. You already know the service providers want you to assume service is waiting and demand access as part of expected amenities.

There are three ways to provide the physical connections to support broadband service in such a concentrated location:

✦ Run new wiring (Category 5 UTP or coax or fiber) to every client location (apartment, office, condo, and so on)

✦ Piggyback new broadband service over existing wiring

✦ Spread wireless access points around the complex

Apartment developers are getting smarter and adding more connections to each unit for broadband services. Office building developers learned long ago to add these extra connections and always to provide service connections to a central point in every new office built.

Depending on the broadband service access provider for your building, you may have a broadband modem, router, or other hardware device in your unit for connection.

If your building doesn't have some type of broadband access wiring in place, the owners probably won't add it for you. The cost of rewiring an apartment building, or any other multitenant property, jumps up pretty quickly. The cost of wiring a new building during construction is minimal.

DSL service providers make a cost-effective option for older buildings without any type of broadband access wiring to each unit. The good news for each tenant is that because the building has its own node, speeds to each unit should be pretty high. Most DSL companies that service buildings guarantee at least 1 Mbps downstream speeds. (Your mileage may vary.)

A few companies, such as www.icetech.net, are starting to sell apartment complexes wireless access service that allows users to wander around the grounds with their laptops or PDAs and remain connected to the network. This will be great for some, but make others extremely paranoid. Security and authentication will need to be at a higher level, obviously, than on the systems where your connection over physical wire helps set your security and authentication. But this does illustrate the increasing reach and capabilities of wireless vendors.

Wireless providers can, of course, provide the edge connection equipment for your apartment or office. You may never know you have a wireless Internet connection because each apartment or office will connect via wire to the edge connection equipment and the router for service provider access.

Apartments

The good news for you, the apartment resident, is some type of service will be delivered to your apartment. In rare cases, you will have a choice. In equally rare cases, a single connection to each apartment will provide all telephone, Internet, and TV services through a breakout box in the apartment.

When looking for a new apartment, ask about broadband access. Equipment vendors always pitch the value of advertising broadband access in their marketing literature aimed at apartment owners. It would make them feel good to have you verify the value of broadband access to the apartment managers by demanding broadband Internet access. Frankly, many apartment residents will use a broadband access service much more than a pool.

If broadband service is important to you (you bought this book, so it must be), verify upfront your broadband service options. Your best negotiation time is before you sign a lease contract, because you can still walk to the next apartment complex and sign a lease there.

If broadband access is not provided, but you really like the apartment complex, check into your options. Services like DSL may be available if you're close enough to a central office. Large apartment clusters in one neighborhood often force the telephone company to put a central office in the area to handle the customer load. If this is the case, DSL of some flavor may be no problem, but you must confirm that fact before you sign a contract.

Because almost every apartment complex already has cable TV, you may be able to get broadband service from the cable provider. Most systems today allow the cable company to split the broadband from the TV frequencies inside your apartment with a splitter. Your Internet connection may have to be close to your TV, but that might not be a problem and could be an advantage.

Verifying your service provider of choice will connect you at the requested apartment. Verifying your apartment will allow the service provider any access necessary to install your connection. Write that information on your contract, or you'll be sorry. Chat sites for broadband include many tales of woe from people dialing in to complain about territorial fights between apartment managers, phone companies, and DSL providers. The companies fight, service never gets installed, and the individuals listen to the modem connection dirge and wish they'd chosen a different apartment.

Although you're verifying things, make sure your apartment broadband access service rate is cheaper, or at least not more expensive, than the rates charged directly by the service provider. Volume discounts from the service provider to the apartment owner should be passed to you. If not, at least you shouldn't be charged extra.

If you're a big wireless broadband access fan, you may be able to put a transceiver on your balcony and get service. But be sure your apartment allows that hardware installation. If the apartment complex has its own service provider, the rules probably outlaw attaching hardware to bypass that service. Verify or regret.

What to ask the landlord

If it seems there are a lot of questions to ask before you sign your lease, you are correct. Let me provide a checklist so you can objectively decide whether an apartment will get you acceptable broadband service.

Notice that you can decide whether a detail doesn't matter in your situation. If you live by yourself, you may not care about concurrent connections, for example. You may prefer to pay for your broadband access as part of your rent, all on one check, or you may need to separate billing for tax purposes. I can't make those decisions for you, but consider the answers to the following questions before you sign your lease:

✦ What type of service is available?
  - ❏ Acceptable
  - ❏ Not acceptable
  - ❏ Doesn't matter

✦ Who supplies the service?
  - ❏ Acceptable
  - ❏ Not acceptable
  - ❏ Doesn't matter

✦ Who manages the service (apartment or third party)?
  - ❏ Acceptable
  - ❏ Not acceptable
  - ❏ Doesn't matter

✦ Who does the billing (apartment or third party)?
  - ❏ Acceptable
  - ❏ Not acceptable
  - ❏ Doesn't matter

✦ What access speeds are available?
  - ❏ Acceptable
  - ❏ Not acceptable
  - ❏ Doesn't matter

✦ Can a different service provider connect you instead?
  - ❏ Acceptable
  - ❏ Not acceptable
  - ❏ Doesn't matter

✦ Can you upgrade service later?
  - ❏ Acceptable
  - ❏ Not acceptable
  - ❏ Doesn't matter

✦ How many concurrent connections are allowed (parent and child on two different computers, for example)?
  - ❏ Acceptable
  - ❏ Not acceptable
  - ❏ Doesn't matter

✦ What is the guaranteed level of service (uptime and access speed)?

❏ Acceptable

❏ Not acceptable

❏ Doesn't matter

It doesn't really matter what your answers are, just that you've thought about the process and understand what you're willing to accept for your broadband service. After you discover what's important to you, making your choices will generate less mental uncertainty.

Keeping your old e-mail address

When you move to an apartment with a broadband service provider and no choices (take its service or dialup) you get a new e-mail address. Some people don't really care, but many people find that horribly inconvenient. If you want to keep your e-mail address, there are ways to do so.

You can always plan ahead and get an e-mail address from one of the free services, such as Yahoo, Hotmail, or iWon. There are a variety of Web sites that provide vanity names or other permanent e-mail addresses not tied to your service provider. Once you have this address, you can forward mail to this account from whatever broadband service provider your apartment building uses.

This plan requires you to plan ahead a year or two, so it won't work for all people. The other ways to keep your existing e-mail address cost money.

You can keep your account at your current Internet service provider after you get broadband service. The ex-provider will be happy to let you do so, because you'll pay the monthly charge but you won't dial in and use one of their modem ports.

There are two advantages with this system: you can keep your old e-mail address (and any personal Web pages) and you have a back-up dial-up option in case something happens to your broadband service provider.

A third advantage, especially if you use AOL, is a reduced price on your old service. Because you connect to the old services (e-mail account) the provider will want to charge you something. But because you don't dialup through that provider's network, the cost of supporting you is lower, and the price for the service drops. Look for the AOL broadband with 5-hour dial-up plan, which costs $15 versus $24 for the regular dial-up plan (as of early 2004). It's not free, but it's nearly half price. If your current service provider has a national presence, it may have a similar option.

If you keep AOL when you add a broadband service provider, which I did because my teenage daughter threatened me with unending hatred if I disconnected her from all her AOL-IM buddies, you make a simple change on the AOL Sign On screen. Tell AOL to connect over broadband (cable/DSL/ISP) in the

Location line on the main screen. The program tests your network connection, finds a broadband service provider already hooking you to the Internet, and zooms through the connection sequence.

If you have a different service provider you want to keep, you keep your same e-mail address and thus you get your mail from the same e-mail server as before. Your outgoing e-mail server, however, must be the one provided by your broadband service provider.

For Outlook Express, the critical name is the outgoing e-mail server name. Figure 9-1 shows the screen on which you change this name. Reach the screen in Figure 9-1 by clicking Start ➪ Outlook Express ➪ Tools ➪ Accounts ➪ Add Mail account. Provide a display name and click Next. Provide the Internet e-mail address and click Next. Provide the e-mail server type, e-mail server name, and (finally) the outgoing mail (SMTP) server name.

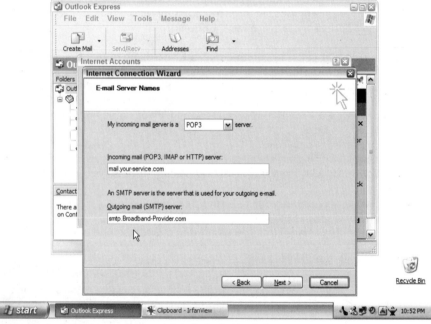

Figure 9-1: Setting e-mail server details in Outlook Express.

Your incoming e-mail server will not be named *mail.your-service.com* but will be supplied by your service provider. In the case of Comcast cable broadband access, the incoming e-mail server is mail.comcast.net. This will be the name you have been using, so you won't need to change this setting.

The outgoing mail (SMTP) server field will include the outgoing e-mail server name provided by your new broadband service provider. Following the example of Comcast in the previous paragraph, the outgoing e-mail server is named smtp.comcast.net.

Tech Bits SMTP stands for Simple Mail Transport Protocol. It's called *Simple* because it was developed before the Internet became a land of spammers, and the security model assumes people using e-mail servers were honorable.

To stop (or at least slow down) spammers and hackers, service providers almost never accept outgoing e-mail that doesn't originate on their service. That's why you can't continue to use your old outgoing e-mail server. If you try to use it, after moving to a broadband service provider, your old e-mail server will reject your messages and perhaps block you as a spammer.

Changing service providers may be a hassle, but you can overcome it. At least you can keep your e-mail address, even if it costs a few dollars a month to maintain service from two Internet service providers (old dialup and new broadband).

Condos

Condos have much in common with apartments as far as broadband access. However, instead of an apartment manager you may have homeowners association, and they can be crazier than any apartment manager.

The good news from the world of condos is they attract the same type of third-party service provider that apartments do. Many people in one place makes for interested service providers, and condos fit that bill

If your condo management made a deal with a third-party broadband service provider, you're in the same position as described in the previous *Apartments* section. The checklist in the *Apartments* section provides all the questions you need to ask your condo management.

One sticky detail with some condos is the homeowners association, drunk with power and governed by aesthetics. You may not have an option to attach any type of external antenna to your property, even though it is certainly your property. If that's the case, your hopes for wireless or satellite broadband access may be dashed. For that matter, so may your hopes for satellite TV.

The restrictions on external antennas will be diligently enforced if the condo developer or homeowners association has a contract with a third-party broadband service provider. If that's the case, the provider picked by the association will be *your* broadband service provider as well. So skip ahead to the next major section entitled "*Security Control Points*" and learn how to protect your computer while using their broadband service.

Executive suites

Individual offices inside a building, with shared amenities, such as conference rooms, telephone services, and (sometimes) a receptionist, are great options for small business people who don't want an office in their home or apartment.

Executive suites offer the look and sound of a company larger than the one person sitting in a rented office.

The advantages, and rationalization for the cost of an executive suite, are the added amenities. Everything a person needs for a company office should be provided, including telephone, fax, receptionist, coffee machine, and network connection. Executive suites usually inhabit a floor inside a commercial building with multiple service providers, and one or more of those providers will supply service to the executive suite.

You may not have a choice of service providers, but you will likely get faster and more reliable service at an executive suite than at any residence. If the executive suite doesn't offer full high-speed network connection options, keep looking for an executive suite that does.

Office parks

Office parks, planned developments built and managed by one company, can offer most of the same advantages as an executive suite does, and probably more. Most include multiple buildings and multiple options for all types of service, not just broadband access.

The other end of the spectrum appears as well, when an office park offers little or nothing except the space you rent. In cases like this, your situation is no different than any business. You must get your broadband service provider connection yourself directly from the provider.

If that minimalist approach was taken by your landlord, ask your neighbors who supplies their broadband Internet access. It may be a phone company, the cable company, or a specialized business-only provider. No matter who it is, any provider that already has one customer in the office park will want to get another one. You may even get a discount if the network equipment installed for your neighbor can support your needs as well.

Service from the landlord

Security in a multitenant situation ranges from absolutely wonderful to abysmal. If your apartment manager and leasing company tries to run broadband access themselves, chances are your security will lean toward the abysmal end of the spectrum. If your apartment management brought in a third party to handle broadband issues for them, you should be in good shape. If the third party broadband access provider takes ownership responsibility for all Internet access and puts switching equipment on the site, you should have great security.

When your landlord tries to perform all broadband access services, you must take extra precautions. Internet access protection in the world of spam, viruses, and hackers requires more technical expertise than most apartment management companies can muster.

You want to protect yourself, from Internet problems and landlord problems. This will take some effort if your apartment management is clueless or malicious.

Billing questions

Money makes people weird. Get billing questions answered before signing the lease. Who bills for the broadband access? Is the service cost rolled into the rent, or is there a separate charge?

If broadband service is included within the rent amount, you will have a difficult time deducting money for poor broadband access without looking like a rent deadbeat. Tenants have some rights, but landlords have more in most of the U.S. states. Can you deduct the portion of the rent payment if your broadband service isn't usable for most of the month? How much is the broadband access portion? Will the landlord report your deduction for poor broadband service to credit agencies as a services dispute, or a rent nonpayment?

The best situation you can hope for is that the broadband service is billed separately and does not reflect on your credit rating if withheld for poor service. But withholding any portion of your rent makes for a sticky situation with rental management.

Separate terms of service

Each landlord includes a variety of thou shalt nots in every lease: that you won't run a criminal enterprise in the apartment, that you won't steal the appliances, and sometimes that you won't badmouth the apartment complex to anyone publicly or privately.

Broadband service providers include Terms of Service in their sign-up contracts: that you won't transfer obscene material through their system, that you won't spam, and sometimes that you won't badmouth them, either.

If your landlord provides broadband access, will conflicts in one area spill over to the next? If your computer is hijacked by one of the multiple viruses running around that turn your PC (they exploit Windows vulnerabilities) into a spam-sending e-mail server, will that violate your rental agreement? If it does, can they throw you out of the apartment with little or no warning?

This may seem farfetched, and I hope for your sake it is. However, read the fine print on your lease and you may be surprised by the rights the landlord holds over your housing status and credit rating. Landlords put all those restrictions in the lease so they can protect themselves and throw you out if you become a problem.

When you find that type of information in a lease, the rental agent will always tell you "that never happens" and personally guarantee you'll never have a problem like that. But unless the agent amends the contract to reflect those words, those promises are just random noises to reassure you until you sign the lease and give up some of your rights.

Service level agreement

Broadband service providers tout their uptime and service reliability. Does your landlord guarantee a certain percentage of uptime? If so, what are the procedures for you to follow if your uptime drops below those levels?

If your cable broadband access connection drops for two weeks, do you get a free month of service, your bill reduced by half, or nothing at all? If the lease and broadband service agreement don't spell out these details, you'll get nothing.

Support contacts

You will, I promise, need a contact to call about broadband access service problems. No matter how good your service provider, there will be a problem.

If your site landlord is your service contact, expect more problems than solutions. Good service departments are rare, and the chances of your apartment management company being one of the few good ones borders on hilarious.

Privacy assurances

Broadband service providers should always list their privacy policies so you can read their idea of privacy before you sign up for their service. Here are some of the questions you should ask:

+ Does the provider resell your name and address to affiliated companies?

+ Does the provider resell your name and address to everyone?

+ Does the provider sell your physical address information, or just your e-mail address?

+ Does the provider track which Web sites you visit and sell that information to other companies?

+ Does the provider notify you when someone official requests your online activity information?

Unfortunately, some service providers do, in fact, resell, track, and monitor constantly. You should know these details so you can decide whether you want to find a more polite service provider.

Landlords have specific rights to monitor and even search your premises depending on the situation and the laws of your state. Do they automatically extend those invasive rights to everything you do on the Internet? If so, they should tell you and let you decide whether to allow these intrusions by signing the lease or going to a less nosy apartment complex.

Update your security

No matter how pleasant or onerous the answers from your landlord are about the issues in the previous sections, you must update your security if your landlord provides broadband access. Go through your computer(s) and verify if the following are in place:

✦ Operating system updates (particularly for Windows versions)

✦ Active and updated virus protection

✦ Active and updated spam protection

✦ Active and updated personal firewall

All of these features are smart Internet precautions, no matter what. But when your apartment landlord provides your broadband access service, they move from smart precautions to mandatory. You don't want to pay the penalty for your management company's Internet ineptitude.

Summary? If your landlord and/or apartment management company provides your broadband service, you may soon be disappointed and eventually look elsewhere. However, if you ask the right questions before signing the lease or contract, you will have more control over your broadband access situation and time to make alternative arrangements if necessary.

Service from a third party

Some questions for your broadband service provider need be asked no matter who does the providing. If your apartment group uses a third-party that specializes in broadband access service you'll have better luck all the way around. It doesn't matter if this company specializes in multitenant systems as much as it does in broadband access.

Support contact

Ask for the support contact when you sign your lease, even before you move in. The more warning you can give the service provider, the better your chances of getting the service you want and having it ready when you arrive.

All Internet service providers have customer support centers of some type, along with information concerning what clients should do to get started. These service centers may not be staffed with phone-answering people 24 × 7, but they will have some type of help online and numbers you can call at least part of the time.

Verify your billing options with the third-party before you get connected. It's easier to get the type of billing you want upfront than it is to change afterward. If the bills come with your rent invoice each month, and the apartment forwards the money to the service provider, ask about receipts or confirmation to avoid potential service hassles later.

Service level agreement and privacy

The service level agreement from a third-party service provider should be considerably better than that from an apartment management team. Service providers almost always offer some type of payment rebate when they drop the ball too often or too long.

Privacy concerns still exist, but service providers tend to protect privacy much more than apartment leasing companies do. Besides, if you a broadband service payment, the provider doesn't get nearly as upset as an apartment manager would. The government can still demand your service details from a service provider under laws associated with the Patriot Act, but your apartment manager can't snoop into your Internet activities if a third-party provider delivers your Internet connection.

Keeping your account

As soon as you find you really like your broadband service provider at your apartment, you'll probably start looking for another apartment for some reason. If the service provider handles one apartment complex, it may well handle others. If you have started receiving substantial e-mail traffic or hits to your personal Web site, you may want to keep the same provider.

If your provider services another apartment complex from which you wish to rent, take care of the paperwork before giving notice at the first apartment. Sometimes these customer exit processes are automated to their own detriment. If you give notice, the apartment contract with the service provider may state to notify the service provider and stop all access at a certain date. They may even scrub your account and leave no record of you or your e-mail address.

Think ahead, and you won't have to fill out the new client paperwork again, speeding your service availability in the new place. Planning ahead will also keep a ton of e-mail from bouncing the week your e-mail address falls into limbo.

Onsite broadband router

If your apartment (or condo or executive suite) supports enough broadband clients, the service provider probably installed some edge connection equipment onsite. Most likely, this unit will be a router of some type paired with a multiplexor handing the cabling connections throughout the site. After all, one of their big selling points, fast service for customers, demands they keep equipment onsite to support the clients.

Your connection won't be much different if it's from a router in the basement or a service provider in the neighborhood. There can be a couple of differences, however, so let me explain two quick things.

Firewall

The router at your location may include a firewall or the service provider may rely on its firewall between the entire network and the Internet. For extra security protection, a firewall at your site is preferable. After all, you have no reason to trust every other client of your service provider. You want to keep a buffer between you and as many people as possible.

If the firewall is at your site, the service provider will have another one at its office as well. When you get the IP addresses and port numbers for game connections, verify you're getting all the necessary firewall client details and your contact knows that you may have a firewall at your apartment as well.

Network address translation

Network Address Translation (NAT) details will appear, in depth, in Chapter 12, but I want to mention something now. Your service provider should use *network address translation* for each router-based site, including your apartment complex. Network address translation converts the private, hidden IP address of your computer into a known, public IP address when your data packets zoom about the Internet. This keeps outsiders from seeing your real IP address and targeting your real computer.

If they don't use network address translation, it means your entire apartment complex will be on one big happy network with little security between you and the weirdo who skulks around the washing machines. Not good, because each client connection should go to a separate physical port on the local router or multiplexor.

This all-on-one method of placing everyone in the complex on one network is stupid, but has been done from early on in Internet history. Demand network address translation on each connection, if possible. Adjust your security mindset accordingly if there's a shared network connection. Check for this networking method by going to Start ⇨ My Network Places and clicking the View Network Computers in the menu on the left. If you see one or more computers you don't know, they can also see you. Oops.

If you can see other computers on your local network, they can see you (over the network, not physically). That means you must complain to the service provider and increase your security profile. Although waiting for help, stay off the network unless you're actively surfing or getting e-mail. Do not leave the computer turned on while connected to your broadband access provider in this situation.

Summary

When you are in an apartment or other multitenant situation, your broadband service provider choice may be completely out of your hands. Verify that the apartment you want to move into has an adequate broadband access system for your needs.

If some adjustments will make your connections better, ask. But ask before you sign the lease, because when the ink dries on your lease, you're stuck with the conditions inside the lease and any additions you made.

Moving from Stand-Alone PCs to a Network

Connecting to a broadband service provider pushes you to connect other devices to broadband as well. After all, for a few extra dollars every computer in the house can enjoy fast broadband surfing.

The software side of networking includes configuring devices, handling network addresses, and a bit about secure network routing. Underneath it all is TCP/IP, the protocol that connects the Internet (and just about everything else in the world today).

More computing means more people making more data and more reasons to protect that data. A little planning will avoid lost files and accidentally deleted documents, and keep your favorite files, photos, and music safe and sound.

Server and Storage Options

No one ever has enough space. Not enough space in their closet, their garage, or their hard disk. After you start relying on your computer, the disk space melts away like a snowball in July.

The solution to this problem isn't to stop relying on your computer but to manage your data better. Adding more storage without a plan makes it harder to find what you're looking for. But adding storage as a way to share data, streamline controlling data, and ensure data is protected makes computing life much easier.

Why You Want a Home Server

I've had friends laugh at me when I've told them they will need dedicated file servers in their homes before long. They accused me of being a shill for server companies. Then I tell them they will need to buy more computer books, and they accuse me of being a shill for publishers.

I won't argue that I'd like to see more computer books sold (especially the ones with my name on them, because I'm being honest), but I will argue with the first part. You can make a home server without buying a new box of any kind. The goal is to gain the important benefits a home server provides.

 Note A server serves, so a home server provides a centralized storage location for files of all types, including documents, photos, music, and financial records. Servers often provide security and authentication for users, blocking those not defined in the system and allowing identified users access to certain areas only (if you wish to be restrictive). Business servers also host databases, Web servers, and e-mail servers.

I walk around the houses of my accusatory friends and start pointing. There's the "family" computer, which usually means it's too slow for the kids to play games on. That means there's at least one computer for the children, and often each child has his or her own computer. If one or both parents work for a large company, there's at least one laptop, and often two.

The conversations tend to go like this: "What's on that computer?" I ask, pointing to the family system.

"Nothing much. Nothing all that important."

"Really?" I ask, looking at their digital camera. "Where are the images from your digital camera?"

Turns out they're on that computer and scattered around the children's computers as well. But when I ask to see the Christmas pictures from 2 years back, no one remembers where they are. A search ensues until I stop them.

"Where are your online banking files? Where are your financial records?" Turns out that "nothing much" computer data includes their financial history.

It also includes e-mails going back years, including some from family members no longer around. Are there printed copies of those e-mails? No. Are there backed up copies? No.

The kid's computer(s) generally include homework, study notes, and personal items like pictures from friends. How would you feel if I replaced that computer with a brand new, faster unit? Kewl. What if all your data went to the dump with the old computer? Can't do that.

What about music? Kids tend to have plenty of MP3 music files on their hard disks, some from downloading and some from copying files off the physical CDs they own. Would you like to play those files on your stereo? Kewl. Just run a long cable from your room to the stereo. Not kewl. Need a server.

Company laptop owners often create PowerPoint presentations on their home computer, and then e-mail them to themselves at work. Why? Getting the presentations from their home computer to the laptop means more effort than they want to face.

The messy side of home computing

A few more questions like these, and the truth comes out. People's computer images, music, and data files are messier than their closets. Look at more than one computer in a household and you find the following:

✦ Files are scattered around.

✦ Backups for critical personal and business data are nonexistent.

✦ Some hard disks are getting full and others have plenty of open space.

✦ There is no way to share a high-speed broadband connection.

✦ There is no way to play music files on another computer or a stereo.

✦ There is no easy way to move work files from a home computer to a laptop and vice versa.

It's painful when family members realize they've spent thousands of dollars on technology they can't control. It's almost funny when they realize some of their aggravation about computers can be avoided with planning and a home network designed to make their computing life easier.

Cleaning up home computing

A home server turns a computer mess into something reliable and useful for everyone. Well, it can, if it's done right. But like most things concerning computers, you can also turn a small mess and headache into a giant mess and a migraine.

My advice for those adding a server is to think of organization first. When properly organized, the rest of the server benefits appear naturally.

Connecting devices

When you tell people they need to network computers (and storage devices and printers and backup devices etc.) together they freak out, imagining wires snaking down the halls and holes drilled in walls.

Relax.

Yes, wires do connect devices, especially devices close to each other. You will almost certainly use an Ethernet patch cable to connect your cable/DSL modem to your router. If a computer is on the same desk, you will use a cable to connect it to the router. These small patch cables will disappear among all the other messy cables computer spawn, such as the power, mouse, keyboard, and monitor cables. But that cable mess is not necessary throughout your home or office.

Cross-Reference

Chapter 14 explains how to choose between wired and wireless connections, depending on your situation. It also explains how to network devices through the power plugs in your home or office, meaning no extra cables at all.

Chapter 15 tells how to connect devices using radio waves rather than wires, the ultimate neat and organized solution. Although wireless vendors like to show people lounging by a swimming pool reading e-mail on a laptop, connecting the den computer to your broadband router without wires is even more useful. Not as photogenic, perhaps, but greatly appreciated.

Organization

People really want to be organized, but it takes time. Once you let a small pile turn into a giant pile, either physically or electronically, attempts at organization meet more of a mental block than an actual physical problem.

With a centralized hard disk for data storage, you can place all the data files in one area, the music in another, the photos in their own section, and on and on. You can do this with folders, or make each area look like a completely separate hard drive.

Each person can keep a stash of favorite files, pictures, or songs on his or her own computer, but still put a copy on the server. This also makes a quick backup copy for recovery from accidents, such as your mouse crawling down to delete the wrong file. Or worse, overlaying a good file with a junk file with the same name. The Recycle bin on Windows won't save you from that little mistake. (Don't ask.) But having a copy on the server will bring that file back in a flash.

Backup

Computers are harsh, inanimate creatures. When you screw up, by clicking Delete instead of Rename on a context menu, computers do what you tell them to without any guilt.

People often consider backups valuable only when their entire computer crashes and burns (sometimes literally). Backups save data then, obviously, but they also work in less disastrous situations. Delete some work files because you think you don't need them anymore, then change your mind? A backup will save them.

All those photos you've been archiving? If they're only on one hard disk, and that disk fails or something else happens, those photos are gone. The MP3 files you copied from your own, legal, CDs? Sure, you can copy them again off the CDs, but wouldn't you rather have a handy backup of those music files?

Businesses particularly need backups, for internal reasons and often to comply with government regulations. Individuals may not go out of business if they lose their files. Want to face your IRS filing deadline after you realize that last year's files were on that PC you traded in for your new one? Learn to make backups.

Share files

You may not want to share your accounting files with the entire family, and you can certainly keep them private on your home server. But you may want to share photos, music files, family trees, electronic greeting cards, downloaded jokes, books online, or sound effects. You can do all that, and more, with shared, centralized storage, such as that provided by a server.

Share printers

Some people believe, and I'm one of them, that the biggest kick start to the local area network industry was the original HP LaserJet printer. Those first printers fascinated businesses as employees demanded to have their own LaserJets.

But because the price was high, sharing printers over a new-fangled network became the plan.

Today you can buy a new inkjet printer for less than you spend on replacement ink cartridges for the same printer (at least for some low-end printers), so the urge to share printers has dropped. Yet some printers, such as high-end photo printers, are far too expensive to put on every computer in the house. Besides, photo printers aren't the best things to use for school reports or business presentations. The modern wired household may have as many printers as computers. With a network and some centralized control, you can share the printing wealth with little effort and no hassle.

Security

Any computer you can get your hands on physically is not a secure computer. If you don't want to share the files on your personal computer with everyone in the house, you can put those files on a server.

Because you don't type or view a server, you can lock it up or hide it in a closet. (I've seen this, believe it or not.) And because some servers have no keyboard, mouse, monitor, or CD-ROM drive, the information inside that server can be reached only by a network user with the correct username and password.

Here's a basic guideline for public and private file storage folder on a server:

✦ Public

- Photos
- Music
- Reference

✦ Private

- Dad
- Mom
- Child-1
- Child-2
- Dog
- Finances

In the folder organization shown, everyone will have access to the Public folder and all folders contained therein. Inside the Private folder, each user will have access to the one folder set up for them and them only. Although I suppose the Finances folder can be shared among the parents only, especially when they're spending the children's inheritance.

The server operating system requires a username and password to grant access to the server resources. When, for example, Child-1 (Alex, in this case) provides the correct username and password, the server allows Alex to see all the Public folder files, but only the \Private\Child-1 folder in the Private folder. As far as Child-1 is concerned, there are no other folders in the Private folder area. Laura, Child-2, can't see the files in Alex's folder, or any of the other folders in the Private area. And I certainly don't want our dog, Hunter, to see we could afford more dog toys than we already buy him.

Do you want to lock Aunt Bessie's family reunion pictures away from the rest of the family? No, or probably not, depending on Aunt Bessie's photos. But a server makes it easy to restrict access to some folders although allowing anyone on the network to see other folders.

Capacity

Personal computers have large storage capacities, especially compared to computers from a few years ago. But when you need to add storage space, it makes the most sense, and is most cost effective, to add space everyone can use.

Servers of any sort, whether full-fledged network file servers with e-mail and Web services along with tight security, or what amounts to an extra hard disk on the network, make disk capacity available to everyone on the network. If your family generates lots of data, which happens quickly when you start using music or video files, a central file server will come in handy. It's easier to put one 120GB drive in a server than it is to add three 40GB drives to individual computers. It's also cheaper.

Media hub

Don't look now, but your TV will soon become computer network savvy. If you have a TiVo or other Personal Video Recorder (PVR), you're halfway there already.

Computer vendors aren't happy with controlling your offices at work and at home. Now they want to control the den at home as well.

High-end audio equipment now includes Ethernet connectors. You can play a DVD in computers now and pipe that video to your TV (with the right extra equipment). The computer and entertainment worlds are colliding. The "media hub" according to vendors is nothing more than a home server.

Of course, when you buy a "media hub entertainment coordinating device," you pay big bucks for the hype and label. But with a home server, you have many of the advantages of the media hub without the huge hole in your wallet.

Why You Need a Small Business Server

Home users, even the most technically advanced and gadget-laden, don't really *need* a server. They can benefit from a home server, and having one will make many things easier and more secure.

Businesses are a different story. Wasting time at home looking for a lost file or trying to replace a deleted photo just keeps you from watching more mediocre television. But losing files in a business, or losing all your files, means the end of that business more often than not.

A U.K. research report from the spring of 2003 laid out the stark details. Small businesses that lost their data due to system failures or a fire (a pretty severe system failure, but all too common), stood only a 50–50 percent chance of survival.

Lose your data systems, and your company stands only as much chance as a coin flip of surviving. Not encouraging.

Even less encouraging was the discovery that only half of small businesses had a business backup plan in place. Another flip of the coin, but one the business owners controlled.

A home-based business can generate plenty of income. A home-based business that loses all data records due to computer failure can't generate any income. The same goes for a small business outside the home. No computers in business today means no business.

Backup

Backing up Aunt Bessie's family photos is nice. Backing up the business records of Aunt Bessie's Photo Emporium is crucial.

Although the primary mover of early network installations was the HP LaserJet, I always maintained the primary benefit of a server was data backup. Centralized servers back up all the data, either manually or automatically from each computer client, and provide one location from which all backups can run. Centralized storage means centralized backup and that means data security.

Chapter 13 covers various backup options, tools, and best ways to make backups easier, but there are two critical areas, both provided by using a server, to consider now:

- ✦ Easy, reliable, regular, and automatic data backups
- ✦ Off-site storage of backed up data

If you have a small business, in your home or in another location, a server may make the difference between you being in business after a problem or throwing in the proverbial towel. Like them or not, computers run the majority of businesses today. Trusting Lady Luck with your data security will likely work out as well as trusting Lady Luck at the casino to make payroll. It might work once or twice, but in the long run the house always wins. In the data security business, the house is fraught with chaos through accidents, worms, viruses, hackers, angry employees, and disasters. That's a lot of luck to rely on to keep your business up and running.

Organization

Some people are naturally organized, and rarely lose a thing. Others are, well, organizationally immune.

Searching through piles of photos at home to find the one Aunt Bessie picture where everyone's smiling can take as long as you want. There's no deadline or time limit.

Searching through marketing images to find the one scheduled for the newspaper ad next week does have a deadline. Wasted time and lost images cost you money, as anyone in advertising will tell you. (A healthy percentage of ads are recreated because the originals disappear.) If you're not on speaking terms with neatness, a central file server will help limit your searches, and make it easier for someone else to help organize items within folders for you.

Sharing

After organizing your data, sharing your data becomes much easier. Unless you run a one-person company, company information must go to others.

Large companies spend millions on customer relationship management (CRM) applications to track and keep customers. The key for all those big buck applications? Shared information.

You can't easily share the files on your computer, because peer-to-peer file sharing breaks down as the demands for information or number of users grows. Central file servers make sharing easier, and the included security options make sharing safer, as well.

 Note Peer-to-peer networking, long popularized by Macintosh systems and Windows starting with Windows 3.11, shares resources between devices without a centralized file storage location or security authentication controls. This works reasonably well for three to four computers, but then the need for security and organization strongly recommend moving to a server of some type. It may be that one PC with a big hard disk acts as the server for the other computers on the group by providing centralized storage space and using its access sharing controls to force some level of security. But a dedicated file server is almost always more secure, more reliable, and more manageable.

Want to provide spreadsheets for quotes? Put them on a file server in read-only mode, and no one will ever again overwrite your carefully constructed sheets.

Security

Computers people can touch aren't secure. Servers can be set on a desk or shelf anywhere and still do their job, because people don't type on their keyboards or watch their monitors (if they even have any). This fact makes it easier for servers to stay hidden in locked rooms (with proper ventilation, of course).

Files on personal computers connected via basic peer-to-peer networking aren't particularly safe, either. Individual computers, especially PCs running Windows, regularly catch viruses. Individual computer users regularly delete the wrong files or overlay files by accident.

Centralized storage adds security by keeping files farther away from bumbling users, and the easy backup options on a server provide even more benefits. You can't look at security as "stopping hackers" but as any and everything that can damage data in any way.

All banks keep money in their teller cages, close to the people. But not too much money. The big money stays in the vault, with extra layers of security.

 Chapter 13 goes into quite a bit of depth on back-up devices, security, and rationalizations. But let me say here that if you don't back up your files, you will lose some sooner or later. That's a guarantee.

Capacity

Hard disk prices have dropped constantly over the past few years, and centralized file repositories make the best use of big drives. Not only are the new hard disks larger, they are faster.

One really, really big disk in a file server makes for faster file access times for everyone. Two really big disks in a file server, writing files to both disks at once (running RAID Level 0 fault tolerance), eliminate the worry of a disk failure taking your company data (and your company) down the drain.

 RAID stands for Redundant Array of Independent Disks. There are multiple levels of RAID depending on how many disks are used to store the data. The basic Level 0 fault tolerant application uses two disks in place of one, so if one disk fails, all your data remains available on the second disk.

Choosing Your Server

So you finally agreed you need a server, right? Now you just need to find the server, or at least the type of server, that will do the best job for you.

The overlap between servers for home and servers for small businesses is quite wide. Don't limit your thinking to a "home" server based on case size or initial price, or you may choose the wrong server for your job at hand.

Let me give you a quick rundown of server features, and explain how those features may help your situation:

✦ **Cost:** Low cost is attractive, but be sure and get enough server capacity to handle your situation today and through the next year or so. A good rule of thumb is to get twice as much storage as you think you need.

✦ **Performance:** Home servers generally don't need fast performance. However, if you plan to stream videos to your home theater setup, performance matters a great deal. Large file transfers need faster servers and hard disks than relatively small digital photos and documents being copied or viewed.

✦ **Upgradeability:** All-in-one devices are rarely upgradeable. If you need to buy small and upgrade, look toward a PC system with added software rather than a server device.

✦ **Wireless support:** Some servers allow client connections wirelessly. Others can plug into the network via a patch cable and service wireless clients who access the network through the wireless router. The result is similar, but wires run faster than radio waves today and probably will at least until new products appear in the year 2006 , so if performance is critical look for wired support.

✦ **Accessible over the Internet:** Some servers expect to be on the public Internet and even run Web and e-mail services. Others are private servers and don't have the security feature set to protect them from hackers.

✦ **Application host:** Some servers run applications, and some only provide centralized file and print services. If you need applications to execute at the server, such as databases for your business, make sure you choose a system that supports applications.

Go through this list, and check which features are the most important for your situation. Then I'll help explain what type of server you need based on your choices.

✦ Low initial cost

❑ Very important

❑ Somewhat important

❑ Not very important

✦ High performance

❑ Very important

❑ Somewhat important

❑ Not very important

✦ Large storage capacity

❑ Very important

❑ Somewhat important

❑ Not very important

✦ Ability to upgrade storage capacity

❑ Very important

❑ Somewhat important

❑ Not very important

✦ Capacity to be your Web and e-mail server

❑ Very important

❑ Somewhat important

❑ Not very important

✦ Option to make files available over the Internet

❑ Very important

❑ Somewhat important

❑ Not very important

✦ Direct support for wireless clients

❑ Very important

❑ Somewhat important

❑ Not very important

✦ Strong security on internal users

❑ Very important

❑ Somewhat important

❑ Not very important

✦ Strong security against outsiders on the Internet

❑ Very important

❑ Somewhat important

❑ Not very important

✦ Management control ease of use

❑ Very important

❑ Somewhat important

❑ Not very important

✦ Ability to run applications on the server

❑ Very important

❑ Somewhat important

❑ Not very important

Get through those questions okay? Good. Now the bad news: every item checked as "Very important" will cost more money. The more features, the more expense. As features pile one on top of another, the meter keeps ticking and speeds up.

The next sections appear in decreasing order of complexity. If your checklist is full of "Very important" checks, you should focus on server appliances. As the number of Very important checks go down, the further down this list you can go and still meet your needs. Or, at least the needs based on this checklist.

Now let me outline the different server types you should look at, depending on what your checklist tells us.

All-in-one server appliances

Personally, I love all-in-one server appliances for small businesses and even some home users. I've used several over the years in my home office, and think they do a pretty good job. This approval rating goes up even more now that broadband service providers do a better job of supporting home and small business networks.

The market doesn't agree with me as well as I hoped about server appliances, however, and many of the best ones over the years have disappeared. In fact, the two best ones (the Cobalt Qube and the Netwinder Rebel) are gone. The good news is that new products are approaching the quality of software from the earlier systems, and the hardware is definitely better today.

Small companies tend to appear, make a great product, then disappear as they run out of money trying to reach their market. Sometimes small good companies are bought by larger ones and killed as when Sun bought the Cobalt Qube line as part of the Cobalt rack server product line they wanted, ignored the Qube for the rack servers, then discontinued all the Cobalt products.

Toshiba Magnia

Toshiba, long relatively unknown in the server arena (great laptops), now has probably the best all-in-one server appliance out today, the Magnia. Check them out in Figure 10-1.

Figure 10-1: Reigning all-in-one appliance champ, according to me.

Go to magnia.Toshiba.com and click the Magnia picture to find this screen. Automated Web sites like Toshiba uses create some incredibly long and ugly URLs.

You can't tell even with the zoomed-in picture, but the case is metal and feels like a tank. The 16 × 2 LCD screen helps with status information during use and particularly during installation.

The Toshiba Magnia includes several excellent features:

✦ Wireless option with addition of PC card (extra $100 when ordered through Toshiba even though this is the same type of PC card you plug into a laptop).

✦ No routing features, but it can be used for a firewall through a dedicated Ethernet connection.

✦ Dial-backup option with addition of PC card modem for second PC card slot so the server can dialup your service provider if the cable/DSL service stops.

✦ Dual disk drives auto mirror of all data with scheduled disk-to-disk copy much like RAID Level 0 for fault tolerance.

✦ Number of Virtual Private Networks (VPNs) to remote sites limited only by load on the system. Most large companies force users connecting from home to use a secure and encrypted Virtual Private Network to link back to the office.

✦ Outstanding internal-use portal with excellent templates for documents, images, and photos makes it easy for small businesses or overly organized home users to present information.

✦ Provides all the network configuration details, such as IP address, for other devices on the network (Dynamic Host Configuration Protocol).

✦ One-click method to download all e-mail from service provider and make it available internally on the Magnia.

Overall quality of the administrative tools, reached via Web browser, outclass all others on the market today. The clearly defined screens contain logical features based on their headings, and warn you when you're drilling down into something that can get complicated.

The Magnia 30 has a 1.2 GHz Intel Celeron processor, and the Magnia 25 has an Intel Celeron running at 566 MHz. That appears to be about the only difference between the two units.

One great advantage of the Toshiba software is the ability to send backup files offsite to a remote File Transfer Protocol (FTP) server. You can also send them anywhere else on the local network the Toshiba can access, but the offsite option gains major points for Toshiba and their thoughtfulness.

Tech Bits File Transfer Protocol (FTP) is a rock-solid method of putting files on a remote server or getting files from a remote server. This protocol does the undercover transfer work when you download files using your Web browser.

Judging the high-end features, Magnia includes an e-mail server that collects e-mail from the Internet and makes it available to your client computer but not a public Web server. Backups can be done offsite, a huge plus for business users. Not a complete 10, but pretty close.

Pricing (as I write this) ranges from pretty good to almost high. The Magnia 25 goes for $899 without the wireless option, and the Magnia 30 goes for $1499 without the wireless option. Add $100 to each price for the wireless card. This puts the Toshiba pricing in a strongly competitive range for the features it includes.

Procom Taurus

Some products and their companies disappear (like Rebel and their Netwinder), some get eaten (as Sun gobbled and discontinued Cobalt) and some products get a second chance after the company disappears.

The Procom Technology (www.procom.com) Taurus is an upgrade of an earlier system by Celestix. Hard to miss the distinctive shape and the large LCD screen that you can see in Figure 10-2.

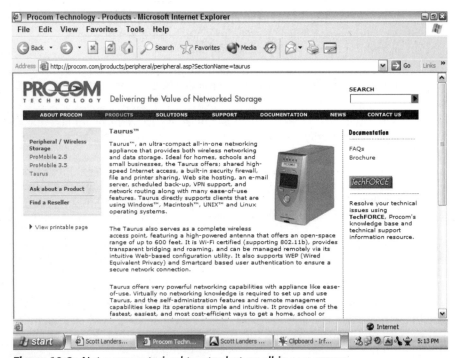

Figure 10-2: Not a computerized toaster but an all-in-one server.

A complete Web and e-mail server suitable for Internet use, the Procom Taurus also includes Wi-Fi support. In fact, the company calls it "wireless storage" as much as an all-in-one server. If you want to create your own Web pages, and make them available for the world of Internet users to see, the Procom Taurus will support you. But I suggest using a Web hosting service until you feel comfortable handling the security necessary to host a Web server and keep it safe from hackers.

The biggest problem connecting new network devices in many cases is aligning an existing computer or network with the new device's IP address assigned at the factory. You have to redo your computer, isolate any servers providing addresses, and then plug in the new device. Then you must change the device and, oh well, the whole process awaits in the Connecting Network Devices section just ahead.

Procom's Taurus skips that painful step, because the front LCD screen lets you set the IP address before you plug the unit into your network. Major headache relief, believe me.

When I tested this box, I set the IP address and then placed the Taurus in between my cable modem and my lab network. In just a few seconds the unit configured itself for the cable modem broadband connection and passed traffic from my PC out to the Internet.

Of course, equipment that becomes the primary firewall for a network should offer some strong management screens, details, settings, and reports. Alas, the Procom Taurus takes the "too simple" way out, giving too little information and too few configuration options.

The e-mail server offers only basic information, but the Web server seems more capable. You can host multiple Web sites on the box, handy for small businesses with multiple ventures. If you're Alex of Alex's Financial Planning and of Alex's CPA Services, you can have two separate Web sites on the same Procom Taurus unit. But remember my concern about security when you host your own Web server.

Pricing ranges from about $1,700 for an Intel Celeron 1.2 GHz processor, 512MB RAM, and a 40GB hard drive to $2,350 for a unit with a 250GB disk. Only resellers and a few online shops carry the unit, so you may have to look around.

Other choices

The EmergeCore IT-100 (www.emergecore.com) advertises itself as a complete "IT Department in a box" but one must always be wary of brightly colored advertising. Following much the same road as the Procom Taurus, the EmergeCore IT-100 offers Web and e-mail servers, firewalls for placing the unit between your network and the Internet, VPNs, and some rudimentary security settings.

Lacking wireless support and coming with only 128MB of RAM and a 40GB disk, the initial version of the EmergeCore doesn't stack up well in the statistics department. It does, however, transfer files faster than any server appliance I ever tested.

Available through resellers at a listed price of $1,400, the EmergeCore IT-100 leans heavily on easy management (but incomplete) and some Web-creation software for marketing traction. But in the hands of a good reseller to configure it properly and integrate into a company network, it can be worth the money.

A new unit I have yet to test could be the killer product of the market segment, it if lives up to the hype. Axentra Corporation (www.axentra.com) touts their new H-25 Multifunction Server Appliance with the longest list of features in the market, surpassing even the Toshiba Magnia.

Of course, seeing (and testing) is believing, but the Axentra makes the following promises:

✦ Broadband routing, content filtering, and firewall security

✦ Web server(s)

✦ E-mail server with spam controls

✦ Universal plug and play for easy installation

✦ Wi-Fi wireless with 802.11g as well as 802.11b (with purchase of optional USB wireless adapter)

✦ Print server (parallel port and USB)

✦ Web e-mail client, publishing, and address book

✦ MySQL open-source database

✦ Bonus Web designing software

All these features supposedly cram into a box about the size of a big book that weighs less than 5 pounds. Great if they can make it work.

The best part: $499 retail, and already available just after release at one online store for $450. Add the USB wireless adapter from the same online store and you will still be in the $500 neighborhood. For an all-in-one server with these features, that neighborhood is still very small and new.

Network-attached storage units

The term, Network Attached Storage (NAS) describes exactly what the units are. They are stand-alone appliances that connect via Ethernet to a network and act as a central file repository. They may sit by the router within a patch cable's reach, or you can use HomePlug connections and place them anywhere

 Cross-Reference See Chapter 14 for more on HomePlug devices.

There is a difference between a NAS and an all-in-one server like the Toshiba and others in the previous section. The servers include more service applications, such as Web and e-mail servers, than a NAS. The NAS clearly limits what it will do: It will share storage on a network with approved users. A NAS trades sophistication of applications for the brute force of buckets of disk space.

Small NAS units today are 120GBs, and some vendors make NAS boxes with tera-bytes of disk space. A bit overboard for homes and small businesses, but one can never tell how many photos Aunt Bessie will snap. If it ranges into the hundreds of gigabytes, there are affordable NAS boxes to support Aunt Bessie's work.

It seems, at least for the low-end Small Office Home Office (SOHO) boxes, just providing storage space isn't enough. Many of the new NAS boxes also act as cable/DSL routers. Another company adds a print server and removable disk trays to add storage quickly and easily.

This market should thrill all buyers. Vendors are adding features and dropping prices with each new product.

Kanguru iNAS-100

Yes, the spelling is correct. The Kanguru Solutions (www.kanguru.com) company offers a wide range of external disk drives, readers, CD-ROM and DVD writers, and other interesting products. The company recently delivered its first NAS and it made a strong impression when I reviewed it.

First, it's pretty small. Figure 10-3 doesn't show it in comparison to anything, but the box is not much bigger than many of the cable modems in use today.

Second, look at the small LCD screen. Only 16 characters on two lines, but they help, and they make some setups easier.

Figure 10-3: Small, clever, handy.

Third, the Kanguru is a full-fledged cable/DSL broadband router, including firewall protection and all the other bells and whistles. Every feature of routers covered already in this book exists in the iNAS-100.

And unlike the other NAS devices, the Kanguru iNAS-100 makes it easy to access files across the Internet. The only caveat is its relatively high price in the market now, but prices have a way of drifting lower as competition increases. The 120GB version has a street price of around $600, the 200GB version is around $750, and the 250GB unit is around $850.

The feature of the Kanguru that puts it above the other NAS devices in this chapter is its remote file access. Although not a modifiable Web server, the Kanguru sports a Web interface for remote management and remote file access. Remember the little LCD screen on the front? That shows the current IP address assigned by your broadband service provider, especially handy on those connections where the service provider reboots during the night and your IP address changes. Put that IP address in your Web browser, connect to the Kanguru, and drill down to files as shown in Figure 10-4.

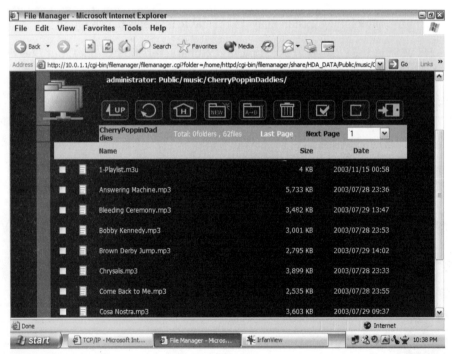

Figure 10-4: The file access screen from the Kanguru (yes, the music files are legal).

 Tech Bits Anytime you leave a server on the Internet, your passwords must be far more difficult to guess than your birthday or your spouse's name. Mix lower and upper case letters and numbers in a password at least seven characters long.

Grabbing files remotely makes life much easier for those who travel, even if just from home to office. Other systems later in the book make this possible as well, but each vendor adds its own flavor, and the Kanguru offers one of the better solutions.

Knowing that the target market is for less-technical home and small business, Kanguru makes the initial setup and configuration simple. Every vendor pays lip service to that, but the iNAS-100 displays the Quick Configuration screen shown in Figure 10-5 the first time the new owner connects to the administration screen.

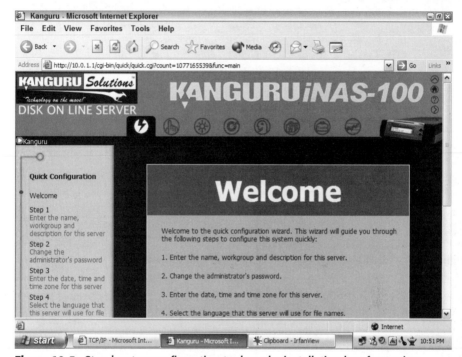

Figure 10-5: Step by step configuration tools make installation less frustrating.

Tritton ASA1120 and brethren and cousin IOGear

One of the true low-cost leaders in this market, the Tritton Technologies (www.trittonsales.com) company offers well-equipped NAS boxes for a retail of $329. The street price? About $270 for the NAS120 with 120GBs of disk storage, and the ASA1120 is $322 (street) with its excellent cable/DSL router, VPN, and firewall.

The physical case and administration screens for the Tritton ASAP I reviewed and the IOGear BOSS (the name comes from Broadband Office Storage Server) lead me to the unalterable conclusion the same manufacturer is making both systems. I don't know who makes the box for whom, but Tritton appeared first and has a wide range of products based on the same fundamental case and Linux-based operating system.

Take a look at Figure 10-6 to see what I mean about the Tritton product lineup. This doesn't prove they make the box, but it strongly hints to me they are closer to the manufacturing process than IOGear is.

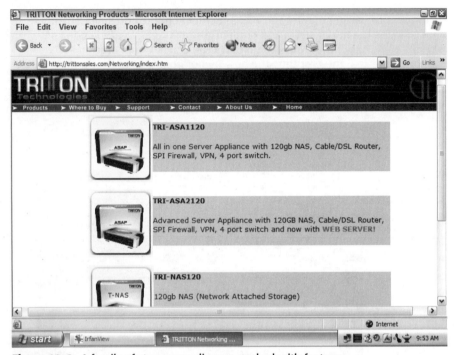

Figure 10-6: A family of storage appliances packed with features.

The street price for the ASA2120 is about $360, and that model includes a public Web server. There is a disclaimer about trying to make this a heavyweight e-commerce server, but most Web sites use static pages full of brochure-ware anyway, and this unit should be just fine for that.

SnapAppliance SnapServers

Perhaps the originator of the SOHO NAS, the Snap company started, was bought, and then later freed itself to be independent once again. It still has a huge market share on the low end with SOHO buyers, but is expanding on the top end as well.

SnapAppliance makes one of the smartest moves in this market by including client back-up software with the Workgroup product line. It also provides ways to synchronize data between various SnapAppliances. Being one of the early market entrants has given SnapAppliance a long history and plenty of time to upgrade software.

Their Web browser administration shows the care and long development. The range of client file systems supported, including Windows, Linux, Unix, Macintosh, and NetWare clients adds to their versatility. Figure 10-7 shows the SnapAppliance Network Settings information page.

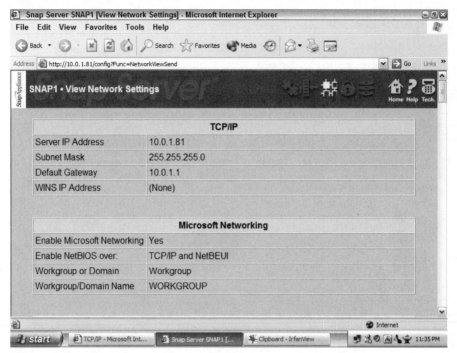

Figure 10-7: Information overview pages help you monitor appliances.

The SnapAppliance 1100 travels easily, and they suggest you unplug it and put it in your briefcase for easy transport. The company's reputation helps it maintain a substantial market share even through its prices are higher for pure NAS-only devices. Street price for the SnapAppliance 1100 with an 80GB disk is around $535, and the 160GB disk is around $780.

Linksys EFG80 and EFG120

One of the biggest names in home and small business wireless, HomePlug, and router products, Linksys (www.Linksys.com) offers expandability and strong administration to the NAS market. Now a division of Cisco Systems, Inc., the friendly rounded shapes of products have been "corporatized" as you can see in Figure 10-8.

The EFG80 on the right is a bit bigger than a shoe box. The EFG120 on the left is about the size of a VCR, although one of the newer VCRs that isn't as wide as they used to be.

It's tough to see in the small pictures, but both products place their disk drive in a tray. You can remove the disk drive, or upgrade the disk to a larger one (the 120GB drive can bump up to 250GB, and the 80GB drive bumps up to 120GB). Adding a second disk jumps the storage capacity, and you can replace the original Disk 1 if you want to have as much as 500GB with the EFG120 unit when fully expanded.

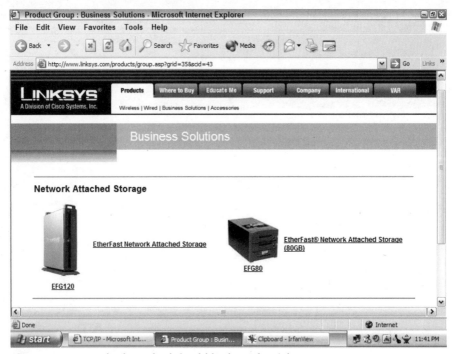

Figure 10-8: New look on the left, old look on the right.

Some of you are wondering how the Linksys operating system survives the replacement of the primary disk that ships with the unit. Good question, and that would be a problem, normally. But Linksys engineers built its operating system into a ROM chip and placed that on the system motherboard. When the unit gets power, the chip wakes and supplies the necessary information to the disk drive(s) as they boot.

Linksys also includes a print server on its NAS boxes. There isn't enough administration and control over the print server, but it does come in handy at times.

Are these the only NAS appliances? Absolutely not. But many of the others lean toward the high end, far outside the budget of home and small business customers. And it appears there will be more vendors, rather than fewer, as hard drive prices drop and users realize the value of NAS appliances.

Turning an old computer into a server

What do you do with an old personal computer? You can always turn it into a server for the rest of the computers on the network.

You might wonder if an old computer, too old to handle the applications you need to run, can be useful as a file server. Absolutely. The reason you upgraded your computer was because the demands of the operating system's graphical user interface grew too heavy. That, and the applications gained in size and complexity and you got tired of waiting for screen updates.

I promise your file speed had nothing to do with changing your computer. Even a fairly old computer can make a good file server. And with the prices of hard disks dropping still, putting a 120GB disk into an old computer to turn it into a file server will cost around a $100. Depending on the type of software you want, that and a few minutes of configuration time may be all you spend on the system.

Using Windows networking

All versions of Microsoft Windows since Windows 3.11 for Networks include the ability to share resources with other computers on the network. It's not great networking, and it's not particularly secure networking, but with the right configuration it will work pretty well.

One big advantage of making an extra computer the new centralized server is that no one will be using the server machine for regular day-to-day work. When you don't ask Windows to do anything on a computer except share some files, its reliability goes up considerably.

Windows XP Home and XP Professional make sharing files easier than ever. They even provide a Shared Documents folder front and center whenever you open My Computer. Figure 10-9 shows the Sharing Document Properties dialog box open for the Shared Documents folder.

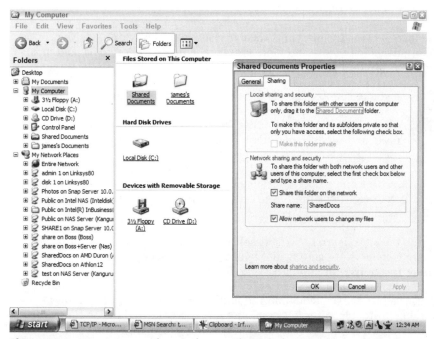

Figure 10-9: You can open the window on the right by going through Sharing and Security or through Properties.

The explanations in the dialog box work well. Check the first box, in the middle of the dialog box, to share the Shared Documents folder. Microsoft does well to tell you other users of that computer will see that folder, as will everyone using Windows networking protocols on your network.

Notice the second check box under the Share name text box? Microsoft gives you two options for file access: read-only, or read/write. That's how computer people put it, but Microsoft includes the nontechnical explanation. They don't do a good job explaining that the first Share check box will only let people read the files as supposed to make changes, but you can't get everything when you are dealing with software.

Similarly, shared printers attached to this computer will be seen by the network users as well. This set up makes it easy to share a printer around the network by hanging one off your old system.

Using Linux

Don't think this Linux reference comes from left field, because it doesn't. Every network appliance discussed earlier in this chapter uses some type of Linux operating system. And why shouldn't they? They get a great operating system, well developed and well tested, for next to nothing when they follow one of the license arrangements used by developers.

I can't describe how to take a Linux distribution and turn an old PC into a file server in the space I have here. There are many books on Linux and servers, but you may not have to have any of them.

People just like you dig into Linux regularly and come away excited. New distributions include more and more graphical administration tools, and most jobs in Linux are now just as mouse-oriented as Windows.

 Tech Bits If you're curious Linux and want help investigating the hottest operating system in the past decade, you're welcome to buy and read *Red Hat Linux 9 Bible* by Christopher Negus. I did, and the included Red Hat disks and other applications means you save money buying the book rather than buying Red Hat directly.

One old PC with a Linux operating system can become your Web, e-mail, and file server. Linux doesn't lack for power, or Google wouldn't use Linux on PCs to run its giant search engines and Web sites.

If you don't want to learn Linux yourself, check around the neighborhood. More and more teenagers are getting into Linux. The old cliché about asking the kid next door to set up your computer is no longer farfetched.

Linux uses a program called SAMBA to implement the Microsoft Windows networking protocols. After it is configured, you may never have to touch the Linux server again, especially if you're just sharing files. Even when running full Web and e-mail services, you'll find that Linux systems stay up and running longer than any Windows systems you've ever seen or even heard about.

Setting Up Users and Disk Shares

Although the term "network administrator" may sound scary because of all the syllables, modern server and storage appliances make user setup pretty easy. Two or three steps are all you need to worry about.

Corporate networks include plenty of file and resource access options with increasing granularity down to the point I can lock you out of an individual file every Thursday from noon to 1:27 P.M. if I want. But homes and small businesses don't need that level of control (if anyone really does at all, anyway).

For each server or storage appliance, you need to perform the following steps:

✦ Define the user (or let everyone access it)

✦ Define whether the user can modify files or just read them

✦ Include users in a group (optional)

As you can see in the first bullet, you can define an appliance as open to everyone, and everyone can use that file system. Technically, you allow guest users to have full access. The users don't even have to provide a name or password because the device accepts everyone who makes a connection.

Security, obviously, comes from different angles. If you and your spouse have a home office together, locking each other out of folders won't be part of the plan. Some storage devices may be completely open for sharing whereas others on the network are restricted to certain users. You have control.

Setting up users and groups

The Kanguru iNAS-100s administration screen provides a nice overview of all the things you can do with users. Figure 10-10 shows the main user control screen reached by clicking the user icon (funny little head) highlighted at the top of the screenshot.

You probably won't care about some items in the list, but they illustrate the flexibility and features of the iNAS-100. Notice the NFS Setting item? That supports sharing file systems between Unix and Linux computers to make remote file systems as available as local disks. Handy for some, but not many SOHOs include peer-to-peer Unix networking.

The minimum you must provide for each user is a username (all one word with no nonalphanumeric characters) and a password. Figure 10-11 shows the Linksys NAS user setup screen.

You enter the following information for users:

✦ **Name:** Use a short, one-word name that includes letters and numbers only.

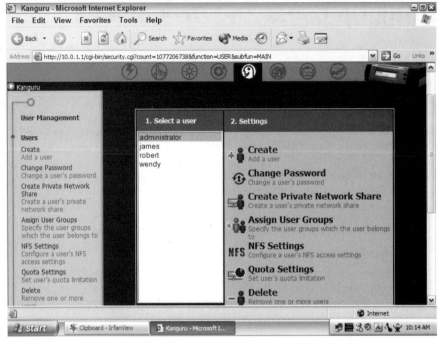

Figure 10-10: User control for the Kanguru NAS.

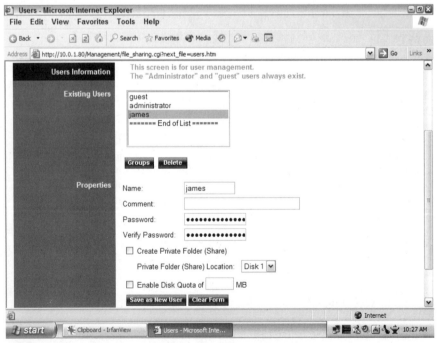

Figure 10-11: User setup and optional configuration details.

✦ **Comment:** Not all systems have this, but it's handy when you have more users to manage.

✦ **Password:** The best passwords have at least seven characters, including numbers, letters, and symbols like $ or *.

✦ **Private folder:** This option is not available on all systems, but gives each user a private space on the storage or server device.

✦ **Disk quota:** This option is not available on all systems, but it's handy when you manage a large group of users and some are digital packrats.

Group inclusion may happen during user creation or you may have to go to a Groups screen to add users to groups. Relying on groups, especially as you get more users, makes management faster and less error-prone. By using groups, you can define the parameters for a group, such as Sales, and every time you add a new salesperson you just plop the person into that group. All the rules and settings you defined for the group automatically apply to the new user in the group, such as allowing them access to the Inventory folder but blocking them from viewing files in the Payroll folder.

In Figure 10-12, you can see the Linksys screen that allows groups access to the disk volumes.

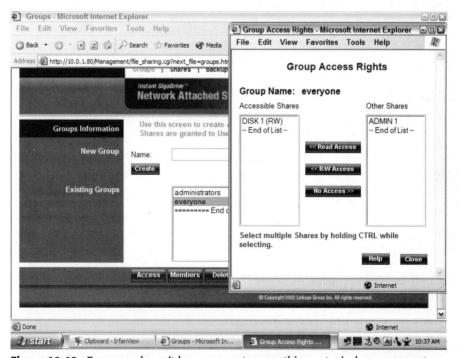

Figure 10-12: Everyone doesn't have access to everything, a typical arrangement.

The Group Access Rights dialog box that pops up when you click the Access command button at the bottom of the screen shows that the group Everyone does not have access to the Admin 1 volume. You can tell by the command buttons between the two lists that groups can have access or not to disk shares, or just read access, or read/write access (the RW Access command button).

Every setting you can make for a group you can make for an individual user. But as your user list grows, taking advantage of groups of users with like access profiles will save you time and prevent you from forgetting a setting for a new user.

Managing disks

Server and storage appliances don't make a big fuss over disk volumes. You can usually leave the entire disk as one big space and carve it up into multiple network shares for organization.

Tech Bits   A volume is a logical storage unit that can be a portion of a single disk or span multiple disks. A share is allowing access to a resource, which in this case, is a folder on a disk.

Vendors handle multiple disk volumes in two ways. First, they can let you allocate a certain amount of space for that volume, and keep track of that space. When you reach the limit of that volume, you're full.

Second, they can ignore the space used per volume, and let the disk space fill up as it gets used. If one volume had 80 percent of the allocated space and the other one has only 20 percent, that's fine. System feedback, such as the free space notation in a directory display, shows the total amount of space on the physical volume.

Setting shares

Low-end NAS and server appliances have a single disk with a single volume. The way to allocate disk space among users and groups is generally through the network share.

Tech Bits   A share in Microsoft networking is a name given to a folder on a hard disk allowing access to that folder and all subfolders. Users cannot move up the file tree and see the parent folder of the shared folder.

Making a network share on a server or storage appliance looks much like making it on a Windows computer:

+ Specify which folder to share
+ Provide a name for the share unique to that host
+ Tell the operating system to share it
+ Add any user restrictions

Figure 10-13 shows the New Network Share screen for the SnapAppliance 1100. Add a name, pick the folder, make a comment if you want, and allow everyone access or make special access arrangements on the next screen. Okay, it may be slightly more complicated than on a Windows system, but not much.

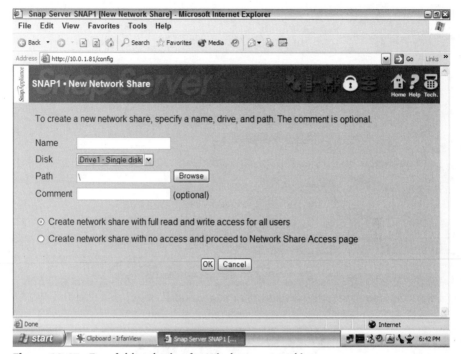

Figure 10-13: Easy folder sharing for Windows networking.

Network shares are assigned under the Security page of the SnapAppliance. After logging in as the Administrator, go to Security ➪ Network Shares and click the New command button for adding a network share. Other buttons let you modify, change who can access them, or delete existing shares.

You can see the shares your Windows PC has connections to by going to Network Neighborhood in Windows 9x or My Network Places in Windows XP.

Disk maintenance

Server and storage appliances include more disk maintenance tools than most personal computer operating systems, but not so much as to be confusing. The Linksys NAS boxes have the most disk maintenance information on one screen, so that's why the Disk Settings page from Linksys is in Figure 10-14.

The Linksys unit is the only one of the storage appliances that offers scheduled disk maintenance. Notice the time settings for Scandisk and Defrag. The drop-down box that says Never in Figure 10-14 offers a schedule to run either utility every day, or any one day you choose.

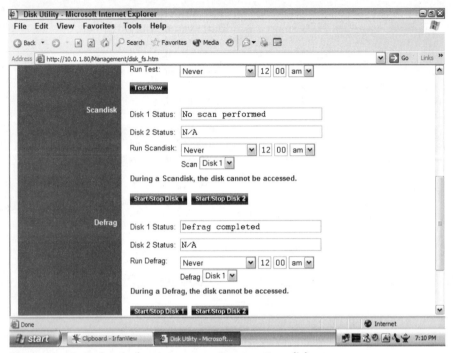

Figure 10-14: Defrag is done, no reason to run a Scandisk now.

Connecting Network Devices

Every network device connects to the network slightly differently, but there are more common configuration steps than different steps. These are the common steps:

1. Set an IP address or tell the system how to get one.
2. Name the device, if applicable.
3. Set the workgroup name for Windows networking.
4. Coordinate wireless channels, if applicable.

Four easy steps, right? If all goes well, the steps are easy, logical, and foolproof. But in technology, as in real life, things don't always go exactly right. So let me show you a few examples of connecting appliances to your network and explain where things may go awry.

Server and storage appliances

Adding a new server or storage appliance to your network requires a bit of planning and several jumps through some networking hoops. The hoops are caused by the vendors being forced to guess whether their appliance is the first server on the network, or you already have an appliance and theirs is an add-on.

The details for Dynamic Host Configuration Protocol (DHCP) are in Chapter 12, but let me hit the high spots now. *DHCP* is a software server that runs on a server of some type and allocates IP addresses to all devices on the network when they ask for information. Systems that ask a DHCP server for an address are called DHCP clients. Many server devices include this capability.

But vendors have no way of knowing whether you already have a DHCP server on your network. If you do, they should (perhaps) set their box to be a DHCP client. If you don't, however, making the new device the DHCP server makes much more sense, and eases network configuration. Unfortunately, you must make the decision before the system connects to the network.

So begins the installation dance. Commonly, the sequence looks like this:

1. Read the Quick Start Guide and see that the box doesn't match your network address scheme.

2. Connect this box and one client to a wiring hub.

3. Configure your PC (vendors almost always demand a PC) to be a DHCP client.

4. Start the box; then start the PC.

5. Make connection from your PC to the new box and start the configuration process.

6. Set the IP address or the DHCP client or server settings depending on your network.

7. Reboot the new appliance.

8. Reboot your PC to change the network address to match that of the newly configured appliance.

9. Verify that the settings match your network.

10. Cross your fingers and hook the new appliance and your PC to the network and start all devices.

A bit disjointed, and certainly not a three-beat waltz, but that's the dance.

Sometimes the dance is shorter. If the appliance really is the first server-type object on the network, the vendor's configuration may well work for you. In that case, you keep the vendor's IP address range and let the new appliance be the DHCP server.

If you already have a DHCP server, such as the router between your cable/DSL modem and your internal network, you must configure the new appliance to become a DHCP client. Or, you may want the new device to take over all the DHCP server chores. Or, you may need to give your new appliance a specific IP address that it will use all the time but not provide DHCP services to other network systems.

This does sound more complicated than it really is. Figure 10-15 shows the Linksys NAS setup. In this case, the NAS has its own IP address, and will not provide DHCP services.

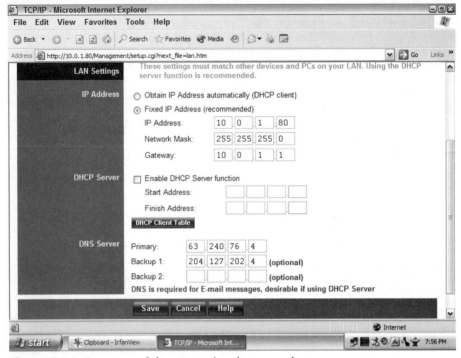

Figure 10-15: Two steps of the connection dance are done.

Personally, I prefer giving all the servers their own IP addresses because it makes it easier to connect to them to run their utility software. If you let a DHCP server give them new addresses, it can be hard to find them on the network. Hard as in nearly impossible, but if you know their IP addresses you can put the URLs in your bookmarks list.

There can be two or more DHCP servers on a network for fault tolerance and to keep addresses available if one server goes down. The trick is to assign the IP address ranges provided by the two servers so they do not overlap.

Now let me show you the Kanguru iNAS-100, which is the DHCP server for one of the lab networks. Figure 10-16 shows the Kanguru screen that matches the Linksys screen in the previous figure.

Notice the assigned IP address for the Kanguru NAS: 10.0.1.1. That's the first address in the network because .0 is reserved and can't be used. Many network administrators put their routers at .1 for every network as a matter of policy, and because it makes them easy to find on the networks.

Yes, the Kanguru NAS is also the router and the gateway, one of its nice features. It uses Network Address Translation (NAT) to hide the internal network IP addresses from the outside. More on that trick in Chapter 12.

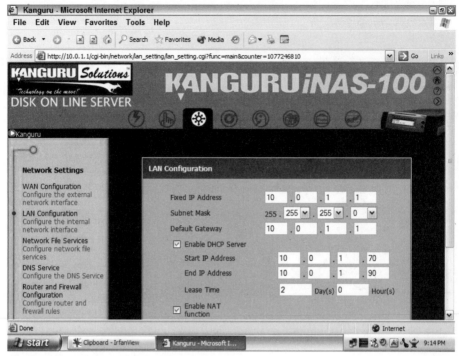

Figure 10-16: The network DHCP server.

Routers

Network routers have to work in two directions: the internal network like the one provided by the Kanguru router in the previous section, and the broadband network provided by your broadband service provider. In very real terms, the Internet comes all the way down to the cable/DSL modem and through to the WAN plug on your router.

Let me show you router connections to a cable broadband provider, then to a DSL broadband provider. The Kanguru NAS/router connects to the cable modem provided by Comcast. This is interesting but easy, because Comcast provides the information to the routers via DHCP. See how nicely the explanations dovetail in this section?

The IP addresses shown in Figure 10-17 all come from Comcast. When the router connects to the cable modem, it asks for network information (DHCP client). The cable modem, under control of the head-end, assigns an IP address and other details to the router.

I put in none of these IP addresses because they all came from Comcast. The top entry, Specify MAC address, adds another layer of security by allowing only preconfigured routers with a known MAC address (an internal number for the

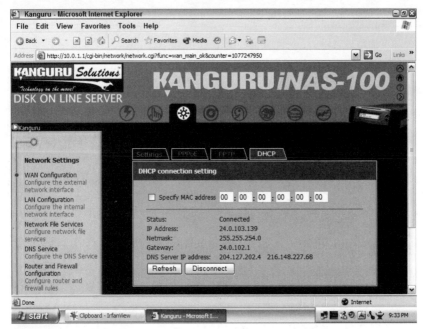

Figure 10-17: The Kanguru router as DHCP client to a cable modem.

Ethernet connection which can't be changed) to connect to the network. A bit of security overkill for a suburban cable modem connection, but useful in some areas or corporate remote sites with increased security needs.

The picture looks a bit different on a DSL router connection. On the network with the DSL modem to SBC Yahoo! DSL, the Linksys WRV54G wireless broadband router must use Point-to-Point Protocol over Ethernet (PPPoE) which requires a username and password.

Figure 10-18 shows the Linksys Internet setup screen. My username and password go from the router to the DSL modem to the central office for verification before I get connected. My setting says to stay connected all the time, and as you can see at the bottom of Figure 10-18, this router also provides DHCP service for the internal network.

DHCP and PPPoE are the two most common router connections used in the United States. Both work reliably and reconnect quickly and automatically whenever the service hiccups and resets the cable/DSL modem at your home or office. Because the internal network IP addresses remain separate from the Internet IP addresses from the broadband service provider, those reconnects do nothing to your computers and other network devices.

Wireless Webcam

Earlier I made reference to, and even showed a picture from, a wireless Webcam from Linksys (Chapter 1). Let me show you how I hooked that up to the network.

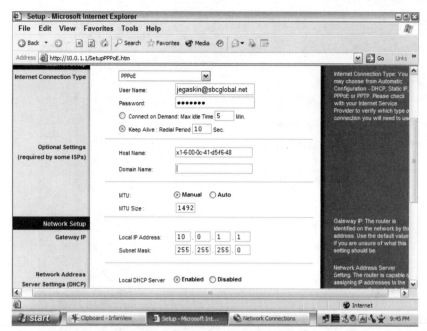

Figure 10-18: The DSL and Linksys version of the Kanguru and cable information in the previous screenshot.

This chore required a typically complicated connection dance, because I had to connect the Webcam over Ethernet to perform the initial system configuration, then make all the wireless links later. That's why I said attaching some network devices requires you to redo your network connections and IP addresses at least twice in most cases.

Configuring the Webcam itself wasn't all that hard, because the Linksys software searches for the intelligence in the camera and makes the link. Figure 10-19 shows the setup software and one of the primary installation screens for the Webcam.

Remember I said you have to name almost all the devices you add to the network? Here I provided the name for the Webcam. On the screen after this one I clicked the Automatic Configuration DHCP button to tell the camera to ask for an address from the DHCP server.

Telling the camera to be a DHCP client takes care of the IP addressing issues, but I still need to configure another setting to make the camera work wirelessly. The Service Set Identifier (SSID), essentially a name used in the header of data packets going over a wireless network to help identify which network each packet belongs to, must be provided.

Figure 10-20 shows the fill-in value of the SSID. I used my daughter's name because she stole my wife's laptop and uses it in the den while watching TV. Because she's the one using the wireless network most of the time, I figured giving her naming rights was only fair.

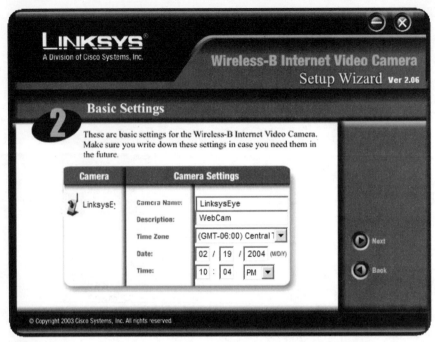

Figure 10-19: The Linksys "name the device" screen for the Webcam.

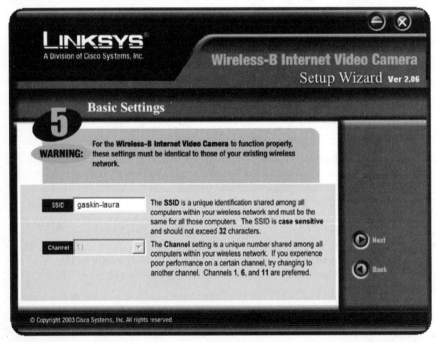

Figure 10-20: Adding the second step of the connection dance, this time for the wireless link.

The SSID doesn't provide any security protection, because the name goes over the wireless network as plain text, but most vendors force you to have something in the SSID field. Anyone using minimal security-bypassing software can get this information. Security details for wireless networks are coming up in Chapter 16.

After all the details are taken care of, the Webcam can capture images and send them winging wirelessly around the house. Handy to keep pointed out the front window when I'm expecting a FedEx delivery.

Server Security

After you include a server of some type in your home or small business network, your security headaches go up. Placing all your critical files in one spot, one advantage of a server, makes it more important to protect those files in that one spot.

Physical security

As I mentioned, if someone can physically touch your computer, that computer no longer has any security whatsoever. You may not be talking about state secrets on your home server, but you don't want the files stolen or destroyed.

If you have the flexibility in your small business, take some of these simple precautions to keep your server or storage appliances safe from accident:

+ Keep it away from crowded areas.

+ Lock it up, if possible.

+ Put it in an area with linoleum or wood floors rather than carpet to guard against static.

+ Make sure employees know it is not available for any other use, particularly when it's an old computer transformed into a server.

Blocking hackers

Every computer visible to the Internet must repel hackers. The great value that NAT support added to router functions is that they hide internal computers and make them invisible on the Internet.

Not only does NAT keep your internal addresses blocked from those snooping around on the Internet, the internal addresses suggested by vendors are prohibited from Internet use at all. The following network addresses will not be passed onto the Internet by any router:

+ 10.x.x.x

+ 172.16.x.x

+ 192.168.x.x

That's the reason vendors almost always assign one of these network addresses, usually either the 10.x.x.x or 192.168.x.x to their equipment. The trend in consumer and small business equipment seems to be to use the 192.168.x.x network address, but equipment for large company use tends to be in the 10.x.x.x range. Neither address will ever be seen on the Internet, so no hacker can try to focus in on your personal computer using an IP address of 192.168.1.23 inside your firewall with NAT enabled.

Cross-Reference Look for much more about hackers and security in Chapters 12 and 16.

Backup planning

Too often people cross their fingers and assume that because they have files copied to a file server of some type, their backup duties are over. Sorry, but that attitude will come crashing around your ears one day soon if that's your only backup plan.

Hard disks fail. Folders full of important files drop out of memory and get left on a retired computer. Critical CDs full of valuable files get lost behind desks.

Adding a server or storage appliance just increases your need for a good backup. Luckily, the centralized storage makes backup easier in many ways. But you must include backup tools in your server or storage appliance budget.

Even if you use RAID Level 0 for fault tolerance to keep your data available if one drive fails, you still need backups. Why? Because when you delete a file, it gets deleted from both disks. That means if you delete the wrong file you will really wish you had read Chapter 13.

Summary

Someday you will want a home server. Someday you will need a small business server. This chapter explained many of the features and benefits of a server or storage appliance for home or business.

Using the servers and storage devices on my own lab networks, for examples, I covered many of the installation and connection issues that beginning networks face on a regular basis. Drilling a little deeper, I showed you several ways to manage users on server or storage appliances.

What You Need to Know About Desktop Networking

You need to know some things about desktop networking that you don't really want to know. Sorry about that. I will try and slip in details now and then during installations and explanations so it doesn't feel like protocol school.

If something doesn't work immediately when you follow the instructions in various chapters, you may have a network issue. Issues concerning operating system configuration changes to support networking are discussed in this chapter, and you can find them based on your client operating system. If the information here doesn't work, flip over to Chapters 18 or 19 and keep digging.

This chapter should be considered a reference chapter, like a collection of frequently asked questions or an encyclopedia. Sitting down to read this chapter like a book, word after word after word, might be a bit dry.

Imagine home and small business networking like that silly song we all sang as kids where the "knee bone's connected to the thigh bone" and you'll get the most important part. Your broadband provider delivers broadband in the form of a connection on your cable/DSL modem. You connect that to your router with a short Ethernet patch cable (almost always). You connect your computer to the router, with another patch cable or radio waves with wireless networking.

You connect your server (if you have one) to your router as well, usually with a wire of some type but sometimes wirelessly. Even when the devices don't physically touch via wires, they are connected. And that's how a Web page comes from the Internet to your screen, by crossing all the connections between your service provider and your computer.

The physical part of the network follows the rules for Ethernet, which is a shared-medium (one long cable electrically called a bus) network with collision detection (when two computers "talk" at once, just like people interrupting each other, they stop for a second) and collision avoidance (one person lets the other person speak first). These rules apply even when talking about wireless networks, were there are no wires.

The software part of the network provides the organization. Network devices can be both servers (they offer something to other network users) and clients (they use resources from other network devices). Again, just like people, you can have dedicated servers (those who always provide resources to others) and takers who never share anything.

Here's a quick list of the types of settings every network-attached device will need, more or less. Servers won't have Winipcfg is specific to Windows 9x/ME, and wireless devices have another group of settings to handle:

✦ **Network adapter:** An Ethernet adapter comes standard with all modern personal computers. If your system doesn't have one, you can attach a network connector to the USB port, or connect a wireless network adapter to the system.

✦ **IP address:** Every connected device needs one. It can be set on the device or provided by a server using Dynamic Host Control Protocol.

✦ **Workgroup or domain name:** Small networks with only one or two servers don't need a fancy directory service to track each user, so I will concentrate on workgroup computing. So every device must be configured with the name of their workgroup to connect to the network.

✦ **Password:** If you have a one-person network with no access from outside, maybe you don't need a password. If you have more than one person able to reach your network resources, they need passwords. If your computer can be seen across the network, it needs a password.

Inexpensive Routers with NAT Support

There is no one "cure all" security product you can buy today. However, an inexpensive router with Network Address Translation (NAT) support will go a long, long way toward making your computers inside your home or office safer from the social misfits called hackers roaming the Internet.

 Note   Some computer "explorers" complain that hackers are judged harshly and called criminals when they are just curious. Sorry, but I don't buy it.

> If you want to see my office but the door is closed, you can't see it. Going through the door without invitation is trespassing. In Texas, trespassers are criminals. In some parts of Texas, trespassers are considered targets.

Chapter 12 goes into the technical details of Network Address Translation, how it works, and how you set it up. But when you get a router from your broadband service provider (or you buy it yourself), the default is usually for Network Address Translation to be turned on, hiding your computers from the Internet. If not, enable NAT immediately. Yes, NAT ASAP. You have to do very little, and it provides excellent protection against many hacker attacks. The settings for Network Address Translation are usually found in a security administration screen, and are often part of the initial configuration steps.

In effect, by using Network Address Translation, you can "hide" your computer from the world. Not physically so your kids can't download more viruses, but hide it so it can't be seen from the Internet. This technique should be the first step in every home or small business network.

The following manufacturers offer low-cost routers that sit between your broadband provider's cable/DSL modem and your computer(s). Even if you have only one computer today, a router with NAT support will make your broadband experience safer.

I have tested routers from the following companies and recommend them:

✦ Linksys at www.linksys.com

✦ Netgear at www.netgear.com

✦ SMC at www.SMC.com

✦ Siemens and their efficient product line at www.efficient.com

✦ Buffalo Technologies at www.buffalotech.com

✦ ZyXEL at www.zyxel.com

✦ Netopia at www.netopia.com

These companies have received good reviews and also offer inexpensive routers:

✦ Belkin at www.belkin.com

✦ US Robotics at www.usrobotics.com

This list does not exhaust the market by any means. The technology for routers with a minimum level of security protection, meaning NAT, is a long list. Any product you find from a reputable retailer, online or physical, will do a decent job. And even a decent job provides much more protection than you'll ever get when connecting your computer directly to the cable/DSL modem and bypassing a router. When you bypass the router, you give up an easy way to hide your computer's real IP address (NAT), address management to automatically give IP addresses to devices, and usually a firewall which blocks all the software addresses used by hackers to get into your local network.

Windows 9x/ME: Keep or Can?

Before you get to the information on making Windows 95/98 or ME work correctly, stop and think a moment. Is upgrading the way you want to spend your time?

Networking hardware and software improvements over the last several years have been nothing short of amazing. Newer products include more features and install and run better than older ones. Integrating older equipment into modern networks takes time and sometimes more money than adding newer equipment.

 Note   Remember: the future of consumerism in America depends on people like you and me replacing our old stuff with new stuff.

All that said, let me lay out some of the reasons you should upgrade your old system, and some reasons you may not feel the upgrade is necessary. Every operating system has strong points and weak points, and networked security happens to be a particular weak point with Microsoft starting with Windows 95. The details are many and technical, but let me just say that Microsoft developers had little experience with the network protocol software they added to Windows 95, and they left some gaps in the security area.

Reasons to upgrade your Windows 9x/ME computer

New stuff is always more fun and exciting than old stuff, especially in technology. So if that's enough to justify upgrading your operating system or your entire computer, great. Skip to the *Configuring Windows XP* section and get to work.

If you (or the holder of the checkbook) require more reasons for upgrading, let me and other experts lay a few reasons out for you. And to be fair, I will include some reasons why you may not want to upgrade your operating system or computer. Just be prepared to live with the consequences of your decision.

Why Microsoft says to upgrade

First, let me tell why Microsoft says you should upgrade your Windows 9x/ME system. True, there is some bias on the part of Microsoft, which benefits financially if you upgrade from Windows 9x/ME to Windows XP Home or XP Professional. On the other hand, Microsoft knows reasons to upgrade that others have yet to discover. This point becomes particularly potent when discussing security.

One of the Microsoft Web pages provides several Top 10 lists for reasons to upgrade. Let me present the reasons I believe make the most sense:

✦ **Less downtime:** This is absolutely true. Windows XP Home and XP Professional stay up longer and resist crashing far better than Windows 9x/ME and even Windows 2000. I say that from personal experience, and other objective experts agree.

✦ **Recovery Tools led by System Restore:** This new feature gives you a mulligan on all system changes. Try the change, and if it doesn't work out, you can roll back your operating system to the state it was in before your changes. Just like a friendly golf partner, Windows XP makes it possible for you to say, "I want to do that again," and be able to do so.

✦ **Improved Internet security and networking:** Microsoft includes an Internet Connection Firewall as well as better default security configuration settings.

✦ **Wi-Fi wireless networking support:** Microsoft calls it 802.1x, but that's primarily Wi-Fi and Windows XP includes support for Wi-Fi automatically. It even works pretty well.

✦ **Updated peripheral support:** Universal Serial Bus (USB) 2.0 specifications made it into Windows XP, and better support for FireWire (especially from Sony computers) makes your Windows box almost as media-connection friendly as a Macintosh. Not quite, but close.

✦ **Encrypting File System:** Particularly critical for laptop owners, the Encrypting File System (EFS) keeps your files safe in case your laptop falls into the lap of someone that's not you.

Microsoft lists other reasons to upgrade that I don't necessarily agree are truly progress in light of its safety record (remote access technologies). However, the six reasons listed make a nice justification in almost every situation.

What Microsoft doesn't say on their Top 10 list is that TCP/IP configuration for Windows 9x/ME, the critical software for networking, wasn't shipped to be secure. In fact, networking security experts relate what I call gaps in security to yawning chasms of operating system holes. But starting with Windows 2000, network software security and ease of configuration took a giant step forward.

If you plan to buy a new name-brand computer, you will be upgraded automatically. All the major manufacturers still demand you get an operating system from Microsoft for personal computers. The barrier is less certain for some server products, which can include Linux, Unix, or NetWare as operating system options, but that probably doesn't apply in your situation. For consumers and small business customers, a new personal computer means an upgraded Microsoft Windows operating system. The only way out of the Microsoft tax is to build your own computer, or buy from one of the auction sites (www.ebay.com and www.ubid.com work best for me) and install your own operating system after you get the computer.

The biggest hammer in the upgrade toolkit for Microsoft came out late in 2003: no more support for Windows 98. Public outcry caused Microsoft to relent and continue to offer support, but that support is no longer free.

Anti-Microsoft folks declared this a typical Microsoft plot to extort money from poor helpless users still clinging to Windows 98. Other, more neutral observers mentioned that no industry supports old products forever. Your new car comes with a great warranty for the first year at least, then fewer and fewer components remain the responsibility of the manufacturer. Microsoft has done little more than phase out warranty support for an obsolete (by two newer major operating system releases) operating system.

Bottom line: Upgrade your computer hardware and software for the most fun and best possible computing experience with your new broadband Internet access.

Why others say to upgrade

I said several things in the previous paragraph, so you can count those as an "others" argument. But I found the following additional reasons for upgrading during my research.

Windows 98 is essentially only a pretty face on a DOS foundation. Critical system components, such as memory space, are severely limited. Did you know every running program in Windows 98 must fight to register application details in an address space on 64KB in size? That's not MB or GB, that's KB. When that memory space gets full, you get error messages about lack of memory even though you may have a gigabyte of RAM in your computer. That gigabyte doesn't increase that 64KB address space one nibble.

Note   You get more for your money if you upgrade your operating system by buying a new computer. Retail prices for Windows XP Home and XP Professional software only range from $100 to $300 per computer. You can get a pretty good brand name system for $400–$600, including the operating system.

Windows 2000 and Windows XP do not rely on these DOS underpinnings and that explains one of the best reasons why they are more reliable and run longer before demanding a reboot.

Here's a list of more upgrade justifications:

✦ Newer application software will not run on older operating systems. This chance of obsolescence increases with every new application released. Particularly at risk are audio and video applications that take plenty of computer horsepower to run.

✦ USB 2.0 devices can't be added unless you buy a special hardware card and insert it into your computer.

✦ More applications added to the system (not running, just installed) bloat the registry and slow down the computer.

✦ The hardware interface options for Windows 98 computers are Industrial Standard Architecture (ISA), defined by PC vendors in the very early 1980s. Expansion slots won't support the newer Peripheral Component Interconnect (PCI) cards almost all vendors sell today. I'm not sure you can even buy an ISA expansion card manufactured this century.

✦ Adding larger hard drives may be impossible because of Basic Input Output System (BIOS) limitations in the older computers.

✦ New memory for upgrades (to support a newer operating system on an older PC) are harder to find. Worse, BIOS restrictions affect total system memory as well as hard disk sizes. Available memory will jump in price as manufacturers concentrate on newer memory connection types not supported by the older hardware.

Add my voice to this list. Upgrade if you can at all, in any way, justify the expense and effort.

Note You don't have to upgrade to Windows. You can buy Linux desktop operating systems for as little as the cost of shipping on up to around $100 depending on included applications. You can get a pretty decent computer, including a Linux operating system, for $200 that will take full advantage of your new broadband Internet access as well as be the operating system and application equivalent of Windows XP with Microsoft Office thrown in.

Reasons not to upgrade your Windows 9x/ME computer

If you want to avoid the expense or effort of upgrading, you may need some justifications of your own. I'm nothing if not fair and balanced (okay, I'm biased in some ways, but I try to warn you), so here's the rest of the story.

Microsoft lists many reasons to upgrade that I don't agree will benefit most readers of this book because of security issues. I don't believe remote desktop control over the Internet and file access control to your computer files really make sense based on Microsoft's poor security record guarding against malicious intruders. Both these options leave open holes that expose at least a portion of your computer to the Internet, and I feel there are better options for both situations.

Microsoft also makes claims about performance that I don't necessarily buy. When Windows XP came out there was great confusion about whether Microsoft's performance-enhanced claims could be verified. New hardware improvements make larger new operating systems seem faster than the replaced software until you put the old software on exactly the same hardware as the operating system.

I never saw a definitive answer concerning across-the-board desktop performance increases I could trust. Some areas of the operating system ran faster, but some did not. Call it at worst a draw, although upgrades in the Windows XP (SP1) may have improved performance enough to make the claims legitimate. Maybe.

The best and final answer for your situation, and your choice to avoid the expense and effort of upgrading, is that you like the way things are working now. In sports, you don't change your game when you're winning. If you're happy with the applications on your computer and the function of that computer, you can just stay where you are.

Most of the broadband connection options discussed in this book require an Ethernet network connection. Windows 98 and even Windows 95 systems often included Ethernet connection support on their motherboards, so you should have one. If you don't, you can get an Ethernet adapter, or use a USB connection. Your choices are limited if you must use USB for your network connection, but they are available. Assuming your PC has a USB port supported by the operating system, of course.

> You can always try something new to extend the life of your older PC running Windows 98: Linux. A Linux desktop operating system will run faster on older hardware than will a comparable Windows operating system. You can get a Linux operating system, which usually includes enough software to equal a full copy of Microsoft Office as well as a Windows XP-comparable operating system, for $30–$100 depending on the vendor.

Configuring Windows 95/98/ME for Networking

Okay, you didn't succumb to the lure of a new computer or even a new operating system because you're happy with what you have. That's fine. I will use Windows 98 for examples because that's the operating system in largest use between the three options I'm covering in this section. Some reports claim 25 percent of home users are still on Windows 98, and millions of corporate computers also lag behind.

The good news is that Windows 9x/ME operating systems are designed to be user systems only and don't include many server-type applications. That means those server-type holes causing problems on other operating systems don't exist to be abused on a Windows 9x/ME system. The three ways to compromise these systems are as follows:

✦ Change configuration remotely

✦ Trick the user (you) into running a malicious program

✦ Get physical access to the system

Of the three, I'm going to ignore the third option. Anyone hostile, who gets physical access to your computer, will probably steal it. That means you'll be able to upgrade your system by replacing it with the insurance money, and you can skip ahead to the Windows XP section.

Basic network settings

Windows does a pretty good job of setting up basic network access when you install the software if there's an active network connection during installation. But those settings don't take into account the modern aspects of broadband access to the Internet and the climate of viruses and hackers today.

Password

You need a password on your computer when you attach it to the Internet. No excuses. You need a password. Password creation is a science, not an art. You want hackers to struggle enough to uncover your password they give up and go to the next potential victim. All personal computer passwords can be broken with enough time, but hackers tend to be impatient and won't spend hours attacking your system when the next one they hit may have a password of "no" or something equally worthless.

Figure 11-1 shows the Password Properties and Change Password dialog boxes in Windows 98 (Start ➪ Control Panel ➪ Passwords ➪ Change Passwords). See the asterisks in place of letters? That's to hide the password from people looking over your shoulder. Guess the developers who started that trend of using asterisks never figured that if someone stood over your shoulder they could just watch your fingers when you typed your password.

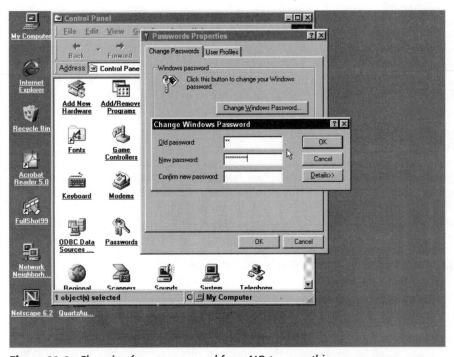

Figure 11-1: Changing from a password from NO to something more secure.

If you're the only one in the house or office using the computer, you may not want to use a password, and you can get away with that security breach. People with coworkers or children tend to be a bit more paranoid.

Smart parents make themselves the only user with administrator privileges on their computers and put good passwords in place. Many applications require a user with administrator privileges to install them, which won't be a problem if you have only one user that accesses everything. Multiple user systems with only one administrator require an extra step. When children need to install software, the parent can perform the installation to help monitor the programs and the installation success. Although some applications can be installed by any user, viruses and worms tend to need more access to system services than just user level security. So you have a chance to monitor installations and stop if something insecure begins.

Network adapter

Your Windows 9x/ME system will need an Ethernet adapter supporting a 10Base-T plug. This plug looks like a telephone plug but is bigger because the RJ-45 connector supports eight wires whereas the telephone's RJ-11 connector only supports four wires (four twisted pair versus two twisted pair).

Most computer vendors have put an Ethernet 10Base-T (unshielded twisted pair wiring rather than the coax cables used before 10Base-T that look similar to the wire the cable TV uses) connector on PCs for years. If your PC doesn't have an Ethernet connector, you can buy one (an Ethernet 10/100Base-T network interface card can be purchased for less than a dozen dollars) and install it or have it installed. But you'd be better off upgrading your computer to a system new enough to include Ethernet support.

Some of the new cable/DSL modems include a USB connection so you don't have to use an Ethernet adapter in your old computer. But if your computer is so old it doesn't include a basic Ethernet connector, it probably doesn't include a USB connector, either. Another good reason to upgrade.

TCP/IP

Transmission Control Protocol/Internet Protocol (TCP/IP) became the only protocol allowed on the Internet since January 1, 1983. Before that, the fledgling Internet included a wide variety of communication protocols developed by different vendors. But TCP/IP won the protocol beauty contest, and has beaten all other protocols, no matter their advantages in certain areas, as the reigning network protocol.

 A protocol is a set of rules that communicates between machines.

Even protocols not called TCP/IP require TCP/IP, or some portion of TCP/IP, to communicate. Although TCP/IP management details fill many thick books, for home and small business users the important thing to remember is that TCP/IP is the networking software that does all the communications underneath your applications. You see an e-mail client, but the Internet sees your TCP/IP address and communication commands.

 More details about TCP/IP await you in Chapter 12.

All you care about now is that every computer on a network (yours and the service provider's and the Internet) must have a unique number. This IP address must be carefully controlled if used on the public Internet, but you have all sorts of flexibility with internal networks.

There are two ways for your computer to receive a TCP/IP address and therefore the ability to connect to a network:

✦ Assign the computer a specific IP address to use every time

✦ Have the computer request an IP address and other network information whenever the computer starts.

Both methods are configured on the same screen, as shown in Figure 11-2. You reach this Properties dialog box by clicking Start ⇨ Settings ⇨ Control Panel and then clicking Network ⇨ TCP/IP Physical Adaptor ⇨ Properties.

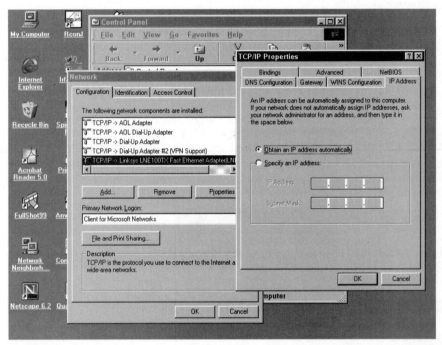

Figure 11-2: Notice in the foreground window on the right that there is no address listed in the spaces.

Checking the Obtain An IP Address Automatically box tells your computer to ask a Dynamic Host Configuration Protocol (DHCP) server to supply a unique address and other information. That server will probably be your router.

If your service providers tells you to put an IP address in that space and gives you the address, it will look something like "24.30.107.139" with periods between every group of three numbers. Yes, there's space for three in every white text box, so you have to press the Tab key to move to the next section if your address has only one or two numerals in that space.

If your service provider tells you to put an IP address in that space, and it's a computer rather than a router, double-check that request. That means your computer is attached directly to the Internet with no firewall or router in between you and the global world of miscreant software developers.

The only time I specify an IP address in my local network is for servers that must be managed via a Web-browser interface. If I let the DHCP server give them an address I have a hard time finding the address of the server when I need to configure or just check something on the server.

Winipcfg

Short for Windows IP Configuration, this Windows 9x/ME program is hidden by Microsoft for some odd reason. Must be scary for some users, but I think it really helps novice and experienced users alike by showing all sorts of TCP/IP information in one handy screen. When things work properly you won't even need to look at winipcfg.

You start the program by clicking Start ➪ Run and typing **winipcfg** in the text box that appears. Press Enter and the application will start by opening a small box on the screen.

Two things you must do to make sense of this application. First, find your network Ethernet connector defined in Windows for TCP/IP networking. Software connectors, such as for AOL, tend to be placed in front of the hardware. Scroll down to find the Ethernet network connection you use for that computer. You will only have one network adapter that is not software and labeled AOL and the like, and that one will almost always say Ethernet of some type like the shot in Figure 11-3.

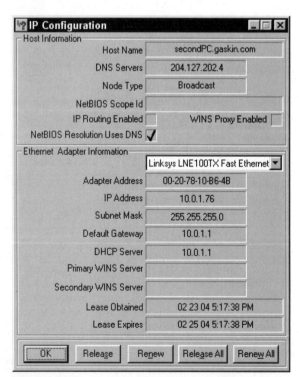

Figure 11-3: Start ➪ Run ➪ winipcfg ➪ More Info command button.

In my case, this is a Linksys Fast Ethernet adapter I added manually to this computer because it did not come with an Ethernet plug by default. Yes, if I used this in a production setting it would be long gone by now. But it works well enough to show a Windows 98 system when necessary.

Second, click the More Info command button at the bottom-right of the Winipcfg application. This pops open considerably more TCP/IP network information and makes it easier to see what's happening, as you can see in Figure 11-3.

You can't change anything directly through this screen, but you can reset the IP address of your Ethernet card. Sometimes, such as when you change a server, or a network connection freezes up in Windows, you must clear the old address and get a new one.

Release your current IP address by clicking the Release or Release All command button. The Release button just releases the network connector shown in the Ethernet Adapter Information text box. Notice the down arrow at the right end of that box tempting you to see what other adapters are running on your system. I always click Release All so no odd connections that occurred in the background stay open and cause me problems.

When you click the Release All command button, the address information you saw in Figure 11-3 clears and you are left with a forlorn computer with no network connection. Figure 11-4 shows a Windows 98 system with no connections, after I clicked the Release All command button.

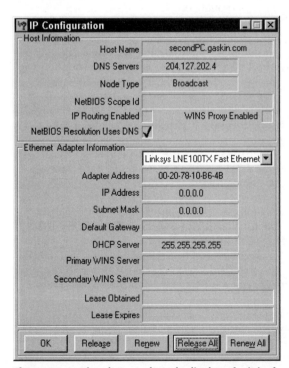

Figure 11-4: The clean and ready display of winipcfg after releasing the connections.

Your computer will keep the Domain Name Service (DNS) server address even after the connections are released, which is why you see 204.172.202.4 in that space in Figure 11-4. The Node Type remains, as does the 16-byte Adapter Address shown just under the double lines. The Adapter Address is the hard-coded serial number of sorts given to every Ethernet adapter when it's built (called the Media Access Controller or MAC address). An international numbering authority assigns the first part of the number so it can track vendors, and the vendors themselves keep track of the rest of the number as a way to keep track of their own product sales.

Chapter 12 will go into detail about the 10.0.1.1 IP address listed twice in Figure 11-3, but that corresponds to the router (Default gateway) that also parcels out the IP addresses (DHCP server). Those default gateway IP addresses will be the same for every DHCP client on the network, because they all get that information from the router acting as gateway and DHCP server.

Play with the winipcfg program if you want, and check out the details shown for the other network adapters in the pull-down menu. You may be surprised by what you see in some listings, but don't let the details worry you, because the IP address and details just described are all that matter when connecting to a broadband service provider and the Internet.

Your workgroup

Microsoft offers two ways to connect personal computers to a network (actually three, but one is officially obsolete). Big companies use Active Directory with server software dedicated to tracking and managing all parts of all client computers. Small companies and homes use the peer-to-peer networking (workgroup networking) Microsoft has provided for years and years.

Workgroups consists of the computers and other resources (printers, storage devices, servers) you are most likely to connect with while using your computer. The connections between systems and resources make up the Local Area Network (LAN) you read about. It matters not whether the connections are wired, wireless, or even run over the A/C power in the walls of your house because those are all ways to make up a network.

For workgroup identification, each collection of resources must use the same workgroup name. The default name for this in Windows 9x/ME is WORKGROUP, a handy bit of redundancy. Yet Microsoft XP Home sets the default workgroup name to MSHOME, which I find inconsistent and egotistical on their part. If they had to change the workgroup name to reflect a home network, couldn't they have used HomeNet or MyNet in place of MSNHOME?

The bottom line is that your workgroup consist of resources on the same local area network all referencing the same workgroup name. Your home links to share your broadband connection will be a small network. Your small business may also use this method of networking, especially when adding server or storage appliances. Remember in the previous chapter when I mentioned all the storage and server appliances appear inside Network Neighborhood (Windows 9x/ME) or My Network Places (Windows 2000 and XP)? They appear because they guess correctly that the local workgroup name will be workgroup.

Figure 11-5 shows the page where you set the computer name, workgroup name, and computer description in Windows 9x/ME. You also set these details when you install the operating system, but they are easy to change if you add networking later.

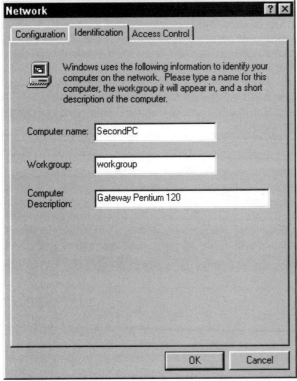

Figure 11-5: Start ➪ Settings ➪ Control Panel ➪ Network ➪ Identification to reach your network identification page.

 Tech Bits Another reason to upgrade from Windows 9x/ME? Every time you change any network parameter, you must reboot. Not true with Windows XP.

You can have more than one workgroup running on one local area network. The workgroup name separates the resources from one network to the other. However, there isn't much reason to make this separation. If your network has enough resources, such as in a small but growing business, moving up to a better network operating system makes more sense than juggling multiple workgroup networks.

Adjusting the default security options

If your broadband connection does not include firewall software on the router between your computer(s) and the cable/DSL modem, prepare for plenty of extra security configuration work. If your computer(s) are Windows 9x/ME systems, your workload just got heavier by as many Windows 9x/ME computers as you have.

With Network Address Translation

Here's the first big security step and easiest way to protect your network: get a router with Network Address Translation and firewall software. Use both, and relax about hackers bursting into your network at all hours. You still have to worry about spam and worms and viruses, but you need to read security and e-mail control books to solve those problems.

There are no complicated examples in all the routers I have in the lab for Network Address Translation. Engaging NAT rarely requires more than checking box like you see in Figure 11-6.

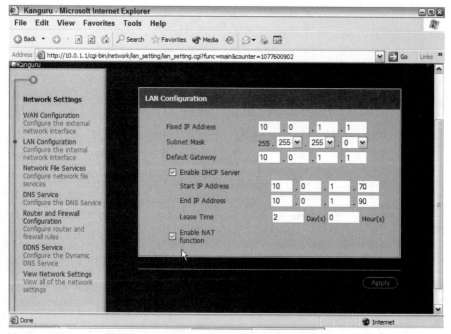

Figure 11-6: NAT takes little effort to engage. See the check box?

The internal address range that your NAT service hides from the rest of the world is the range set by your DHCP server. In the case of Figure 11-6, this is the

IP address network 10.0.1.1. Clients requesting IP addresses will get those addresses, on a first come first served basis, from the range 10.0.1.70.

Network Address Translation software tracks which clients send data packets to the Internet. When the packets go through, the NAT software adds a port number to the NATs IP address. When response packets return, the NAT software knows which client sent the request because the response comes addressed to that port number.

Outsiders looking to cause trouble can send queries to known port numbers, like Port 80, which supports Web servers. Hackers like to find Web servers because so many of them aren't well protected, especially those at smaller companies with small security budgets.

But scanning a range of IP addresses on Port 80 won't pass the NAT filter smell test. Because no packets that left were tagged with Port 80 on the way out, no return packets have permission to go through the filter using that port number.

Using Network Address Translation doesn't solve every network security problem, but it covers most attacks from the outside. It certainly protects you from hackers scanning for easy targets, because the hackers can't see any computer on the far side (for them) of your NAT barrier.

Without Network Address Translation

Most people consider their files the most critical resource on their computer or small network. If you don't have a functioning Network Address Translation barrier in place, turn off as many network shares as possible.

The easiest way to do this is to stop each Windows 9x/ME computer from sharing files by turning off that switch for the complete computer. Figure 11-7 shows the small dialog box with the appropriate check boxes to stop sharing any file from this particular computer.

Reach this dialog box by clicking Start ⇨ Settings ⇨ Control Panel ⇨ Network ⇨ File and Print Sharing. Click the File and Print Sharing box and you're in business.

The File and Print Sharing dialog box offers you two clever options: Share Files, and/or Share Printers. One choice doesn't affect the other, and few Internet hackers are looking for printers to invade.

If you have no firewall and/or NAT barriers between your computer and the Internet, you will be advertising your shared resources to the world. Remember the discussion of early cable networks and the fact you could often see the shared files and printers of your neighbors? The lack of firewall and NAT filters allowed that to happen then, and it can allow that to happen today.

If you have no firewall and/or NAT barrier between your computer and the Internet, turn off all resource sharing. Then look at the *Inexpensive Routers with NAT Support* section earlier in this chapter and go buy a router immediately.

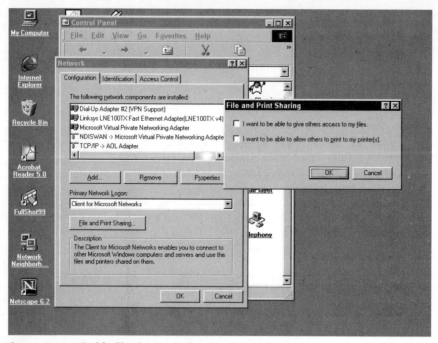

Figure 11-7: Disable file sharing by leaving these check boxes unchecked.

Closing exposed security holes

The only truly secure computer is one that is turned off, unplugged, and still in the box. You don't have that option, but you can close some security holes to make your broadband life a bit safer.

I'd tell you to update the security files from Microsoft for Windows 9x/ME, but because Microsoft declared Windows 98 obsolete, few, if any, changes are being made to the source code. This means security patches and safety upgrades will appear rarely if ever again. Yes, that's a hint to upgrade.

Unbind TCP/IP

Windows 9x/ME doesn't have any of the server software options that later Windows operating systems include, but it does have a relatively poor implementation of TCP/IP. Microsoft added TCP/IP support directly into Windows in Windows 95, and Windows 98 still had some growing pains in the TCP/IP area.

You don't need TCP/IP to communicate between computers within your home or small business. You do need TCP/IP to communicate with the Internet. But you can turn off TCP/IP support for your local network, making it that much more secure.

Figure 11-8 shows the page within TCP/IP properties to unbind (disconnect) the TCP/IP protocol from the network interface card so that protocol won't be used

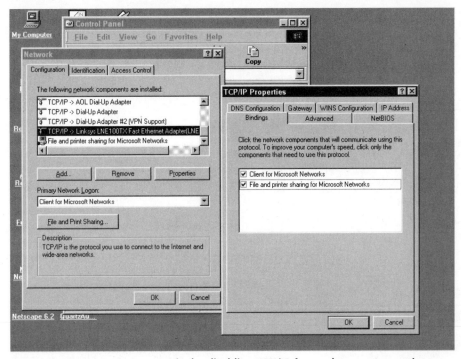

Figure 11-8: Improve your security by disabling TCP/IP for workgroup connections.

as a client for Microsoft Networks. Uncheck both boxes, and you'll make your Windows 9x/ME safer from outsiders.

Notice the description in the Network dialog box to the left of the TCP/IP Properties dialog box? The description, as shown in Figure 11-8, reads, "TCP/IP is the protocol you use to connect to the Internet and wide-area networks." Does that mention local shared folders? No it does not. Reach this dialog box by clicking Start ➪ Settings ➪ Control Panel ➪ Network Interface Card Properties, and then click the Bindings tab.

Repeat this process for every interface connection that reaches the Internet, including any AOL adapters in the Network ➪ Configuration list of installed network components. Because this is Windows 9x/ME, you will have to reboot to make the changes stick.

Turn off file sharing

When you're ready to share files, get a server or storage appliance like the ones discussed in Chapter 10. Then put the appliance on your private network on the inside of a router. If you're not ready to do that, at least turn off file sharing on your Window 9x/ME computer.

Refer to Figure 11-7. Notice the two check boxes? Make sure the top one, "I want to be able to give others access to my files" is cleared. You can share your printer with the world, if you want. It's your paper.

Setting passwords for file sharing

Because you don't want to turn off file sharing, or really can't, let me show you how to set passwords to keep those resources at least slightly safer. Figure 11-9 shows the screen where you set passwords for an individual shared resource. You must configure passwords for each and every shared file resource. Get to this screen by right-clicking the folder to share then choose Sharing.

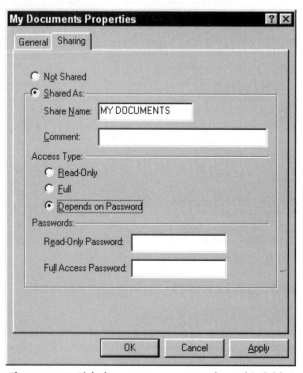

Figure 11-9: Pick the way you want to share this folder.

Figure 11-9 shows the Properties page for My Documents, but it could just as easily show any other folder you wish to share. You can drill down to the folder to be shared, or share an entire disk drive if you want. When you find the folder (or disk) to share, right-click the item to open the context menu. Sharing is about halfway down the list.

Give a better name than "My Documents" to the share in the example to distinguish it from the My Documents folders all Windows operating systems include. Comments are optional.

Notice under Access Type you have three choices: Read-Only, Full, and Depends on Password. This selection makes pretty good sense. If you grant users read-only access, they can view and copy your files in the folder but can't mess them up. Full access, or read/write access, allows all those with the password to fold, spindle, and mutilate your files to their heart's content.

Use real passwords, not just quick and dirty passwords.

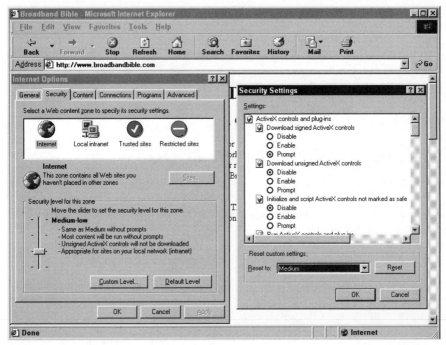

Figure 11-10: Setting your security comfort level for surfing with Internet Explorer.

Tighten Internet Explorer

The world of Web sites became a minefield over the last two years. Clever hackers started running applications within visiting Web browser software to infect the computer. Yes, now even looking at a Web site can cause problems. And unfortunately, a NAT layer won't help.

Hackers use ActiveX components or Java applets to attack your browser. You can turn off these internal settings to block their use or at least prompt you to allow ActiveX or a Java script on a site you trust. Figure 11-10 shows the Settings page. On the Internet Explorer menu, choose Tools ⇨ Internet Options ⇨ Security ⇨ Custom Level.

You want to set the following to either Disable or Prompt (scroll down to find them all):

✦ Script ActiveX controls marked safe for scripting

✦ Run ActiveX controls and plug-ins

✦ Active Scripting

✦ Scripting of Java applets

Depending on the types of sites you visit on the Web, you may prefer setting everything to Prompt rather than Disable. That way you can see how often, and how, you get asked to open the soft underbelly of your computer to the rabid dogs of the Internet.

You do have choices in Web browsers, even for Windows 9x/ME. Netscape, for instance, makes a better browser in many ways than Microsoft does. You can get Netscape, and its brother Mozilla, free from www.netscape.com and www.Mozilla.org, respectively.

Configuring Windows 2000 for Networking

If you have Windows 2000, I won't pressure you to upgrade at all. You get the advantages of better reliability from Windows NT (not DOS with a graphical interface like Windows 9x/ME) with graphical improvements over Windows 98 Special Edition. And you don't have to reboot nearly as often.

Security with Windows 2000 improved over Windows 9x/ME, but you must still be careful. If you completely separate your internal network (or even one computer) from the broadband service provider's network with a router or gateway, you have done the best thing to protect yourself against malicious outsiders.

Note   Privacy advocates feel that Windows XP goes too far in collecting PC information and relaying that information back to Microsoft. Microsoft says the data helps support product troubleshooting and future development, but once someone else has your data you have no control over that data. The technology exists within Windows XP to track an enormous amount of Internet-derived tracking and transaction data and name the individual sitting at that computer. That makes privacy advocates nervous, and they stick with Windows 2000, Linux, or Macintosh systems.

Unlike Windows 9x/ME, Windows 2000 does include server-type programs used on a regular basis. Big in the corporate world, Windows 2000 Professional makes remote desktop management easier than Windows 98 but not as easy as Windows XP (see the progression?). So there are more things to worry about concerning remote access, but more tools to handle and monitor the situation.

If you don't have a router with minimum security controls, such as Network Address Translation, jump back to the beginning of this chapter and read why you must have one. Life on the broadband Internet will be much safer and more secure with a router between your computer(s) and the cable/DSL modem.

Basic network settings

Settings for every network device include many of the same configuration details. The good news about Windows 2000 is that there are fewer than with Windows 9x/ME, but they must be applied to every Windows 2000 system on your network. So get ready to adjust some security options Microsoft leaves too open for safety and shut the door on some hackers, such as:

✦ Turn off services offering access to the system.

✦ Disable Internet sharing through the Windows 2000 system.

The look of network configuration screens in Windows 2000 echoes those of Windows 9x/ME. One advantage is that you can reach the networking components with one less mouse click. Windows 2000 adds a link to network connections to the Settings submenu off the Start menu. But to complicate things, Microsoft moved the advanced functions away from the Local Area Network Properties page to the Advanced menu choice on the Network and Dialup Connections window.

At least the primary page where you set the PC to ask for an IP address (DHCP client) from a network server stayed put. Figure 11-11 shows how to tell your PC to become a DHCP client. Reach this screen by clicking Start ➪ Settings ➪ Network and Dialup Connections ➪ Local Area Network ➪ Properties ➪ Internet Protocol (TCP/IP) ➪ Properties.

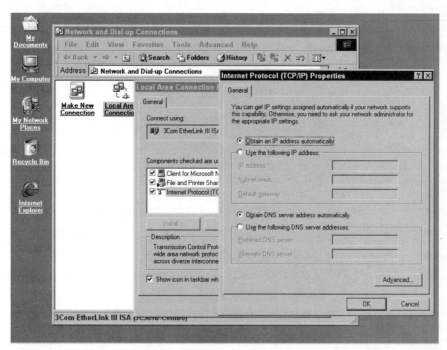

Figure 11-11: Setting Windows 2000 to request an IP address from a Dynamic Host Control Protocol server on the local network.

Your Dynamic Host Configuration Protocol server (usually your router) will provide the gateway IP address along with the Domain Name Server addresses. Setting those at your DHCP server makes it easier to change or update that information, because every computer queries the DCHP server for that information each time it is logged in to the network or has to release its IP address.

Computer Name and workgroup/domain settings are part of the Windows 2000 installation routines, but you can make changes. Microsoft actually made the change screen slightly easier to find and slightly more helpful.

Figure 11-12 shows the Identification Changes that may be necessary if you want your newly networked computer to see other systems on your local area network. The computer name must be unique within your network, and the Workgroup name must be the same as all other computers in your workgroup or you won't be able to see them as easily. Reach this screen by clicking Start ⇨ Settings ⇨ Network and Dialup Connections ⇨ Local Area Network ⇨ Advanced (top menu) ⇨ Network Identification ⇨ Properties.

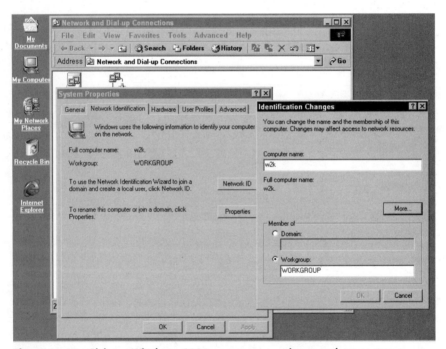

Figure 11-12: Giving a Windows 2000 computer a unique workgroup name.

The default name for the workgroup is Workgroup, which makes it easy when configuring multiple new computers. This also means that everyone knows the default name is Workgroup and anyone looking for openings in your network will try the Workgroup name first of all.

Adjusting the default security options

If you don't need to share the folders on this PC, don't do so. Shared folders are an invitation to others to see what's inside them.

The default setting for Windows 2000 is to add TCP/IP for all connections even if that isn't necessary. If you have no router with firewall and NAT protection, you should unbind the Internet protocol, TCP/IP, from your local file and disk sharing protocol.

Figure 11-13 shows the disconnection of TCP/IP from local file and print sharing to keep your internal network out of harm's way. Notice the arrow pointing toward the Client for Microsoft Networks setting, which must not be cleared. Find this dialog box by clicking Start ⇨ Settings ⇨ Network and Dialup Connections ⇨ Local Area Network ⇨ Advanced (top menu) ⇨ Advanced Settings ⇨ Adapters and Bindings.

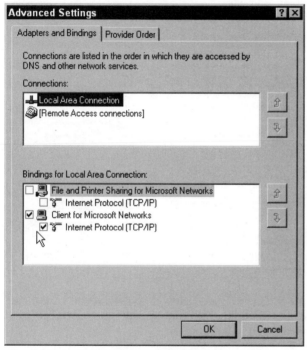

Figure 11-13: This Windows 2000 dialog box looks different from the similar one in Windows 9x/ME, but the results are the same when configured.

Again, this step isn't necessary with a router between you and the broadband world. But if your broadband service provider gives you an IP address that belongs only to you, you're hanging directly from their Internet connection and everyone on the Internet can see your computer.

Services to disable

Windows 2000 starts many services you may not need. Turning them off saves time booting and leaves more memory for applications you do want. Even if you don't have a security need, turning off services you don't need makes good sense.

My concern now is with those programs that provide some type of host environment for others. Windows 9x/ME didn't have this issue to deal with, but Windows 2000 and XP are powerful enough to act as servers in some capacities as well as clients.

Turn these services off, one by one, checking machine stability after each operation Figure 11-14 shows the Services control page. This dialog box is reached in several ways, but the most direct is Start ➪ Setting ➪ Control Panel ➪ Administrative Tools ➪ Services.

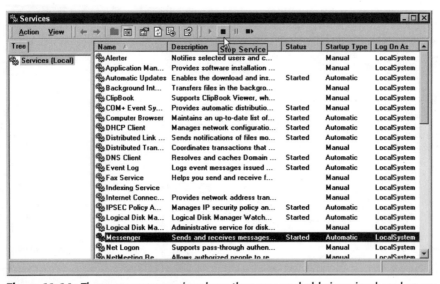

Figure 11-14: There are more services here than you probably imagined, and many are not necessary for normal computing.

All the services remain on the system and are ready to go even if you stop them. In fact, you must change them to Manual rather than the Automatic startup command so they don't restart when you reboot

The Messenger service highlighted in Figure 11-14 should definitely be stopped. That's what sends pop-up messages to your desktop.

Notice I put the cursor on the Stop Service button, which you can see in the middle of the screenshot at the top. You can also right-click service names and stop them that way.

Try stopping these services to improve network security:

✦ **IP SEC Policy Agent:** An improved IP security driver that doesn't help if you're not in a network domain. Provides no value to workgroup clients.

✦ **Messenger:** Bringer of dreaded Alerter service messages co-opted by spammers and popups.

✦ **Net Logon:** Passes through user name authentication for logon services in a domain. No help for workgroup clients.

✦ **Performance Logs and Alerts:** Gathers local and remote computer performance data then writes data to a log or alerts an administrator.

✦ **Remote Desktop Help Session Manager:** Controls Remote Assistance, where a remote user takes over your computer just as if they were at the keyboard physically rather than across the Internet.

✦ **Remote Registry:** Allows remote users (and management tools) to modify Registry settings.

✦ **Routing and Remote Access:** Allows dial-in access.

✦ **TCP/IP NetBIOS Helper:** Resolves NetBIOS names and runs NetBIOS packets on top of TCP/IP data packets.

✦ **Telnet:** Remote user login application allowing programs to be executed remotely. The default is to start manually, but be sure and check that setting.

✦ **Universal Plug and Play Device Host:** Universal Plug and Play (UPnP) allows machines to communicate and configure access to each other without involved humans. Not a safe or smart plan, and a regular hacker target.

Try stopping these services to improve general performance:

✦ **Network DDE:** Dynamic Data Exchange providing network transport and security for enterprise-type application. Again, rarely used in a workgroup setting.

✦ **NT LM Security Support Provider:** Security for Remote Procedure Call (RPC) programs that don't use named pipes. Sound like a workgroup application?

✦ **SSDP Discovery Service:** Sniffs out UPnP devices on the network.

None of these suggestions are anything more than suggestions. You should find your level of comfort and act accordingly. However, if you don't have a router with the proper protection in place, I suggest you stop more of the services than you allow.

Figure 11-15 shows the Properties page that appears on each service when you double-click them. The Startup type listing, pulled open for display, shows that the Messenger default is to start automatically whenever the system boots. Your choices are to make it a manual startup process or to disable the service so it can't run even if some user or applications really wants it to run. Click Start ⇨ Settings ⇨ Control Panel ⇨ Administrative Tools ⇨ Services. Then right-click the service and choose Properties.

Internet Connection Sharing (ICS)

This feature was a big deal early on, as Internet service providers could use it to help users get more than one computer connected to its service. And when routers with firewalls and Network Address Translation were hard to find or expensive, using one Windows computer as a gateway to the Internet made sense. Kind of.

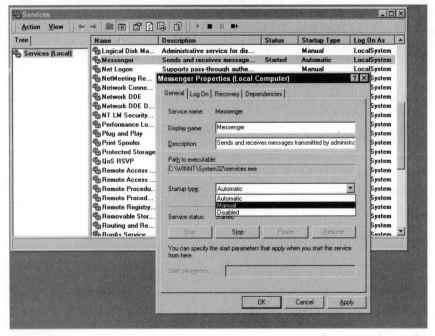

Figure 11-15: I say set the services you don't want to Manual settings. That makes it easy for start them if realize later you really need them.

Okay, this didn't make sense because of the security problems Microsoft had in the past and continues to have. Trusting one computer to stay safe when directed to the Internet through your broadband service providers is a stretch. Trusting that one computer to keep the rest of your network safe from hackers, viruses, and worms is a lot to ask.

Routers are too cheap today to run the risks of putting one computer directly on the Internet and linking the rest of your computers to that computer. Buy one of the low-priced routers with a decent NAT module and you'll be far better off in the areas of performance and security

Closing exposed security holes

If you read part of the Windows 9x/ME section, you know the security holes are greater there than in more recent Windows operating systems. Yet there are some security issues that will never leave.

Having a working router with Network Address Translation at the least and full-fledged firewall, at the best, closes the security holes in Windows 2000. The holes I will help you close are holes everyone has to some degree.

First off, you can turn off sharing for your hard disk. Go to My Computer, right-click your hard disk, and choose Sharing. It looks much like Figure 11-9, but click the Do Not Share This Folder radio button, and your shared folders on that hard disk will no longer be shareable.

If you want to go deeper, you can. In Windows 2000, file sharing for the entire system is controlled by the Server component inside the Services listing. Change that service to start manually rather than automatically. You can't see Server in the list of services in Figure 11-5, but it's there. Double-click that listing and turn the Server off and you close most of your security holes.

If you're nervous about turning off a service that "Provides RPC support and file, print, and named pipes sharing" you can go to all resources around the home or office and see if anyone took the "Sharing" bait by seeing if your computer file folders appears in their My Network Places folder. Someone probably did, because Windows makes sharing the default, and the option to share any resource appears in the context menu that pops open whenever you right-click a sharable resource like a folder. Because this is peer-to-peer networking, without a centralized network operating system controlling access to network resources, you have to check each computer. Or, you can just stop the Server service and see who complains.

If you find an active share in a place you didn't expect, close it up. Then look around carefully, because the person who made that share probably made more than one. If that's the case, stopping the "Server" service may be your best option. People tend to take the same actions time after time, so a "sharing" person yesterday will likely be a "sharing" person tomorrow.

Configuring Windows XP for Networking

Windows XP became the "official" Windows when released in 2001. Microsoft wants everyone to move to the new operating system, of course, and all new PCs come with Windows XP of one flavor or another.

Windows XP Home looks and feels exactly like Windows XP Professional. The primary differences between the two products are enterprise networking support for domains, Active Directory, and remote manageability. Home and small business users have no reason to pay extra for the Windows XP Professional version.

Just like with Windows 2000, there are a few details to clean up in Windows XP for added security. You will turn off unneeded services to increase security and decrease the load on your computer, and close a few other network security gaps.

Why You Should Upgrade to Windows XP

Visually oriented people want to upgrade because Windows XP looks so much more finished and sleek than Windows 2000 or Windows 9x/ME. That is, of course,

Continued

Continued

if those visually oriented people didn't already buy a Macintosh, because that visual interface sets the bar that Microsoft Windows seems to always reach for but just miss.

The majority of the reasons I feel you should upgrade to Windows XP are listed at the top of the chapter. Quick recap: more stable, System Restore, Wi-Fi support, and better peripheral support with USB 2.0. There are a few other reasons, now that you understand more of the reasons for some of the changes we've been making to earlier Windows versions:

✦ Sharing is not the default for all network resources

✦ New personal firewall included

✦ More controls for TCP/IP networking management

✦ More resistant to system damage due to failures such as power outages

And, like I said, it looks nicer.

Basic network settings

If you have an active Ethernet connection on the PC when you install Windows XP of either flavor, the system will accept any network configuration it can find. It may not do it completely right, but you will get a good start.

Figure 11-16 shows the Network Connection Status box. You can disable your network connection here with the Disable command button, and then click the Local Area Connection icon to enable the connection. This process resets the network interface card and reinitializes most of the networking software in your PC. Reach this dialog box by going through My Network Places ⇨ View Network Connections ⇨ Local Area Connection ⇨ Status.

Notice something interesting in that listing? The last line in the Connection area at the top of the window says "Signal Strength." That's one of the improvements in Windows XP to support wireless networking.

One more click to drill down to more information that's useful on a regular basis. Click the Support tab in the Local Area Connection Status window to pull open the Detail windows shown in Figure 11-17.

These two interesting windows provide more information than you got from Windows 2000. The window on the left, the Local Area Connection Status window, is the first drill-down from the previous screenshot. This appears when you click the Support tab at the top of that window.

The Internet Protocol (TCP/IP) information echoes the information received from the DHCP server allocating IP addresses on the network. The Address Type listing tells us this: Assigned by DHCP. This means the DHCP server on your

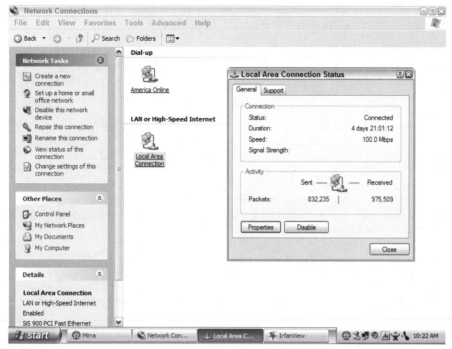

Figure 11-16: Monitoring the status of your local area network connection.

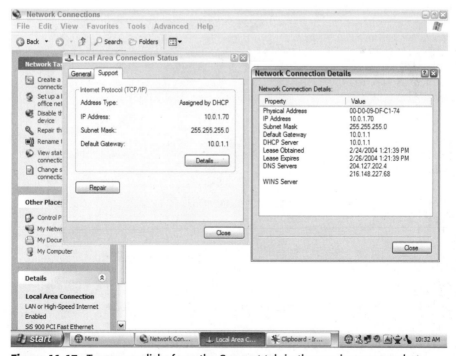

Figure 11-17: Two more clicks from the Support tab in the previous screenshot.

network did its job, and your PC client software requesting an IP address and other information did its job as well.

IP Address tells us the IP address is allocated by the DHCP server. I'll show you more details about DHCP servers in the next chapter. But the IP address, 10.0.1.70, fits within the range I set. The Default Gateway, 10.0.1.1, is the router for this network.

Curious about the Details command button? That pops open the Network Connection Details window on the right side of Figure 11-17. This echoes some information from the window to its left but adds more.

Let me save the details for Chapter 12, but the nice lesson for this section is that Windows XP does provide more network information than previous versions. When you start worrying about changing your network or troubleshooting, the more details you can get, the better.

The configuration screen to tell your computer whether to be a DHCP client and to specify some of these other details looks similar in Windows XP as in earlier versions. Figure 11-18 shows the window, which should look familiar. Get there through Start ➪ My Network Places ➪ View Network Connections ➪ Local Area Connection ➪ Properties.

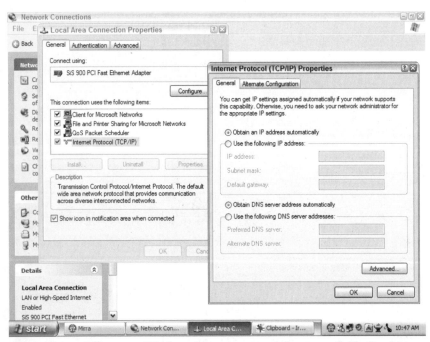

Figure 11-18: Telling your Windows XP system to ask for an available IP address.

The Local Area Connection Properties windows to the left show the Network Properties screen that appears in Windows 9x/ME and Windows 2000 but dressed up in Windows XP style. I opened the Internet Protocol (TCP/IP) Properties window when I highlighted the last entry in the list in the background window and clicked the Properties command button.

All you need do to become a DHCP client is to check the Obtain An IP Address Automatically radio button. Your network will have a DHCP server because your router (you have gotten the router, right?) will almost certainly include a DHCP server module along with the Network Address Translation function that's so important.

You don't specify the IP address of the DHCP server because you can change the server, and have multiple servers if you want. Clients do the electronic equivalent of standing on a street corner and yell, "Can someone tell me who I am, where I am, and how to get out of here?" The DHCP servers respond by providing an available IP address, other network information, and the IP address of the default gateway.

 Chapter 12 includes all types of details on getting to this point if your Windows XP system has not yet been set up for networking. But if your computer's included Ethernet plug works as it should, all you need to know to network your Windows XP computer is in Figure 11-18. But you'll still need to check out Chapter 12 to learn to configure the DHCP server.

Adjusting the default security options

A new setting for Internet security appeared with Windows XP Home and Professional: a personal firewall. They call it Internet Connection Firewall, and you can see it in Figure 11-19. Reach this by clicking My Network Places ⇨ Local Area Connection ⇨ Properties ⇨ Advanced Tab.

This screen looks simple and provides extra protection not afforded by Microsoft operating systems before. And it's easy to configure: check the box and click OK, and you have more protection after than before. So check the box and relax a bit more. But don't turn this on if:

✦ You have a third party firewall such as Norton, Symantec, or Zone Alarm.

✦ Your router includes a good firewall.

 More details about the Internet Connection Firewall settings are in Chapter 12.

The second largest security hole, standard folder sharing, opens your computer up to all sorts of investigations and possible attack and has been closed by default. That's a nice improvement from Microsoft, although long delayed.

File sharing should be turned off unless you are using your Windows XP as a server of sorts. Using the newest computer, which probably includes the largest hard disk, makes sense to configure as the server for many people. If so,

Figure 11-19: Turn on your Internet Connection Firewall if you have no network router with firewall capabilities.

don't worry about the file sharing as long as your router has Network Address Translation running. Right-click any folder if you're curious, and choose the Sharing context menu option to see if the resource has been offered to the world.

You should also consider making the oldest and least exciting computer the server rather than the newest. Heavy file activity slows the server. If it's an older system no one is using, no one cares. If it's your system and someone's dragging your performance down, you care quite a bit.

This option keeps your Windows XP system one step farther away from hackers, because you won't share any files or folders directly from your system. You can still get attacked and have some trouble, but your primary machine, not being a server, wouldn't be the primary target.

Closing exposed security holes

About the only other critical security option to address are the open services that support remote connections to your Windows XP computer. Like Windows 2000, Windows XP offers quite a few services to other computers (and people) on the network.

You should close services immediately if you have no router (then go get a router). If you have a router, feel free to close the services anyway to speed up your computer and release memory and CPU cycles running services no one should be using.

The first option to check is your Universal Plug and Play settings. This feature, handy for Microsoft-only networks, opens the door to many remote exploits controlling devices with poor security.

Services look pretty much the same in Windows XP as in Windows 2000, as you can see in Figure 11-20. You do have to go through a slightly different route to get there, and interpret the new look of Windows XP a bit. Reach this screen via Start ➪ Control Panel ➪ Administrative Tools ➪ Services.

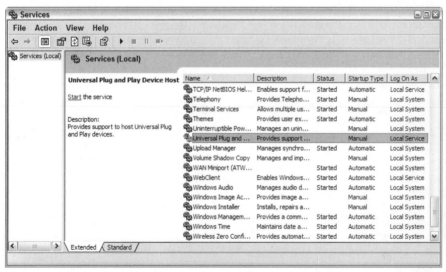

Figure 11-20: The look should be familiar, but there are a few new services running in Windows XP.

UPnP in my system is off. Yours should be off as well.

The rest of the remote service options listed in the Windows 2000 section apply to Windows XP as well. There are a few other services you may think of turning off, depending on your network:

✦ **Terminal Services:** Support remote connections from other PCs to your system.

✦ **WAN Miniport ATW Service:** Added by AOL and usually left behind if AOL is uninstalled

✦ **Wireless Zero Configuration:** Allows Windows XP to try and configure wireless devices rather than letting the vendor tools do the job.

And Internet Connection Sharing? Turn it off and buy a router.

Configuring Other Systems

Other systems, primarily Macintosh and Linux, are ahead of Microsoft in some ways, and even with them in others. Peer-to-peer networking, the equivalent of Microsoft's workgroup, has long been a standardized and well-oiled service for both Macintosh and Linux systems (and the Unix systems before them).

Remember the famous tag line that "The Network is the Computer" from Sun Microsystems? That came out in the 1980s. That's why experts say Microsoft has been catching up, not leading the market.

Microsoft does lead the market in volume, however, which has made the Mac and Linux communities learn to interact with Windows workgroup networking. And so it goes on today.

One excellent Linux desktop system, Xandros 2.0 (www.xandros.com) provides a perspective into non-Windows systems that may surprise you. Take a look at Figure 11-21 and decide if that looks like what you've seen other places in this chapter.

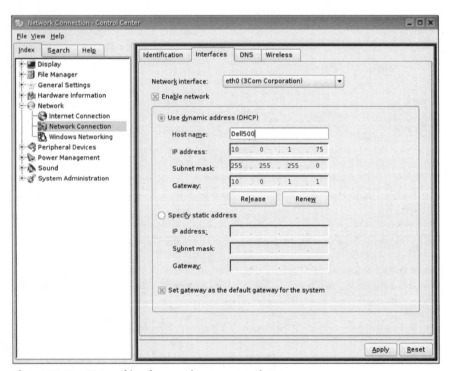

Figure 11-21: Networking from a Linux perspective.

Cross-Reference

To me, using Xandros or one of the other new Linux desktop systems takes little mental readjustment from Windows. Notice how I checked the Xandros system to use the same DHCP services the Windows computers use. No problem. Want to put a dedicated IP address for the Xandros system instead? Again, no problem (more details about why to do that in Chapter 12).

Using Shared Resources

It seems I've spent the bulk of this chapter telling you to disable shared resources. Yet sharing resources defines the essence of networking. But Microsoft's security for shared resources in the workgroup does not stand up against Internet hackers, so I must nag on and on about separating your local network from the network hookup to your broadband service provider.

Now let me show you how to share those resources, find the ones available, and make repeatable connections for later use.

Finding and linking to shares

Finding shared resources doesn't take much work at all: Click My Network Places or Network Neighborhood (Windows 9x/ME) and all the shared documents and shared folders will appear. Figure 11-22 gives a look at one of my lab networks.

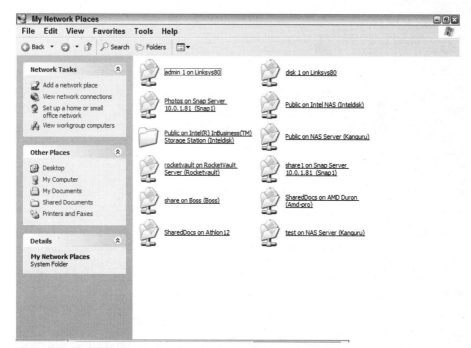

Figure 11-22: Click My Network Places in the Start menu and here you are.

You can set your display to show the listing in various ways, but the view in Figure 11-22 seemed the best way to show the shared folders in enough detail to be visible. Can you see the difference between the third icon from the top in the left line versus the other icons? That one indicates shared documents.

Ten of the 12 icons represent server or storage appliances rather than other computers. The 10 icons come from six different appliances, so you can have more than one share per device. Two icons represent other personal computers. Can you tell the difference? Not without reading the names you can't.

You can find some network shared resources in the My Computer screen as well. Figure 11-23 shows a My Computer listing for a Windows XP Home system. Notice the bottom icon on the screen? The one labeled Network Drives?

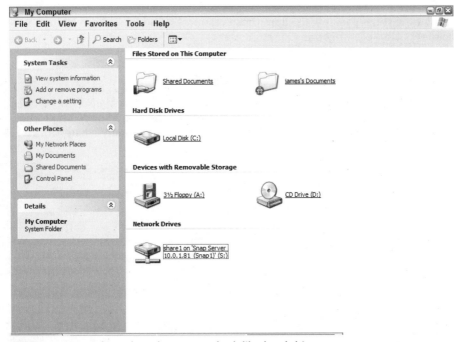

Figure 11-23: Making shared resources look like local drives.

The trick to making a shared resource appear in the My Computer listing rather than just the My Network Places is to "map" a drive letter to that shared file resource. Just as your main hard drive is (usually) Drive C and your CD-ROM drive is (usually) Drive D, you can assign a letter to be a network shared folder as well.

This is simple to do, and you start from the My Computer screen if you want (or any other screen with the Tools menu item). Selecting Tools ⮕ Map Network Drive opens the small window in the left side of Figure 11-24, and clicking the Browse command button next to the Folder field opens the Browse for Folder dialog box shown on the right of the screenshot.

Figure 11-24: Map a drive via Start ⇨ My Computer ⇨ Tools ⇨ Map Network Drive.

In a network with multiple server or storage appliances, you may be listed as a different user on one or another shared resource. For example, a network attached storage device for use by everyone may have a default username (guest) and password (password) to make connections easy. Another network attached storage device may be more restricted, and you'll need a specific name and password. If this happens, you will have to tell that resource who you are and your password. Windows will save the information to make connection easier the next time. The dialog box to map a network drive allows you to login with a different name and password if necessary. You can have as many mapped drives as you have alphabet letters available.

Old Timer Alert: Mapped drives like this show up in the DOS window (or at Windows command prompt) and as a local link in the Folders display. If you remember what the command prompt looks like, and use it now and then, the mapped drive letters come in handy. Type **NET USE** at the command prompt to see your connections, and those with mapped drive letters will use those letters in the display.

Sharing resources

Windows XP makes it easy to share resources, perhaps too easy. That's why I'm glad Microsoft now includes a link for users to learn more about security and sharing in the screen where shares are created. I just hope people read that extra section if they're a little unsure about what they're sharing or why.

On a Windows XP system, right-click a folder (directory for some of us), and choose Sharing and Security from the context menu. The Properties dialog box opens, titled with the folder name (Broadband Properties in Figure 11-25).

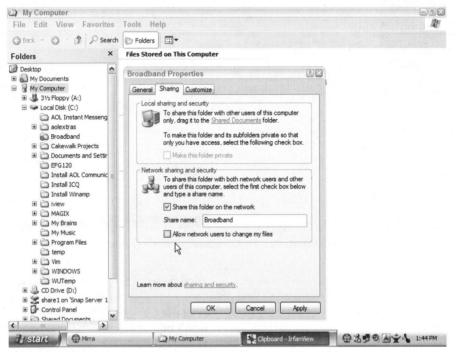

Figure 11-25: Right-click a folder and click Sharing and Security; then pick your option.

Windows XP still clings to the idea that multiple users may be accessing this computer, so the top section explains local sharing and privacy. Quaint, but still possibly useful.

The Network sharing and security section makes it easy to share the folder with one click. You can see in Figure 11-25 the cursor pointing to the Allow network users to change my files check box. In other words, shares are read-only unless you explicitly set them to read/write.

This looks nice and easy, but it's a step backward in security control. Windows 2000 offers more security over the files shared inside the folder, and even Windows 9x/ME asks for passwords immediately. Take a look at Figure 11-26 and see what Windows 2000 offers as way of security on shared files.

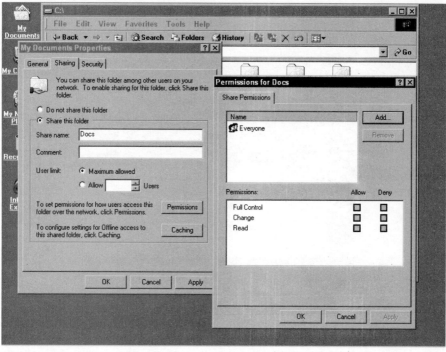

Figure 11-26: Sharing with an extra security step.

Windows 2000 enables you to limit the number of users that can access the shared resource. Interesting, but it probably won't be an issue in your home or small business. But after I clicked the Permissions command button, the extra window (on the right) opened and I have more options.

Want to add a single user who can access to read, but not change, the files? Windows 2000 allows you to do that. So do most of the storage and server appliances in the book discussed earlier. That may be a problem with Windows XP, however, so be careful there.

The Kanguru iNAS-100 network attached storage device (with included router) shows a nice representation of assigning access rights. Figure 11-27 shows the screen, and shows that everyone has access to the Public share.

Kanguru lists options as Full access (read/write), Read-Only, and Deny access. Normally, you don't need to specify Deny access because everyone not allowed by name or group is automatically denied. But if you have someone you want to block from something, and that person is a member of a group with access to that resource, you can deny access individually, although retaining the same profile for the group.

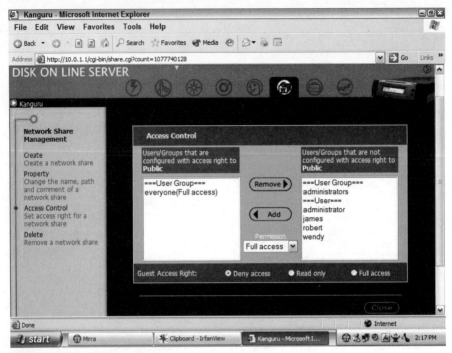

Figure 11-27: Sharing a Kanguru.

Summary

First, upgrade your system. Then get a router with Network Address Translation. Then have fun. Then you wake up.

Windows operating systems older than Windows 2000 have more security holes and require more effort to configure and secure than you probably want to spend. Upgrade if at all possible.

Every networked computer should be secured appropriately with the network situation. The more people on your network, the more need for passwords to guard network resources.

No networked computer is really secure. The best you can do is to close all the obvious security holes, keep your Microsoft operating system updated, and use a router with Network Address Translation and a good firewall.

What You Need to Know About TCP/IP Networks and Routing

Y ou're going to have an interesting situation when
you get more than one computer ready to connect
to your broadband access point. You will have to use the
same type of networking protocols, software, and
configuration routines used by the biggest companies
and universities powering the Internet. But you need to
know only enough to make your small network run
properly. The key points for this chapter are:

+ Networking protocols (often called the protocol
  stack), which provide a standardized way for any
  type of network device to talk to any other type of
  network device, without the user or application
  knowing the details.

+ Networking software, most TCP/IP commands, that
  interface with the networking protocols so
  developers can network their applications.

+ Address management to ensure every IP address
  on your network is unique.

+ How Network Address Translation hides your
  internal IP addresses from the world.

+ How firewalls leverage TCP/IP software access
  points to keep your network safe.

This chapter, even more than the previous one, is a
reference chapter. Dip in where you need to get the
answer you need, and get back to playing with your

computer. Reading this chapter from start to finish goes beyond dry. It would be considered cruel and unusual punishment, so I'll sprinkle in some snide asides here and there to relieve the technical load.

TCP/IP Details

Transmission Control Protocol/Internet Protocol (TCP/IP) runs the world of networking today. By law, all networking books must have a diagram of the Seven Layer OSI model (don't ask, but it starts at the physical layer, includes software that communicates to the physical component and handles transport across the network, and the application software). Because this book doesn't have "network" in the title, I'm going to risk it and refuse to put the diagram in here. Just think of TCP/IP as a supporting layer between the physical (wired or wireless network devices) and the application sending or receiving packets, and you'll be okay.

If it sounds like TCP/IP is a long name for one protocol, that's because it's really two global networking standards. They just work together so well everyone now mashes them together.

Most of the descriptions of TCP/IP focus on the IP portion. They show data streams being split into multiple packets that travel across the Internet via different routes, and even arrive at the far end out of order, forcing the receiving system to reassemble the packets to makes sense of the data.

Imagine sending a letter with 100 words, by putting each word in a separate numbered envelope, and mailing that from your house to an address across the country. I have little doubt the letters would travel through different mail-carriers hands and trucks. They would not all arrive at the same time, and some letters may be lost. And the recipient would have to assemble the letter by arranging the contents based on the number of the envelope. That's how IP works.

IP became the standard because it uses best-effort delivery, which is usually good enough. Besides, a best-effort delivery mechanism uses few resources at either the sending or receiving end.

On the other hand, TCP guarantees the data arrives by establishing a connection between the two hosts (usually computers or routers) involved. This is like you hiring a courier to deliver a package directly to another person. The courier establishes the connection between the two of you. The TCP packets travel the same path across the Internet and arrive in the same order they left.

But that guarantee carries a price on the Internet just as in real life. A first class stamp costs far less than a courier. Even a hundred first class stamps cost less when you factor in distance. If the courier goes across town, it's expensive. If a dedicated courier goes across the country, faithfully carrying your package in hand all the way, the cost will be outrageous. Tying together the two endpoints, along with the route between them, takes resources from many systems.

Why are people excited by phone calls over the Internet? Because a typical phone call works like TCP, making a connection between the caller and called. But phone calls over the Internet (VoIP for Voice over Internet Protocol) use IP and best effort, counting on the fact that a few dropped or out-of-sequence packets won't ruin the call quality. This reduces resources needed and means cheaper phone calls with acceptable quality.

TCP/IP isn't necessarily the best protocol in the networking world, but it won the popularity contest for a variety of good reasons. It offers robust networking over huge networks. Other protocols offer that as well, but TCP/IP offers ways for devices to join networks without needing to have their addresses listed in an authentication database of any central server. This method eliminates the types of bottlenecks (overloaded authentication servers) that can choke networks.

Why TCP/IP?

You may have heard that the Internet was developed by the Pentagon to continue communications after a nuclear war. Close. The Internet was developed out of a series of networking projects funded by Defense Advanced Research Projects Agency (DARPA) to link existing networks. That's where the term *Internet* came from: Interconnected Networks gave way to Internet.

Early on, universities (often while funded by DARPA) connected their existing campus networks to the new DARPA Internet. Technically, the Internet is a network of networks.

Other protocols developed based on the requirements for local networking. Connections between systems were assumed to be reliable and speedy. TCP/IP designs assumed the networks were not local, connections were not reliable, and bandwidth for high speeds was not available. TCP/IP developers tested the protocol on wireless and satellite networks from the beginning.

Why did TCP/IP become the only protocol allowed on the Internet starting on January 1, 1983 (called Flag Day, although not the one on your calendar)? The following reasons highlight the features that made TCP/IP the protocol of choice.

✦ **Connectionless Packet Delivery Service:** This is the IP part of the feature list. Until this technology, most networking (like the telephone network) had to create a link between end devices. That meant the connection protocol had to understand all the details of the network between the two devices. IP skips this problem by mapping directly onto the underlying hardware (or now wireless network links) and traversing the connecting devices linking different hardware networks. Lost packets in a sequence are requested when the receiving end realizes the packets are lost.

✦ **Reliable Stream Transport Service:** This is the TCP part of the feature list. When applications need a direct link and will be disrupted by packet loss (which happens with IP), the programmers demand TCP. The network connection gets established by making a link across the Internet reliable like a wire between two systems. The sending device won't send Packet 2 until the receiving device has acknowledged the accurate receipt of Packet 1. (There are ways to speed that process, such as acknowledging seven received packets at once, but they aren't important now).

The following features, along with the maturation of TCP/IP starting in the late 1970s (work started in the early 1970s), made the Internet technically feasible.

✦ **Independent network topology:** The protocols are separate from the underlying hardware, because TCP/IP is a standard implemented by every hardware vendor who makes network equipment. As long as the hardware supports TCP/IP, the packets zooming around don't care whose name is on the router, computer, network interface card, wire, or wiring hub. They all support TCP/IP, just like the road doesn't care what type of car or truck runs on top of it.

✦ **Universal interconnection:** By using unique addresses, any two computers on the network can communicate. The address uses a form recognizable to all other systems on the network, and each packet of data (often called a datagram in the early days) holds its source and destination addresses. Because each data packet knows its destination address, it routes through the Internet to reach it independently of other data packets.

✦ **End-to-end acknowledgments:** Some early networks tracked progress across each and every connection point along the way. In other words, each router a packet passed sent an acknowledgment back to the source of the packet. That caused an enormous amount of extra traffic, and didn't really tell whether a packet reached the final destination. The Internet protocols decided to rely on acknowledgements from the end points, rather than interim points. This end-to-end acknowledgment scheme gave the crucial information (destination reached) without the extra traffic, and works when the end points don't share any direct links to each other.

✦ **Standards for applications:** Although the lower part of the protocol stack looks to the transport support details, the upper part provides support for applications. Developers can use these existing services to provide communication support for applications rather than trying to write their own communication protocols.

TCP/IP wasn't discovered. These protocols developed after long years of hard work by networking pioneers. Some funding and technology came from the U.S. Government, some from universities and other research sites, and some from the early vendors making the newly designed hardware and software products.

This process called for everyone to share information rather than hoard it. Groups of individuals gave up their time to meet and hash out differences to ensure all parts of the developing network fit together properly. Many of those groups (with new members, of course) still remain to watch Internet development, but the aggressive push of some large companies has distorted the process away from a spirit of community to a spirit of commercialization. Not all changes bring advancement.

Addressing

I wrote an article for *Network World* magazine in August 1996 called *Finding Your Way Through TCP/IP*. The following is the first line of the article.

"If TCP/IP's addressing scheme brings back memories of new math, take heart: you're not alone."

Doing that article allowed me to talk to many of the smart people developing the next generation of TCP/IP. I also talked to managers and designers of large TCP/IP networks. All of them missed their time estimate for when the current version of TCP/IP would run out of addresses and the next version would appear to add billions of new addresses.

IP address format

IP addresses represent four numbers of 8 bits each for a total of 32 bits. The numbers appear as a group of four octets, or four groups of 8-bit numbers.

If you think IP addresses are confusing, be glad you're not seeing the real IP address. When you see an address such as the following:

    204.251.122.127

The computer actually sees this:

    11001100.11111011.01111010.01111111

Now doesn't 204.251.122.127 look better?

All IP addresses (in IPv4 which is still the current version) must have four numbers separated by the periods. If you don't see three numbers in each of the four address octets, they are still there. Several times I've used an address like 10.0.1.1 for an example of a router on my lab network. Technically I should write it 010.000.001.001, but that gets confusing. Your computer will understand 10.0.1.1 just fine.

The highest number you can have in any of these octets is 255, because that's the highest decimal number you can represent with eight binary digits (the bits). Yes, the number is really 256, but binary digits start counting at zero, making the decimal maximum 255.

Note   One of my favorite computer jokes is "There are only 10 kinds of people in the world: those who understand binary and those who don't." If you don't understand binary send me a note and I'll explain.

You may have noticed the IP address 255.255.255.0 in some of the screenshots. That's called a *subnet mask* and helps separate the IP address into network and host (computer) addresses. Subnet masking used to be a pain, but new advances in software make it much easier because your broadband service provider has to do all the work now.

There are three major groupings of IP addresses: Class A, Class B, and Class C. These addresses separate the network and host addresses at the periods between octets. You can tell which class an IP address belongs to based on the following list:

+ **Class A addresses:** 1-127.0.0.0
+ **Class B addresses:** 128-191.0.0.0
+ **Class C addresses:** 192-233.0.0.0

There are only 127 total Class A addresses, and those were gone long before anyone outside the Internet development pioneers knew about the Internet. Numbers of hosts per class are as follows:

+ **Class A:** 127 total networks, nearly 17 million unique host addresses per network.

+ **Class B:** Over 65,000 total networks, over 65,599 unique host addresses per network.

+ **Class C:** Nearly 17 million total networks, 254 unique host addresses per network.

Companies almost never get assigned "networks" anymore, because the Class A addresses were snapped up in the early 1980s and the Class B addresses were running out by the mid 1990s. Class C addresses are usually assigned to service providers who slice and dice the network address numbers to allocate the least number possible to each client.

Now you have an idea where your single IP address fits into the scheme of the global network.

Using the IP addresses from your provider

Many times, your service provider assigns you a dynamically allocated IP address for your cable/DSL modem. That means your cable/DSL modem requests an address when it starts, and a server at the provider assigns your cable/DSL modem an available address.

If that's the situation for your network connection, you don't need to know any of these IP addressing details. You're welcome to stay if you're curious, however. There won't be a test but at least you'll learn something new.

When your broadband service provider assigns you multiple IP addresses, which is what happens when you buy a business plan from some service providers, things work differently. But the service provider must have some way to tell its network devices which part of your address is the network part and which is the host part.

This used to be done with the subnet mask, that 255.255.255.0 address. That subnet mask marks the first three octets of the IP address (the 255.255.255) as the network address, leaving the last octet (the .0) as the host portion of the address, a standard Class C address.

But addresses are in short supply, so giving a home or small business user a Class C address with 254 IP addresses wastes the majority of them. So service providers slice the number down by increasing the number of bits for the network portion of the address and decreasing the number of potential hosts on those networks. There are two main ways to slice these addresses:

✦ Classless Inter-Domain Routing (CIDR)

✦ Variable Length Subnet Masks (VLSM)

You don't have to choose which option you receive because that decision belongs to your service provider. But many small office service provider options include six IP addresses you can use for Web and e-mail servers and the like.

The configuration details of Network Address Translation (NAT) are deeper in this chapter.

Reserved addresses

Some IP addresses are set aside for internal networks connected to the Internet through a NAT service, and I'll discuss those later. But two addresses are restricted in every network address scheme, internal or Internet:

✦ xxx.xxx.xxx.0 is forbidden for use by individual devices because that number refers to the entire network.

✦ xxx.xxx.xxx.255 is forbidden because that's the number used for broadcast messages.

If you use a server to provide IP addresses to clients this will never be a problem. If you type individual addresses into each network host, be careful and avoid these numbers.

Running out of IP addresses

There are over 4 billion IP addresses available using the scheme in place now, IPv4. Some experts believe only 5–10 percent of all IP addresses allocated are actually used. So how can we be running out?

Because address allocation is done inefficiently, that's why. A Class A address has the room to provide IP addresses to nearly 17 million unique devices. Companies don't have that many, so maybe 99.9 percent of those IP addresses are wasted.

Even small networks waste space. I once was assigned the Class C IP address 204.251.122.0. (I guess I still "own" that address but my service provider from that time is long gone now.) I have a huge number of systems in the lab for a two-person office, but I never used more than a dozen addresses at a time.

Experts I interviewed in 1996 were sure the IP address space would run out soon. One positive engineer declared that IPv6 networks would be rolled out by 1998 (oops).

That turned out to be far too soon, as Network Address Translation became popular and allowed service providers to control their numbering schemes. Now my service providers assign me a single IP address for the cable and DSL modem connections that's usually defined dynamically.

One of the big advantages of IPv6 is the hugely expanded address space. After all, cell phones and beepers and data watches and PDAs all connect to the Internet now and more will do so in the future. Here's how the IP address numbers work:

IPv4 has a 32-bit address space. IPv6 has a 128-bit address space.

✦ IPv4: 2^{32} unique IP addresses
✦ IPv6: $2^{32} \times 2^{32} \times 2^{32} \times 2^{32}$ unique IP addresses

How many addresses does that mean? Even if we allocate IPv6 addresses as inefficiently as we have IPv4 addresses, that still leaves us over 1,500 IP addresses for every square meter of dry land on Earth. That should even cover the cell phones.

Short take? Don't worry about IP addresses. By the time we need them, service providers will have their networks updated and will pull you along with them into the future with unlimited IP addresses.

Routing

Routing is the process of moving a data packet from its source to its destination in general terms, and specifically moving a data packet from one network to the next network using the best pathway across the network. Routers can be hardware appliances, as discussed earlier, that you place between your cable/DSL modems and your network or software modules inside other servers.

Bridging is like routing, but not as complicated. When a data packet arrives at a bridge, the bridge software checks the low-level packet destination address. Then the bridge makes a simple decision: is the address on the side of the network where the packet already is? If so, ignore the packet. If not, pass the packet to the other side of the bridge. These are great devices for segmenting high traffic networks, but they aren't smart enough to make complex decisions.

Router software examines data packets at a higher level of the stack of networking protocols than do bridges. At this level, the router can see where the packet came from and where it is going, and make a judgment about the best direction to send the packet. The routing table in each router holds information about optimal network routes for data packets coming to the router.

Your router will have a very easy decision to make, because it will connect to your service provider. Any packet leaving your internal network will go upstream to your service provider and then out to the Internet. Your service provider has some serious routers, however, and fights with them daily to keep them up to date, active, current, and processing packets at the highest speed possible.

 Note Cisco has an excellent TCP/IP tutorial including most routing protocols at `cisco.com/warp/public/535/4.html`

Any routing information necessary for your situation will come directly from your service provider. But unless you start getting into multiple network connections or virtual private networks, you can usually avoid diving into the world of routers.

Dynamic Host Configuration Protocol

I've mentioned Dynamic Host Configuration Protocol (DHCP) several times while dealing with network setup. Now you get to see what it is, why it's useful, and why you will like it.

DHCP is an internal network management tool. If your network has one computer connected to a broadband service provider, network administration means nothing. Even if your network is in a small business with 25 computers, network administration will not ruin your day (at least the DHCP part won't).

But imagine your job revolves around corralling a thousand computers across multiple internal networks. Imagine the thousand computers include 50 different ways to set their IP addresses for communicating to the network. You do remember that each IP address must be unique on the network, right? That's a thousand addresses to track on multiple networks.

Early on in networking, the pioneer administrators realized something had to change. Tracking a bunch of computer IP addresses on a piece of paper to remember which computer used which address seemed downright stupid. They were computers, after all, not desk chairs. The computers should help the process.

Thus developed Boot Protocol (BOOTP, pronounced Boot Pea). One BOOTP server on the network watched the wires for a BOOTP request from a client trying to boot up and get onto the network. The BOOTP server responded to the request with a packet of information telling the client its network IP address and the location of a file on the server to boot the client. This was back when hard disks were so expensive even Unix workstations didn't always have their own.

And BOOTP was good, but limited. More complex networks demanded more complex boot arrangements. BOOTP required preconfiguration of a host database and didn't handle the developing dynamic networks in which hosts come and go and clients look to connect to the hosts without having to configure their connection database.

Thus developed DHCP. Supporting dynamic allocation of network addresses and support for newly attached hosts, DHCP became the successor to BOOTP. Even nicer in a world of expanding network-attached devices, DHCP includes a way to recover IP addresses no longer needed so another device can use them.

Tech Bits A *DHCP server* is a device that provides network configuration information when queried

A *DHCP client* is a device that broadcasts a query packet to the network asking for network configuration information.

By 1996, DHCP was well defined and marching through the Internet standard protocol process. Before the world of personal computers really discovered the World Wide Web, DHCP was ready to handle increased network IP addressing chores.

What DHCP servers do

Any number of different routers and server/storage appliances include a DHCP server. The server software isn't that complicated and provides value for all small networks, and especially when the appliance is the first server-type device on the network. In fact, in my test lab, the following devices include a DHCP server:

✦ Every network attached storage unit

✦ Every server appliance

✦ Every wireless router

✦ Every wired router

Essentially, just about every server-type device of any kind includes a DHCP server. Wiring hubs and HomePlug wiring (TCP/IP over home power connections) seem to be the exceptions. Oh, and the wireless Webcam doesn't act as a DHCP server. Maybe that will come with the next software version.

The majority of DHCP servers manage the following for their clients:

✦ Provide client IP address

✦ Provide client's subnet mask

✦ Identify the default router for the network

✦ Provide other DNS or netbios settings if needed

DHCP can also supply the following if tweaked:

✦ Host name

✦ Available routes

✦ Application and directory-specific settings

I don't want you to push the DHCP envelope, although I'm not sure if you could use the tools delivered with storage and server appliances. But at least the various products display DHCP in a way that won't confuse people.

The DHCP servers you will be working with provide the following to clients:

✦ IP address

✦ Subnet mask

✦ Default gateway

✦ DNS server addresses

✦ Length of time to use the address

When a network device configured as a DHCP client starts its networking connection—whether that happens when booting up, when started, when restarted, or when restarting the network interface card—the client sends a broadcast packet looking for a DHCP server. The server sees the packet, checks for available IP addresses, and provides one of those addresses to the client.

A network can have two or more DHCP servers as long as its client IP addresses don't overlap. Using two servers on a large network provides fault tolerance and redundancy. You won't need that in your home or small business network.

Redundancy means two independent devices performing a similar job.

Fault tolerance means two or more devices connected in some manner so that their resources remain available even after a failure of one or more units.

Some DHCP servers, even those in network appliances, offer a way to assign a particular address to a particular client. You must configure the Media Access Control (MAC) address, the nonchangeable address set in the network interface card hardware, into the DHCP server. When the DHCP server gets a request from that device, it supplies the specific IP address you configured for it. This is handy in larger networks, but won't matter in a home or very small office setting. This feature may be called something like Address Reservation.

Besides, some of the DHCP servers in the routers aimed at this market assume they are the only DHCP server and do not provide an IP address for the default gateway and automatically use their own addresses. That leads to trouble as it tells the clients the gateway to the Internet is through that router, when in fact another router actually connects to the cable/DSL modem. If you want a second DHCP server for redundancy or to provide IP addresses in two different ranges, make it one of the storage appliances that doesn't act as a gateway so it will provide the correct gateway IP address.

DHCP server settings

Connect your router running your DHCP service to the cable/DSL modem. This causes the fewest problems, and that way your DHCP server gets the DNS server addresses provided by your service provider directly from the cable/DSL modem. That means the DNS addresses provided to your clients won't have to be configured (by you) in your DHCP server settings.

For clients

Figure 12-1 shows the DHCP server section of a Netgear WGT624 wireless (802.11g) router and firewall. Netgear sells many products through retail, and you can see this router provides plenty of helpful information on the screen where you must put that information to use.

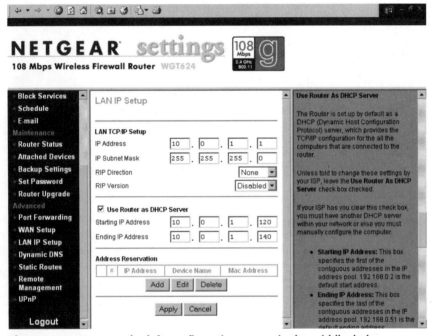

Figure 12-1: Menu on the left, configuration screen in the middle, help information on the right.

Because the Netgear puts its DHCP server settings under Advanced LAN IP Setup, the screen includes some networking options not found in older routers. But when you read the help information on the right part of the screen, Netgear tells you to leave the two Routing Information Protocol (RIP) settings at their defaults unless told otherwise by your broadband service provider, because you will almost never have to specify which version of the protocol used to communicate between routers (RIP) on your broadband network.

Most routers don't consider DHCP service as part of the "Advanced" network sections. Providing IP addresses for clients on a small network ranks as one of the most important functions for routers in this market, so they put the DHCP functions under an easily found label on their configuration screens.

One storage appliance/router, the Tritton ASAP, adds an interesting touch to its DHCP services. Like many routers in this market, the Tritton includes four Ethernet 10/100 Base-T ports to plug in computers directly or wiring hubs from existing networks.

That's pretty normal. But the Tritton adds a way to assign different IP client address ranges to each of the four Ethernet connections. Look at Figure 12-2 to see what I mean.

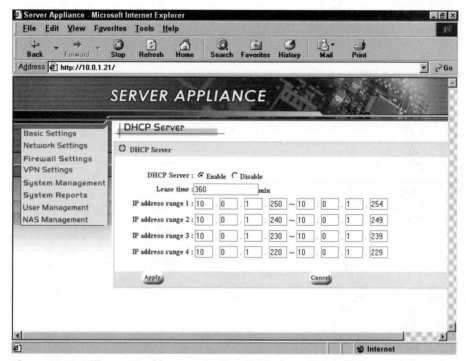

Figure 12-2: Different IP address settings available for each Ethernet connection.

Notice the default lease time for each IP address: 360 minutes. That's the default for the Tritton device, but that's a shorter time period than any other DHCP server I've tested.

Set your DHCP Address Lease Time to at least one full day. Many broadband service providers reset your cable/DSL modem every day or two, and if new information is provided to your router you want the clients to receive that information fairly quickly.

Some clients, networks, and applications have trouble with short DHCP leases, however. If clients disconnect from servers, or act weird in other ways, lengthen the DHCP lease time to a week and see if that helps. Some DHCP routers allow you to set lease times as long as 999 days, so check out your model.

For broadband connections

Your DHCP settings for the router connected to your cable/DSL modem can receive configuration details from your service provider. That's the smart way to configure your router so network changes are passed to your client(s) whenever they join the network.

The Kanguru iNAS-100 has a nice connection screen with good detail. Figure 12-3 shows the Wide Area Network (WAN) configuration, which controls how the router connects to the cable/DSL modem. Your broadband service provider will tell you whether to use PPPoE (Point-to-Point Protocol over Ethernet) or DHCP (see more information in the *Connection Options to Your Service Provider* section later in this chapter). Either option used for connecting to your service provider will still provide the DNS server addresses (the servers that translate IP addresses into host names) for your router to pass along to your clients.

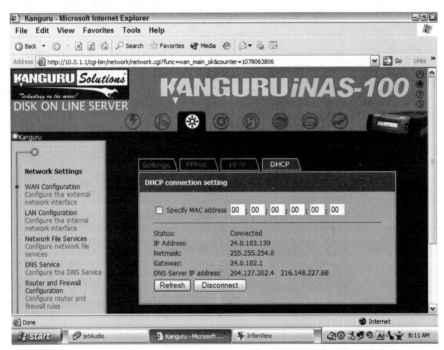

Figure 12-3: Notice the DNS Server IP address listing at the bottom of the screen.

This screen shows the WAN connection, but in the Kanguru NAS/router this is where you find the DNS server IP addresses. Notice there are two DNS server names. Fault tolerance in DNS name servers means the difference between surfing the Web easily or being locked out of the Web if your only DNS server drops offline or you can't reach it anymore. Having two DNS servers listed makes it easy for your client to keep going if one DNS server is out of touch.

Did you notice the gateway IP address makes no sense based on my lab network? That's because that address shows the gateway IP address on the service providers network, where the cable/DSL modem sends packets bound for the Internet.

The IP address just above that listing is the Wide Area Network IP address for the router to use to find the cable/DSL modem. This IP address, provided by Comcast Cable, tends to change every day or two. The only reason I know this is because the Kanguru iNAS-100 displays that IP address on the front panel LCD screen, and I notice the numbers are different on different days.

Yes, this means that a device can be a DHCP server and a DHCP client at the same time. That's how IP networking works so well, by sharing resources. And devices can certainly provide resources to some while using resources from others.

DHCP client settings

This is a snap. The designers of Microsoft Windows operating systems got smart when they installed TCP/IP software and made use of DHCP servers on the network. Now, Windows XP makes setting your client for DHCP use a one-click job. And the default network setup for new clients is to look for a DHCP server automatically.

Figure 12-4 shows the Windows XP Home networking configuration screens. You can reach the Local Area Network Connections Status screen various ways, including by right-clicking the network icon on the task bar and choosing Status.

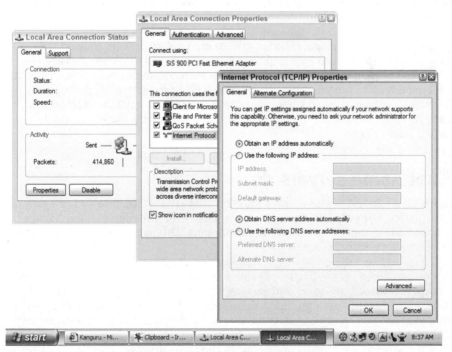

Figure 12-4: The default Windows XP DHCP client setting.

Reach this screen by highlighting your Ethernet network connection in the Local Area Connection Properties window, the middle one in Figure 12-4. Once highlighted, click the Properties command button to see the final window labeled Internet Protocol (TCP/IP) Properties.

You have a place to put in a specific IP address for your client. That is often necessary on larger networks or remote offices where links back to HQ require special configuration. Your home or small business network shouldn't use dedicated IP addresses for regular, run of the mill client stations.

The same advice goes for DNS server addresses. Your broadband service provider will send the addresses to your router and DHCP server, so accept those addresses. Large networks may have good reasons for specifying DNS servers, but home and small business networks rarely do.

Windows now (finally throwing notebook computer users a bone) offers an Alternative Configuration page in Windows XP. This page allows you to set another, completely different network IP address configuration. Very handy for those taking notebook computers between their home network and the office, or traveling between offices.

Domain Name Service

Sometimes called the Domain Name System, when you see the acronym DNS it means the way to translate IP addresses (such as 64.236.16.20) into readable names easier to remember, such as CNN.com.

Originally developed for local Unix systems on a network, a centralized DNS server replaced the need to put the IP addresses and host names of every networked system into a local HOSTS file on each computer. You couldn't find a machine if it wasn't in your own machine's HOSTS file. With a handful of machines, you could make something like that work. 50 machines turned that manual system into scramble city. The Internet, obviously, made a manual system impossible.

What name servers do

There are a handful of global "root servers" that are the ultimate authority for all DNS queries. For years the Internet ran on just seven root servers, but hacker attacks against those servers and the expanding Web made the addition of a few more root servers necessary.

One reason some people like to call this a Domain Name System is that the root servers for various networks and service providers constantly reference and update each other. Although home users looking for an online bargain CD outlet will never directly query one of the main root servers, they will query their ISPs DNS root server, which queries a root server upstream, which queries a root server upstream, which may query one of the root servers.

It may look complicated, and it is complicated to keep running and expanding, but you'll never see the complication. All you need do is provide your client the IP address of one or more DNS servers. When you look for CNN.com, the name server at your ISP tells your browser to go to 64.236.16.20, and CNN.com pops up in your browser window.

Very rarely, a name server high up in the authority chain will go down or be disconnected by accident or malicious intent. None of the main root servers have had this happen, even though hackers have tried.

When a name server at your broadband service provider goes offline for any reason, your surfing will suffer. Root server connections time out after just a few seconds and the name server querying that server will shift to a secondary name server. But those delays can cause hiccups in name service, causing your Web searches for sites to fail.

Luckily, the fail-over time to a new server is only about 5 seconds, and service providers have a range of options to keep name service up and running. Although some worry about a global DNS shutdown, or hackers boast about their ability to cause such, the name service structure remains solid, redundant, and well protected.

Finding name servers

A name server provides some type of naming or directory service. DNS is a name server of sorts, but doesn't work as a typical directory service.

Your broadband service provider will do one of the following:

✦ Give you the names of name servers to list in your TCP/IP configuration

✦ Automatically assign name servers through DHCP to your cable/DSL router

In almost every case today, your broadband service provider will send the name server details along with the DHCP setup for your cable/DSL modem. You shouldn't ever have to search for name servers.

Name servers must be listed when creating a new Web site. Your Web site host will give you those names, or if you're hosting your own server, check with your service provider.

If your router doesn't pick up the proper name servers, you will have to call your service provider. Or, first, reset your cable/DSL modem and your router, in that order, then check back. If your devices don't have a reset button, unplug the device, wait 30 seconds, and replug the device. That's a serious reset you should really call a reboot.

No name server means you can't resolve any IP addresses into names and therefore can't surf the Web. You can see your name server addresses in

Windows XP in your Network Connections Details window, as shown in Figure 12-5.

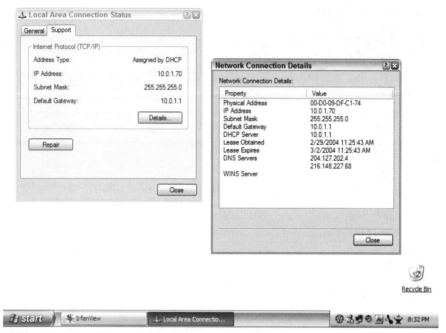

Figure 12-5: Details in your Windows XP connection.

Reach this point by right-clicking Network Connections (either in My Network Places or in the task bar if the icon appears there when you network) and click Status then the Support page. Then click the Details command button, and a window that should look amazingly like the one on the right in Figure 12-5 will appear.

If you need to set an IP address on a client, you need the addresses of at least one name server. Do yourself a favor and copy down the information from this page, and you can supply the IP address of the DNS servers in the space requested when you write in a specific IP address for a client.

Static IP addresses

Standard residential broadband service plans almost always come with a dynamically allocated IP address for your cable/DSL modem. When you configure your router to use DHCP to get an IP address from your service provider your cable/DSL modem gets a different IP address every time the modem restarts or your broadband service drops and resumes a connection. That IP address information goes to your router.

When you're going out to the Internet, it doesn't matter what your IP address is, as long as it's unique on the network. But users who want to connect to your

Web or e-mail server need a way to find you. That means you need a stationary location on the network. That means you need a static IP address.

Pros of a static IP address

Web servers have static IP addresses (with an exception I'll explain in the Dynamic DNS section upcoming). E-mail servers have static IP addresses.

Broadband service provider plans always include options for one or more static IP addresses.

Here's why Earthlink believes you should pay $15 per month more for a static IP address:

✦ Home teleworkers will benefit by easier passage through corporate network firewalls and connections to Virtual Private Networks.

✦ Game players will be able to sign up for more multiplayer games.

SBC/Yahoo DSL doesn't say why you should pay $25 per month extra for five static IP address offered with residential service, but it has a price plan in place.

Verizon told me why I should have a static IP address, but called it a feature of DSL rather than of IP addressing. Verizon echoes Earthlink's reasons for having static IP:

✦ You need it to host Web sites.

✦ You need it to host e-mail servers.

✦ You need it for conducting e-commerce activities (I guess with the Web sites).

✦ It facilitates remote user access to business networks (VPNs).

Verizon didn't show me a price for residential service with a static IP address, but the charge is an extra $30 per month for the small business package.

It's clear: If you want to host a server of any type (Web, e-mail, File Transfer Protocol, or game) you need a static IP address. People can't find you if you don't stay put, and a static IP address lets you stay put in the world of the Internet.

It was interesting to me that no service provider I found in my search offered reaching a Webcam in your home as an advantage of a static IP address. Guess the Nanny Cam craze hasn't hit the service providers yet.

Cons of a static IP address

Money. It costs more for a static IP address from every vendor of residential broadband I checked, or at least could find on their Web sites. Having a static IP address costs you more money.

Why? It costs the provider more money. As I showed earlier in this chapter, IP addresses are running out (some believe they are running out in the near term, some believe in the far term). Supplying customers with IP addresses of their own means the service providers can't put those IP addresses in the DHCP pool and lease them out.

Another reason some people avoid a static IP address is that is *does* make you findable on the Internet. Security by obscurity can't be your entire plan, but having your Internet address change now and then makes it harder for hackers to find and target you. Whether that's a real advantage with the fast-acting tools hackers have today is a matter for another book.

So far, the arguments against a static IP address include the following:

✦ It costs more money.
✦ It's slightly less secure.

Now if your company is paying for you to get broadband at your home, the price difference won't come out of your pocket. And if your company's network security requires you to have a static IP address, that's what you'll have.

But if you just want to host a Web and e-mail server, go another direction entirely and sign up for a hosting service. With a hosting provider, you'll get much better network throughput. Providers have big, fat, and fast connections to the Internet and they will keep the servers up and running. Running your own Web and e-mail server, even with a server appliance, may be less fun than you expect.

Dynamic Domain Name Service

Another option if you want to host your own Web and e-mail server but don't want to pay the high markups from service provider for their static IP addresses is to check into a provider of Dynamic DNS. There are a variety of them available, and you can find them by searching for "dynamic dns" on your favorite search engine.

Essentially, a Dynamic DNS service company keeps address listings for your Web or e-mail servers (or Nanny Cam) on its hosts. An application resides on your computer (or server) that notifies the Dynamic DNS host when your IP changes. It doesn't matter if your broadband service provider reboots every night and changes your address, because the local application will quickly update the information on the DNS service company.

When others look for your Web site by typing the www.YourWebSite.com URL, the DNS servers around the Internet will point them to your Dynamic DNS host. That host will point them to your current IP address. Bingo, you have a connection. And that connection costs less than any of the static IP address options I found from broadband service providers (FYI).

Network Address Translation

Chapter 11 made it clear you need a router, and your router needs Network Address Translation (NAT). That router must be between your computer(s) and your cable/DSL modem. If you don't have a router like this with NAT enabled, you are not taking security seriously.

Some people think of NAT like a disguise: Your packets are really sent from a computer with an IP address of 192.168.1.34 but the Internet services you visit believe your IP address is really 24.0.103.139.

Some people think of NAT like a translator: Your packets come from a private network, and a system in between (your router with NAT software) translates the private language (er, IP address) into something the rest of the Internet devices can understand.

Either way you want to think of it is fine with me. Just enable NAT on your router yesterday.

Tech Bits *Proxy servers* are devices that act in place of other devices. Some people consider them NAT devices; some people consider them more than a NAT device, and some don't know what to call them. If you use a proxy server for caching Web activity or as a connection to outside Instant Messaging servers, they do perform a type of NAT service. But they really aren't the same thing as a NAT, so don't let people confuse you.

Public and private addresses

Remember that in the IP addressing sections earlier I said that every device connected to the Internet must have a unique address. That's the public address that everyone else on the Internet can see. It's not only a public address but also a global address when you talk about the Internet.

Private addresses are those that are not seen on the Internet. In fact, the Internet standards bodies created three separate IP address ranges that will never be seen on the Internet because all routers must change or ignore those addresses before passing on the data packets.

The private address ranges are:

✦ 10.0.0.0–10.255.255.255

✦ 172.16.0.0–172.31.255.255

✦ 192.168.0.0–192.168.255.255

You may have noticed one of these address ranges, especially the last one, when looking at the default IP address of new routers and other appliances. The 192.168.0.0 network range is the most popular for new devices to use out of the box. Many network appliances favor the 192.168.1.1 address for themselves, and their DHCP settings start numbering at 192.168.1.2.

Large networks make good use of these private addresses because they provide far more flexibility and quantity than available public address ranges. The 10.0.0.0 network range can host nearly 17 million individual hosts and is easy to remember.

 Note See an advantage for DHCP here? Network managers can renumber all their network devices by changing their DHCP servers rather than changing their clients.

Because these private network addresses don't go across the Internet, someone on the outside can't directly address any of your network devices (meaning computers). Hackers can't launch an attack against your computer, because they can't see it unless they're on your private network.

Configuring NAT

Even back in the mid 1990s when private addresses became available, configuration was straightforward and relatively simple. The good news is that vendors haven't found a way to make NAT more complicated.

There are two critical pieces to the NAT configuration puzzle: your private network address range for internal use and the IP address of the device running NAT which is publicly viewable. The NAT device will be your router, and the IP address it uses to connect to your cable/DSL modem is the public address. You set your private IP address range when you configure your DHCP server (also your router for convenience).

Figure 12-6 shows the most complicated NAT configuration of any of the routers in the test lab.

The Kanguru iNAS-100 is the only router with a specific check box to configure NAT. How common is NAT? Every other router assumes NAT. If you enable the DHCP server, the public address used is that of the router itself.

Translating the address

Behind the scenes a little bit more goes on than it appears with one check box. But the process is straightforward. One explanation is to imagine you send a letter from a PO box, using that PO box for your return address. The "public" world of the Post Office and the recipient see only the PO box address. When the response comes addressed to the PO box, you carry it back to your home or office. Only you know your home address, and the outsiders only know the PO box address.

But I need to show the send/receive dance with IP addresses. Let me simplify the steps that occur when you send and receive a packet through NAT:

1. You request a Web page from the Internet.

2. The data packet leaves your computer bearing your private IP address of 10.0.1.23.

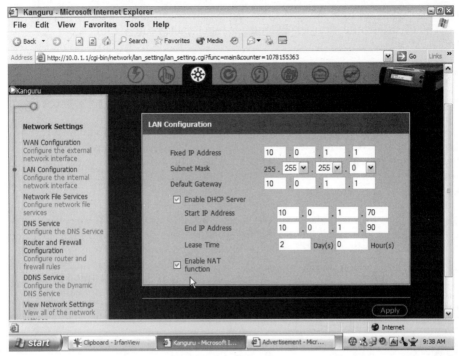

Figure 12-6: Check the box, and NAT is configured.

3. The router receives the outgoing packet.

4. The router replaces the 10.0.1.23 IP address with its own IP address of 24.0.103.149.

5. The router adds a port number to the outgoing IP address so it now looks like 24.0.103.149:5788.

6. The router makes an entry in a database table to track all incoming packets addressed to port number 5788 as belonging to 10.0.1.23.

7. The Web site responds and sends a packet to 24.0.103.149:5788.

8. The router receives the packet addressed to port 5788 and checks the address table.

9. The router changes the IP address to that of your computer (10.0.1.23) and delivers the packet.

Actually, there are a few more details in there with port number tracking for the internal and external addresses and port numbers used to address Web pages and the like. But all this happens under the covers, out of sight, and literally out of mind. This stuff works, and works reliably.

A port number just specifies a software address and allows the router to track outgoing packets and match the incoming packets to the correct internal device that requested the packet. The other port numbers get involved because when you send a packet to a Web page you really send it to 129.201.34.7:80 because port 80 identifies the software listening for Web page requests.

Is NAT enough security?

Short answer? No, but it's a good start.

Security experts always advise layers of defense. Your home exemplifies a layered defense, for example. You have locks on the door. You have an alarm system. You have all your jewels and extensive gold coin collection (fun to pretend, right?) locked in a safe. You have insurance on your jewels and gold coins.

Your excellent lock and alarm system keeps burglars out, like NAT keeps hackers out. But the locks and alarms do nothing to stop someone you let into your home, like the FedEx or UPS person, from getting to your jewels and gold coins.

NAT does nothing to stop worms, viruses, and Trojans. It does nothing to back up and protect your files. It keeps your internal devices hidden, but only from outsiders.

NAT limitations

Many new network features, such as multiplayer games and peer-to-peer networks, want a direct connection to the actual device, not a NAT server. Sometimes remote office connections, such as Virtual Private Networks, have a problem with a NAT server, although this problem is easing quite a bit.

A new function called Realm Specific IP (RSIP) works for large companies by adding the public address at the client (your computer) rather than the NAT server. The NAT server routes the new public address out of the network to the Internet. This requires a new server to hand out the public IP addresses and related port numbers and some new client software. Good for large companies, but home users and small businesses won't employ this for a while.

NAT products make allowances for more game playing and other peer-to-peer network connections today. One feature of Universal Plug and Play (UPnP) will address this issue to upgrade NAT to eliminate the current limitations. Not yet, perhaps, but soon.

Firewalls

You know people tell you without a firewall you're open to the world of hackers and other Internet deviants. Good news is that your NAT service acts as a firewall, and in fact is one of the main components of good security. In fact, a "firewall" is really a collection of services that provide protection, not some single item with magical properties.

The features that make up a "firewall" vary depending on who's selling the firewall. Here is a list of most common functions:

✦ **Packet filter:** Examines each packet leaving or entering the network and accepts or rejects that packet based on rules configured by the network administrator. Difficult to get working correctly.

✦ **Application gateway:** Tightens security on specific applications such as various servers.

✦ **Circuit-level gateway:** Controls TCP and Universal Datagram Protocol (UDP), which is part of the TCP/IP suite connections.

✦ **Proxy server:** Hides all internal network addresses.

✦ **Network address translation:** Hides internal addresses and functions as a special type of proxy server.

✦ **Stateful inspection:** Verifies that incoming packets match a request from an internal user. Can examine many parts of the packet, focusing on addresses, applications, or ports requested.

Firewalls, at least the better ones, use two or more of these techniques. Again, a firewall guards the gates of your network but doesn't automatically secure and protect everything on your network against worms, viruses, or user mistakes.

There are a boatload of books and Web information on the care and feeding of firewalls. Dig in as much as you want, but it's not a casual subject, and not one that home users or even small businesses need to worry about as much as they do. Both groups need a firewall, but default configurations from newer firewalls are better than expert configurations done by security consultants a few years ago.

Router-based firewalls

Yes, many routers have firewalls. But because NAT falls under the definition of a firewall, you must verify that you're getting the level of protection you paid for, if you paid extra. And before you pay extra, make sure you will use the features if they are there. Configuring firewalls requires more time and experience than many people (including me in most cases) want to devote to the project.

The good news is that if you want a firewall, the router is the place for your firewall. Your broadband service provider has security and firewalls on its side of your cable/DSL modem, but can't check your traffic.

One good job for firewalls is to show when packets are leaving your computer. These warnings are meant to alert you to Trojan applications sending out information. All I ever see, however, are messages leaving some type of Windows XP software subsystem to the Internet. And Microsoft wonders why people accuse them of gathering information and personal data from PC users.

If you want tighter security, you need to configure you own firewall. Your firewall location options are the router and your computer.

Configuring a router-based firewall

Most routers advertise a firewall, but remember that NAT falls under the firewall umbrella. But many routers, especially the newer ones, include more firewall settings and options than you probably realize.

The new Netgear WGT624 Wireless Firewall Router (108 Mbps wireless when things work right) includes extra firewall services. The configuration screen, shown in Figure 12-7, is about as easy a firewall configuration as you'll ever see.

Figure 12-7: An easy but limited firewall setup screen.

Two features you want in a firewall are already configured for you: the Stateful Packet Inspection (SPI) filter and Respond to Ping on Internet Port rejection. This configuration, straight out of the Netgear box, means that the following:

✦ Packets coming in are rejected unless they match packets going out.

✦ Hackers testing your address to see if something is there won't get an answer.

The second option about the ping response is often called ICMP response or the like. Internet Control Message Protocol (ICMP) is regularly used to verify that a device is up and running at a particular IP address (among other things too tangential to examine here). Hackers send ICMP packets to every address on a network to see which addresses have active devices. If a device is active on a particular IP address, the hackers can start trying to cause trouble.

On the other hand, network administrators rely on ICMP for troubleshooting and testing. Another example of a good tool warped by bad use in the hands of bad actors.

Figure 12-8 shows a firewall setup that is considerably more complicated. The Kanguru iNAS-100 includes plenty of firewall configuration options because it offers service to outside users on the Internet as well as routing and firewall services for internal network users.

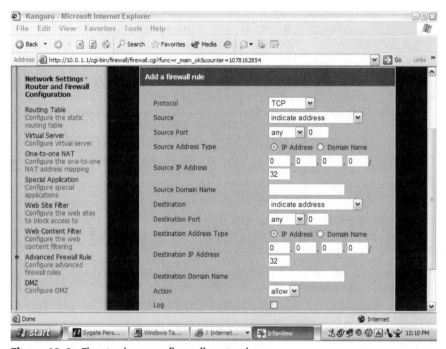

Figure 12-8: Fine-tuning your firewall protections.

Let me show you what's in the drop-down menus you can't see, and explain some of these options. First, the protocol options are TCP, UDP, and TCP/UDP. For our purposes, UDP is the same as the IP packets discussed at the beginning of this chapter. UDP packets are not guaranteed to be delivered and set up a connection but make their "best effort" to do so.

✦ Source menu includes Indicate address (showing), Exclude indicate address, and Any address. The address referred to is the Source IP Address listed later in this list.

✦ Source Port options include any (showing), WWW (World Wide Web), FTP (File Transfer Protocol), FTPDATA, SMTP (Simple Mail Transfer Protocol), POP3 (Post Office Protocol version 3 used in most e-mail transactions), Telnet (remote terminal connection), and Other. When you select one of the options in the drop-down menu, it automatically fills in the port number. For example, pick WWW and port 80 will appear in the window. If you want to block or allow another port number, use the Other option and type the port number directly in the field.

✦ Source IP Address allows you to list the exact IP address, or network range, to include or exclude. If you want to allow all connections from your office back to your home computer, for example, you would put the IP address of your computer at work in this field. If your company uses a NAT or a proxy server, you can put that address in. If your company has multiple NAT or proxy servers installed, you can allow the entire range of IP addresses.

✦ Source Domain Name works like the previous field, but uses domain names instead. Want to block all future packets from `www` `.AllSpamFromHere.com`? Put `www.AllSpamFromHere.com` in that Source Domain Name field. Too bad that's only an example I made up and not real.

✦ Destination field refers to the internal device, which is the subject of this firewall "accept or deny access" exercise. You can put indicate address, exclude indicate address, or any address in this field.

✦ Destination Address Type can be either a single IP address or a domain name.

✦ Destination IP Address refers to the internal IP address mentioned in the previous listing if you clicked IP address.

✦ Destination Domain Name refers to an internal domain. Internal domains are rare in home and small business use, so this will not apply to you unless your situation is extremely unusual.

✦ Action is the critical choice, where you allow or deny the rule you are creating.

There's plenty in that firewall rule setup screen, isn't there? But not all offer so much configuration detail. Frankly, unless you have e-commerce servers and active peer-to-peer connections across the Internet, you won't need this level of configuration detail. But it's nice you can get this level of protection at a price reasonable for home and small office users.

Figure 12-9 shows a new Linksys WRV54G VPN broadband router, which also includes plenty of firewall-type protections. Yet the configuration screen doesn't require as many decisions from you.

The screen shows the default settings, which I will tell you how I amended for better security.

✦ **Firewall Protection:** Turns on or off the Stateful Packet Inspection filter. Enabled (default).

✦ **Filter Proxy:** Controls packets trying to bypass security by using a WAN proxy. Enabled (changed).

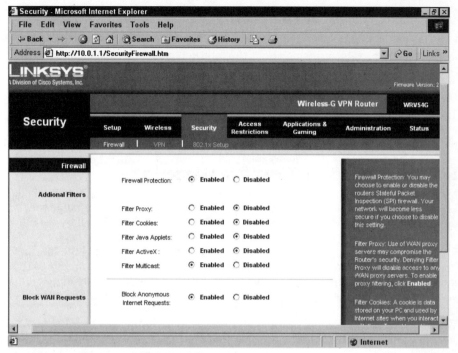

Figure 12-9: The new Linksys firewall configuration screen.

✦ **Filter Cookies:** Blocks cookies attached to Web site traffic that can compromise security but are required for many Web pages to function properly. Disabled (default).

✦ **Filter Java Applets:** Java applets are programs running on Web pages which can execute inside your browser, compromising security, but they also provide needed functionality for many programs. Disabled (default).

✦ **Filter ActiveX:** ActiveX is another programming language for Web pages using Microsoft technology. I block this, but I don't play online games requiring ActiveX support, either. Enabled (changed).

✦ **Filter Multicast:** Allows one data stream to connect to multiple computers at once. Used for Web video and audio, so blocking them may stop audio and video playback. Disabled (changed).

✦ **Block Anonymous Internet Requests:** Refuses to acknowledge ping packets from outside, as discussed earlier with ICMP. Enabled (default).

Personally, I prefer to accept all the group definitions, such as those shown in Figure 12-9, that are available. Trying to drill down and specify individual addresses to block specific protocols, as you can do with the Kanguru router/firewall is something I recommend you leave to the administrators of large networks, unless you have online game issues, which are covered soon.

Using a personal firewall

You may feel a personal firewall provides you the required peace of mind to make you comfortable cruising about the Internet. If so, you're in luck, because there are a variety of them and some are free.

However, if your home or small business network has a working router with NAT and at least minimal firewall services, and you're not hosting servers on your internal network, you may not need a personal firewall. You may even find having both causes some aggravation without increasing real security.

Internet connection firewall in Windows XP

Microsoft made plenty of public relations noise with the inclusion of its Internet Connection Firewall (ICF) in Windows XP. It even went so far as to change the default with the Support Pack 2 version of XP and enable the firewall by default.

Thank you, Microsoft, for once again misunderstanding the world of the Internet. You can only use Microsoft's ICF if that particular PC is connected *directly* to the Internet. When you turn on ICF inside a router with a firewall already in place, your PC networking gets weird and you must change the Windows XP setting.

You check your ICF settings inside the Advanced page within the Local Area Network Connection Properties window. Right-click the network icon in the task bar or click Network Connections inside My Network Places and the General window will open. Click the Properties button then the Advanced tab to open the page with the ICF check box. Click the Settings command box in the lower-right corner, and the window you see on the right of Figure 12-10 will open.

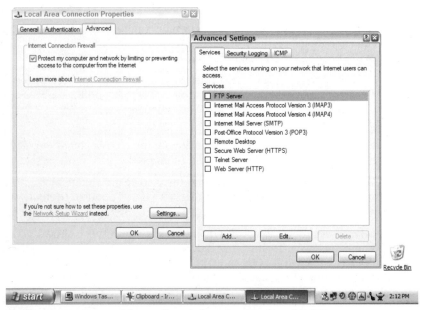

Figure 12-10: Some of the setting options for Windows XP ICF.

All the services you might host on your PC that Internet clients would want to use are disabled by default. If you run an FTP server, check the box allowing FTP access. The same advice goes for all the others, all the way down the Web server. Yes, your PC can become a Web server on the Internet, but you probably won't do that within a Windows XP system.

If you've been curious about the variety of ICMP messages (send a packet to see if a device or software service is running), you'll love the Advanced Settings ICMP page. Take a look at Figure 12-11.

To *ping* something in the network means to send a packet to see if the service is up and running. If you hear computer people talking about pinging someone it just illustrates how another technical term moved into common usage.

Each item to be or not to be checked includes an explanation in the bottom of the window as you can see in Figure 12-11. Nice of Microsoft to include that information, and the definitions are accurate. Might be nicer to tell people what type of problems they can get into when checking any of those items, but that's what help screens are for, right? Oops, the F1 help key only echoes what's in the bottom of the screen.

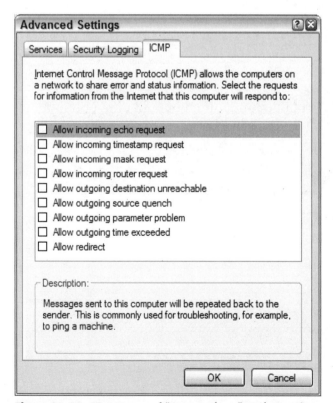

Figure 12-11: More types of "are you there" packet options than you'll ever see in one place.

Here's my suggestion: Don't turn on any of these. Then move back one screen to the Local Area Network Connections Properties page and click the link to Learn more about Internet Connection Firewall so you'll understand when you should use it. Then get a router anyway, because you never know when some program will reset your configuration details and open your PC up to the world.

Other software firewalls

You can spend money on personal firewalls, or you can get them free (even more than the one in Windows XP). To me, free is always good when the product works. Home users have multiple free options as several personal firewall providers make free versions available as a gesture of goodwill (and of advertising their products, of course).

Perhaps the most popular over the years has been Black Ice Defender (blackice.iss.net). Second to them may be the personal Zone Alarm application (www.zonelabs.com). One that I find interesting is the Sygate Personal Firewall (Smb.sygate.com).

Figure 12-12 shows the main screen from Sygate's product. The two graphs on the left keep running all the time. I've seen no attacks in the graph on the right, but this is sitting behind a firewall router, so I shouldn't see any attacks.

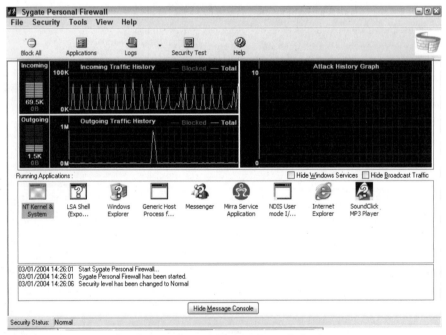

Figure 12-12: A graphically interesting personal firewall display.

See the nice list of large icons in the bottom half of Figure 12-12? The one with question marks on their faces are ones I must approve to send packets. Notice the Messenger service in the middle? I told you to turn that off, didn't I? See why I suggested that? The Messenger service sends invitations out just asking for trouble (in my opinion).

You may not be able to see it clearly, but the last icon to the right has little blue boxes in the bottom corners. This shows that it is transmitting packets out to the Internet, and that's correct. I'm streaming audio from the SoundClick music server (www.soundclick.com) and the client application (Soundcast player) must tell when it's ready for more music.

The rules for blocking traffic in a software firewall look much like those for the firewall in the Kanguru router/firewall shown earlier. Each application has its own configuration screens with varying degrees of complexity.

If you feel the need for a personal firewall, download the options mentioned earlier and others before you decide. See how automatically each application blocks the type of traffic that suits you the best.

Use the personal software that satisfies your security needs with the default settings. No matter how good your intentions, you won't create a proper set of firewall rules. Even highly trained network managers for huge companies have trouble creating the right set of firewall rules to be really safe.

Configuring firewalls for online games

Gamers have it rough at times, because hosting games on their broadband service connection makes the service provider mad (too much upstream traffic) and firewalls block other players from joining the game. But there are ways to open some ports in your personal firewall to allow gaming, and they may even work with your router/firewall appliance.

When you initiate connection to a game, your firewall matches incoming response packets to your outgoing request. All is cool. You don't have to do anything to join a game.

When you create a game and invite others, you have a problem. When outsiders respond, they are not allowed into the network. Bummer.

The best way to show how to do this is to show a configured firewall rule. Figure 12-13 shows a rule in the Kanguru iNAS-100 allowing a user on the network to play Warcraft III.

Warcraft III requires TCP port number 6112 open for remote users to connect. I put in the UDP port because earlier versions of the game (Warcraft II) demand UDP as well and I'm afraid there may be a leftover need now and then for some UDP packets.

Your game providers will make the necessary port numbers and protocols available, because they want you to play the game. So if there's a gamer in the house, a more finely controlled firewall will be necessary than for a network without gamers.

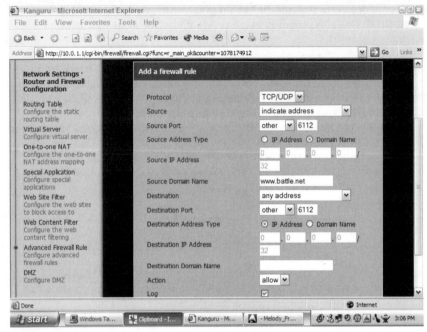

Figure 12-13: Opening a door to marauding war parties but not hackers (cross your fingers).

Proxy and cache servers

Your broadband service provider may use *cache* and *proxy servers* when providing a connection to your apartment building. A cache (pronounced cash) speeds data access by keeping the most recently downloaded content in fast memory, close to the user. Service providers often run a cache server to increase speeds. Imagine a neighbor downloaded a song from www.Ampcast.com, and a moment later you download the same song. If the music file is still in the cache at your service provider, you can start downloading it immediately rather than waiting for the music site to send it across a thousand or more miles again.

When you read several pages of one site, graphical elements of the site such as logos, images, and navigation buttons repeat from page to page. A cache server will provide those from closer memory than you'll get from the remote server.

You can't always see a cache server because some of them work on all traffic. Other cache servers are one part of a proxy server, which you must know about to connect to it properly.

A proxy server acts as you'd expect with a name like "proxy." It acts on the behalf of another server. In this case, a proxy server may filter traffic, cache traffic, and increase security by providing firewall protections. You must set your client computer to use any particular proxy server, as shown in Figure 12-14.

You reach this screen through Internet Explorer ➪ Tools. Click Internet Options to open the Internet Options window you see in the left of the figure. Click the

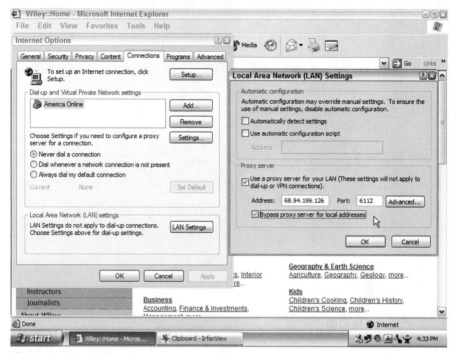

Figure 12-14: Setting the proxy server address.

Connections tab, and then the Settings command button in the Local Area Network (LAN) settings area to open the Local Area Network (LAN) Settings window.

There are three ways to find and connect through a proxy server. Most service providers give you an address and a port number. You can see in the bottom portion of the right-side window in Figure 12-14 that I've put in an IP address (68.94.199.126 in this case) and a port number (6112). Your service provider will give you the exact IP address and port number to use.

The section at the top of that window, Automatic configuration, is most often used by large companies with involved networks. But if your service provider tells you to configure that section, at least now you know where it is.

Summary

This is nowhere near all the information about networking and TCP/IP that is available. Fat books dedicated to the subject can't cover all the details. However, these are the areas with particular concern to home and small business networks connecting to a broadband service provider.

Between the information in this chapter and helpful hints in the troubleshooting chapters, you will be able to handle all the networking chores necessary for a home, home office, or small business using a broadband service provider. Enjoy your network, and don't let IP addressing schemes cost you any sleep.

Backup and Disaster Recovery

Bad things happen to good computers. And the most dangerous threat to most data? Users.

Most people assume backups are to protect you against disasters, such as fires or the upstairs bathtub overflowing and pouring soapy water into your computer in the office below. But users delete most files by accident. For example, with one twitch of the mouse a user might highlight the wrong file, or a user might think format means to put into data columns when it really means to erase a hard disk.

An insurance company in the United Kingdom did a study in the spring of 2003 and learned that nearly half of all small firms that have disasters, such as a complete system failure or fire, never recover. Nine of ten firms that lose data in a disaster are forced to close within 2 years.

More bad news? Less than half the small businesses studied had any type of contingency plan such as backed up computer systems to help them recover from a disaster. Because you're smart enough to pick up this book, I assume you're in the half who wants to prepare.

Tools to protect data exist in greater numbers, work better, and cost less today than ever. I will show you a dozen different ways to protect and backup data. You can do this automatically, manually, to tape, to CD-ROM, to hard disk, to online service, and even to paper, but please do it.

More Backups Mean Less Frustration

People make mistakes. People lose things. People name their files in weird ways.

Hard disks die. Application updates blow up. Operating systems upgrades fail halfway through.

Anytime one of these six "things" happens to you and your data, frustration appears. When you're in a hurry and one of these things happens, frustration brings your family members aggravation and anger. Then depression arrives as you realize what you once had has now disappeared.

I don't know about you, but I have enough frustration in my life, so I don't want any more jumping from my computer. I can't promise you that computers won't be aggravating and frustrating on occasion, but I can promise that reliable data backups shorten frustration and avoid depression.

What to backup

The easy way to determine what to backup is to determine all the things you don't want to repurchase, retype, download again, or rescan. Because to get back to where you are today, you may have to perform one or more of those onerous and potentially expensive tasks.

If you use your computer for work, all work files need to be protected. Writing the Great American Novel? Save it. Write music? Save it. Have a hard disk full of digital photos? Save them. Do all your personal finances on the computer, as many do? Guess what you should do with those files.

How about e-mails? Many people realize, too late, that they used their e-mail folders as a history for all types of information that can never be reclaimed after their computer hard disk grinds to a halt, or worse, when a child erases space to make room on the hard disk for a new game.

If you or your family members are music fans, backup the music files and any license information you paid for. Windows Media Audio (WMA) files, created by Microsoft Media Player and locked into the Digital Rights Management (DRM) controlled by Microsoft, must have the license file on the same computer as the music files or you will hear nothing.

Be selective?

Many hesitate to start a back-up process because they have no idea how to copy everything on their hard disk onto some type of back-up media. But you don't have to duplicate everything. You just need your data in most cases.

Those who worry there's so much data they can never capture it all should relax. I've been writing professionally for 16 years, and that includes 14 published books before this one. All my word processing files, in Microsoft Word (.doc), basic text like Notepad creates (.txt)), Rich Text Format (RTF), a standard file type for formatted text, and WordPerfect (WP) formats add up to less than 200MBs of data. I can store 16 years of writing work on one-third of a CD-ROM disk.

Research (by back-up vendors) tells us that despite the huge hard disks in today's personal computers, the vast majority have only 4–6GBs of unique data.

And here I have only 200MBs. So selective backup is an excellent option for many users, if you believe me or the back-up vendor research.

You already have backups of all your operating system and application files: the CD-ROMs in the package. You can count the original CD-ROM disks as a backup with complete justification.

Backup everything?

The other option some people favor is to backup absolutely every bit of every byte on their entire hard drive. That's fine too it just requires a different approach.

Many users download applications constantly, and that trend continues to accelerate as vendors increasingly sell online rather than through retail outlets. If you buy your software online via download, there are no backup CD-ROM disks that came with the product. So those applications must be treated like data.

There is no right back-up philosophy; there is only the answer that is right for your situation and comfort level. You must decide how much risk you can tolerate versus how much time and money you want to spend to alleviate that risk.

Please, do something. So many people do nothing about protecting their data it depresses those of us in the business. Backing up your data will save you more grief for less money than anything else you can do with your computer.

Configure your PC for easy backups

No matter how you plan to back up your data, you can make the process simpler with a little preparation. After all, the easier the back-up process is, the more likely you are to make those backups.

My secret for configuring your PC to make easy backups is to establish a data partition separate from the partition booting my computer and holding my applications.

This separate *partition* (a separate section of your hard disk set aside and formatted to look like a different physical disk to the operating system) can be part of the one disk in your computer, or it can be a separate disk entirely. Network servers, and even some of the server appliances discussed in Chapter 10, can get complicated with volumes and storage pools and partitions, but the hard disk in your PC can be handled in a straightforward manner.

I always do one of the following:

- ✦ Partition a disk for applications (3/4 of the space) and data (1/4 of the space)
- ✦ Add a second hard disk just for data

I prepare every PC of mine used for anything other than lab testing in this way. Why? So I can copy all the data and have an easy time restoring data to another PC, if necessary.

With the amount of data I have, using 3/4 of the disk for applications (the programs themselves) and 1/4 for data works out fine. Your recipe may be different. If you have but one application, such as a music program to create and mix music on your computer, rethink that ratio. In that case, you would probably reverse my ratio or at least start out with equal size partitions for applications and data.

A partitioned disk looks like a second disk to your operating system. So instead of having two disks (hard disk and CD-ROM) show up in the My Computer display, you will have three disks. Nothing else changes, except you tell your applications to store data on the data partition rather than the same partition as the application program itself.

Prepare your disk(s)

Of course, new computers always come with the disk formatted in one large partition. I even reworked the Windows XP Home computer used in the screenshots for this book and didn't think it was necessary to create the data partition. So now you get to see the process.

When I start Windows XP Home and look for a place to add a partition to a drive I see no place to add a partition to an existing drive unless I reformat the drive and start over. That means erasing every program on the drive, and I don't want to do that. Microsoft does not include drive partitioning software in its operating systems for desktops.

The third-party program I use for handling disk partitions is PartitionMagic. This product was just acquired by Symantec late in 2003, so you may still find it listed as PowerQuest Corporation (but go to www.Symantec.com to find it now).

PartitionMagic 8.0 also includes a nice back-up software program called DataKeeper. The software watches all your files and backs them up to a network shared folder after every change to your local file. When you open a document, change two words, then close it, DataKeeper copies the changed document before you know what happened.

Figure 13-1 shows the opening screen of PartitionMagic running on a Windows XP Home operating system. The existing local hard disk, nearly 30GBs worth, is highlighted in the upper-right third of the screen.

Figure 13-1 shows a healthy, barely used hard disk. Notice under 5GBs of space have been used on this drive, almost all due to Windows XP Home. A tiny bit of the drive, 7.8MBs, is not partitioned.

My first step is to create empty disk space to use. It's hard to see in Figure 13-1, but only 7.8MBs of disk space was open. By that I mean not in a partition, because disk preparation often leaves some bits unusable because of the drive

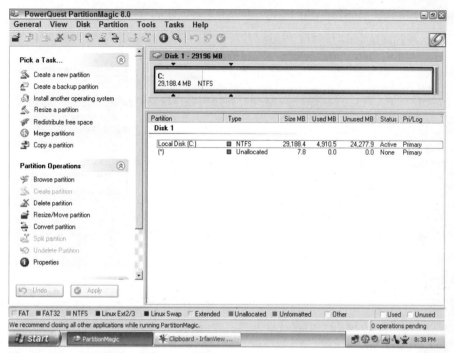

Figure 13-1: A single hard disk partition.

configuration and the way the operating system divides available space. I used PartitionMagic's Resize/Move command to make the primary disk partition, the one I'm using already as Drive C, about 7GBs smaller.

This follows my formula for application space versus data space. A quarter of a 30GB disk is a bit over 7GBs, and that's close enough for my purposes.

My second step is to create a new partition in the open space. Figure 13-2 shows the creation step, after I configured the extra space.

Notice I didn't make the second disk partition NTFS (NT File System) like the primary one. I don't need the low-level security NTFS offers, because I'm not on a network with a lot of people. And, I can always recover data from a partition formatted with FAT32 much more easily than one formatted with NTFS.

Note   FAT32 (File Allocation Table) is a disk formatting method that dates back to the early DOS days. The FAT32 upgrade uses 32-bit addressing for the disk directory to handle modern large disk drives.

NTFS (NT File System) arrived with Microsoft's Windows NT. The newer format improves performance, management, and security controls, which made it popular for NT servers. Microsoft recommends using NTFS for all Windows XP hard disks.

Trust me, when the low-level NT-based disk booting routines get all buggered, you're, ah, frowning. In all my years messing with Windows, I've never been able

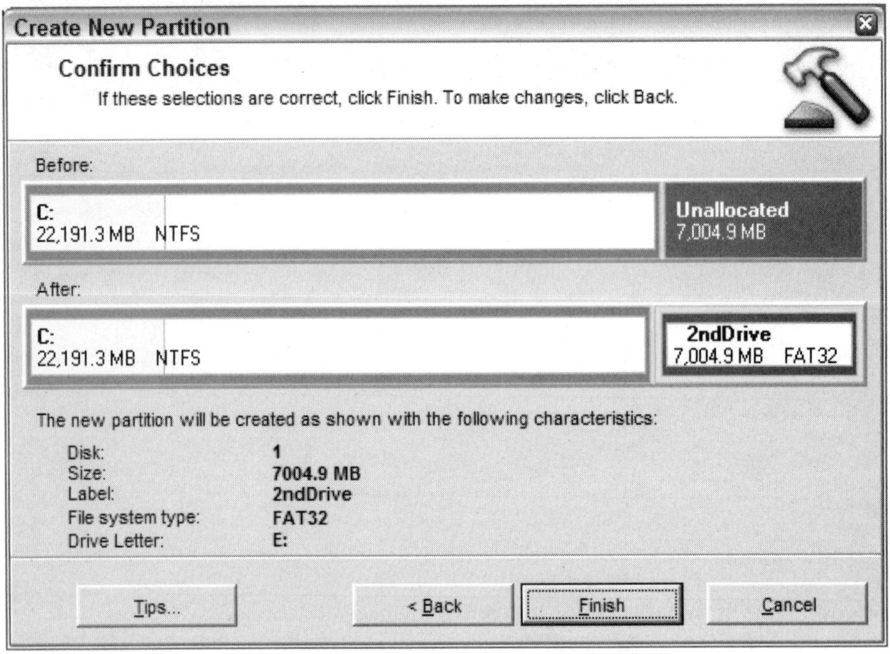

Figure 13-2: Now there are two hard disk partitions (almost).

to save a disk when the NT boot loader error messages started appearing. Not with Windows NT, not with Windows 2000, and not with Window XP. Perhaps I'm not smart enough and there's something simple I'm missing, but when NT boot loader errors appear I just curse a time or two and reformat the hard drive partition.

PartitionMagic queues the proposed changes and applies them all at once, requiring at least one reboot to make everything work. After the reboot, I have a second disk partition for data completely separate from the boot disk. When I have to replace the operating system on the boot partition because of problems or upgrades, the data partition won't be touched. The screenshot in Figure 13-2 provides a nice before and after shot, showing what the disk will look like after the partition operation.

I can also, if I want, change the drive letter of the new partition to Drive D. That requires three steps:

1. Change the CD-ROM drive letter to F.

2. Change the second disk partition to Drive D.

3. Change the CD-ROM drive letter to Drive E.

I don't think I'll go through all that for this exercise, but some users feel strongly that the CD-ROM should be the last drive letter in the chain. I try to be flexible, but you can be however you want.

Move the My Documents folder

Microsoft Windows makes many assumptions for users, and not all of them work to the user's advantage. The My Documents folder, for instance, is the default location for saved files. But the folder is three levels deep in the directory structure and is filled with other directories, making them four levels deep.

At least Microsoft made it easier to move the My Documents folder in Windows XP than ever before. You can move the folder in Windows 2000, but there are more steps. And making it move in Windows 98 wasn't worth the effort.

My plan is always to put data files on the second partition of the disk. In the case of the PC shown in the first two figures, that means putting My Documents on Drive E. Figure 13-3 shows the steps involved, which aren't many with Windows XP.

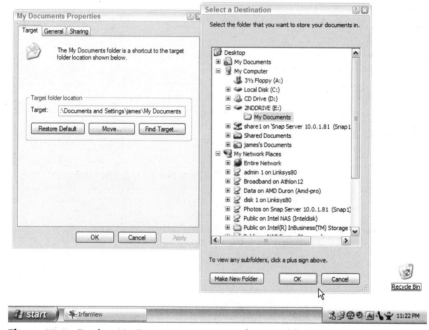

Figure 13-3: Putting My Documents on your data partition.

Here are the steps:

1. Open the Start menu
2. Right-click My Documents
3. Click Properties
4. Click Move
5. Choose (or create if necessary) a folder on the second partition
6. Highlight that folder and click OK

You don't have to name the new directory "My Documents" if you don't want to, but that may look more familiar to you. Calling it DATA always works for me, and I create subfolders inside the DATA folder.

Windows will politely ask if you want all the documents and folders from the old location to move to the new location. I said yes. When the default save location is My Documents, you'll know they are on the second disk partition. Many applications prefer to put files in the My Documents folder, and now those files will be on the data disk.

Did you notice in Figure 13-3 that Windows XP enables you to save My Documents on a network shared drive? That can be a handy option when you want everyone to save their files on a network folder for easier backup.

Windows 2000 enables you to relocate the My Documents folder, but the process is a bit different:

1. Open the Start menu.
2. Click Documents
3. Right-click My Documents
4. Select Explore
5. Right-click the My Documents in the folder view
6. Right-click and select Properties
7. Click Move
8. Choose (or create if necessary) a folder on the second partition
9. Highlight that folder and click OK.

Again you have the option of using a network folder for My Documents with Windows 2000. That's a good option for coordinating backups among a small workgroup.

If your My Documents folder is still on your Desktop, you can shorten the process of moving it. Right-click the folder, click Properties, and then click the Move button to open the dialog box with the Select Destination process.

Personally, I prefer to name my top folder DATA with subfolders. After all, not all the files you create on a computer can honestly be called Documents, can they? My Files would be more accurate, or you could call the top-level Projects and label subfolders with the names of each project (Smith File, Reunion, Taxes, and so on). It's perfectly fine to store all different types of data files inside one folder.

Back-up technology overview

Back-up technology's goal is to enable you to move information from one medium or location to another to keep it out of harm's way.

Early mainframes used those huge reel-to-reel tape drives shown in all the movies in the 50s and 60s. Don't forget that data printed on paper is also backed up in a way. However, the person you force to retype all the information from paper into the computer won't be your friend anymore.

On a high level, there are a few options for back-up data storage. Here's how I break down the market players:

✦ Floppies

✦ CDs and DVDs

✦ Tapes

✦ Disk-to-disk for one computer

✦ Disk-to-disk over a network

✦ Online storage services

Full and Incremental Backups

Different back-up applications make a big deal about how they handle full back-ups versus incremental backups. Full backups are what you expect: everything you want backed up is done in one pass. These backups make file and folder restorations simple, but the majority of the files copied don't change from day to day, yet you're still backing them up. This takes time and storage space.

Incremental backups check to see which files have changed since the last backup, and only backup those files. This saves time and storage space, but makes it harder to restore files because you may have to search a bit to find the last time the file was included in the incremental file backup list.

Each option has advantages and disadvantages. Let me explain exactly what I mean with each back-up technology now. Then I'll list all the pros and cons in the next section.

Floppies

People sometimes believe these are the original backup media, but only because they're too young to remember cassette tapes. Early Apple][computers, as well as the first IBM PCs, had cassette deck plugs on the back. Personal computer pioneers used the cassette tapes to load programs and save data. One soon learned to change tapes before saving data (ahem).

For the majority, however, floppies were the backup of choice. The early IBM XTs had a 10MB (yes, 10 MegaByte) hard disk, and the 360KB floppies could back up the entire disk in a manageable manner. Of course, this era also sold complete applications, such as word processors, on a single floppy with room for some of the files you created.

By the time hard disks grew into the 40MB range with the IBM AT, floppies were the backup choice of last resort. No one I knew ever reliably backed up their computer with floppies more than twice. Too painful and boring.

Floppies do have an important place in backup today, but they are for individual files rather than entire disks. You can, I guarantee you, put an entire novel's worth of words on a single floppy.

CDs and DVDs

The advent of the CD burner excited many people for many reasons, but back-up fans realized there was a 600MB backup storage location with relatively cheap and relatively sturdy media. Use the "data copy" method of burning a new CD and that becomes a great back-up option.

Just about every back-up utility program takes advantage of writeable CDs for storage. With 600MB+ of room, they make good options. Writeable DVDs, with 4.5GBs of room, make even better options. I say that because I'm a big fan of complete backups every time rather than a full backup followed by incremental backups.

Tapes

Individual tape drives with up to 20GBs of storage on a single compressed tape cartridge make excellent back-up options. The problems appear with tape when you try to restore a tape made from one drive with another drive, because sometimes that doesn't work. Tape drive heads are touchy, and misalignment means no tape restore. Sometimes a tape made months earlier can't be read on the same drive head after wear and tear change the tape head alignment slightly. Verify tapes regularly by doing restores from the tape, not just by trusting the tape software that said it verified the files as they were written. If you can't restore files to another system, the tape backup is useless.

Disk-to-disk for one computer

I break down the disk-to-disk backup option into two categories: for one computer, and for a network. With one computer, you can use an external hard drive with excellent success. With multiple computers, you really need to use a network-attached disk like some of the server and storage appliances discussed in Chapter 10.

Advancements in hard drive capacity coupled with decreases in drive pricing now make external disk drives with plenty of capacity inexpensive enough for worry-free acquisition. When you can get an external hard drive with USB 2.0 connections with 120GBs of storage for about a dollar or so a GB, you have a great product.

Disk-to-disk over a network

Chapter 10 included discussions about the type of storage appliances that make great back-up tools. Network Attached Storage (NAS) systems can hold many times the storage capacity of all your networked computer drives totaled together and make that space available to all.

Online storage services

Now that you have (or will soon have) a broadband connection to the Internet, online storage services begin to make sense. And there are great advantages to such a service, as well as a variety of vendors ready to rent you storage space "in the sky" so to speak.

Pros and cons of back-up options

Wouldn't it be wonderful if all back-up options worked great for all users, regardless of circumstances? And if the Easter Bunny left Faberge eggs?

Unfortunately, the first assertion is just as fanciful as the second. What works great for one back-up situation may be terrible for another. Relying on your neighbor's stock pick from his "insider" friends will cost you less money, in the long run, than trusting your neighbor's back-up system to work for you.

Back-up system decisions involve a mix of the following considerations:

✦ Cost

✦ Speed

✦ Lifespan of media

✦ Backup file availability for restoration

✦ Number of systems to back up

✦ Offsite storage plan

✦ Disaster recovery needs

The trick is to find your perfect back-up system in the range of product options available. There are far more options than you have the time or money to investigate, I promise, so let me help you narrow down your choices.

Your decision points

✦ How many computers do you have? Simple problem: the more computers to back up, the more complicated the backup becomes, and the fewer back-up options you have.

❏ 1–5 (2 points)

❏ 6–20 (10 points)

❏ 21–50 (20 points)

❏ 50+ (50 points)

✦ How much total data do you have to back up? The more data, the more resources. 5 points puts you out of the CD-ROM burner category into tape or separate hard disk products.

❏ Under 600MBs (2 points)

❏ 600MB – 2GBs (5 points)

❑ 2GBs – 10GBs (10 points)

❑ 10GBs – 100GBs (20 points)

❑ 100GBs and more (25 points)

✦ How much time can the total backup take? If time is not a problem you have more options. If time is critical, such as needing a backup completed in less than an hour, you move out of the tape, CD-ROM, and online products into hard disk products.

❑ Overnight (2 points)

❑ Less than 6 hours (5 points)

❑ Less than 2 hours (10 points)

❑ Less than 1 hour (20 points)

✦ Manual or automatic process? Will it bother you to start the process? If so, you add points.

❑ Manual (2 points)

❑ Automatic (10 points)

✦ Ease of carrying backup media offsite? Offsite data storage is the most critical component of disaster planning. If you can carry a burned CD home from your small business and leave it there for safekeeping, that's wonderful. A writer friend of mine walks his dog from his home office to the bank where he puts tapes into a safety deposit box. Those who can do something of that nature will do their backups more regularly and store data offsite more often than others.

❑ Very easy (2 points)

❑ Medium easy (5 points)

❑ Difficult (20 points)

✦ How long can you be without your data? If you accidentally erase your DOCUMENT file and click the wrong button on the recycle icon and erase the files inside rather than recover them, how long can you do without those files? The sooner you must have them the more resources you must devote to keeping them close at hand.

❑ 1 day (2 points)

❑ 4 hours (5 points)

❑ 1 hour (10 points)

✦ How fast must your disaster recovery be for one computer? If you spill your morning coffee into the computer and get snapped to clarity by shooting sparks and a small fire, how long can you wait to recreate everything you had on the old computer onto a new one?

❑ 1 day (2 points)

❑ 5 hours (5 points)

❑ 1 hour (10 points)

✦ How fast must your disaster recovery be for two to ten computers? If the air conditioner leaks water onto your computers and fries them all, how long can you wait to recreate your systems using new hardware?

❑ 2 days (10 points)

❑ 1 day (20 points)

❑ 1 afternoon (50 points)

✦ How fast must your disaster recovery be for 11 or more computers? You have some serious business back-up decisions to make. I can't help you here except to tell you to sign up with a disaster recovery service with hot site protection and co-located servers.

❑ 3 days (20 points)

❑ 1 day (50 points)

❑ 1 afternoon (100 points)

Scoring your choices

My scoring is unscientific, because I want you to come to a back-up process decision you can live with and use reliably. The higher the score the more resources (hardware, software, and time) you will need. You can feel free to move up a level and implement a hardier back-up process than your score indicates. But if you move down the suggestion ladder, you run the risk of being extremely frustrated and angry one day.

✦ **40 points or less:** You have few back-up problems. A CD-ROM burner will do all that you need. But this score almost guarantees you have one or two computers in a noncritical situation, such as home entertainment use.

✦ **40–80 points:** Now you're bumping into the advanced home user or home office category. Number of computers, data volume, and/or recovery speed likely drives your score up. You need a dedicated back-up device and probably an online service for offsite storage.

✦ **80–120 points:** Business systems are in order. More than one back-up system (one for data, one for recovering computers from scratch) should be on your budget. More offsite storage room will be needed.

✦ **120 and more points:** You need everything in the previous category, but if your need for uptime bumps you to this score you probably need hotsite or server co-location services. You definitely need a full, business-oriented back-up system with local NAS storage and offsite storage to go along with the remote hotsite support.

My recommendations

Unless your backup needs are small (see the first two scoring answers in the previous section), you may need more than one option for backups. The tools that grab lots of data quickly are not the same tools that recreate systems after a disaster. The higher your data score, the more options you may have to use to cover your self, and your data, acceptably.

First recommendation: Do a complete backup data set every time.

I always back up everything at once—no incremental backups. Incremental backup systems capture "all" your files, then later (and usually on different backup tapes) saves only the files that have changed since the first full backup.

The problem with this method comes when restoring such a system. Yes, the software is supposed to keep track of where the files are spread across your tape library, but there are often problems with those systems. And because tape cartridges are expensive, the more you use for incremental backups the higher the cost and the slower the recovery.

If your back-up system does incremental backups, make sure it stores the updated files as part of the same file-set it created during the full backup. This is generally how the hard disk back-up systems work, and I like that. A full restore of a data partition will restore all the files in their most current version.

Second recommendation: Always send data offsite one way or another.

The problem with hard disk backups is carrying your data offsite. Believe me, if the unthinkable happens and your computers burn up, the Network Attached Storage box sitting beside your server will burn up as well. For that matter, so will the tapes thrown into the cardboard box sitting beside the tape drive. Tapes have no secure offsite advantage if you don't take them offsite.

You must send your data offsite or your data is not safe. If not, you do not have an acceptable back-up process in place. Period.

Online back-up storage sites offer easy ways to send data offsite, and my favorite back-up tool, the IntraDyn RocketVault, makes this simple. The RocketVault is highly recommended if your score is above 60 on the earlier decision points, but I'll talk more about this excellent backup for small to large businesses in upcoming sections.

Third recommendation: Set up a system you will use every day. Period.

Great intentions do not recover critical files deleted three weeks ago. Good back-up systems do that. And they can only do that when they're used regularly.

Back-Up Tools

There are many, many backup tools available. These tools range from free software that backs up files to your CD-ROM writer (most CD burners include this software as well) to automated tape storage units that cost over a hundred thousand dollars. I doubt you need one of the latter (but if you do buy one, put me down for my commission).

Let me show you five back-up tools. Two are software, three are hardware.

✦ The first product is DataKeeper from PowerQuest (now Symantec) mentioned earlier. It came with the PartitionMagic 8.0 software, so the price is certainly right. In addition, the SnapAppliance folks include the software with their Network Attached Storage products, and I received a copy with the SnapAppliance SnapServer 1100.

✦ The second product is from Acronis Inc., (www.acronis.com) called True Image 7. This includes features, such as disk cloning and shortcuts to add new disks to your system and get the right information on the right drive.

✦ The third product is Mirra Personal Server from Mirra, Inc., (www.mirra.com). This is a customized system that connects to the network and uses Windows share networking to pull files from PCs on the network. You can also access the files over the Internet and even invite others to view shared folders full of fun stuff like vacation photos (there are fun things, really).

✦ The fourth product is an external hard disk from Olixir Technologies (www.olixir.com) that connects via USB 1.1 and 2.0, FireWire, and PCMCIA card on laptops. It functions as a separate hard drive when plugged into your PC, but there's also specialized back-up software. This product differs from other USB hard disks used for backup because it is shock mounted and can be linked with other units to form a much larger storage space. It comes with Retrospect Express Backup software from Dantz Development Corp., (www.dantz.com).

✦ Finally, the best backup system I've seen so far is RocketVault from IntraDyn, Inc., (www.intradyn.com). This customized computer sits on the network like the Mirra, but it also forwards files to remote online storage facilities, including well-priced storage offered by IntraDyn. I have it set to send critical documents to a hidden directory on www.BroadbandBible.com.

Notice I don't have any tape back-up products in here? I prefer hard disk backups combined with online storage over tapes. External hard disks used for backup are bootable with the right software; whereas tape drives are never bootable. And the cost of online storage for offsite security is less per month than most tape cartridges.

Backing up a desktop

This section shows examples of backing up a single desktop to CD-ROM, tape, or an external hard drive. You can also back up desktops to other network drives. The other drive can be on a Network Attached Storage device or even another computer. I recommend that you use a storage or server appliance rather than another PC, however, because other PCs have users and thus are prone to suffer from accidents. Storage appliances don't have users trying to run applications on them all the time, and so are less likely to experience mishaps.

Backing up three or four desktop systems doesn't differ all that much from backing up one. But once you have two or three systems to back up, the manual method using things like CD-ROM and tape start because they become inconvenient are likely to be neglected. That's the time to begin looking for a network-based solution that works automatically.

CD-ROM or DVD backup

You have two good options with most CD burners: Run a specific back-up routine included with the CD burner, or configure a writeable CD as another hard drive and use other back-up software to write to it. DVD writers, being newer and more expensive (not to mention with much more space) tend to have better back-up software included.

Remember to change the CD after you use it. Remember to take filled CDs offsite for safekeeping.

Tape backup

I said that I prefer not to use tape, but you can make your own choices. The prices for individual computer tape back-up drives with low capacity tape cartridges aren't too high. You can usually find internal tape back-up units with a capacity of 10GBs (up to 20GBs with compression) for under $400.

A single tape drive for a single PC may be overkill, but it will still work. The internal tape drives are less expensive, but harder to use on other computers because you can only backup shared folders across the network

Also worth considering is one of the new Iomega Zip drives. They hold 750MBs of data and read and write more quickly than tape drives.

Any system with removable media like a tape drive or a Zip drive must be managed properly. Remembering to change the tape and to rotate tapes offsite for safety will mean the difference between a working back-up system and an expensive failure.

External hard drive backup

There are over 150 back-up programs available on www.Download.com, and at least five are completely and forever free for personal use. Surely one of those applications will feel comfortable for you.

Figure 13-4 shows the backup configuration screen for DataKeeper from PowerQuest (now Symantec). This is the first screen that appears when you start the program.

Remember the My Documents folder we moved to the new partition? In Figure 13-4 I'm backing it up to the SnapServer 1100 storage appliance using the DataKeeper software that come with PartitionMagic.

DataKeeper allows an immediate backup, but it monitors the folders you tell it to monitor for any file changes. Notice the cursor arrow in the bottom-right of Figure 13-4. Can you read the info message? It says, "Monitor selected folders for

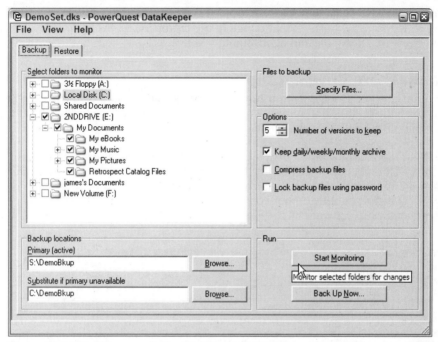

Figure 13-4: Backing up only the My Documents folder on the drive space created as an example earlier.

changes." A piece of the DataKeeper program stays active and sits inside the task bar. When a file in a monitored folder changes in any way, DataKeeper updates the back-up copy on the remote drive you specified.

Backing up a laptop

Because people don't back up their desktop systems often enough, how often do you think they back up their laptops? Even less to never, that's how often.

Laptops don't stay put, so they magnify the back-up problem. But they are more prone to suffer from accidents than desktops are, and often the data on the laptop disk is worth more to you or your company than the laptop itself.

Even the largest corporations with plenty of computer technicians struggle to keep laptops backed up. Desktops left on overnight can be backed up automatically by a central storage server. Laptop users have to purposefully perform a backup. Human nature being what it is, many laptops don't have a recent backup and some have never been backed up.

CD-ROM or DVD backup

Some laptops make life easy by including a CD burner. Some newer systems even have DVD burners, meaning a single disk back-up session can hold over 4.5GBs of laptop data.

Even owners of the thin laptops built for portability may still be able to use CD burners. External CD burners that attach to the laptop via a USB 1.1 or USB 2.0 connection are affordable and lightweight.

External hard drive backup

When the laptop connects to your home network at the end of a trip, you can back up all the information to a network drive. Or you can carry a hard disk in an external housing with you at all times. Heavy perhaps, but safer for your data.

The Olixir Mobile Data Vault puts 80, 120, 180, or 250GBs into a box about the size of a VCR tape, but much heavier. Olixir brags that its Mobile Data Vault can withstand up to 1200GBs, and I'm inclined to believe that based on its heavyweight chassis with rubber corners I can hold in my hand. Figure 13-5 shows the backup software included with the Olixir drive.

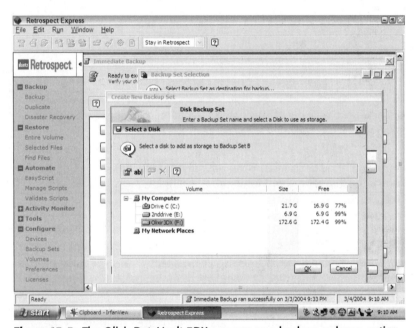

Figure 13-5: The Olixir DataVault 3DX appears as a back-up volume option in the Retrospect software included with the drive.

Some of the newer external hard drives, like the Olixir, can actually boot the system if you have the right connection, such as a new Serial Advanced Technology Architecture (SATA), which is a type of hard disk controller installed in a desktop. For laptops, the Olixir software creates a bootable CD-ROM with a file snapshot on the external 3DX hard disk to boot and restore a laptop so garbled it won't even boot.

External hard drives tend to be heavier than you may want to carry in your briefcase with your laptop and its power supply. But the rugged Olixir 3DX erases any worries about the safety of the hard drive when thrown into a checked suitcase, which is thrown again (and again) by baggage handlers.

Online backup and storage

Traveling laptop owners should thank their lucky stars every day for online back-up services, and back-up options back home that make it possible to retrieve files remotely. The growing number of hotels that include Ethernet connections to the Internet in every room makes it possible to perform complete backup or restore operations quickly enough for impatient executives.

Almost every online back-up service enables users to update incrementally files that have changed since their last update. These updates, often just a few files changed while the laptop owner creates and modifies data during a trip, upload fairly quickly even with a dial-up Internet connection. The back-up service software varies according to vendor, but will generally merge changed files into the complete back-up set to be ready if a full data restore is necessary.

If you have a laptop that you carry around the country, make a full backup over your network from home to the online storage service of your choice. Then every travel day, no matter what, hook your laptop to the hotel phone line and back up all your changed data files. You can turn on the back-up process before you head to the hotel gym for your daily workout (hey, it could happen) and the process will be complete when you return.

Backing up network-connected computers

Here is where you have the most options, which is good because this situation is the one with the most variables. Remember the scoring list a few pages back? I listed different scoring depending on whether you have 1–5 computers, 6–20, 21–50, or more than 50 computers. That's because your approach must change as you increase the number of systems under your management.

With five or fewer computers, the tools listed for individual computer backup work perfectly well. For example, handling two computers the same way you handle only one doubles the time spent but doesn't really add complexity to the problem and solution.

When you get to four or five computers, however, the time element can start to become burdensome. This leads to trouble as backups slide down the priority ladder, because people (even you and I) tend to avoid unpleasant tasks. By the time you have six or more computer to manage, you better start thinking of network-based solutions or your backups will be done adequately.

Don't fall into the trap of thinking that once you start a network backup all the tools you used for individual computer backups are worthless. You will need to think of a way to rebuild systems quickly after they are lost to hardware failure (dead disk drive) or how to load all the data to a new computer. The individual computer back-up tools you used for your two computers still provide data security even after you have a dozen or more computers.

After you start getting more than a few systems to manage, the need to keep data copies offsite becomes critical. One or two computer's worth of data you may be able to recreate in case of a disaster, but a dozen computers? That implies much more data and many more transactions to recover. You need complete data sets stored offsite if you want your company to survive even minor disasters.

Storage appliances to the rescue

Here's where I believe Network Attached Storage (NAS) devices really come into their own: small but growing networks that need shared file space and backup but can't afford the expensive and feature-overloaded server software offerings from Microsoft and others. An inexpensive storage appliance, like the ones discussed in Chapter 10, really make sense for a small network.

It's nice when these appliances include their own back-up software, especially because Windows XP Home doesn't provide a real "back-up" program. But the opinion of many computer consultants (this one included) is that trusting Microsoft for data security can be dangerous. Use a different back-up program than Microsoft's offerings, even when one is included.

System Restore does good things for Windows XP Home users, but relying on System Restore and the Recycle Bin alone will not protect your data as much as it should. Having old versions of files available through generational backups, which some vendors provide, can save the day. And long-term storage of archived files, available with storage appliances and the right software, can really cover your, ah, bacon.

Go Beyond System Restore and the Recycle Bin

The Recycle Bin in Windows makes life easier on many people. However, you can't trust it to be your only backup.

Why not? Not all deleted files move to the Recycle Bin, especially files deleted from a command line or by some applications. Also, Murphy's Law dictates you will empty your Recycle Bin the day before you realize which file you desperately need.

Microsoft's Windows XP include a pretty good System Restore utility. This allows you to roll back your PC to the time before you mistakenly changed the system in some disastrous way. But rolling back the system for a file may undo other changes you want to keep.

And neither option provides any way to move data offsite for safe keeping.

Yes, any shared network disk can be considered a storage appliance for my purposes in this section. If you converted an old PC into a dedicated file server in Chapter 10, the upcoming comments will work with that system as well. But it won't be as compact and friendly looking as the Linksys EFG80 in Figure 13-6.

You can make use of a networked storage device for backups with little effort. In Figure 13-7, I'm configuring the DataKeeper backup software to save my files to a folder named \\Kanguru\Public\Users\James for my personal back-up area.

Figure 13-6: Network Attached Storage unit with expandable storage and print server.

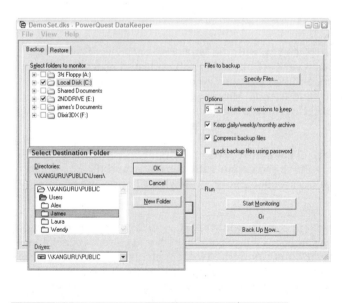

Figure 13-7: My changed files will now go to the Kanguru NAS and the software will keep five versions before overwriting any changed files.

You can set every user's My Document folder to a network storage device so all their stored files go there. Then when you back up that one storage device, you get everyone's files. However, nothing stops applications or users from storing files in other folders on their computer. That means your wonderful back-up method no longer works, because you won't get the new local files scattered over the user's hard disk.

The advancement in network storage devices over the past year has been amazing. Not only are prices coming down (because the hard drives are getting downright cheap) but new methods of backing up systems and implementing data security are appearing.

Two really nice products appeared late in 2003 that improve the storage picture for home and small business users considerably. Let me show you the home product first, the Mirra Personal Server (www.mirra.com). Then I'll show you my favorite network product for all of 2003, the RocketVault Server Management Vaulting System from IntraDyn, Inc., (www.intradyn.com).

Mirra Personal Server

The Mirra Personal Server is an interesting mix of network storage, automatic backup for any and all files on your computer, and sharing mechanism over the Internet. It's not too small and not too big, as you can perhaps tell in Figure 13-8. Just over five inches wide, it stands about 11 inches tall and 10 inches deep.

This product is aimed at home users, but the market penetration of network storage in the home market is less than tiny. Perhaps growing numbers of broadband connected families will increase that percentage, but Mirra has to do something beyond backups. And it does.

You can share the folders backed up with the Mirra Personal Server over the Internet. Mirra works this cleverly by managing authenticated users through its www.mirra.com Web site, and you can send an e-mail with connection instructions to your family and friends. Mirra signs in the users, checks your Mirra box for approval, and then makes the connection between the user and your Mirra shared folders. You can share all or none of your backed up folders.

Figure 13-9 shows the Mirra client software. Each PC (and only PCs right now) must run the Mirra client software to connect the computer and the Mirra device. This main screen offers a good overview of what's happening on the Mirra device.

When you load the Mirra client software on your PC, you first make a connection to the Mirra server on your network. Once established, you can set local folders for backup whenever a file in those monitored folders changes. If that sounds like some of the other back-up software discussed earlier, that's exactly right. Applications can easily watch your file system and copy every file changed.

You can monitor and back up only local folders, not any attached network folders. But you can load the Mirra client software on as many PCs as you want on your local network.

Figure 13-8: A combo system: backup and remote sharing device, the Mirra Personal Server.

Notice in Figure 13-10 all the folder icons have a small red dot in their bottom-left corner. It's red, trust me, and it mirrors the round red Mirra logo. Even when you run local folder tools, such as My Computer, the red dot on the folder appears. This way you always know which folders are backed up by Mirra and which aren't.

See the File and Folder Tasks window in the bottom-left of the Mirra screen? There, you can perform the following operations:

✦ **View files in this folder:** Drill down in the folders to find the individual file if you need.

✦ **Copy folder to new location:** A useful feature in all good back-up software, this function enables you to copy a folder from the Mirra

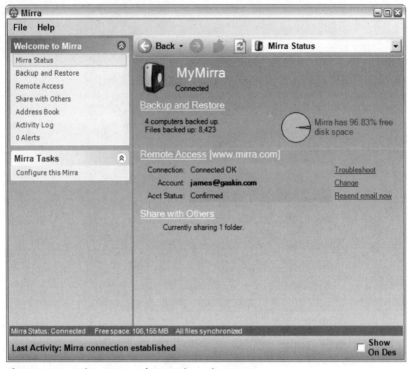

Figure 13-9: Mirra Personal Server's main screen.

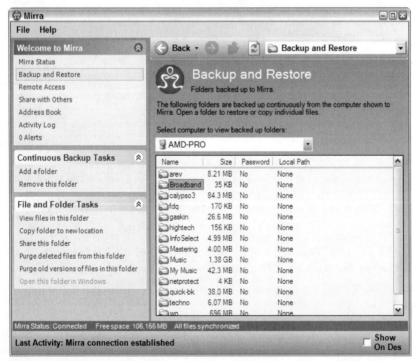

Figure 13-10: Backup and Restore screen for the Mirra Personal Server.

to your local computer, even if the folder was backed up from a different computer. You can't copy files or folders to network disks, however.

✦ **Share this folder:** Send an e-mail invitation to someone to access this folder over the Internet.

✦ **Purge deleted files from this folder:** Mirra holds on to deleted files so you can undelete them if you want, or you can clear them for more disk space.

✦ **Purge old versions of this file in this folder:** If you need space, you can clear the eight older versions of files kept by Mirra, folder by folder.

✦ **Open this folder in Windows:** If this folder is from your computer, you can click this to pop open a Windows Explorer window of this folder from your local hard disk.

At the office and need a file from home? Traveling and need a spreadsheet to keep track of your expenses from the office? Your Mirra Personal Server makes this simple.

Figure 13-11 shows the remote part of the Mirra Personal Server. Over the Internet, you can connect to the Mirra Web site, give your name and password, and they will fetch the file information from your Mirra Personal Server.

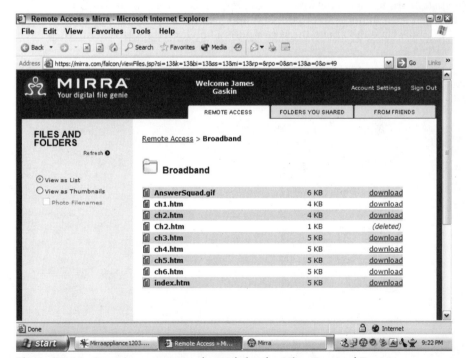

Figure 13-11: Remote access over the Web for the Mirra Personal Server.

Notice something interesting about this Files list. Remember I said that Mirra tracks deleted or updated files for eight versions? Notice there are two `Ch2.htm` files, and the second one is marked (*deleted*) in the file listing. You can undelete and download that file if necessary. The others are available for immediate download, so that expense spreadsheet you need is only a few clicks away with a Mirra Personal Server.

As cool as this product is, there are some caveats. This product does not make it easy to store your backed up data sets offsite. You can, for example, download all your data from a remote location using the Mirra remote connection, but that's a manual process and must happen one downloaded file at a time. That's not good enough to be a reliable offsite back-up mechanism.

You can't treat this like a typical network attached storage device, either. The only way you can get files to the Mirra is to declare the folder for backup today and forever. Doable, but it requires extra steps.

The good part is that the Mirra Personal Server, at least in the spring of 2004, is priced comparably or less than any other network attached storage device. So you get most of what a NAS device gives you, but you also get the easy remote access through any Web browser from anywhere on the Internet.

RocketVault

The RocketVault from IntraDyn, Inc., (www.intradyn.com) sets a new high standard for small network backup appliances. (See Figure 13-12.) This is, at least in my opinion, the first and best back-up device a company can get from the time they have three computers networked together until they have hundreds.

Figure 13-12: RocketVault is built into a Shuttle PC case.

As one might expect, large companies struggle with backup all the time, and an entire series of products has been developed called data vaults. The process for grabbing files and moving them somewhere offsite and safe is often called vaulting. That's why RocketVault calls itself a "Server Managed Vaulting System."

Here's what RocketVault does:

✦ Copies files from client computers using Windows file share networking on a preset schedule.

✦ Sends the files and folder you specify offsite to a secure storage location at IntraDyn or a remote server of your own.

Two of the three critical components of a successful back-up system, to me anyway, are capturing data without user intervention, and storing that data offsite to be safe in case of disaster. RocketVault does these things, and also makes for easy restorations, which is my third criteria for a successful back-up system.

Setting up RocketVault isn't difficult, but there are steps to watch to keep the security straight. You tell the RocketVault which share you want to copy, give the username and password for that share if it doesn't match the default username and password for all shares you can set, and repeat the process for all other shares you want copied.

You can list quite a few shares, because the low-end RocketVault has 240GBs of disk space. The first step is to name a group for this back-up process, and I used Images. Figure 13-13 shows the next part of the share-defining process.

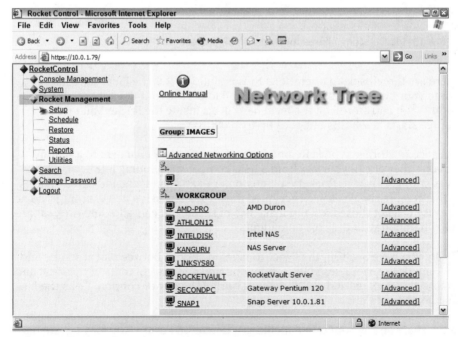

Figure 13-13: RocketVault sees the entire network.

The RocketVault then opens all the shares on that computer. Notice there are several hidden shares that the SnapAppliance never shows normally to Windows network clients, but RocketVault picked them up with no problem. Figure 13-14 shows these formerly hidden shares, and my name and password so RocketVault can now back up the Photos share.

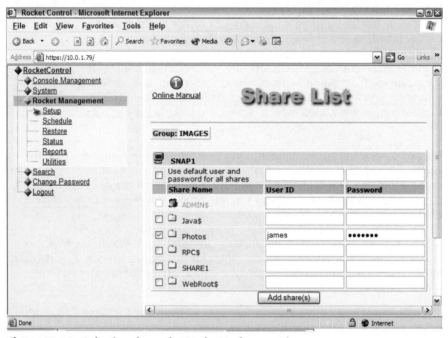

Figure 13-14: Selecting shares for RocketVault protection.

There are three back-up operations to schedule. First is the local schedule, where your files are pulled from the shared folders across the network by RocketVault and stored on the local hard disks inside the RocketVault (local storage starts at 240GBs but goes up to 1000GBs).

The second storage type is RemoteVault. This schedule connects to a remote server, either one of yours or from a host company (including IntraDyn, who rents storage space to RocketVault customers), and sends the indicated share(s) to that remote site. Files are encrypted during transmission and in storage, so no one else can get those files and make use of them. You can schedule every share at a different day or time for uploading.

Finally you have SychDR, the synchronization service between local shares and the remote storage. These files can be updated and the contents of the local and remote shares equalized multiple times during the day or continually as the files change on the PCs.

Every share storage operation includes a Retention Period. You may set shares copied on a daily bases to be retained for 14 days, or two weeks. You may set shares copied on a monthly basis to be retained for 12 months, giving a full year of safely backed up and protected files. Certain transactions, such as banking operations, need to be saved quite a while to protect yourself and cover any mistakes you must correct at the bank.

There are two ways to restore files. You can restore entire shares, based on the date they were backed up. So if your retention period was long enough, you could make a share look exactly the way it did three months ago. Figure 13-15 shows the restore by share and date method.

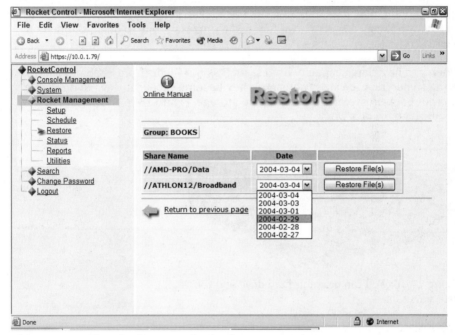

Figure 13-15: Choosing leap year day for the restore point.

The other way to restore files is to search for the filenames in the Search page. You can search by complete filename, a keyword that filenames should include, and even several words that are in filenames. You must select the group and storage area (LocalVault or a remote location), and specify whether you want the search terms to be case sensitive and whether all words are required.

When the search is executed, you see multiple entries for the same file. They are arranged by date, taking into account the retention rate you configured for each share.

The starting price for RocketVault as I write this is $1,495 for the 240GB version. All versions include stout security (256-bit encryption) and local and remote storage. Although the price may be high for a three-computer network, it's amazingly reasonable when compared to high-capacity tape drive units and for the security it gives your data. This level of data security was far too expensive for small and medium companies until RocketVault appeared.

External hard drive backup

Great for laptops, as mentioned in the previous section, external drives that connect via USB ports do a good job on desktop computers as well. Systems such as the Olixir 3DX understand backing up multiple computers onto one hard drive unit, and their software will keep the different computer data sets separate. And there are many more external hard drive back-up systems than just the Olixir, of course, and all provide value.

The problem with external hard drives when you get more than three or four computers is the manual part of the process. Someone must carry the unit over to a computer, plug it all together, run the backup software, and carry the hard disk unit to the next system. Not fun, and a process prone to being skipped on busy days.

When you have large capacity drives, such as the Olixir (from 80GBs to 250GBs in the same VRC-tape sized housing,) they become excellent ways to duplicate another back-up system for easy offsite storage. Figure 13-16 is a picture of the Olixir 3DX hard disk brick.

Figure 13-16: You can drop this hard drive and your data stays safe.

Say you have a storage appliance in place, and it grabs all the data from each of your four computers overnight. First thing in the morning, plug the external hard disk into a networked computer and copy the latest backup from the night before. Then put the external hard drive somewhere far away in the office from the server you just copied. If you can't get the data offsite, at least get it as far away from the other systems as you can.

Tape backup

Tape back-up systems remain more expensive and more error prone for the small and medium business situation than the RocketVault. Disk-to-disk back-up systems have been trying to take over the tape market for years, and the convergence of less expensive hard disks and faster broadband connections to move data offsite for safe storage are hitting their stride. I don't expect RocketVault to be the only back-up system using a combination of local disk and automatic remote storage for very long, but I don't believe that tape drives will be able to drop in price to match them.

Servers (like Microsoft or Linux or NetWare servers) often have tape back-up systems built in, but that jumps the price up too high for home office and small business customers. Those servers with appropriate software often cost two or three times as much as the server appliances discussed in Chapter 10. Tape systems to back up 100GBs+ in one operation cost thousands of dollars, not hundreds, and their tape cartridges are expensive as well.

Many people still like tape, and that's fine. If you're one of those people, please do these three things:

✦ Make sure you can get a full backup in one pass, either with high capacity cartridges or autoloaders that automatically flow backups across multiple tapes.

✦ Verify that the cartridges can be read by your tape drive on a regular basis.

✦ Test file restorations at least once a week so you don't lose too much when a tape gets too worn to read properly.

I did review a Sony StorStation tape drive with new Advanced Intelligent Tape (AIT) technology. Essentially an 8mm video tape with some electronics onboard the cartridge to help track and locate files on the tape and speed search operations, the StorStation or equivalent tape technology is the only type I would consider for a small business network. Even a home office with a serious amount of data (photographer, artist, music recordings, or composer, etc.) can benefit from a tape that holds 90GBs.

If you love tape and can get a system like Sony's, feel free. Otherwise, save yourself some grief and get a RocketVault.

Online backup and storage

One of my three critical issues for backup is some type of offsite data storage. You can carry a newly burned CD out in your pocket, send files over the Internet to your Web site, or pay a service to store information offsite, but data has to be offsite to be safe and useful for disaster recovery.

The availability of high-speed data connections now makes it feasible to move large amounts of data over the Internet to secure storage that's way, way offsite. Huge companies with mainframes have done this for years, but now the services are priced for small businesses and individuals.

There are nearly 50 online back-up services listed at Yahoo alone (http://dir. yahoo.com/BusinessandEconomy/BusinesstoBusiness/Computers/ Services/Backup/). You may find others, and companies offering other services may include online backup as well, such as IntraDyn, which rents space to service its RocketVault customers.

You can create your own online backup service if you want. There are two ways to do this:

- ✦ Make a deal with a similar sized company and you store their data whereas they store yours.

- ✦ Buy Web hosting space from one of the zillions of Web hosting services and send the files there yourself.

Online back-up services provide client software, much like the back-up software discussed earlier in this chapter, to schedule backups and coordinate uploading the files from individual computers or servers. These remote services offer excellent back-up options for travelers carrying laptops around. In fact, they may be the only way many laptop users ever backup a file.

How Your Small Business Data Can Survive Disasters

As I mentioned at the beginning of this chapter, most data must be restored from backup because of user error or mistakes rather than disasters. Other data restoration efforts help set up new replacement computers with data from the old obsolete system. Be glad you don't have disasters often.

But disasters don't have to be worthy of a team of Hollywood special effects magicians crashing asteroids onto your computer. Not all disasters require a visit from the fire department. Much more mundane events can accurately be described disasters when you realize what they have done to your data.

What if an employee gets really, really mad and deletes all the files on your storage appliance, then leaves without telling anyone. Could you recreate accounting files from 7 months ago under your tax filing deadline? That's a disaster.

Wondering what happens to companies who get hit hard by some virus infestations? Wiping all the operating systems to disinfect the computers and restore everything from backup is one sad possibility.

What if your youngest child thought your CD drive tray was the perfect size for his or her sausage biscuit? That could be a disaster as well.

Have you ever seen someone pour water into an office plant that dripped onto a computer? How about a mug filled with coffee into a computer case? I've seen both. Those are disasters if you have no data backups.

Many disasters involve police reports and insurance claims. What would it do to your home office or small business if you came in one morning to find holes where your computers used to be?

Cross your fingers and hope your disasters don't involve huge fires, floods, or nuclear explosions. But understand that your data is still gone if the cleaning crew kicks over a PC and crashes the hard disk.

Offsite storage saves the day

If a disaster of any kind destroys your computers, you must have data stored somewhere to reload on your new replacement computers. If you have back-up tapes and you must get a new tape drive because yours disappeared with your server, you have only about a 50/50 chance of getting your data back. You need to move your data offsite in one of the following ways:

✦ Burn CDs and carry them home in your pocket at night

✦ Make tapes and carry them home in your pocket at night

✦ Use a Mirra Personal Server (and remember the Kanguru iNAS-100 offers remote file download) and copy files to your home computer

✦ Use a RocketVault and combine fast local data backup with automatic online storage

✦ Use an online back-up service from your single PC and know you can retrieve the files anywhere you are with Internet access

Imagine a chemical leak closed the building where your small company is, and you couldn't go back to your office until the EPA gave the area a clean bill of health. Could you rent a few computers, install all your data from your offsite backups, and be back in business? You can if you move your data offsite with one of the options I've been nagging you about.

Here's a scary thought as you do your taxes: the IRS can seize your computers and keep them for 90 days. Completely legal, I guarantee you, because I did consulting for some IRS branches once upon a time. When they returned your computers on that 91st day, would you still have a business?

Tools that rebuild systems quickly

Many back-up software packages restore data to only working systems. That means if your hard disk goes psycho and you must reformat it, you must go through a full operating system installation before you can restore your data.

Some software back-up applications make what's called a disk image rather than a copy of the files. A disk image is the exact copy of everything on the hard disk you can save as one giant file for copying to the hard disk, if necessary.

One new product from Acronis, Inc., (www.acronis.com) covers both the backup and disk image angle. True Image 7.0 enables you to recover the full system image or pick and choose certain files to restore. Figure 13-17 shows the opening True Image 7.0 screen.

The two leading applications in this market, by most accounts, were Norton Ghost and PowerQuest Drive Image. But Symantec bought both companies over the past couple of years, and whether Symantec keeps the two competing products is up to the powers that be at Symantec.

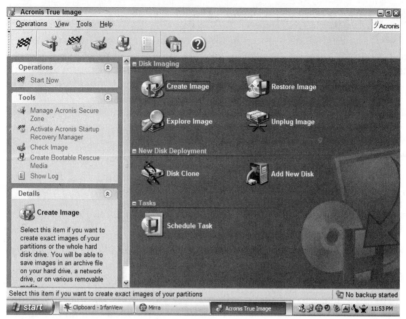

Figure 13-17: A new contender in the disk imaging market.
Acronis, Inc. Used with permission.

Creating a disk image is one thing, but making it possible to rebuild a crashed system means you need some way to boot the system. True Image 7.0 includes options to create a variety of bootable media, including DVDs. This addition is handy, because copying most disk images to CD-ROMs requires you to burn several disks to get the entire image. DVDs, with over 4.5GB of space, stand a much better chance of putting a complete system image (especially when compressed) onto one disk.

Note Remember that many of the details inside Windows operating systems, especially Windows XP, are tied to the exact system where they were installed. You can't take a disk image of one computer and overlay another computer's hard disk with that image, because the underlying computer details wouldn't match, and Windows XP won't work properly.

If you partition your disk and keep the applications and data separate, you have much less problem restoring a complete data set to a computer, even if that computer is a different one from whence the data came. But even with this method in your toolkit, it is handy at times to have a way to restore an operating system back to a known good point. Acronis True Image 7.0 can do that, and gives you plenty of flexibility for storing the disk image and booting the system as well.

Data retention rules for businesses

Storage issues create enough headaches under normal circumstances, but new federal rules for data retention are making life even more miserable. Not only must you keep all types of electronic data now, you have to be able to produce that data within 24 hours.

Worse, there are conflicting requirements between federal and state laws, although various government branches argue among themselves and catch businesses in the middle.

There are two phrases that strike fear in many business hearts lately: HIPAA and Sarbanes-Oxley. The first covers medical record privacy, including retention, and the second covers business records.

Here's how long you must keep records of various types (at least a best guess):

✦ Permanently:

Audit reports

Cash books

Deeds and mortgages

Retirement and pension plans

Insurance records

Labor contracts

Tax returns

✦ Almost forever:

Employee medical records (30 years after last day of employment)

✦ 8 years:

Bank statements

Paychecks

✦ 7 years:

Accounts payable

Purchase orders

Sales records

Voucher payments

Withholding tax

✦ 6 years:

Payroll records

✦ 3 years:

Employment applications

Notice that electronic mail records must be kept if they discuss any of the items in the preceding lists. Because those items cover just about every business topic most people may every use, which means your e-mail must be kept just about forever.

Even instant messages now fall under the umbrella of electronic communications which must be kept, just like e-mail. One might think these laws are made by hard disk vendors and back-up application developers.

Summary

Computers and their data run the world of business today, from the largest companies down to the person putting knitting patterns up for bid on eBay. All these computers create all sorts of data, and that data must be kept in good shape and able to be recovered after anything dreadful happens to your computers.

Remember: you must be able to capture data without user intervention, store that data offsite, and restore that date reliably to have a back-up plan. If you can't do all three of those things, you don't have a back-up plan, you have a potential disaster. And you never want "disaster" and "no backup" to ever occur in the same sentence.

Linking Your Network Devices

Knowing about networking protocols and software is one thing, but actually connecting devices together is another. Use wires? Go wireless? Is it safe? Is it secure?

You have more flexibility in networking options today than ever. So many options, in fact, that I put in a checklist to help you decide which option will give you the best network for your location.

Wireless security is a new concept to most, but it doesn't have to make you nervous. There are some extra precautions to take, but once configured properly, the data flying over your wireless network can be just as safe as if it traveled in armored cars instead of radio waves.

Wired Connection Options

Computers have to hook together somehow. The most common choice is to use wires, or network cables between computers and other network devices. The alternative is not to use wires, meaning wireless.

This chapter discusses the ways in which you can use physical wires to connect devices. Some of those wires will be new, and some of those wires may be in your home, apartment, or business at this very moment, waiting for you to discover their value in a networked world.

Let me gather your choices together here so you can find what you need to get your network up and running. Your network will likely include wired and wireless connections. Information on how to select and use wireless devices is in Chapter 15, but this chapter will help you decide where to use wires and where to go wireless.

For the wired connections, you have a full toolkit of options to cover a wide range of installation situations. Here are your major choices and a quick overview of their strengths and weaknesses.

Here's a look at the good points of Unshielded Twisted Pair (UTP) Ethernet wiring:

+ Widely available, and UTP connections are included in every network device
+ Highest networking speeds
+ Inexpensive

These UTP characteristics may give you pause:

✦ Neat installations require drilling holes in walls and floors

✦ You may feel tethered, especially if you use a laptop or other portable device

Good and bad points aside, when your network components are in one place, using UTP patch cables makes great economic and installation sense. Running inexpensive patch cables between your cable/DSL modem, router, computer, and other networking devices works great, especially if you can hide the cables under a table.

HomePlug devices send Ethernet networking signals through the power lines in your home or office. The connections are not as fast as UTP Ethernet, but these devices are great tools for linking areas to your network without having to run any UTP wiring through walls or floors.

HomePNA (Phoneline Network) devices were an early competitor to the HomePlug groups. Although still available, HomePNA trails far behind HomePlug.

Cable TV type coax cables are the transmission media of choice for some new vendors. These have value in new installations tying in home entertainment devices, but are not yet mature and won't help retrofit an existing home or office.

Choosing Between Wired and Wireless

Connecting network devices with wires is the time-honored method for data communications. But the convenience of wireless connections beckons. You must choose the right set of physical network connections to make your home or small business network communicate within itself properly.

 One important note before diving in: I include wireless network connections under the label of "physical" because they are. I understand that you can't see the radio signals, unless you're a visiting alien from a planet where vision evolved to cover the radio frequency spectrum in addition to the visible light we Earthlings use. But networking protocols treat wireless connections as the physical layer of the network. It's just a funny trick of technical language that the physical layer in this case is no more physical than the connection used by your cell phone.

For purposes of this chapter and the next, any network device with a wire connected to the network will be considered wired. Any network device without a wire connecting it to the network will be considered wireless.

Your particular situation will determine the best fit for your network. Many times the choice between a wired or wireless connection comes down to a coin flip. But because it's your coin, you make the final decision. I will lay out the most common options and network designs, along with cautions and warnings where necessary.

Pros and cons of wired versus wireless

It would be nice if the pros and cons of the wiring options played out neatly so decisions were easy. Unfortunately, a disadvantage for one person may be an advantage for another, making the pros and cons listing somewhat arbitrary.

Let me go down the list of important considerations in your wiring (or nonwiring) choices and see if I can make your decision easier. The good news is that the levels of performance and reliability in wired and wireless products make it hard to pick something that's absolutely wrong for a home or small business network.

Each area for consideration includes a number of line items (or factoids). Feel free to check or notate items that make sense for your situation.

Security concerns

Security in this case focuses on keeping outsiders on the outside of your network. Nothing in this section addresses other data security cautions such as worms, viruses, or file safety through backups.

You may not feel security matters for a home network, but you are mistaken. When you have any type of shared files on your network, you want to be sure only authorized users see those files. Any type of financial information or material that would facilitate identity theft on a shared computer resource becomes open to outsiders if you don't take security precautions.

Always assume someone else can get into your network in some way, especially when you are connected to a broadband service provider. Put passwords on all network resources, even if you tell your network client software to fill in the name and password automatically. The security breaks if an outsider sits at your computer but makes an eavesdropper find a valid username and password to gain access to your network resources.

No home or small office security precautions will be able to stop a determined attacker, just as no locks on the door will keep out someone who really wants to enter into your home or office. For a home network, you want to make security breaches difficult enough that budding teenage hackers in the neighborhood give up and move to someone else to attack. For a small business network, you want to make things difficult enough that an outsider or malicious employee can't wreak havoc by gaining access to critical information.

Wired Ethernet network security advantages:

✦ Wires contain their signals and do not leak out into the air.

✦ Devices must be physically connected to the network and tampering is therefore visible.

Wired HomePlug network security concerns:

✦ HomePlug connections can spread beyond your home or apartment through connected power lines.

✦ Outside electrical outlets allow the opportunity for eavesdropping.

✦ Radio signals are sent over the power lines and may radiate for a short distance, allowing eavesdropping.

Wireless network security concerns:

✦ Signals radiate out of your location to the rest of the world.

✦ Default settings on most wireless equipment bypass all security settings.

✦ Other Wi-Fi clients in the area may latch on to your network by accident.

✦ Eavesdropping tools exist in a variety of mobile devices (see Chapter 17).

When security tops your priority list, wired Ethernet devices protect you the best. HomePlug devices are relatively secure, but signals wander a short distance, so close neighbors could get on your network. Of course, wireless networking devices broadcast your network information by default, and neighbors will be able to connect easily if you don't take precautions. For these reasons, access passwords on all network resources should be used without fail.

Speed

Everyone in the computer and technology business dreams of running faster and jumping higher. The race winners for high speed always start with wired connections and then the wireless folks catch up, or at least get real close.

The speed hierarchy runs this way:

✦ Fiber optic cabling

✦ Coaxial cabling

✦ Twisted pair cabling

✦ Wireless

✦ HomePlug over home powerlines

Speed over distance with wired connections is a function of signal integrity. Cables that keep the signal tight and focused, like fiber optics, provide the highest speeds over the longest distances. Coaxial cable wiring uses shielding around the core wire to keep the signal focused, which doesn't work as well as the fiber cables. Twisted pair wires use the twists of a pair of wires around each other to reinforce the desired signal and reduce interference, but the lack of shielding limits the distance to about 100 yards (300 meters or so).

Listed speeds on technology equipment lie just as much as your car's speedometer. Sure, the car says 120 miles per hour or more, but do believe your car could do that? Absolutely not.

When you read speeds on the box of wired and wireless connections, you must think of your speedometer. Yes, 100Base-T has a theoretical throughput of 100 Mbps. But after you get through the technical time delays in applications, protocols, physical layer interface devices, and errors on every transmission media, you can figure roughly 50–60 percent throughput of the rated maximum. I generally figure about half the theoretical limit will be about the upper limit I'll reach, and I don't expect to reach that too often.

That same formula works for wireless connections as well. And the wireless products have to take into account signal distance, which doesn't create a limit for wired connections.

Distance affects wired transmissions as well, but those devices tend to work and work and work until they reach their limit and the signals fall apart and don't work at all. Wireless tends to work more and more slowly until you can't receive a signal, for a gradual decrease in performance over distance.

Wired Ethernet network speed advantages:

✦ Speeds remain constant until you pass the allowable range of the cable (300 feet for 10/100Base-T) and the signal degrades suddenly.

✦ 1GB (one gigabit) over twisted pair wiring equipment is now affordable and in general use in many company networks and even down to some desktop systems.

✦ 10GB network equipment is now on the market using fiber optic cable but work on twisted pair versions has started.

✦ Even in loaded networks, speed remains fairly constant.

✦ Hard-core game players may not like the increased latency HomePlug introduces over 10/100Base-T wiring connection devices.

HomePlug Ethernet speed advantages:

✦ HomePlug has a speed rating of 14 Mbps with practical throughput of between 6–8 Mbps (faster than cable/DSL broadband networks today).

✦ HomePlug connections run faster than inexpensive wireless devices.

Wireless Ethernet network speed advantages:

✦ Speeds have increased from 11 Mbps to 108 Mbps (rating, not actual) over the past 2 years and will continue to improve.

✦ Installation time for new wireless devices is nearly zero, meaning you start networking faster (hey, that's a speed).

✦ Wired devices almost always transfer data faster and for less money than wireless do.

✦ Wireless speeds catch up in a few years.

Wired 10/100Base-T UTP Ethernet wins the speed race every time. HomePlug runs faster than the 802.11b wireless networking standard (in-depth info in the next chapter about wireless standards) but newer wireless devices are faster than HomePlug. But those wireless devices cost more money than HomePlug devices, and HomePlug will speed up with the next version. All of these offer faster transfer speeds than your broadband provider will deliver, so you will only notice speed differences for large file transfers within your network.

Distance

Every network technology has a distance limitation. Homes and small businesses rarely, if ever, hit those limitations in most areas.

The trickiest technology for distance operations is wireless networking. Power settings for client devices are usually rather low (about 50 milliwatts for most brands of client networking transceivers) and affected by distance and interference. Higher-power client products and special antennas can often improve a tenuous wireless networking connection enough to be usable, however.

Hybrid networks (wired and wireless components together) provide solutions to distance problems in most cases.

Wired Ethernet distance advantages:

✦ Repeaters, hubs, routers, and switches extend the distance of 10/100Base-T considerably. Network devices can communicate across four hubs end-to-end for about 1,200 feet of distance.

✦ Routers and switches reclock the data stream and extend that distance even more.

✦ HomePlug wiring networks cover all the distance inside a typical home (99 percent of all homes were completely covered because the guideline is 5,000 square feet) with no dead spots.

✦ HomePlug distance is limited to about 900 feet (300 meters).

Wireless Ethernet distance advantages:

✦ Wi-Fi equipment limited to about 100 meters (300 feet).

✦ Every obstacle (wall or floor) between wireless devices reduces their effective distance.

✦ Wireless devices connect through walls without knocking holes for wires.

✦ Wireless coverage in one room allows a mobile device to wander around the area easily.

✦ Inexpensive antennas or placement adjustments can greatly improve signal distance.

✦ Wired connections don't fade as they run longer.

✦ Routers and switches extend wired distance, but there are limits to the number you may have between any two devices (four hubs is the maximum without a router or switch involved).

✦ Directional antennas provide a huge improvement in wireless distances.

✦ Use a mixed network to extend wireless distance.

Wired connections almost always win the distance race, but may require extra wiring devices for long stretches. Wireless signal reach can be greatly increased with extra antennas, but those cost money. Networks that stretch over a wide area often need a mix of connection methods to link everyone.

Tech Bits Do-it-yourselfers will have a great time buying and installing all sorts of products from www.smarthome.com.

Interference

Every electrical signal can suffer from, and create, interference. ElectroMagnetic Interference (EMI) is junk radio waves created by electronic devices that interfere with useful waves. Running a vacuum cleaner by a radio usually introduces static in the radio signal because of junk radio waves from the vacuum's electric motor. Of course, those signals inside shielded wires resist interference far better than wireless signals broadcast in the open air. Some wireless devices, for instance, stop functioning when a microwave or cordless phone close by starts up because all devices use radio waves in the same frequency range.

Your job is to make sure you have options when interference ruins one part of your planned network. Being able to mix and match wired and wireless devices will generally give you the options you need to beat an interference problem.

Products are designed to handle the interference problems of normal homes and businesses. If your home or office is next to an industrial area, you may have problems. If your neighbor has a huge ham radio system, you may have problems with wireless and be forced to use wired connections.

The wired product interference resistance ratings are outlined in the following list:

✦ Twisted Pair Ethernet is more resistant to interference than wireless so microwaves and portable phones don't slow the network.

✦ HomePlug network devices include several advanced networking algorithms to allow them to ignore interference caused by other devices connected to the power lines.

✦ HomePlug networks do drop their transmission rate when interference disrupts the signal. Connecting a plug-strip full of other electronic devices into the same outlet as a HomePlug device will slow down your network.

Wireless product interference resistance ratings are outlined in the following list:

✦ Older wireless products (802.11b) have less resistance to interference than newer products do.

✦ Antenna placement can make a big difference in interference effect.

✦ Added antennas can often overcome interference problems.

Interference, especially in the 2.4 GHz frequency range used by early wireless devices and cordless phones and microwaves, can shut down your wireless network. Spectrum management tools, used by large companies to survey their interference problems, are far too expensive for home and small businesses.

Because you can't really control interference (it may come from outside), you may have to use wired network components to supplement your wireless ones. Another option is to use directional antennas in some areas (see Chapter 15). Either way, you can almost always find a way around interference.

Compatibility between vendors

Networks run on open standards set by a variety of international committees made of representatives from vendors and large customers. No proprietary network technology has made a major dent in the market, or even been introduced, in at least a decade.

That said, early versions of standards leave questions and vague areas the vendors must interpret when they make products. Therein lie the gotchas for early product versions as minor incompatibilities in the standards get worked out. After a product generation or two, the vendors and standards groups work out the vague areas in the standard and compatibility between vendors becomes a reality.

There are no compatibility problems between wired devices from different vendors. There are few compatibility problems between wireless devices following the 802.11 family of standards.

802.11b products have been in the market the longest, and work well together. 802.11g and 802.11a (you'll get the details about b, a, and g in the next chapter) work together pretty well. Some vendors are adding extensions to the 802.11g standard to up the speeds, and those products are not compatible between vendors because they do not follow the standard.

Wired compatibility advantages:

✦ Every Ethernet device will work with all other Ethernet devices from any vendor.

✦ HomePlug products from different vendors usually work together. Balky units may work fine when plugged into different sockets.

Wireless compatibility advantages:

✦ Products from various vendors supporting the 802.11b (11 Mbps) standard almost always connect and work together.

✦ Products released recently from various vendors supporting 802.11g (54 Mbps) usually work together.

✦ By design, 802.11g wireless devices work with 802.11b devices.

✦ Early products supporting 802.11g shipped before the standard was approved and will likely have trouble connecting to products from another vendor.

✦ Enhancements to the standard, such as "turbo mode" and the like, rarely work between product lines.

Compatibility between vendors summary:

✦ Wired Ethernet products (10/100/1000Base-T) almost always work together.

✦ Update wireless firmware and client software to improve chances of connecting between products from various vendors.

If a device connects with wires, it will be compatible with devices from other vendors. That's true across the board for Ethernet and HomePlug devices.

Wireless devices are touchier about compatibility between vendors, but second generation products almost always connect across company lines. You may wish to buy all your wireless products from one vendor so you have a single supplier or only one management interface to worry about, but wireless compatibility is no longer a major concern. But all bets are off when you get products with turbo modes and other enhancements not in the standard.

Future network devices

Network research and development groups work with wired connections first because wires (copper and fiber) are well-known and well-controlled entities. Some technologies run at such a high bit-rate that the cables connecting devices can only be a few feet long (like disk cables from servers to high-end disk subsystems).

Breakthroughs happen with cable and then spread out from there. If you want to add the fastest and best new products to your network over the next few years, make sure you have some physical network connection points available.

Some business and consumer technologies go against this trend. Wireless products obviously arrive at the market ready for wireless deployment. So my advice about wired connections works for all new products except those that are meant to be wireless by nature.

Wired advantages for future devices:

✦ Wires are a known media. They are resistant to interference and provide low transmission error rates that are attractive to new product developers.

✦ Faster products almost always use wires at introduction and maybe, but not always, offer a wireless version later.

✦ Adding wireless networking to a new product, such as network appliances, introduces an extra variable for users to manage during initial setup and configuration.

Wireless advantages for future devices:

✦ Consumers love wireless products and many cool new innovations are released as wireless products only.

✦ Mobility for personal data products (PDAs and entertainment devices) is a huge selling point, leading to wireless devices.

✦ Laptops sell just about as many units as desktop systems in many market sectors, and people like wireless laptops.

✦ The Wi-Fi "HotSpot" craze encourages more wireless devices.

✦ Wireless is more convenient for any device that may move around.

✦ Vendors are starting to link to home entertainment systems to play streaming audio and video files from the Internet, and are using wireless connections to do so.

The future belongs to wireless for the cool stuff, because portability and location flexibility matter to consumers, and wireless delivers those features. Devices that remain in one place, such as your router, servers, and desktop computers will continue to use wires for transfer speed and convenience.

Pros and cons summary

After all the listings of advantages and disadvantages of your two wiring options, are you clear on what you want or are you more confused? That's okay, most people in the networking business stay confused, so you're in good company.

A few situations force one option or the other onto your network design, such as walls you can't drill through or distances too far for wireless links, but otherwise you can use what you feel most comfortable using. I certainly can't make a claim that one option, wired or wireless, always works better and should be your first choice.

Wireless wins the cool factor, although wired products win the "higher speed" and "better security" awards. I believe the trend for personal and household items leans in the wireless direction, because of the cool factor. Network devices that stay put, such as routers and server/storage appliances, are already adding wireless support to their marketing pitches.

Many new routers include wireless support as well as 10/100Base-T Ethernet connections. Only one device I know of, from Siemens, is a cable/DSL router with Ethernet, HomePlug, and wireless support in one box (Siemens SpeedStream 2524 Power Line Wireless Cable/DSL Router - SS2524). It may be listed by some vendors as from the Efficient product family, because Siemens bought the Efficient company several years ago.

Don't box yourself in. Be flexible, and look toward using all the tools you have, including wireless, twisted pair Ethernet, and HomePlug where they make sense in your network.

Where to use wires

Perhaps because I'm a creature of habit, I look to wired products first. There are wires all over the lab network in my office, 100Base-T patch cables are cheap, and wires generally work. But then, most of my computing devices have no inclination to wander around.

Note

Wired network products tend to be less expensive than their wireless counterparts that serve the same function.

Closely located devices connected to a wiring hub or network router through patch cables are cost effective and controllable as far as I'm concerned. Stack them up, bundle the patch cables as neatly as possible, and you're done.

Security issues may be the only ones that dictate that you use wired connections, and those wired connections mean 10/100Base-T primarily, rather than HomePlug. The data transmitted over HomePlug uses radio frequencies similar to wireless and can leak off and be intercepted if an eavesdropper is close enough (next door or the next apartment).

Those of you building a new home can, for relatively little money during construction, have the builder run a cable bundle to every room. See the upcoming section on Twisted Pair Ethernet Wiring for details on cable bundles and why you may want one. You will also need to decide on a common location where all the wires from the home congregate. That will be your future control center, and you will be in great shape for all types of data and entertainment networking if you install the cabling during construction.

Note

Get construction advice and a thousand products to wire your new home front to back and top to bottom at www.smarthome.com.

Wiring multiple rooms of an existing home can be a giant pain. The effort and expertise needed to drill holes though floors and walls may be beyond what you have. Businesses tend to have an easier time wiring between offices because drop-panel ceilings give access to the spaces between walls. Many office spaces are refurbished between tenants, and building in your network connections during remodeling will save you much time and effort.

My approach is to use HomePlug devices in residential situations to reach areas wireless doesn't reach easily, such as from the basement to the upstairs. But I don't have to support 100 Mbps transmissions across the network as you may want to for business or hard-core game playing.

If you want a hard and fast rule on where you should and shouldn't use wired devices, security is the biggest reason for using wired devices. After that, you can make the decision that works best for you.

Where to use wireless

If you're a creature of habit and love wireless, you probably look to use wireless connections before wired connections. That's fine with me.

Wireless device options give network designers, even those worried about designing a home network, wonderful flexibility. Here are some places you really want to use wireless:

✦ In historical homes and buildings where drilling holes in the walls and floors requires permission from oversight groups and diminishes the historical flavor of the site

✦ When architectural barriers (glass bricks, a cement wall) make wiring impractical

✦ By your pool in the back yard

✦ In your treehouse

The cost of adding wireless connections to an existing wired network does not include construction and remodeling. That's one of the great advantages to wireless networking: you can easily add it to your existing wired network.

Twisted Pair (10 and 100Base-T) Ethernet Wiring

For most of the network world, twisted pair wiring *is* Ethernet wiring. That's because 10Base-T became the standard for convenient Ethernet wiring before the World Wide Web and Internet took off. Those of you who jumped into the world of the Internet after about 1993 have no clue how much pain and aggravation twisted pair wiring saves you when you run cabling anywhere.

First, however, you need to understand just a little about Ethernet and how it works. There were many other types of network transmission systems in the 1980s and early 1990s, but Ethernet won over them all. Let me explain how and why this happened.

A quick overview of Ethernet

Let me describe a problem much like that facing some people today: a new employee was told to figure out a way for coworkers to share a new, expensive laser printer. The difference? This was in 1972, for the Alto personal computer developed by Xerox, for a newly developed one-page-per-minute laser printer.

Dr. Robert (Bob) Metcalfe, a newly minted Ph.D. from Harvard and MIT, went to work. For the first time ever, there were more than one or two huge computers in the building. There were dozens of small computers that actually fit on desks (and used graphical screens with windows and a mouse, but that's another book).

Ethernet developed over the next several years until by 1979 it ran at 10 Mbps and many of the details were set and ready for commercial use. Here are two of the details that matter today for your home or small business network:

✦ Ethernet uses a shared-bus architecture. That means one electrical circuit connects all the stations on the network, like one subway connects all the stations.

✦ Ethernet uses a method of determining when data packets collide on the network because two devices send a signal that overlaps called Carrier Sense Multiple Access Collision Detection (CSMA/CD).

The first bullet seems simple, but includes an important concept. Any device on the network can "see" and send or receive packets to and from, any other device. That means there is no central authority deciding which device can send a packet at what time.

The second bullet seems complicated, but is actually simple. Because every device on the network can hear every other device, they all listen for a period of silence before sending a packet. Imagine a group meeting where people wait until no one else is talking, to start talking themselves.

That process works great unless two people start talking at the same time. Similarly, when two devices put data packets on the network at the same time, they mash together and garble each other. In fact, that's what happens in the meeting, too. Just like the bored meeting attendees, the Ethernet devices wait a random number of milliseconds before trying to "talk" on the network again.

As you'll see in the wiring sections coming next, modern twisted pair Ethernet does not look like a single network with all devices on the same string. But that's what it is, at least electrically.

Category 5 (CAT5) cabling

The term Category 5 (CAT5) relates to the grade of cabling and the speed rating for that cable. CAT5 used to be the top end, but now you can get CAT5e and CAT6. The ratings for the cable categories stack up this way:

✦ **CAT6:** Highest rating available today. For 1000Base-T (Gigabit Ethernet) and one day soon 10GB Ethernet over twisted pair.

✦ **CAT5, CAT5e:** Up to 1000Base-T (Gigabit Ethernet).

✦ **CAT4:** Non-Ethernet networks

✦ **CAT3:** 10Base-T (10MB)

✦ **CAT2:** Telephone voice lines, alarms

✦ **CAT1:** Too low, not rated for anything.

Yes, you can technically use CAT3 cable for your 10Bast-T network, which may be okay for your network device. Yet so many computers, wiring hubs, and network appliances ship today with 100Base-T support you'd be running the risk of network problems using such low rated cable. Stick with CAT5 at the minimum, although CAT5e is now easier to find and CAT6 prices are dropping to almost the same level as CAT5e.

Premade cables are available from thousands of locations (even your local Radio Shack). Figure 14-1 shows a good picture of a CAT5e cable from the people at Smarthome, Inc., (www.smarthome.com).

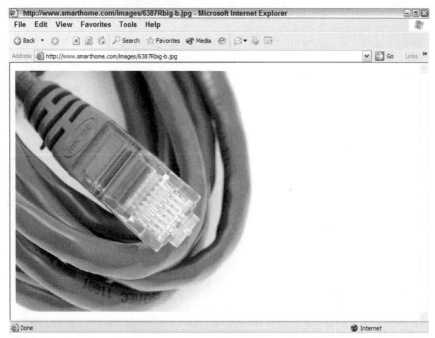

Figure 14-1: A close look at a CAT5e cable with four twisted pairs of wires inside.
Smarthome, Inc. Used with permission

Be sure and get a "snagless" or "booted" cable, which refers to a plastic hood over the clip on the connector. If you have more than a couple of cables behind your desk, pulling a cable out that doesn't have a hood guarantees you will snag it on something at least three times. Snagless cables are lifesavers when the cables get thick.

There are eight wires in a CAT5 unshielded twisted pair (often shown as UTP) cable arranged in four pairs. At least two pairs must be wired for 10/100Base-T to function. The connector is called a registered jack, wiring pin diagram 45 (RJ45). Your telephone cable is called an RJ11.

10/100Base-T cables come in a variety of lengths, generally from three feet to 300 feet already made with RJ45 connectors. Many standard premade lengths are available, including 3, 5, 7, 10, 14, 25, 50, 100, and 300 feet (although it's sometimes hard to find a premade 300 foot cable). Boxes and rolls of raw cable used for installation are available in 500' and 1000' lengths. Many suppliers make custom lengths and apply the connectors for a small charge if you need a cable that's 128 feet long, for example.

Wiring your network using bulk cable is the cheapest alternative by far if you don't spend too much money on the installation (you do it yourself). For less than a hundred dollars, you can buy 1,000 feet of cable and all the connectors you need to support a small network in your home or office. You will also learn more than you wanted about crimp tools and how much your hand hurts after crimping a few dozen connectors.

If you want to wire parts of your home for every conceivable current and future digital entertainment connection need, check into bundled cables. These bulk cable sets include multiple cable types within a sleeve to make running the entire bundle much, much easier.

Smarthome offers two standard cable bundles they call SpeedWrap (other vendors may have different names for a similar product). You can see in Figure 14-2 that Smarthome include enough cable options to handle networking today and in 10 years. These are perfect products to install in new home construction if you want the flexibility to put a media center in every room.

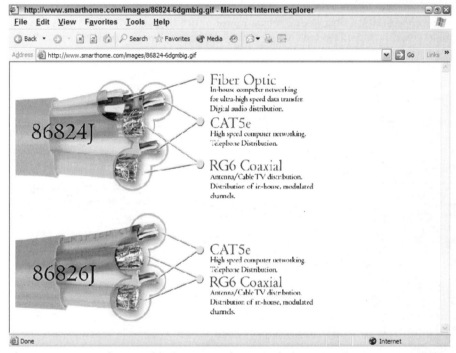

Figure 14-2: SpeedWrap cable from Smarthome includes twisted pair, coax, and fiber cables.

Smarthome, Inc. Used with permission

Think fiber optic cable is overkill? Maybe you'll need it in 10 years? Think again, because even consumer devices include fiber connections today. Check out the back of high-end audio and video equipment and you will see a TOS-link connector or two. That's a fiber optic cable wrapped in black protective insulation about the size of spaghetti with a small connector on each end.

Wiring hardware

If your home or office arrangement looks like mine, where the feeds from the cable and/or DSL service providers terminate on the wall beside a table with the cable and/or DSL modem and wiring hubs, you don't need to worry about wiring hardware. If you want to provide connections to other rooms or offices, however, you will need to run wires through the walls. When you reach the room or office to be connected, it's considered bad form to just knock a hole in the wall and leave the cables dangling out.

Network hardware suppliers got smart years ago and started collecting multiple connectors on a single faceplate to save wall space and speed installation. That type of thinking now must be used for home installations because we're determined to fill every room (potentially) with floods of data, audio, and video.

Products collecting telephone and network connections onto the same faceplate appeared first; then other connectors jumped into the mix. Figure 14-3 shows a four-connector faceplate with room for telephone, network, and dual coax cable connections.

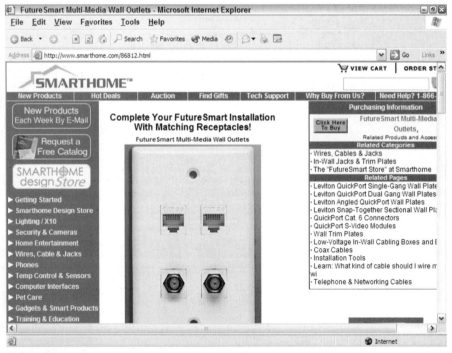

Figure 14-3: A wall connector to support SpeedWrap cable.

Smarthome, Inc. Used with permission

RJ45 connectors are used to support multiextension phones, which some larger homes have today. The phone connections, as well as distribution panels for the various network and coax cables, congregate at one location in the basement, garage, or utility closet. Some homes include a wiring closet, just like you find in offices, behind the wall supporting the home theater setup.

When you use bulk wire for installation, whether SpeedWrap or the old-fashioned kind, you must terminate that cable somewhere. A distribution panel collects the lines run from locations around the home or office and terminates each cable at one point on the panel. Patch cables then connect the lines, which must be connected on the panel, or link them to wiring hubs or routers. Figure 14-4 shows a distribution panel from HomeTech Solutions (www.hometech.com).

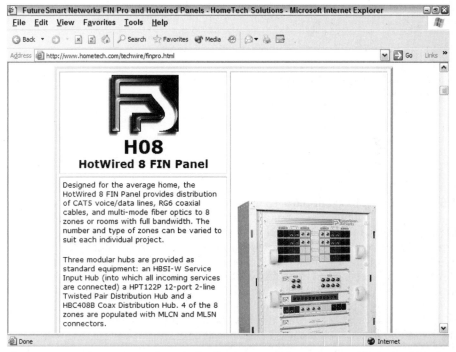

Figure 14-4: A FutureSmart (.com) distribution panel from Honeywell via HomeTech.

Can you put anything available to commercial wiring companies in your home? Absolutely. You should check around with various home theater retailers in your area for products and lists of certified installers. Many of the initiatives that include network wiring around the home are driven by the home theater and other entertainment industries.

Wiring hubs

Back in the pre-twisted pair wiring days, each network device connecting to an Ethernet network had to "tap in" to the cable. The first Ethernet cabling scheme used "thick Ethernet," a heavy yellow cable about the same size as a garden hose. Connectors actually clamped on to the main cable. The most popular was the vampire tap, which included teeth to hold on to the cable and a screw to drill a sharp pin through the insulation to the copper center conductor. This was obviously inspired by a medieval torture device.

Life in the network trenches improved greatly over the past 30 years so that now you can use a neat little box with RJ45 female connectors ready for your RJ45 patch cables running from the network device to be added.

Wiring hubs replicate the same electrical environment as a piece of coax. Each device connected to the hub sees all the packets and can send packets to all other device. Figure 14-5 shows a small Netgear wiring hub for 10/100Base-T devices.

Figure 14-5: A Netgear wiring hub.

There are three important parts to the wiring hub in Figure 14-5. First of all, you can see the four RJ45 female connectors in the front panel. That allows four network devices to connect to this device. You can see, barely, a button on the far right of the hub that says Normal/Uplink. This supports a connection to another wiring hub or router, which expects a crossover cable to keep the transmit and receive pairs coordinated. In place of a crossover cable, you can just push the button to make the hub cross the pins electrically. Much easier than trying to remember which is a crossover cable, because they look the same as a regular CAT5 cable but they don't work in most situations. Aggravating, and the switch on the hub eliminates some of that aggravation.

Tech Bits

A crossover cable changes the wire order to directly connect two work-stations or two hubs. The crossover connects the transmit data to the receive data pins on the connected device, such as you need connecting two PCs without a hub in between.

You can also, somewhat, see the lights on the left side of the hub. These lights show when the hub has power (the power connection is in the back) and when ports are in use. Lights on the plugs themselves light up when connected to a powered device and flicker as data goes through them.

There are no smarts in a hub, except that they keep the 10 Mbps connections on a separate data path inside the hub from the 100 Mbps connections. This keeps the 100 Mbps devices connected to the hub from monopolizing the bandwidth from the 10 Mbps devices.

Hubs come with 4, 8, 16, and 24 ports. When you see more than 24 ports, or the price seems oddly high, you have stumbled upon a switch rather than a hub.

The electronics controlling the network switching makes them much more expensive than unintelligent hubs.

Wiring switches

Where a hub electrically replaces a coax bus-type network, a switch isolates each connection from the others so that connection has the full bandwidth available to the devices on that switch port. Usually the switches run at 100 Mbps but support 10 Mbps connections. You don't need switches for a small network, but they have become so inexpensive many router makers use them rather than hubs.

Network designers connect hubs to switches, so the devices connected to the hub have the full 100 Mbps bandwidth available without sharing any of the bandwidth with other devices plugged into the switch. When a packet on the hub needs to go to a device not on the hub, the switch takes the packet and then connects it to all the other devices on all other switch ports.

Switches look almost exactly like hubs because the only difference between the two is the electronics to isolate each connection as a separate network. Figure 14-6 shows a Linksys switch about the same size as the Netgear hub shown earlier.

Figure 14-6: A Linksys five port switch for home and small office use.

Unlike the Netgear hub, the Linksys puts its RJ45 connectors in the back. This has become a popular option for many manufacturers so that all the connections and messy wires go in the back rather than the front. This leaves the front panel free for advertising and, oh yes, information about which ports are used and how busy they are.

Switches come most often in 4,8,16,32, and 48 port models. Even Gigabit switches, supporting 1000Base-T (Gigabit Ethernet) are now affordable. Perhaps not necessary for your home network, they have great value in larger companies where a server attached to each Gigabit port has maximum throughput available to the network.

Wiring devices in routers

The joy of electronics is the constant size reduction of components necessary to perform certain functions. One great example of this is the huge number of available cable/DSL broadband routers with wiring hubs or switches built right in. Many also have wireless connections built in as well.

Many people with a home broadband connection will find this type of combination device does all they need. They run a short CAT5 patch cable from the router/hub/switch/wireless device to their cable/DSL modem to establish their link to their broadband service provider. Then they run another CAT5 patch cable to their desktop system right next to the router, and use the wireless connection to handle their laptop when they're lounging by their Olympic size pool overlooking their acreage and polo pony barn, or when they're sitting on the couch in the den watching TV while checking e-mail.

The Netgear WGT624 108 Mbps Wireless Firewall Router in Figure 14-7 is fast, easy to manage, and about the size of a paperback book. The lights, from left to right, are power (on) Internet (your cable/DSL modem connection), wireless (the little ice cream cone radiating outwards) and the four LAN connections (1 and 3 are lit to show they are connected to at least one working network device). The wireless light blinks on and off and the LAN connections blink when they have traffic.

Figure 14-7: It's a router for wireless connections with a router built in for wired connections.

A small router with one or more Ethernet connections for the local network can do a good job for a single home user and do the same good job for a small business with 20 or 25 people. You won't find, with any of today's products, that your router is your network bottleneck. Save that blame for your broadband service provider, because they are the weakest link in the performance chain.

HomePlug: Networking through Your Power Outlets

Walk into a typical but empty home as if it was a foreign world and guess how the occupants communicate. Phone jacks come to mind, and there are phone jacks in several rooms. Water? Only a few places in the house. Gas? The lines only go to the kitchen and the garage for the water heater. Heating and air conditioning vents? They go to every room, which is a good sign.

Electrical plugs? Hey, they're all over the place and in every room. Many rooms, especially in homes built in the last 20 years or so, have at least one plug on every wall. If I were doing a survey for the StarGate team, I'd bet the power plugs were critical to all sorts of life activities, including communications.

Guess what? Those little plugs are valuable to communications. The world of HomePlug vendors wants you to take a close look at how many ways they can help you network your home or small business.

You might think this was one of those head-slap moments where something easy had been overlooked. Unfortunately, running high-speed data services over electrical circuits is not easy. Problems with interference from other things plugged in, such as motors that introduce an enormous amount of noise into the circuits, stymied vendors for years. Circuit breakers used to cut a huge chunk of the signal every time one was in the direct path between devices.

What made HomePlug possible, oddly enough, were all the advances made in wireless and DSL technologies. By applying things learned from developing those methods of communications, the HomePlug vendors finally made reliable networking a reality through the humble electrical plug hiding under your desk and behind your dresser.

HomePlug overview

You might want to think of HomePlug devices as a translator, or bridge. They translate Ethernet signals from 10/100Base-T twisted pair wiring into signals that the electrical circuits can transport. HomePlug devices turn your electrical wires into a new physical media that Ethernet can traverse.

Official HomePlug speed is 14 Mbps, so if you get half that on a good day count yourself lucky. In fact, half of any Mbps rated speed using TCP/IP at the client (such as a computer on a local network) tops out as the best possible realistic speed you will receive, so I'm not picking on HomePlug. Figure 14-8 shows the best place to go and get information on the world of HomePlug.

Figure 14-8: The Web home of the official HomePlug Powerline Alliance.

If you remember way back in the DSL section, the transmission technique used is Orthogonal Frequency Division Multiplexing (OFDM). This is also used by television signals, which is why I say that HomePlug designers looked around and choose reliable, proven ways to send Ethernet over power lines. To handle the odd nature of running over 120 volts of AC, HomePlug uses burst mode transmissions and adds some other data transmission techniques.

Tech Bits You MUST plug all HomePlug equipment directly into the wall plug. Do not use an extension cord or plug strip of any kind. The only way for the HomePlug devices to work is to be connected directly to the home or office wiring.

HomePlug devices connect to personal computers via Ethernet patch cables or USB connections. When using Ethernet, most HomePlug devices appear as a normal Ethernet connection to computers and other network devices. The USB connections need some type of driver (in almost every case) to connect the computer to the HomePlug network. CDs with appropriate drivers accompany the HomePlug hardware.

The majority of HomePlug devices look like one-port wiring hubs: one Ethernet cable in on one side, one power line going out from the other side. Some of the newer models look like battery-eliminators (wall warts) that plug directly into the power line and have a plug in the housing for your Ethernet (or USB) cable. Figure 14-9 shows an early entrant into the market from Linksys.

Figure 14-9: One of the most popular brands, the Linksys Instant PowerLine Etherfast 10/100 Bridge.

All the early HomePlug units looked more or less like the Linksys in Figure 14-9. Some are plastic, like the Linksys, and some are metal. But second versions got small as the market increased, manufacturing volume picked up, and new components shrank and designers made custom chips that incorporated the functions of several earlier chips, reducing the size of the electronics.

The results of these advances mean smaller units provide more flexible mounting options. One of the later entrants into the market, Netgear, now sells a very sleek and small wall-mounted HomePlug unit. Take a look at the wall-wart XE102 Wall-Plugged Ethernet Bridge in Figure 14-10.

Figure 14-10: The new look of second generation HomePlug devices, this one from Netgear.

Crowded office floors behind desks, where cables come from all directions and emulate spaghetti, will have one less device to entangle. Sure you must run a cable to this, but at least the cable won't terminate somewhere on the floor into a box half-hidden by other cables. You do have to give up a real wall socket, sometimes a precious commodity, but plug strips are cheap even if you do the right thing and buy one with surge protection. Plug that into the other wall socket and you're in business again.

Neighbors, at least those within about 900 feet and within the same electrical wiring from the distribution transformer, will see your signals. Most HomePlug devices now offer 56-bit encryption. This level won't stop determined hackers, but will stop your neighbors from reading the shared files on your network. That assumes, however, that you have turned the encryption on by putting the same password in all your connected HomePlug units. And I always recommend good passwords for all shared network resources, HomePlug passwords or not.

HomePlug and Ethernet

HomePlug devices aspire to be invisible, if not physically, at least electronically. When your computer connects to a HomePlug unit instead of a wiring hub, router, or switch, your computer should never know the difference.

For the most part, HomePlug works invisibly. The primary network design shown by most HomePlug vendors is one device at your router by your cable/DSL modem, and a second device at a convenient location for another computer, such as a child's room or the den. In fact, some early products only worked with two HomePlug devices on the network. Now you can have up to 16 HomePlug devices in one network.

Notice that in Figures 14-9 and 14-10, both products called themselves bridges. That's in keeping with the idea that the HomePlug device "bridges" your Ethernet network over the electrical wiring and delivers your packets back to your Ethernet network as if nothing happened. You know, just like a bridge over a river connects the road on either side. Sometimes electronic nomenclature steals directly from the real world, and this is one of those times.

Interference does cause problems to HomePlug devices. Every time an electrical motor starts up, it inserts an enormous amount of noise on the electrical line. Ever turned on a vacuum and thought the lights dimmed for a second? They did, because the vacuum noise on the line disrupted the electrical flow at startup and the new load of the vacuum motor dragged down the voltage as well.

HomePlug uses spread spectrum frequencies to handle interference, just like wireless Ethernet in the next chapter. When something new adds to the noise on the electrical circuits, the HomePlug devices hop around the frequencies looking for clear frequencies to use. That search and hop disrupts data transmission speed.

Note A Web site with many HomePlug products gathered together for comparison and online sale is www.HomePlugs.net.

Fewer available frequencies means slower transmissions. HomePlug is rate adaptive, another term for the process of looking around to find new transmission frequencies when one disappears because of interference. But one of the ways to find clear space on the circuit is to lower the data transmission speed.

HomePlug security and compatibility

There isn't much to HomePlug security, to tell you the truth. The standard calls for 56-bit encryption between HomePlug units. This isn't much, honestly, but on the other hand your signals don't travel as far or lend themselves to eavesdropping as much as wireless signals do.

56-bit encryption can be broken but the hackers must still gather many of your transmissions, analyze the patterns, and start churning through possible keys. This takes time, and the hackers must do this while physically plugged in to electrical wiring shared by your home or office.

Part of the shortcut to a security challenge for an outsider is to guess your password outright, without having to analyze and churn. How do they do this? By guessing your password based on the default passwords supplied by vendors. Look at the default password for a Siemens 2524 in Figure 14-11.

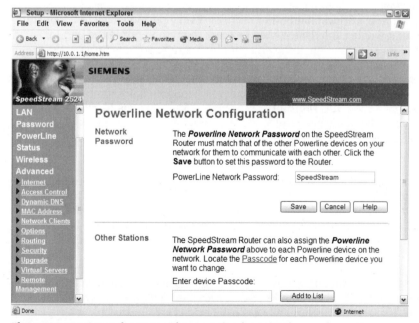

Figure 14-11: Setup for HomePlug security doesn't take much.

This password is the name of the product line. Why do vendors do this? For compatibility's sake. If you buy your HomePlug devices from the same vendor, they will automatically have the same password and all will be well. They will work together and have some level of security. If you mix products from multiple vendors, one of two things will happen:

✦ The passwords won't match so the units won't communicate.

✦ The units will communicate because security won't be engaged.

Don't be too hard on HomePlug vendors, because all manufacturers with secure products walk the line between enforcing strong security or making life a bit easier for their customers. Did you know that some reports show that fully one third of all safes installed in the United States still have the default combination assigned by their maker? If people buying a safe to protect expensive valuables don't bother to change the "password" for their safe, how can we blame home users who don't change their HomePlug passwords to protect digital photos of Grandma's birthday?

Security experts admit that appropriate security for the situation doesn't always look like much security at all. If you see a state of the art car alarm on a brand new Porsche, you think that's appropriate. If you see one on a 1994 Ford Tempo with a crumpled rear end, bald tires, smoking engine, and wrong-colored hood from a junkyard, you would laugh.

The Siemens 2524 in Figure 14-11 is the unit that includes wireless (802.11b at 11 Mbps max speed), HomePlug, four local 10/100Base-T twisted pair Ethernet connections, and a firewall and other security. Every possible way to connect comes in that single cable/DSL router. I expect them to upgrade the unit for faster wireless speeds soon, if they haven't by the time you read this.

If you don't recognize the Siemens name, don't feel bad. They take a lower profile than most huge global conglomerates, but you probably have some of their products. The Yahoo SBC DSL modem I have is a SpeedStream 5100 from Efficient Networks. Recognize the SpeedStream name? Siemens owns Efficient Networks and makes deals with many of the cable and DSL service providers to use their cable and DSL modems.

Every HomePlug device I have examined requires a Windows PC of some flavor to run configuration programs (if there are any). Sometimes, as with the Siemens Web-based configuration shown in Figure 14-11, all management occurs through browsers. Any browser will work, although a few vendors still (foolishly) write pop-up windows and controls that work with only Microsoft's Internet Explorer.

After configuration, HomePlug devices take any and all Ethernet signals from any network device and bridge them to your power line "network" for transmission. Why is this important? Because all network devices are compatible with configured HomePlug devices, which provides great flexibility in arranging your network to your home or office.

HomePlug and wireless

You can connect any wireless router or access point into a HomePlug connection and extend the length of your wireless reach. Alternately, you can bypass problem areas for wireless connections, such as thick walls that cut the signal down too much. Or you can put access points on different sides of your home or office, using the HomePlug devices to link wireless-enabled areas.

I'm amazed how often this combination of HomePlug and wireless works to solve aggravating network problems. I'm surprised at how often smart people never consider using the two technologies together.

Perhaps "surprise" is too strong a word. Many people know and use wireless products, but HomePlug hasn't reached the same market awareness as wireless. All the wireless products, especially in new laptops and PDAs, seem cool and futuristic and high tech. Power plugs, around for more than a hundred years, seem pretty dull and low tech by comparison.

Next time you face a problem with wireless reach, try this:

✦ Connect a HomePlug device to your primary router. That may be your wireless router plugged in to your cable/DSL modem or a separate unit.

✦ Connect a second HomePlug device to your power socket in the area out of wireless reach.

✦ Connect a wireless access point to that second HomePlug device.

✦ Verify your wireless device(s) in the remote area can communicate with your access point.

✦ Verify your remote wireless device(s) now reach your router and the rest of your network connected to the first HomePlug device.

Will you be able to solve every aggravating wireless problem by adding distance with a pair of HomePlug devices? Not every problem, no, but you will be surprised at how often a little more distance fixes a wireless hiccup. And the HomePlug devices will extend your wireless reach as far as 300 meters (900 feet or so).

HomePlug pros and cons

Time to wrap up the HomePlug story into a simple pros and cons section. Unfortunately, the answer won't be simple and clear cut. Every network installation is different, and your network situation is no exception to that rule. But I can provide what I see are the strong and weak points for HomePlug inclusion in your network design.

Pros:

✦ No extra wiring required

✦ Second generation products highly compatible

✦ Very similar to plug-and-play devices when used in pairs

✦ Smaller units that house all electronics in the plug portion save desk and floor space

✦ USB HomePlug units readily available for non-Ethernet devices like printers

✦ Works in all outlets, both 2 and 3 prong types

Cons:

✦ Slower than other wired network communication options

✦ Electrical interference slows HomePlug data transmissions

✦ Can't plug in to a surge protector or plug strip

On balance, I believe HomePlug products work reliably and provide an inexpensive option for connecting devices.

 Note One of the lengthier and more complete HomePlug collections of Frequently Asked Questions is at www.asokausa.com/support/faq.php.

HomePNA: Networking through Your Telephone Line

Before the HomePlug folks got their act together, the Home Phoneline Networking Alliance took a bite of the apple. Designed like DSL to run over existing phone lines, but this time inside the home or office, the HomePNA group released its 1.0 specifications in the fall of 1998.

No earthshaking accompanied the announcement for a 1 Mbps transfer rate over standard residential telephone lines. Unfortunately for the HomePNA, earthshaking acceptance continues to elude them.

Why has HomePNA not done as well as HomePlug? Mostly, I believe, because of wireless. Many, many vendors are big in the wireless market, public acceptance runs higher every day, and speeds for wireless devices continue to increase.

See for yourself what the HomePNA group has to say (www.homepna.org).

Also check out the friends of the HomePNA at the self-described "Source For Home Phoneline Networking Links And Information" at www.homepna.com.

Do I think HomePNA is a good idea? After all, they now have version 2.0 products available that run at 10 Mbps, giving a maximum throughput of roughly 5 Mbps, which compares favorably with HomePlug. And, of course, 5 Mbps far outspeeds any broadband service provider's feed to any of us in the real world.

Yes, HomePNA is a good idea, but I'm afraid the window may be closing. I suggest you look to HomePlug for the following reasons:

✦ More vendors make HomePlug products.

✦ There are 45 plugs in an average U.S. home but only five phone connections.

✦ Three major online vendors I checked had no HomePNA products listed.

✦ HomePNA released 3.0 specifications, including speeds up to 128 Mbps (theoretical) in mid-2003 but no products are listed on their Web site as of Spring 2004, 9 months later.

Putting network connections where the phone plugs are seems to make sense when you first look at it. My home builder put a phone connection in the master bathroom, but I don't consider that a good location for a network device. Even Microsoft gave up the idea (search for Microsoft and public bathroom Internet connections for what may, or may not, have been a great April Fools joke) of computers in bathrooms.

Telephone installers use the cheapest and lowest grade wire available, CAT2. Remember the chart showing CAT5 as the minimum standard for twisted pair Ethernet, and how CAT5e and CAT6 were taking over the market? There is no CAT1, making CAT2 the lowest grade of data cabling possible.

If you get a good deal on HomePNA products and you need a limited number connections that won't conceivably increase in the mid to long term, go for it. If those conditions vary even a little, stick with HomePlug and wireless. Most analysts started saying in early 2003 that HomePNA lost the marketing battle. Although I'm not a fan of most analysts, they may have made the right choice here.

Of course, nothing says that HomePlug will be able to survive the increased reach of wireless. I may have to revise this book in a year and say that HomePlug is a good choice only if you get a great deal and don't plan any expansion. Time will tell.

Networking through Your Cable Wires

A fairly new company recently announced a way to network Ethernet through the majority of U.S, homes: coax cable. The same cable that feeds your cable TV or maybe cable modem can transfer Ethernet. Rather than HomePlug or HomePNA I guess this could be labeled HomeCOAX.

Coaxsys (www.coaxsys.com) makes an Ethernet bridge for coax. You put their hub at the entrance of the coax to your home or office, then put connect to other coax lines from that hub. Figure 14-12 shows the Coaxsys Web site and big pitch.

I haven't seen any of these products in action yet, so I can't offer a review. The company makes a good point that coax cables tend to congregate at the TV, so running multimedia over these wires makes sense. It claims that its Pure Speed

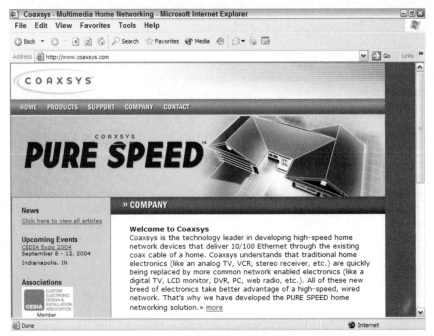

Figure 14-12: A new contender in the home networking market.

equipment runs at 100 Mbps and supports 10/100 Mbps Ethernet connections with no problems.

Coax in the home certainly has the most bandwidth available of any other cable type. There won't be the interference problems experienced by HomePlug or wireless, either. But I remain unconvinced because I have yet to see it personally and judge the added value above standard data networking cables and connections.

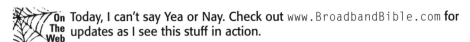 Today, I can't say Yea or Nay. Check out www.BroadbandBible.com for updates as I see this stuff in action.

Summary

Many pages and several new wired networking technologies later, the summary is that twisted pair Ethernet offers the best option for most people. If, however, you don't want to, or can't, run CAT5 cabling through your home or office, wired alternatives exist.

I have been lucky using HomePlug devices to augment 10/100Base-T twisted pair Ethernet and wireless connections. When you get to a barrier, and wireless doesn't work and there's no easy way to run a cable, check back to the HomePlug section and see if something catches your eye. You may solve a problem without much effort or much money. That's always a win–win situation.

Wireless Connection Options

I n the last chapter we covered wires, so this chapter covers nonwires, or wireless. Plenty of folks love the wireless connections on their networks, and plenty more folks can benefit from understanding how to construct a network with at least some wireless components.

Yet just like the different types of wires discussed in the previous chapter, wireless products have a variety of standards, applications, strengths, and weaknesses. Knowing which wireless products best fit your network situation will mean smoother installation, increased security, and more productivity when the network is up and running.

Wireless Advantages Inside Your Building

All during the last chapter you heard about easier ways to run wires around your home or office. What if you didn't have any wires to run anywhere? What if everything worked as easily as turning on your radio to hear music?

That's where everyone in the technology business wants to get to, I guarantee you. After all, most developers leave home in the morning by turning a key in their car's ignition without any clue how to tweak, adjust, or configure anything in their car except the radio. And how wonderful is the radio? Turn it on and you get music, anywhere you drive. Smaller ones fit into your pocket and give you music, news, weather, and sports without a single wire to trip over.

Yes, wireless advantages are marvelous for many users, but sometimes people get a little carried away. They tell you how wonderful it is that they can put a wireless access point at the top of their warehouse ceiling and network the entire place. But did they mention having to plug that wireless access point into a power outlet?

Okay, the wireless access point depends on (power line) wires. But the connections between that device and the network clients use no wires whatsoever. Go to a warehouse sometime and look at a forklift. Know what you'll probably see? A wireless terminal on the forklift talking to the network and an inventory application somewhere telling the forklift driver where to find the next product to move to the shipping dock.

The previous chapter mentioned the advantages for wireless connections in buildings with barriers to new wire installations, such as historically significant sites. Architectural barriers create problems as well. The vaulted atrium between wings of a building, for example, may require hundreds of feet of 10/100Base-T twisted pair Ethernet to reach around the opening. That may all be eliminated by using wireless connections.

Someday, my friend Art will no longer be able to ask his "horseless carriage" question. When did we stop calling a car a horseless carriage, or a network without wires a wireless network? When will we stop distinguishing between a network connection over copper and one over radio waves? When will we just call it all networking and not worry about the details anymore?

Sorry, Art, but I think that's a few more years away. However, many home and small business users can approach their network design with the flexibility and mobility wireless networking provides. When wireless won't work, then you can pull out the HomePlug or CAT-5 cable and go back to copper.

Wireless Standards Overview

Standards drive the computer business, and today, the big companies drive the standards. That works to your benefit, however, as companies can "beat" the standards products out the door with products that are technically proprietary but usually pretty close to the upcoming standard.

The wireless world follows this model more than many areas in the technology world. Not only do companies have to work with each other to develop the standards, they have to coordinate with governments about which radio frequencies are available. In the United States, there have been several "spectrum auctions" for the cellular phone world. It hasn't come to that for wireless networking yet, but the scramble for "licensed" and "unlicensed" spectrum (range of radio frequencies) can get pretty intense at times.

Developing, coordinating, and managing the standards for most wireless networking products fall into the domain of the Institute of Electronics and Electrical Engineers, Inc., (IEEE `www.ieee.org`). All the wireless products you can now buy so cheaply at your local retailer or online were created, developed, and manufactured thanks to the work of the IEEE. Figure 15-1 shows the IEEE Web site for the 802 network family: Ethernet, Token Ring, Wireless LANs.

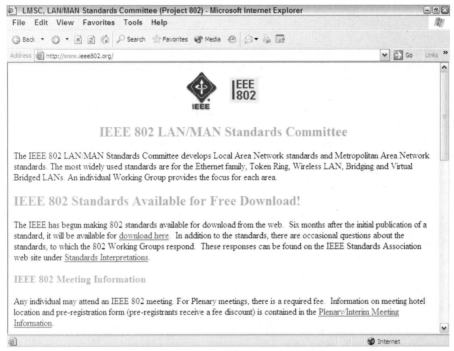

Figure 15-1: The group that makes it possible for your laptop to connect to the Internet in Starbucks.

The standards for wireless networking don't seem to make chronological sense, because you would expect the slowest technology to be labeled earlier than a faster technology. But all is never what it seems in the world of government bureaucracy and technology.

Frequencies, controlled by governments, can be a crowded mess at times. The world set aside the Industrial, Scientific, and Medical (ISM) band for general, nonlicensed use.

Why are wireless network connections subject to interference in the normal home? Because spread spectrum applications (like 802.11) can broadcast with only 1watt of power, but microwave ovens can use up to 900 watts because they're supposed to focus their broadcasts (but some leak). So when you take a popcorn break, don't get mad if your network slows to a crawl while the microwave works its popcorn magic.

802.11b

Those of you who looked at the table of contents wonder why I'm not starting with the 802.11a standard. After all, A comes before B in most alphabets.

But not in all technical alphabets. Letters were assigned based on when the proposal delivery to the working groups of the IEEE 802.x committees. A group defined and delivered a proposal for 802.11a (54 Mbps throughput using frequencies in the 5 GHz range) first, so they got the "a" designation.

A second group appeared with another proposal using frequencies in the 2.4 GHz range with a maximum throughput of 11 Mbps. They got the "b" designation.

Then the 802.11b folks got their standard details worked out sooner and got products to market. Slower throughput leaves more margin for error, and the 2.4 GHz frequency range provides greater connection distance than the 802.11a standard. The 802.11b folks became the embodiment of wireless local area networks as far as most people were concerned.

Check out the details for 802.11b in Table 15-1.

Table 15-1 802.11b Specifications	
Specification	**Description**
Frequency Range	2.4 GHz (2.4 GHz to 2.4835 GHz)
Throughput	11 Mbps maximum
Distance	100–150 feet indoors depending on obstructions
Advantages	Most common, least expensive
HotSpot Access	Common
Disadvantages	Frequency range competes with microwave ovens, cordless phones, medical equipment, Bluetooth devices, and others

For most people, 802.11b is what they think of when they think of wireless networking, even if they don't know it. Companies have provided equipment using 802.11b technology for several years, and the prices have dropped to downright cheap in many cases for 802.11b products.

 Tech Bits

Wireless fans may wonder what happened to Bluetooth, the standard for short range connections that was going to eliminate cables around your desk? Sorry, but you'll likely see Bluetooth connecting only cell phones on your belt to the headphone wrapped around your ear. However, Personal Area Networks (PAN) may revive the standard and put more Bluetooth products on the shelves.

Now that 802.11b defines the low end of wireless network speeds, the vendors focus on higher speed equipment (802.11g mostly) and present 802.11b as the entry level networking. If entry level to the vendors means faster than any broadband connection from a service provider to your location, take advantage of that. The throughput for 802.11b in the real world maxes out around 5–6 Mbps, but many of us only dream of a broadband connection over 1 Mbps.

Tech Bits 802.11b signal encoding technology uses only Direct Sequence Spread Spectrum (DSSS). This technique provides increased resistance to interference.

Intel's Centrino chipset uses 802.11b. Many criticized Intel for building 802.11b equipment into the world of laptops right before 802.11a and 802.11g become commercially viable. Why not wait, the critics asked, and get something just much faster?

In technology, you can make that same argument each and every day about each and every advance. I believe Intel did a pretty good job cementing the bottom end of wireless networking using 802.11b as its foundation. After all, many laptop hard drives can't stream data much faster than the maximum throughput they will receive from an excellent 802.11b connection. Making laptop customers (and by extension PDA users and other wireless network devices) expect at least a promised 11 Mbps raises the bar for wireless networking far higher than it's been raised before. Good for Intel.

802.11a

First to the standards finish line, barely, but way behind the race to market. 802.11a let 802.11b get a major head start before entering the race. Worse, the difference in frequency range (5 GHz rather than the 2.4 GHz used by 802.11b) made early systems incompatible with existing equipment. Not a debut meant for future fame as a Harvard Business School successful case study.

The higher speeds in 802.11a come at the expense of distance. On the surface, it looks like a good trade, because you cut your distance about in half but get five times the bandwidth (theoretically). Real-life speeds don't ever come to more than half the promised levels, but you can definitely tell the improvement moving from an 802.11b connection to an 802.11a link using the same devices in a test.

Check out the details for 802.11a in Table 15-2.

Table 15-2
802.11a Specifications

Specification	Description
Frequency Range	5 GHz (5.725 GHz to 5.850 GHz)
Throughput	54 Mbps maximum

Continued

Table 15-2 *(continued)*	
Specification	**Description**
Distance	25–75 feet indoors depending on obstructions
Advantages	Higher speed than 802.11b, far less frequency congestion
HotSpot Access	None
Disadvantages	Not compatible with 802.11b or g, shorter range, least common, more expensive wireless option. Coming 5.8 GHz cordless phones may cause interference

802.11a deserves better than it will get, no doubt, but you and I can't help that. The increased speed makes wireless networking useful for streaming audio and video applications, but the short range will be a problem.

There are fewer 802.11a devices for sale, by far, than 802.11b. That's not surprising, because 802.11b came to market first. But there are starting to be more 802.11g devices than 802.11a devices. That is a problem for 802.11a fans, because they will lose the distance comparison as well as price comparison with 802.11g products. The fact that 802.11a products don't connect to 802.11b or 802.11g devices means they will gradually disappear.

 802.11a signal encoding technology uses only Orthogonal Frequency Division Multiplexing (OFDM). This technique transmits on multiple frequencies concurrently to reduce crosstalk and interference.

If you have 802.11a devices already, don't throw them out. Many users prefer wireless connections even when devices are within easy reach of 10/100Base-T patch cables to keep down the clutter. Offices with several 802.11a devices will continue to work fine, but try and use the 802.11a devices in smaller, contained areas to maximize their value and minimize their shortcomings.

Locations with high interference in the 2.4 GHz band, such as a microwave and cordless phone testing center (it could happen) will be glad to have 802.11a as an option. Pick the right tool for the right job and success comes easily. It's when you try and force an 802.11a round device into a square 802.11b or 802.11g hole that you create problems for yourself.

802.11g

Now this is what you've been waiting for: compatible with the earlier 802.11b equipment, yet five times faster at 54 Mbps versus 11 Mbps for 802.11b (all numbers theoretical rather than real world). 802.11g will be the dominant base standard for home and small business use for the next few years until 802.11n arrives. The prices for "g" are higher than for "b" but that difference will narrow as more vendors get into the business of making "g" products. 802.11a prices are highest, 802.11g products are in the middle, and 802.11b prices are the lowest.

802.11g takes a dual approach to frequency management. Under 20 Mbps, it uses the same techniques as 802.11b, which is why it's compatible to the earlier standard. Over 20 Mbps, it uses the same technology as does 802.11a. Of course, throughput always depends on signal strength (meaning distance) so an 802.11g connection can drop to slower speeds (11 Mbps range) yet still provide decent network throughput.

Check out the details for 802.11g in Table 15-3.

Table 15-3
802.11g Specifications

Specification	Description
Frequency Range	2.4 GHz (2.4 GHz to 2.4835 GHz)
Throughput	54 Mbps maximum
Distance	100–150 feet indoors depending on obstructions
HotSpot Access	Common because of 802.11b compatibility, but many public places are adding 802.11g support
Advantages	Compatible with 802.11b equipment but faster because of different signal encoding technologies at high data rates
Disadvantages	Frequency range competes with microwave ovens, cordless phones, medical equipment, Bluetooth devices, and others

Distance for 802.11g makes a big difference in throughput. If you stretch your luck (and distance) or go through a wall or two, your standard 802.11g product will essentially become an 802.11b product.

Tech Bits 802.11g signal encoding technology uses Direct Sequence Spread Spectrum (DSSS) below 20 Mbps but Orthogonal Frequency Division Multiplexing (OFDM) for higher speeds, like 802.11a.

Although 802.11g uses the same type of frequency encoding at higher speeds as 802.11a uses, the two standards are not compatible. The frequency ranges differ, and 802.11g vendors seem inclined to push their combination 802.11 "b and g" products rather than some of their earlier 802.11 "a and b" combination products.

That said, the Linksys people have introduced the WRT55AG Dual-Band Wireless A+G Broadband Router. Although the name may be long, the product is pretty small and includes all three 802.11 network standards in one small box. Figure 15-2 shows the WRT55AG.

When one company makes a product like this, others usually follow. If you have a mixed bag of 802.11a and 802.11b products, keep an eye on your favorite vendor and see if they come up with a combination router like this one from Linksys, for example, the D-Link AirXpert Dl-774 wireless router.

Figure 15-2: The small friendly box that connects all wireless clients you may have.

802.11g nonstandard enhancements

People are never satisfied. Give them a fast network and they want a faster one. That's the drive behind 802.11g vendors who are goosing the speeds using a variety of nonstandard techniques.

The value of standards becomes clear when you try and mix products from various vendors. After a couple of generations of 802.11b products, I could finally mix and match products and expect them to work. That's with a single defined standard, yet early products, which supposedly followed the standard, wouldn't work together.

When you get away from standards, you lock yourself into a single vendor. That may be fine in your situation, and many home and small office users won't need more than the two or three stations they install for their initial network. And if you buy from one of the major vendors, you stand a pretty good chance of being able to find additional compatible units at a later time anyway.

It didn't take long for vendors with 54 Mbps 802.11g products to realize a great truth in consumer behavior: users want their network to run faster. Because sales jumped with the advertised speed bump from 11 Mbps to 54 Mbps, some wondered how high would they jump if it said "108 Mbps*" on the box. The * would refer the users to fine print, hopefully not read until after the product was purchased, that included all the various disclaimers.

Methods used to increase speeds

Different vendors obviously use different methods to ratchet up their 802.11g speed ratings. On top of this, the three vendors of core chips driving the 802.11g products have built-in limitations that must be accommodated if the products are to work correctly.

Here are the most common methods used to boost speeds. Your favorite vendor may use a different name for one or more of these techniques, but you should be able to figure out their methods.

✦ **Channel bonding:** This is a popular speed-boost method at the root of some vendor mudslinging. Sometimes called "multi-channel bonding" or "double-channel bonding," this method uses two of the wireless channels available and "bonds" them together. The device treats the bandwidth of the combined channels as if they were one larger channel. This works best in networks in which all devices use 802.11g, because packets from a single-channel device can cause the router to revert to single-channel mode. Effective distances are increased, according to most vendors and some independent tests. That alone may make this technique (or trick, depending on your viewpoint) worthwhile.

✦ **Packet bursting:** Based on the draft standard (the working groups have a fair amount of work done but all the details are not yet finished and approved) of 802.11e for Quality of Service (QoS), packet bursting crams more data in each packet and sends more packets at a time than usual. When fully defined, this technique should keep 802.11g streams fast while still accommodating 80.211b traffic on the same network.

✦ **Fast frames:** This technique increased data throughput from packet bursting by putting more than one data packet into a data frame. This delivers more data per data frame header (addressing and other details), increasing throughput. Also from the 802.11e Quality of Service work, this technique will fall back to normal packet content specifications when communicating with a node that does not support fast frames.

✦ **Hardware compression and decompression:** Just like popular Zip file programs (PKZip and WinZip, for example) compress files before storage, this new technique compresses the data packets before transport over the wireless network. Hardware chips in both ends perform the compression and decompression, speeding the process to make it possible in real time.

✦ **Select mode or mixed mode:** When all network devices use the same performance enhancing techniques, stations will no longer have to watch each packet to see whether it must be handled by gearing down to a lower speed. Mixed mode supports nonturbo-charged devices, and select or turbo mode works only when each device improves performance the same, nonstandard way.

Anytime vendors stroll off the standards path to make their own modifications to "improve" the standard, compatibility with other vendors goes out the window. Some pundits say no vendors should ever deviate from formal, adopted standards. Good luck.

 Check out Netgear's white paper on their Super G wireless technology at www.netgear.com/pdf_docs/108_Mbps_Super_G_WhitePaper.pdf and the D-Link announcement at presslink.dlink.com/pr/ ?prid=123.

People aren't built to follow rules blindly when they can tweak those rules and give themselves an advantage. Besides, would you rather vendors respond to customer complaints to add new features to their products, or just wait for the standards committee to get around to it? I prefer letting the people selling and supporting real live customers help design the features of the next network. After all, don't you want real customers to have some input?

Interference issues

Claims and counter-claims between vendors are nothing new, and the world of wireless turbo networks has not escaped this drama. Some people (vendors) have come forward and accused other vendors of causing enormous amounts of interference because of the way they handle channel bonding.

The best explanations I can find, and my own testing, show the following:

✦ Channel bonding causes interference in "turbo" 802.11g mode near a standard 802.11g network.

✦ Separating network devices by 50 feet considerably lessens the interference problems.

✦ A neighbor using an enhanced 802.11g network in the next house will be hard pressed to interfere with your network because of the distance and two exterior walls. If you live in an apartment and share a wall with this other network, you might have some issues.

✦ Not all manufacturers interfere with each other, even at relatively close range.

✦ These issues appear with first versions of the enhancement software and hardware. By the second generation, interference problems are limited to devices uncomfortably close to each other.

One site doing some testing recorded usable throughput at almost 300 feet because of the new 802.11g enhancements. That's a benefit everyone will enjoy. Improvements are reducing the signal drop as it goes through walls as well. Soon, wireless will be the network of choice for most people.

Wi-Fi

Technically, this is the same 802.11b discussed at the beginning of this section. However, the branding and marketing, along with Intel's Centrino chip set advertisements, has made Wi-Fi bigger than 802.11b in several ways.

Coming from marketing types rather than a standards committee, the name Wi-Fi stands for "wireless fidelity." Not sure why they picked fidelity, a term associated with music or monogamy, but they did. The Web home page for the Wi-Fi Alliance is at www.wi-fi.com.

Now the push from marketing types tries to make Wi-Fi mean any wireless product. Hard to demand the nickname remain tagged to a single type of wireless connection when it's all marketing hype anyway. Rather than referring to 802.11b as in the beginning, now the Wi-Fi Alliance lays claim to the entire 802.11 family.

The Wi-Fi Web site also offers plenty of advice for designing and building your own wireless network. The site's information tends to be correct but a bit generic. It also has trouble advising use of 10/100Base-T and HomePlug cabling where that may really make sense. But bias on a marketing Web site certainly shouldn't surprise you today.

One of the most critical functions for the Wi-Fi Alliance is to certify products. Over 175 products from all the major wireless players have been certified, meaning they will work in conjunction with comparable products from other vendors with the same certification.

Certification takes time and costs money, however, and some vendors jump into new certifications immediately and others wait to see whether customers need or even care about such certifications. Sometimes that leaves a disconnect between the Wi-Fi Alliance, vendors who certify immediately, and later vendors in line for certification.

Because the new Wi-Fi Protected Access (WPA) security ratings were put forward in late 2002 by the Wi-Fi Alliance, some companies have jumped in and others are waiting. Vendors complain about the constant "shake down" of various certification groups, as if various certification labels were required for protection of their products in the market. Hmm, maybe they are.

Details of WPA await you in the next chapter, so you can see for yourself how important or not the certification label is for your network products. Seeing the details should also make you appreciate the effort vendors expend to make confirming products and the time and money they spend on the process. But if a new product from a major vendor name in the wireless space doesn't have a WPA sticker, it may be more a matter of timing or other considerations than an admission that the product has no security.

802.11 futures

Two sections ago, the 802.11e Quality of Service draft standard made some news in the discussion about nonstandard enhancements to the 802.11g standard. Because the 802.11e QoS standard has yet to be ratified and accepted at this writing, that certainly falls into the realm of a 802.11 future enhancement.

Wi-Fi fans are like all other technology users: they want more sooner. Work progresses on a variety of enhancements, including the following:

✦ **802.11e:** MAC enhancements for Quality of Service

✦ **802.11i:** MAC enhancements for security

✦ **802.11j:** 4.9 GHz–5 GHz operation in Japan

✦ **802.11k:** Radio resource measurement of wireless LANs

✦ **802.11m:** Maintenance update

✦ **802.11n:** High throughput

✦ **No number:** The Wireless LAN Next Generation Standing Committee

Where are these working groups trying to go? Several analysts believe that 802.11 networking speeds will be up to nearly 300 Mbps in 2006. Perhaps the technology will first tease us with about 100 Mbps by 2005, if some other analysts are correct.

Interestingly, the rumors are that the 100 Mbps service may use the 5 GHz frequency range. That could make those almost-orphaned 802.11a devices a hot commodity in the future.

Of course, analysts often confuse their mission of objectivity when telling vendors who are buying their reports what they want to hear. The list of wrong analysts guesses never ends, because some of the worst technology analysts continually spout off just to get their names in the paper.

However, the trend of all networking players is to run faster. There are bandwidth and technology tricks aplenty to get your wireless devices talking at two or three times the speed they talk today. Bet on it; just don't bet on the arrival date.

Choosing the Right Wireless Local Area Network Hardware

Now you get to have some fun and actually start playing with some of the wireless toys, er, network devices. If you're new to wireless, let me tell you three things that everyone who builds a wireless network learns the hard way:

✦ Installation won't go as easily as you hope.

✦ Signals won't run as far as you hope.

✦ Wireless won't run as fast as you hope (but it will be faster than your broadband connection).

You will learn these facts as well. Even though you may believe me at this moment, you will be taught these lessons.

But all is not lost. People set up wireless networks every day, and you will get yours running. It may be slower than you expect, but it probably won't be slower than your broadband connection. Even on the best day with my cable broadband service I don't get better than 3 Mbps download speed. 802.11b actual throughput speeds on a good signal will beat that (5-6 Mbps) or equal that (fallback to 2.5-3 Mbps at longer distance).

Now you need to decide what to buy for the wireless portion of your network. If you have some network pieces already, you will have fewer choices. If you're starting a network from scratch, you have more flexibility. The good news on this front is that falling prices have made almost all the network components you will need so inexpensive in the last few years you won't have to "make do" with subpar equipment because of money.

Every wireless network needs one or more of the following items:

✦ **Wired-to-wireless connection point:** If your network router supports wireless, as many do, that will be your connection point. If you don't make this connection in your router, you will need a wired-to-wireless bridge. This is usually a wireless access point that connects to a wired network.

✦ **Wireless access point:** A device with an antenna for wireless client connections and an Ethernet plug for linking into the wired network. Some access points have no Ethernet connections and should really be called wireless repeaters (and sometimes what's called a wireless repeater is really an access point).

✦ **Wireless connection device on every client:** Clients can only connect to a wireless network if they have a wireless network adapter of some kind. These devices are often integrated into PDAs or laptops, and come in the form of PCI cards for use inside a computer or USB connections for use outside the computer.

You may have a perfectly acceptable wireless network that consists only of your network router with wireless support and a laptop with built-in Centrino 802.11b connection hardware. Or, you may have two dozen wireless clients connecting to multiple access points scattered around your business.

Router

This device will anchor your network. Your broadband service provider will leave you with a cable/DSL modem with an Ethernet plug. Every cable/DSL modem I've seen has only a single Ethernet plug, which makes it almost mandatory to connect a router to that Ethernet plug.

Technically you can connect your Windows PC to that plug, but that's a bad, bad idea. And I said Windows PC on purpose, because few if any broadband service providers can support a Macintosh or Linux system connected directly into the cable/DSL modem. Most have configuration software, and all the software I've seen is Windows-centric.

This router (or whatever you have plugged in to the cable/DSL modem) must provide security for your network. Even if your service provider allows you to connect a PC directly to the cable/DSL modem, don't do it.

Cross-Reference If you need a security refresher refer to Chapter 7.

Choosing your router

Here's a critical question: What type of network will plug into your router? After all, the router defines the network to a large extent, so you will save time and trouble by picking the router that best supports your planned network.

Figure 15-3 shows the product page for Linksys. Notice how the wireless products are subdivided into access points, routers, and gateways followed by network adapters.

Figure 15-3: The Linksys product Web page does a good job of laying out your options.

You may or may not need a wireless print server or specialty products, but you will certainly need a router device and a wireless connection device for each client. So use the following checklist to figure out what best fits your network needs:

✦ Router connections:

❑ Wired only

❑ Wireless only

❑ Wired and wireless

✦ How many local Ethernet ports (if any)?

   ❑ One

   ❑ Four

   ❑ More than four

✦ Must this router support HomePlug?

   ❑ Yes

   ❑ No

✦ What wireless 802.11 standard(s) must this router support?

   ❑ 802.11b only

   ❑ 802.11g only

   ❑ 802.11a only

   ❑ 802.11b and g

   ❑ 802.11b and a

   ❑ All three: 802.11a, b and g

✦ Will you have a separate Ethernet wiring hub or switch?

   ❑ Yes

   ❑ No

Notice an option missing from the checklist? Usually network decision trees like this include "how many users" type questions. But for home and small business networks with less than 25 users, all the wireless routers discussed will provide adequate service. If you have more that 25 active Internet-surfing, wireless-using clients hammering on your network all day long, you need another book after you finish this one.

No distance questions were asked. When you're dealing with only wireless product options, distance becomes a big deal. But because wired options to handle distances were covered in the previous chapter, I don't think spending a lot of time rehashing the distance profiles of the various wireless standards is necessary.

It shouldn't surprise you that most vendors have ways to help you decide which products fit your needs. Figure 15-4 shows the D-Link configuration page that pops up whenever you click the Which Wireless Technology Is Right For You? icon. All their answers include D-Link products, of course, but you can still learn quite a bit here and use a comparable product if you prefer.

I find seeing multiple product options displayed on one page helpful. You can't blame a vendor for displaying only its products in the assisted decision screens. But this should also point out how different vendors coin different names for product features.

Figure 15-4: Helpful, if product specific, wireless choice chart.

Another option missing from the decision checklist earlier is pricing. Everyone has a budget, no matter how small or how large (lucky you).

Books have trouble detailing prices, because prices change quickly and books take months to print and stay available (I hope) a long time. But let me give you some relative pricing notes to help you compare routers:

✦ Single feature products cost less than multifeature products.

✦ More plugs on the router cost more than fewer plugs (local Ethernet ports).

✦ Single wireless standard routers cost less than multistandard routers.

✦ Routers with all three wireless standards cost most of all and limit your choices most severely.

✦ 802.11b support costs the least of all.

✦ Buying a combination router will be cheaper than buying two single-function routers.

Although reluctant to list solid pricing because of the fast-changing marketplace, I will mention that I just saw a name brand 802.11b wireless router advertised in the newspaper for a price, after rebate, of $10. Pricing has become a nonfactor for most network decisions now, at least in the range of home and small business equipment discussed in this book.

Besides all these carefully reasoned explanations, understand that this is a competitive market with several major players working to increase their market share. Pricing is one of the easiest changes they can make, so special deals come and go regularly. New products constantly force lower prices on their predecessors, so if you can find last year's product the savings may be substantial.

Placing your router

The standard location for your router is right beside your cable/DSL modem. Either your router or your cable/DSL modem (or both) will probably include an Ethernet patch cable. Use the patch cable to connect the cable/DSL modem to your router.

But "standard" doesn't mean mandatory. You can place your router quite a distance away using longer 10/100Base-T twisted pair Ethernet cables or even a HomePlug bridge between your cable/DSL modem and your router. These options become important when your broadband service provider puts your cable/DSL termination point in a spot convenient for them rather than convenient for you.

Installation technicians put cable/DSL modems in strange spots. One of my neighbors has his cable modem, and his router, in the master bedroom closet. For some bizarre reason, that's where the cable connection wound up.

You will almost never have to touch your router after it's up and running. The only times you may have to touch it are when you add or subtract a new device to the router or you have to reboot the router because your broadband service has gotten "confused" and you need to reset everything. These situations won't happen often for the lucky but may happen daily for the unlucky.

Configuration screens for routers are accessed via a browser to the router's internal Web server. You can be anywhere on the network, or anywhere in the world in some cases, and still configure the router.

Client connection hardware

Most people consider clients to be their own workstations, and that's the typical use. In this situation, however, a client will be anything connected to your network. If you have a network device, it's a client. Backup server? Client. Small business server appliance? Client.

Clients have these options for Ethernet or wireless network adapter connections:

   ✦ Desktops almost always have an Ethernet port on the motherboard.

   ✦ Desktops have a Peripheral Component Interconnect (PCI) slot inside the machine for a PCI Ethernet or wireless network interface adapter card.

   ✦ Desktops almost always have a Universal Serial Bus (USB) connector.

   ✦ Laptops (especially newer ones) may have 802.11b built in (Intel's Centrino chipset).

✦ Laptops almost always have an Ethernet port.

✦ Laptops almost always have a PC card slot for network interface cards.

✦ Laptops almost always have a USB connector.

Figure 15-5 shows the three types of client adapters in a nice concise display.

Figure 15-5: Your three choices for client adapters.

Network appliances always include at least one 10/100Base-T twisted pair Ethernet connection. Some of them, in particular server appliances, also include wireless connection options.

The Taurus server appliance from Procom Technologies comes from a company that makes many storage products, and half the time it advertises that box as a wireless storage appliance. But it includes routing, Web and e-mail servers, and a variety of other features as you can see in Figure 15-6.

The Taurus server has a very handy LCD screen on the front. Unlike a few other products with a screen, you can actually make configuration changes through the screen and front-panel buttons.

Toshiba's Magnia server line also includes wireless support as an option, but its Web site redesign makes it impossible to find the page describing the Magnia servers. Sorry, Toshiba, but I can't find a good screenshot.

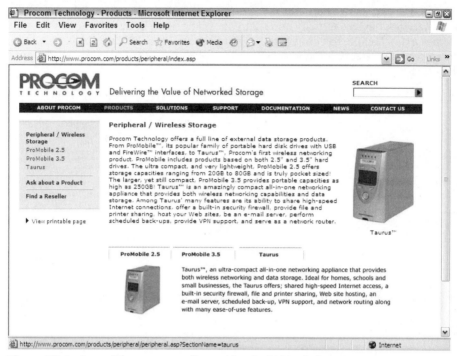

Figure 15-6: One of the server appliances that include wireless support.

Pricing, always risky to state in a book, will be affordable for the standard wireless client connection device. Many laptops have everything you need already, so no additional purchase will be necessary. And if your network is a mixture of wired and wireless, as it likely will be, you can always connect the 10/100Base-T twisted pair Ethernet connections on desktop systems to a wiring hub or a port on your cable/DSL router.

Hardware configuration tools

In this section, "tools" means software. Rarely if ever will you need to take a screwdriver to your hardware. However, you may be tempted to adjust your computer with a sledgehammer on a regular basis. I have to fight those urges now and then.

Because these are network devices, you must configure them to match your existing network. If you are building a new network, chances are you will still have to configure them to match your plans for your network.

Initial hardware setup

Product vendors have egos, just like everyone else. However, almost all vendors treat their router or other network appliance as if it's the lead device in a brand new network. Few vendors make an effort to play nice with others and take into account the possibility of an existing network.

This means you will have to use a single PC (a Windows PC) to configure most of your network devices initially and that you will need an Ethernet port on your PC and a patch cable to connect to the network router or other appliance for the initial setup. Figure 15-7 shows the Windows XP screen configured to ask for an IP address.

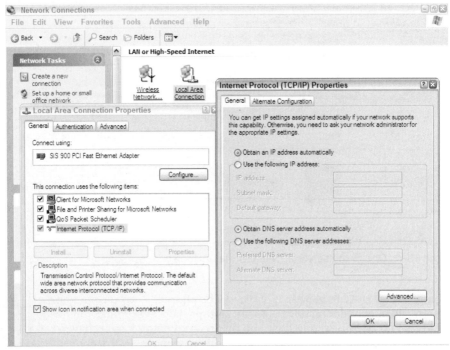

Figure 15-7: Setting your Windows XP Home system to accept IP address information from another device.

Read the installation instructions for each piece of equipment, of course. But here is the general outline of how to configure a router, storage appliance, or server appliance:

1. Click Configure your Network Connections ⇨ Local Area Network Connection ⇨ Internet Protocol Properties and check Obtain an IP address automatically.

2. Turn off your PC and the network device.

3. Connect the patch cable between your computer and the device. If your device comes with a crossover patch cable for use during configuration, be careful to mark it so you don't mix it up with the regular 10/100Base-T twisted pair Ethernet patch cables.

4. Turn on the network device.

5. After a minute or so (or indicator lights tell you the device has booted properly), turn on the PC.

6. Let the network appliance give your PC the necessary network IP address and other information.

7. Start your browser and go to the IP address shown in your installation instructions. This will usually be 10.0.1.1 or 192.168.1.1 but it may be something else.

8. Provide the username and password shown in the network device's documentation. If you can't find these, try "admin" and "admin" or "administrator" and "admin" and hope for the best.

9. Configure the network device's IP address to match your network (if you have one). If not, perform all other configuration options necessary.

10. If you change the network device's IP address, you must reboot that device and then reboot your computer before you can reconnect and finish the job or even verify the changes.

11. Verify the configuration and reboot and retest everything before you allow yourself to believe you are finished.

This all looks more complicated than it really is. You must let the network device configure your PC with the network parameters set as the default in your network device. After your PC and device can talk, you can configure the unit using your browser. Figure 15-8 shows the administration login screen for the Kanguru router/NAS unit.

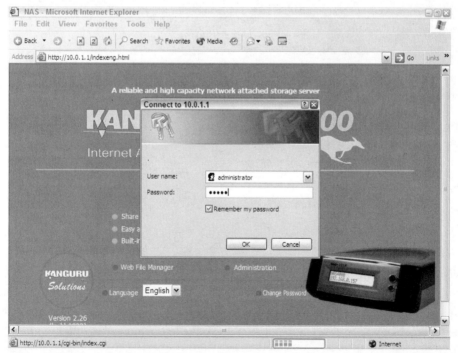

Figure 15-8: Providing the default name and password on the Kanguru iNAS-100.

If the network device manual tells you the IP address of the unit, you can configure your PC manually to that network range and skip some of the steps listed. Best to let the network device's Dynamic Host Control Protocol (DHCP) server provide the details, however, because sometimes the manuals represent some type of alternative reality and not the network device you must configure.

After you have made connections with your network device, follow the instructions for configuration. (Sorry I can't be more helpful here, but I don't know what device you have.) The good news is that many devices are getting much better about providing users an easy configuration process. Change your network device passwords immediately if there is any chance of others misusing your equipment or network connections, or if the device can be seen on the Internet.

Two of the better setup procedures are in the Kanguru and the Netgear WGT624 108 Mbps Wireless Firewall Router. Figure 15-9 shows the Kanguru Quick Configuration initial screen.

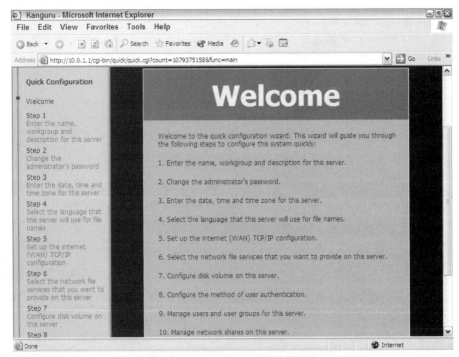

Figure 15-9: How nice to see the upcoming process listed to allay fears.

Not only does Kanguru give you a list of what will happen in the main screen, the left menu helps as well. Each menu step down the left menu will highlight as you step through the process. You can then see what you've already done and what's left to do at every step in the process.

The Netgear router has an automatic process, but doesn't provide all the step-by-step assurance. However, Netgear does provide much more help information on the right side of the screen, as you can see in Figure 15-10. And if you let the newer network devices try to configure things themselves, you may be surprised at how often they do the work pretty well.

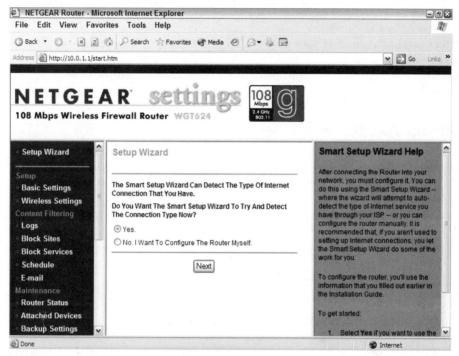

Figure 15-10: Another automated setup sequence.

Changes during use

If you're lucky, you won't have to change many things on your network after it's up and running. Be aware, though, that big-company network managers don't manage the network, they really manage the changes to the network. The same will happen with your network.

Network storage and server appliances may need changing at times, depending on whether you add or delete users from your network.

 Cross-Reference You may tighten security on wireless connections after you notice a strange computer name on your network, but that will appear in Chapter 16 about security.

Keep a file with the quick install guides for every network device. I write the username and password directly on the covers of the install guides so I don't have to read the thing to find the details. If the devices have assigned IP addresses, meaning (for me) servers and storage appliances managed via Web browser, I write the address on the installation guide as well.

Physical Design of Your Wireless Network

Networks all in the same room or office together don't need a design, they just need a place to sit. Networks that span two rooms with one wall between them still don't need much in the way of network design.

After you start spreading your network around a home or small business, you may need to start paying attention to where you put various network components. You will have placement options to choose from, depending on whether you need security or distance.

Designing for security

It may sound funny that you can design your wireless network in a way that improves security. But just think of the way radio waves work, and you may start seeing how device placement (network design) really affects your performance and security profile.

Remember that 802.11 × radio signals do the following:

- ✦ Penetrate two or more walls (b and g)
- ✦ Penetrate glass as if it were invisible (all)
- ✦ Reach farther when higher up
- ✦ Change signal direction based on antenna angle
- ✦ May go for 1,000 feet outdoors

To avoid the problem with signals going through walls, place all types of access points (wireless bridges, routers, and gateway) as close to the center of the room as possible. This placement also helps cover the room with a strong signal.

Avoid putting wireless transmitters of any type near windows. This includes desktops and laptops. Yes, the windows are scenic, but they stop radio waves as well as they stop light waves (not at all, in other words).

Place transmitters as high as possible. Many companies even make antennas that stick on the ceiling to get the best coverage possible. If your placement choice is on a desk or on top of a bookcase, choose the bookcase.

If your office shares walls with other companies, place your access point (wireless router) as far away as you can from the other company and still cover your clients. Shared walls make the need for strong passwords on all network resources, along with various wireless security issues to be discussed in the next chapter, more critical than ever.

There are new products coming that may help secure the perimeter of your wireless network, if you can believe it. Newbury Networks (www.newburynetworks.com) of Boston recently released Wi-Fi Watchdog. This enterprise-level tool effectively blocks those outside your perimeter from receiving any wireless signal from your network. You train the system with locator points that track you as you walk around the office boundaries. Passive sensors help the system define walls and doorways and other entrance and exit points.

Short answer? Newbury Networks really can stop hackers from intercepting signals leaking out of your network. It's expensive and difficult to set up in the beginning (at least in the initial version tested by my friend Tom H), but it works.

Designing for distance

Now, a contradictory option for designing your wireless network. Because the previous section outlined how errant signals from your network are a serious security threat, extending the reach of your transmissions must be done carefully. But many situations require a long signal yet are nowhere close to another home or office to intercept those signals. Just be aware that one of the primary concerns for many wireless users is the idea that someone in a van in the parking lot can intercept their signals and roam their network.

You can take advantage of small details to greatly increase your range and coverage. If these tips are not enough, check out the Options heading in this section for a few other tricks.

Quick checklist for distance improvements

Vendors know the most about their equipment, of course, and here's a collection of tips I culled from various wireless vendors to improve transmission range:

✦ Place routers and access points close to the center of served client devices.

✦ Place routers and access points high in the room.

✦ Keep line of sight between clients and access points whenever possible.

✦ Stay away from water, including fish tanks, water heaters, water coolers, and full bathtubs.

✦ Stay away from metal fixtures, such as sprinklers and large light fixtures.

✦ Standard antennas must be as vertical as possible on routers and access points. The weakest signals are below and above (better) the antennas, so you may need another device on the floor below.

✦ Interference from microwaves and some cordless phones will reduce distance, so move either those objects or your wireless devices.

✦ Aim client antennas toward the router or access point by pretending you're working with an old TV and rabbit ears.

✦ Move laptops, especially those with antennas built into their viewing panel, around the desk a bit to improve reception.

✦ Make sure your antenna is fastened tightly to your wireless device.

✦ Space wireless channels used on different routers farther apart. Try channels 1, 6, and 11 for maximum range in a large network.

Sometimes small location differences make a big improvement in signal strength. Many times the improvement comes from a change that wouldn't seem to be able to make a difference, but it does. Radio waves are always logical and predictable, but because you can't see their interaction with the environment, keep moving things for better reception.

Options

There are two great ways to extend your wireless range after you've exhausted all the easy ways mentioned previously:

✦ Get special antennas.

✦ Connect your wireless extra router or access point to a HomePlug device.

Every wireless device comes with an antenna or two, even if you can't see it. Laptops often wind antenna wires around the LCD panel because that part sticks up in the air, giving better reception. Routers and access points may have an antenna or two that can be rotated and position slightly.

Buying add-on antennas may be less expensive than extending your wireless network some other way. Figure 15-11 shows most of the D-Link catalog of extra antennas.

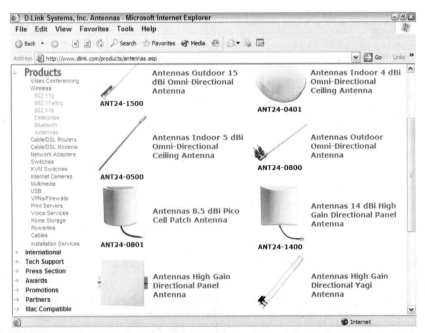

Figure 15-11: More solutions to the wireless range problem.

Notice the antenna in the bottom-right of Figure 15-11? The Yagi antenna family is highly directional. This focus of radio waves transmitted greatly extends your range while enabling you to control the wave pattern for security. If your home office overlooks a long yard in one direction, a Yagi antenna or some other directional option would be more secure than placing a regular omni-directional antenna in the middle of the area.

Of course, because I'm not selling wireless network products, I can also tell you to mix and match wired and wireless to extend your range. HomePlug is a great way to sneak data connections through walls or other barriers.

If a concrete wall in your basement office or thick flooring in your home blocks your wireless signals, don't automatically reach for the antenna catalog. You may have more success by connecting an access point to a HomePlug bridge in the area you're trying to reach.

Just as a wireless bridge can help reach across a void like an atrium, a HomePlug bridge can reach through a barrier. Home office in the basement, but you want to use your laptop on the second floor? If the signals won't reach, try a HomePlug bridge. You may be surprised at how often a low-tech solution can solve a high tech shortcoming.

Channel settings

As you'll see in the next chapter, 11 channels are used for wireless networking in the United States (13 in Europe). How did 11 get to be the magic number? Because about 550 MHz of spectrum bandwidth is allocated for wireless broadcast use in this frequency range, and developers wanted about 5 MHz for each channel. Hence 11 channels of about 5 MHz bandwidth each.

Radio signals weaken with distance due to interference and loss of wave integrity as it spreads. You can see this yourself by watching the ripples in smooth water after something is dropped into the water. As the resulting ripples run, they get smaller and less distinct. So do radio waves.

The primary "ripple" for a radio wave is plus or minus 11 MHz from the center frequency used. The secondary "ripple" extends that reach out to 22 MHz (for 802.11b but only about 10 MHz and 20 MHz for 802.11g).

Oops. See the problem? Channel 6, right in the middle, sends waves that stretch out and interfere up to 22 MHz away up and down the spectrum. But because each channel is only 5 MHz apart, Channel 6's broadcast interfered seriously with Channels 5, 4, and 3 on the downside and Channels 7, 8, and 9 on the upside. So you really don't have 11 usable channels, you have only a few that can broadcast without stepping on the toes of other channel broadcasts.

Most advice for channel selection says to use only Channels 1, 6, and 11. This spread gives maximum room to avoid interference. If you have only one or two routers or access points, this advice works fine. Because one router or gateway will support 15–20 wireless users, you may be in good shape.

If your network density stretches these limits, however, you have another option: using more closely packed channels. One company, Cirond Technologies, Inc., put out a white paper explaining how four channels can be used and without causing too much interference.

 Note Check out the Cirond Technologies white paper here: www.cirond .com/White_Papers/FourPoint.pdf

Essentially, using four channels (1, 4, 8, and 11) keeps enough distance between frequency ranges and resulting interference although adding a fourth channel option for wireless access points in a congested network design. Channels 1 and 4 may be closer together than some people would like, but if you put a router or access point using Channel 11 between those two, you have plenty of distance for radio waves in one channel to decay before interfering with waves from another channel.

Will this be a critical installation tool in your design kit? No, but it's nice to see ways around roadblocks that "everyone" says are insurmountable.

Summary

Wireless network design isn't difficult for the majority of home and small business users. Simple placement techniques can improve distance while maintaining some level of security.

Don't fall into the trap of believing that your network must be all wireless. That's great for design papers from wireless vendors, but you have choices. Wireless is a great tool, but a great tool misused is only the wrong tool. Pick wireless components for your network when they make sense, but always keep your eyes open for options.

Wireless Security in Depth

Those trusting souls who don't believe in layers of security to protect their data may want to avoid wireless networking. Because of the medium used, wireless forces layers of security onto you because you must protect the network (wireless transmissions) as well as your network resources.

Examples of layered security you may well implement, include:

✦ Firewall on your wireless router

✦ Encrypted message traffic

✦ Directional control of wireless access points to keep radio waves from leaking to the world

✦ Unique usernames and passwords on all network resources

✦ Physical protection of servers and computers

✦ Extra security to laptops used wirelessly when traveling

All of these options make sense on their own, and they make more sense when used in combination. Saying layered security is just shorthand for saying multiple security protections in place.

Be prepared. When wireless networking works, it's wonderful and simple and joyous. When wireless networking doesn't work, which is much of the time at the beginning, it's painful and aggravating and horrible. Wireless networking gets weirder and crankier as you enable security, so get a grip on your temper before you start.

There are concepts in here you may never have seen before, such as encrypting network traffic and aiming radio waves. That's okay, because you've never tried sending your data connections winging through the air before. Depending on your network's use and the data you have to protect, you may take a relaxed attitude or spend your time anxious and nervous as you wonder who's listening in to your network. Of the two, I suggest you lean away from relaxed and more toward nervous, but only as far as alert and informed.

Wireless Security: An Oxymoron?

I Googled "wireless-security +oxymoron" and received 970 results. That's bad for wireless fans who need security. The good part is that many results were from articles declaring that wireless security is *not* an oxymoron. In other words, you can have a wireless network and still sleep at night.

You can make a wired network secure, or at least secure your network resources and connections so that an outsider gets no benefit from wardriving and using a portable wireless packet capture program to check out your network. You can make it so secure your users revolt. So you need to find some point in the middle where your network is blocked from outsiders but usable by insiders.

Every writer of a security chapter has an obligation to say this: Insiders will cause you more data security nightmares than outsiders. That's based on history, looking at common network problems. Don't lock the gates on the outside and leave things completely unprotected on the inside. That's the reason I have mentioned using passwords and access lists for internal network resources all through this book. However, this advice does not mean an outsider can't cause you serious grief, just that an insider will likely cause you more grief. But grief is the constant when dealing with computers.

Start Thinking Security When Wireless

Now that I've scared you with the difficulties of wireless security in particular and the grief of computing in general, let me start filling in the holes in your security profile. First, of course, you need to start understanding that you actually have a security profile, which may be a new thought for you. But if you go wireless, you have a security profile, which is an organized approach, and the steps you take, to protect your security.

Not only do you have a security profile, you have one that's exposed. If you just use two wireless connections in your home, you are exposed (but not too much). If you have dozens of wireless connections at your business, your profile goes up much higher. When your exposure becomes noticed by the wrong people, you become a target.

When you activate your first wireless network connection, you pass the "security forever" point of no return.

At the wireless router/gateway

The entry point to all your network resources is your wireless router, gateway, or access point. Your wireless clients connect to your network proper at this point, and so can outsiders.

Your wireless router/gateway/access point (let me just say router from now on) must do several things:

✦ Connect to the wired portion of your network

✦ Provide access to your broadband service

✦ Accept or reject wireless clients seeking access to the network

Outsiders looking to get into your network must breach your router to do so. Plan on some type of strong authentication so your router allows only those into your network you want in your network.

You can't run your router free and open to the wireless world and hope for the best. Adding security measures can be somewhat time consuming, but replacing data stolen or trashed by a hacker will take even more time.

At the laptop client

The majority of wireless clients tend to be laptops, because they're the computers most likely to move around. Desktops can certainly use wireless network connections, but things that stay in one place are pretty easy to tie down with a network cable.

Laptops that travel out of your home or office have extra security requirements, especially when you use them to make wireless connections elsewhere. HotSpots at the coffee shops are great, but you better start thinking of your laptop less like a computer and more like a brick of money, because that's what it will cost you if it's compromised.

A staggering number of laptops are left at airports every day. 96 were left at security checkpoints at Denver International Airport over a two-week period in early 2002, for example (according to *USAToday*). That's not to say almost a hundred people lost their laptops at the airport, that's how many people forgot to pick up their laptops after going through the x-ray machines. No telling how many others were left at bars and restaurants and the like.

Many companies make laptop hard drive encryption software that effectively renders a laptop useless if someone doesn't know the password. Do you have something like that on your traveling laptop?

How about dial-in numbers, access codes, and passwords saved so you can connect to the home network with a single click? Many people configure their laptops that way to make connections quick and simple. That means thieves have a quick and simple connection to your network as well.

Do you share your laptop hard drive? If so, anyone who can get onto your network can also get onto your laptop hard drive. If that happens, that person may as well have your laptop in his or her lap.

All the security details upcoming must be applied with extra diligence on laptops used for wireless networking. Not to do so puts your entire network at risk. Losing a laptop is expensive. Losing a laptop that contains the keys to your personal or business bank accounts can move from expensive to outrageously exorbitant and blindingly painful.

Service Set Identifier

The Service Set Identifier (SSID) is the most basic security portion of any wireless network, although it's a stretch to call it a piece of security. Essentially just an unencrypted password that sits in the header of every data packet, the SSID isolates networks from one another if there are several in the area.

All traffic inside one Broadcast Support Service (BSS) must use the same SSID or the packets will be rejected, because the BSS performs the same function as the Workgroup setting in basic Windows networking. Because packet rejection is involved, you can kind of call the SSID a level of security.

The SSID setup is about the easiest of all settings, but there is a catch: every station on the same wireless network must have the exact same SSID. If you enter a typo in a wireless client, it won't see the network..

Immediately change the default SSID for your wireless network devices (every wireless device has an SSID). Hackers know all the default SSIDs used by various vendors (such as "wireless" or the name of the vendor) and check those when looking for open networks.

At the wireless router

Start your configuration at the router. You will have to use a wired connection to reach the router configuration screen, or you may have to configure a client to match the default setup of your router. For this example, I'm assuming you have an existing wired network and are adding a wireless component or two.

Figure 16-1 shows the Wireless Setting page for the Netgear WGT624. There are several settings on this page I will get to, but look at the first one, the SSID.

Notice the SSID: Gaskin-Test-1. That's a good start at a secure network name (what the SSID is, essentially), but not a great one.

It includes letters and numbers, which is good. It includes punctuation, the dashes, which is also good. It includes upper- and lowercase letters, also good. But it doesn't have nonsense names to guard against a *dictionary attack*, where hackers run through common words and names while trying to crack passwords.

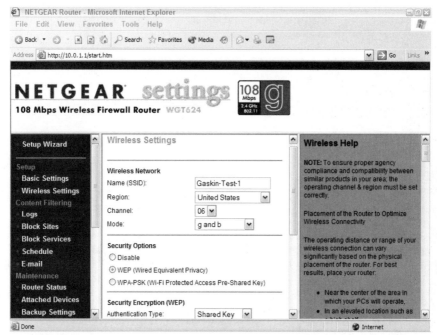

Figure 16-1: Network name is a good explanation for SSID.

SSIDs are case sensitive. NetworkName is not the same, to the computer, as networkname.

A better way to create an SSID that is just as easy to remember as the one in Figure 16-1 is to scramble the letters. You may want to substitute a couple of numbers for letters, such as Ga5kin-T3st-1. This is just about as easy to remember, but takes out almost all the words in the dictionary. Perhaps a better SSID would be Ga5k1n-T3st-1. That changes every word, or part of a word, that may be in the dictionary.

The SSIDs entered in the clients supported by this router must be written exactly as the SSID is written in the router. Typos or changed capitalization will look like a different (and wrong) SSID when they reach the router.

Usually, the router shows the SSID on one of the status screens. In this Netgear example, the status screen shows quite a bit of information about the wireless connection. Figure 16-2 shows it all.

The router can broadcast the SSIDs into the world. This feature works great for HotSpots where clients don't know any details about the available routers and needs to find them, but it's a terrible idea when you want to hide your router from outsiders.

Figure 16-2: Wireless port configuration status screen for the Netgear WGT624.

Every router I tested comes with the SSID broadcast turned on. You need to find that configuration screen and turn SSID broadcast off before putting your network into production.

Figure 16-3 shows where to turn off the SSID broadcast for the Netgear router. Notice you can also completely turn off the Wireless Router Radio (fancy name for the wireless portion of the router) if you want to hide your network when you're not using it. Almost all wireless routers include a way to turn off the wireless portion if you're just using it in a wired-only network.

Does this plan work? Absolutely. In Figure 16-4 I made a connection with a client computer to two different wireless routers. The first one was the Netgear router in Figure 16-3 I turned the SSID broadcast feature off earlier. I grabbed this screenshot after the broadcast name disappeared.

Notice the second router on Channel 1 has no WEP security (Wired Equivalency Privacy, the next security step, will be important in just a bit). Notice the second router has its SSID broadcast turned on, so I (and anyone passing by) can see the network name. That's a second reason the lack of WEP security will be critical in the next section.

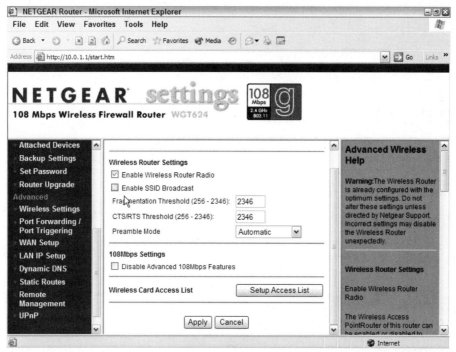

Figure 16-3: Turning off the SSID broadcast helps hide your network.

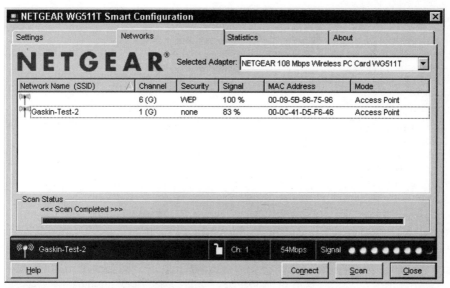

Figure 16-4: The top network router has SSID broadcast turned off, but the second router remains active and completely unprotected.

To wrap up the SSID router details, you must always perform the following actions:

✦ Make the SSID a good password.

✦ Turn SSID broadcasting off at the router.

At the wireless client

When SSID broadcasting is turned off, clients must know the SSID network name to find a router. That's an improvement in the security world. Making your network resources (and your router is a valuable network resource) hard to find improves your security profile a bit.

Every wireless client configuration utility includes a place to put in the SSID. In the ZyXel USB wireless network adapter configuration screen, the SSID text is near the top of the screen. Figure 16-5 shows this client-side utility and the aforementioned SSID.

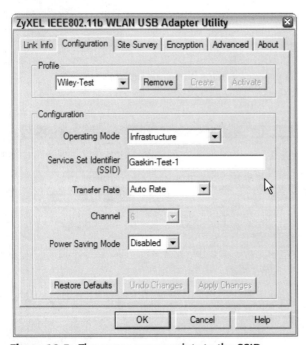

Figure 16-5: The cursor arrow points to the SSID.

Isn't it nice of ZyXel to tell us what SSID means? Be prepared for different clients to call the SSID something other than what you've seen here, such as just identifier or SSID with no explanation.

Take another quick look at Figure 16-5. Notice the field just above the SSID named Operating Mode with a value of Infrastructure? Your other option for

Operating Mode is ad hoc. You always want infrastructure, because that tells your client to make a connection to a router or access point. Ad hoc allows each wireless client to be a server as well, and pass along packets from other devices through its connection, sort of a peer-to-peer wireless network. Security with ad hoc wireless networks is pretty low, so always use infrastructure and let your wireless router earn its keep.

Every client has some way to search for network routers advertising their SSIDs. Figure 16-6 shows the ZyXel client configuration page with Site Survey listed on the tab.

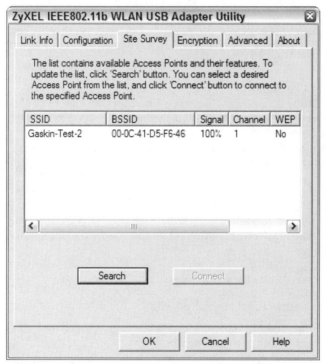

Figure 16-6: The wireless site survey finds only the one router broadcasting its SSID.

In an active environment, the clients may list several networks available to them. What's more disturbing is when you start your wireless network configuration at home and you see the broadcast SSIDs of your neighbors. In high-density areas, such as a street corner in a business district, you may see a dozen or more wireless networks blasting their SSIDs to the world. But do you see the router with the SSID of Gaskin-Test-1 on this list? Exactly.

I hope you're honest and able to turn back the temptation to look at your neighbor's network. And if you don't enforce security on your network, I hope your neighbors are equally honest.

Copy your SSID carefully to each client so they can find your router. The only way for a client to find a router that is not broadcasting its SSID is to have the SSID configured beforehand.

Wired Equivalency Protocol

Wired Equivalency Protocol (WEP) gets a bad rap today. Although called 64-bit security, the WEP developers were forced to stay with only 40-bit security when first released because of export restrictions in place by the U.S. Government. The 40-bit of allowed encryption for the data packets keeps out some people, but will not keep out determined eavesdroppers and hackers.

 Tech Bits WEP encrypts data traveling over wireless links, but the short security keys makes it possible to break the encryption in a relatively short amount of time.

Yes, WEP is vulnerable, but keep this in context. Your car door locks are really pretty useless, too, but if they discourage thieves or joy riders enough to convince them to move to the next car, that too has value. WEP won't keep out corporate spies bent on penetrating your network, but it can be enough to encourage a wardriving hacker to move to the next business and stop snagging signals while sitting in your parking lot.

Although WEP can't stand for long, some reports say that hackers must gather about 4,000 data packets before they can start the process of cracking your WEP keys. And 4,000 packets doesn't guarantee they will break your encryption; They just provide enough raw material to work with to start the process of elimination to find your encryption key.

WEP provides three important security advantages:

✦ The encryption prevents causal eavesdropping.

✦ It increases the authentication barrier for hackers so they have to work harder to gain access to any network resources.

✦ The checksum (simple error detection technique) used by WEP prevents any tampering with transmitted messages.

Many security experts consider WEP, even at 40-bit levels, to be enough security for home users and small businesses. I buy the home user part, but not the small business part. If you run a business and want to stick with WEP only, at least use the 128-bit level and buy yourself a little more protection. That's only a bit more work on your part to make the hackers work a whole lot harder.

At the wireless router

Creating the WEP key has gotten easier, so there's no excuse not to have at least WEP enabled on your network. In Figure 16-7, you can see the process underway on the Linksys WRV54G Wireless-G router shown earlier in the book.

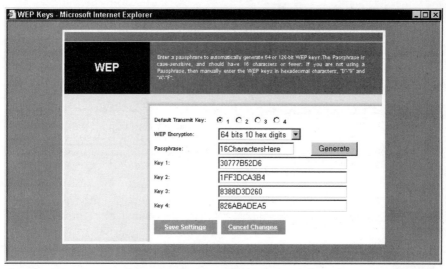

Figure 16-7: Use a 16-character phrase and generate your keys.

For the 64-bit security setting (WEP has 128-bit security because the U.S. Government has relaxed some of the security export rules) a 16-character phrase will be turned into four 10-character hexadecimal keys. Hexadecimal is Base 16, so after 0-9 letters take the place of the next numbers, making A-F numbers in this part of high school math you and I both forgot.

After filling out the passphrase all I had to do was click the Generate command button and the four keys were inserted into the proper places. Each client must transmit exactly the same key expected by the router or the packets will be rejected.

Tech Bits Encryption keys are used in an algorithm to decrypt messages. The longer the key, the more secure. Key lengths have grown over time because faster computers can encrypt and decrypt messages more quickly because of their increased number crunching abilities. Keys of 40 bits (64-bit keys including the overhead) took weeks to break on old computers in the 70s takes hours today. Hence the move up to 128-bit, 256-bit, 512-bit, and 1024-bit keys and beyond. The increase in processing time to encrypt and decrypt is far below the time needed by someone trying to crack the code and identify the key.

One handy way to rotate keys (a good idea in the security biz) is to pick a day every week or two and move from Key 1 to Key 2 and so forth. If someone has cracked your network, changing the key will close the door. After the fourth key has been used, issue a new passphrase and start with new keys.

If you get wireless gear that doesn't include the passphrase option, you'll have to create your own hexadecimal keys. Not too hard, but you have to remember the rules and make keys with exactly 10 characters.

At the wireless client

Using the 128-bit WEP encryption improves your security profile considerably. Figure 16-8 shows the ZyXel USB wireless client WEP encryption screen. Notice there is room for a 32-character passphrase.

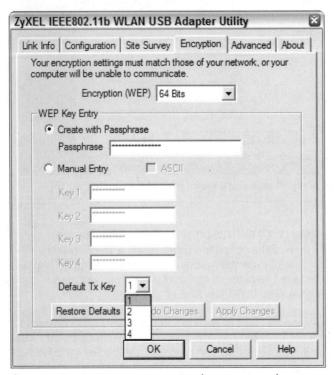

Figure 16-8: Here you can use a 32-character passphrase.

Using the longer WEP key improves your security enough to make using WEP really worthwhile. Sure it can still be broken, but if hackers want your business records that badly they can probably get all they need by going through your dumpster at night.

Note Data security threats never rest. More business secrets go out in the trash from most companies than ever go over the wireless network.

Again, your client and router must match exactly or your packets will be shunted off into the void somewhere. You may find them with the socks your drier eats, but that's only a theory.

Simple rule: activate WEP on your network. Clients and routers must match exactly to communicate. Change your keys regularly. The newer client and router configuration tools make all this much easier than ever before.

Media Access Control Filtering

You may remember way, way back in the discussions about Ethernet interface cards that every Ethernet card in the world has a unique MAC address. MAC stands for Media Access Control, but you can think of this as a serial number for every Ethernet card.

A central numbering authority issues each Ethernet adapter vendor a unique company identifier, and the company then keeps track of every MAC address in its address range. It's a nice, neat system that provides some excellent security advantages when used correctly. Imagine the wireless router checked each incoming packet for a fingerprint, and it had to be the fingerprint of your client device or the packet would be rejected. The MAC functions as that fingerprint. You can think of it as a hardware-based serial number if you prefer.

Again, newer configuration screens make your life much easier. The Netgear WGT624 lists each active workstation connected to the router and allows you to enter the MAC address, along with a device name (defined on the computer in the operating system) with a single click. Figure 16-9 shows this handy screen.

Figure 16-9: The easy new way to enter MAC addresses.

After you have all your approved clients attached to your router, simply click and integrate them each into the MAC address database. To make things easier (they think) the vendors often hide the name MAC address. In Figure 16-9 they call this the "Wireless Card Access List" of which you see the setup screen.

The old way was more trouble, believe me. Let me show you why you will greatly appreciate the new way to capture MAC addresses.

The Linksys WRV54G provides room for 20 MAC addresses, as you can see in Figure 16-10. Each "00" of the six in each space must be replaced with a hexadecimal (that again, unfortunately) number corresponding to one of your network clients or devices.

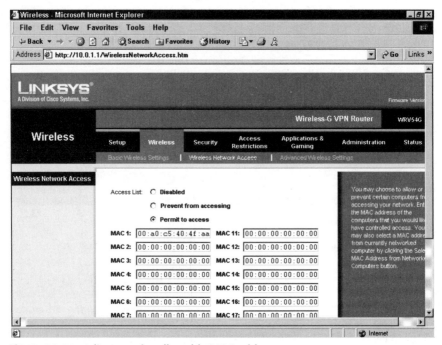

Figure 16-10: A list page for allowable MAC addresses.

Linksys calls this the "Wireless Network Access" page rather than Wireless Card Access List in the Netgear router. But it's all the same thing, and both configuration screens talk about what a MAC address is in their right-side help screens.

Don't let me leave you with the idea that it is horribly difficult to configure the MAC addresses for the Linksys. You can't see in the screenshot, but at the bottom of the 20 entry spaces there is an active Select MAC Address For Networked Computers button. Click that and a window opens showing the connected systems known to the router. All you have to do is click the Select check box and the Linksys integrates the MAC addresses as easily as the Netgear.

MAC address authentication does a great job of restricting network access to only the network clients and other devices you configure. As you may guess, this can become a pain for large networks. But small networks with stable client populations (you aren't adding and subtracting stations all the time) find this an excellent security control.

Technically, this is only an authentication control, not a complete security option. You need to find an option you're comfortable using that includes authentication and encryption. Although this is another good layer of security, you still need to put passwords on your network resources just in case someone gets access to your network through some other avenue.

Virtual Private Network Connections

VPN is another lovely three letter acronym, but one that's fairly self-explanatory. *Virtual* signifies something that isn't real, but acts like it is. A *Private Network* keeps your data traffic safe because no one else can see it. Thus a Virtual Private Network provides a way for you and your data to feel like it's running through a data tunnel built especially for you, even though the traffic goes over the Internet with all the other billions and billions of bytes flying around.

VPNs can be worth an entire book themselves (several, actually), but I don't have that much space left. So let me show you one quick way to connect a VPN over my wireless network.

Does it make sense to go to the trouble of configuring a VPN for use within your own office? If you want complete wireless connection security, it does.

In my case, I want a VPN to one of my server appliances to use as a file server. So I created a VPN to go over the wireless link between the ZyXel USB wireless network adapter and the Netgear WGT624 Wireless Firewall Router to the Tritton ASAP 120GB Network Attached Storage unit. The important part is getting access to the remote network by linking to the VPN device on the far end. After you make that connection, your computer thinks it's on that network.

Windows XP clients have all you need for the client side of the VPN. Here's the process for enabling VPNs for the client:

1. Open Network Connections (Start⇨ My Network Places⇨ View Network Connections).

2. Under Network Tasks (the left-side menu) click Create A New Connection; then click Next.

3. Click Connect To The Network At My Workplace; then click Next.

4. Click Virtual Private Network Connection; then click Next.

5. Provide the Connection Name for future reference.

6. Provide the VPN Server Selection (server name or IP address).

7. Click Finish to create an icon for this VPN connection.

Yes, the connection wizard assumes you're connecting over the Internet to your workplace, but that's okay. You may do that as well with this same wizard, but for now let me just get the link to my file server.

Figure 16-11 shows the Windows XP wizard asking for the name for this connection. Give this a descriptive name if you have more than one connection.

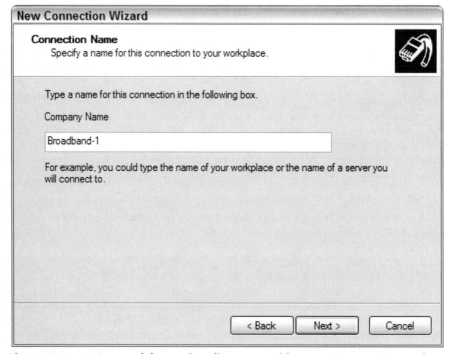

Figure 16-11: In Step 5 of the previous list, you provide a name you can remember for the connection.

Broadband-1 may not be descriptive enough for you, but it works here for me. Feel free to give your icon the name of the file server, for example, so you can keep track.

The next step asks for the VPN server name or Internet Protocol address of the end-point connection. Because this is all on my local network, I prefer to use an IP address rather than a name like `http://tritton.gaskin.com` because using a name forces me to have a local Domain Name Server running in my local network.

Cross-Reference

Refer to the *Domain Name Service* section in Chapter 12 if you want to check out running your Domain Name Server in your home or business, but most small companies don't. They use Windows networking for connecting to Workgroup assets, and rely on the name service provided by their ISP for Internet name translations.

Figure 16-12 shows the IP address I listed for the Tritton ASAP file server. Remember when I said I prefer to give all my network devices specific IP addresses rather than let them grab an address from the pool? This is why: you have to list the exact IP address of the connection point. You can't give an exact address if that may change after a device reboot.

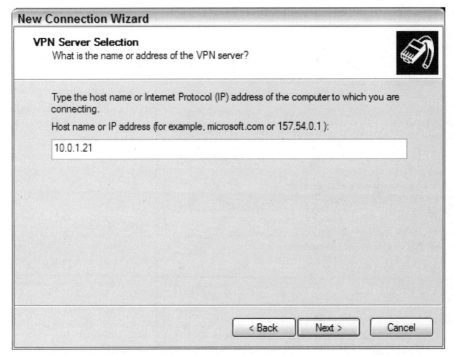

Figure 16-12: Specifying the far-end connection of a VPN.

I don't want to put the IP address of my router in here, because the router is not the endpoint of my VPN (my final destination). The whole idea is to convert an open-air wireless connection with no protection into a secure communication conduit. That means I want every stop on the network traversed by the VPN, not my open-air wireless signals to keep the traffic between me and the network attached storage device encrypted for the entire trip.

Your network must have an intelligent VPN device on each end of the connection. In this case, the ends are my PC running Windows XP Home, and the Trident router/gateway/network attached storage unit. If I was trying to reach the SnapAppliance server and storage device instead, I would make the router the endpoint of my network. Because the Tritton includes VPN capabilities, I'm securing my wireless connection all the way to the folders on the Tritton.

After you click the Finish button, Windows XP Home creates a new icon in the Network Connections page. In my case, the icon is named Broadband-1. Now I do wish I'd picked a better name.

You can check all these settings by right-clicking the VPN icon and choosing Properties. The information you configured, plus many options and security details you may not want to dive into at first, are all displayed for you.

Figure 16-13 shows the Networking page of the Broadband-1 Properties window. The other choices under Type of VPN are Automatic and L2TP IPSec VPN. You won't need to use them unless the device on the far end requires their use rather than the Peer to Peer Tunneling Protocol (PPTP) shown.

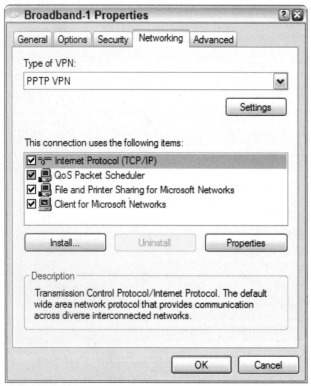

Figure 16-13: Checking on the VPN defined in the previous screen shots.

The General tab enables you to set the IP address of the destination device again, which is the Tritton storage device in my example but could be another router in your case. The Options tab sets dialing behavior. (Microsoft still treats this like it's an old-fashioned data connection over a modem.)

The Security tab includes authentication and validation information. If your company uses a Smart Card for security, you would have to register that with the Windows XP Home software as well any reader you have to use.

The Advanced tab includes another chance to turn on the Microsoft Internet Connection Firewall. I don't recommend that because I prefer using router and gateway products because of their better coverage and low hacker-attack profile. You can also turn the computer for which you are creating the VPN into a gateway for all your other network devices (but I don't at all recommend that). Because we're connecting to a wireless router on the same network, I think we'll leave this one blank and keep the router and included firewall as the primary defense from outsiders.

Finally, my goal is reached. Figure 16-14 shows a directory listing of my Tritton ASAP server appliance retrieved over my private VPN. It doesn't look much different than any other Explorer directory listing, but it does go over the VPN.

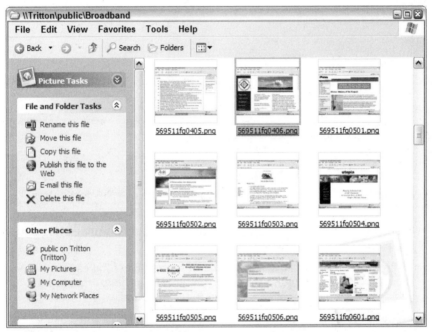

Figure 16-14: A safe and protected directory listing through my new VPN to the Tritton file server.

The next figure, Figure 16-15, shows the Broadband-1 connection Status page. I only supplied some of the information, as you saw earlier, and the rest comes from the defaults programmed by Microsoft.

In case you can't read it, here's what this page shows, along with a few words about each:

✦ **Device name, WAN Miniport (PPTP):** Uses Microsoft's favored Point to Point Tunneling Protocol to encrypt the data flowing across the connection.

✦ **Device type, VPN:** Virtual Private Network, and the "device" is the network connection (Broadband-1)

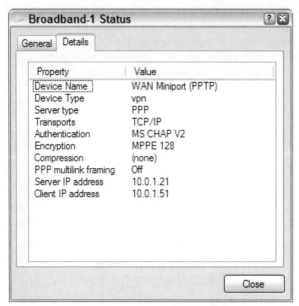

Figure 16-15: A safe and protected directory listing through my new VPN to the Tritton file server.

✦ **Server type, PPP:** Point to Point Protocol, defined by the destination device.

✦ **Transports, TCP/IP:** Networking protocol providing the underlying data transport.

✦ **Authentication, MS CHAP V2:** Microsoft's version of Challenge Handshake Authentication Protocol that encrypts the username and password dynamically even to set up the connection.

✦ **Compression, Off:** Data compression may be necessary when using dialup, as many are forced to use, but that's not as important with a broadband connection.

✦ **Server IP address, 10.0.1.21:** The destination server's IP address.

✦ **Client IP address, 19.0.1.51:** The client's IP address defined by Microsoft and based on the IP address provided by my broadband service provider.

I provided the PPTP (Point-to-Point Tunneling Protocol) option, along with the server IP address (the destination device). The other information came from the default choices in the configuration screens. I didn't need to change the Compression setting, for example, because this is a short VPN not going over the Internet where compression could really help performance.

 Some good places for VPN information include `www.vpnlabs.com`, `vpn.shmoo.com`, `www.linksys.com/edu/page12.asp`, and `www.GaskinGuides.com`.

True, most people consider VPN a remote office connection technology rather than one used for local home devices. On the other hand, nothing in the VPN descriptions I've read mentions any distance limitation, short or long. A safe, encrypted data tunnel can run as far as you want, even if only a dozen feet.

 Tech Bits Point to Point Tunneling Protocol (PPTP) was developed by Microsoft and some partners (U. S. Robotics and others) to wrap your data IP packets inside the PPTP encryption scheme so the traffic can ride over the public IP network (the Internet) without being readable by anyone else. Because Microsoft drove the development, they included it inside Windows XP. This makes a very convenient VPN option.

If you truly want your wireless network to be usable without worrying about every little security hiccup, getting a VPN for your local wireless traffic will allow you to rest easy. When every wireless connection occurs over a secure link, your network wiring security solution is pretty much complete.

On the other hand, a VPN takes some level of client setup. With a few computers, that's not a problem. If your business has a large number of systems, keeping everyone configured properly may be more difficult and time consuming than the effort justifies. A security protocol built into the wireless gear, like with WEP, makes life easier. That's especially true if your wireless routers and client hardware all support the newest wireless security connection, Wi-Fi Protected Access (WPA).

Wi-Fi Protected Access

The 802.11 portion of the Institute of Electrical and Electronic Engineers (IEEE) spends much of its time wrestling with security. 802.11i, a draft working its way through the process (too slowly for many people) will improve security in multiple ways. One of those ways, now available as sort of a "future attraction" is WPA.

How WPA works

Similar to WEP, WPA relies on many of the same security concepts but adds several critical differences:

- ✦ The Pre-Shared Key (PSK) is a longer key value than used with WEP.
- ✦ The Temporal Key Integrity Protocol (TKIP) includes mixing and sequencing functions to change the key.
- ✦ It offers 500 trillion values to try and crack.
- ✦ It facilitates automatic key modifications over time.
- ✦ The entire data packets are encrypted, not just the data payload.

Yes, eavesdroppers could listen to your data transmissions and try and crack WPA. But they have to decode each piece of the data, track the key values, and decode them before the key changes. With current technology, the estimate is that it will take about 2 years to collect enough data from a normal wireless network to crack the WPA encryption. But eavesdroppers don't have 2 years, because the key changes constantly (every few seconds) during data conversations.

No security system is bulletproof, because people have to implement the security and people make mistakes. However, a properly configured network using WPA will be as close to complete protection as any wireless network (outside the U.S. military) has ever been.

Configuring WPA

Because the home and small business users who need security may not have servers installed to support WPA, the Wi-Fi Alliance allows manually entered keys to be used. These Pre-Shared Keys are nothing more than passwords (actually passphrases) entered into the configuration for the router and each client. After that, WPA takes over.

The WPA for nonserver environments requires authentication (the matching passphrase in the client) so it keeps eavesdroppers out of your router. Then it starts up the key-changing rotation so keys mutate every few seconds. This makes even the smallest home wireless network secure.

At the router

The Netgear WGT624 includes WPA, because it's brand new on the market. Older systems may be upgradeable via firmware updates from the manufacturers. Starting in the spring of 2004, almost all the new wireless products you will find for homes and small businesses will support WPA.

In the same security setup screen I've shown you before, the Netgear includes WPA support. The security folks have done a good job of making this simple to use. Figure 16-16 shows the space for the passphrase, which can be from 8-63 characters long. Because the WPA screen real estate doesn't require much room, the arrow cursor points to the text field.

Type your password or passphrase, save the configuration changes on the router, and you're ready to go. Of course, now you must make sure the clients have the exact same passphrase, including the case of every letter.

At the client

Just as the router portion of the WPA security improvements doesn't require much configuration, the client side is a relative snap. Figure 16-17 shows the client configuration program from the Netgear WG511T wireless PC Card in a laptop.

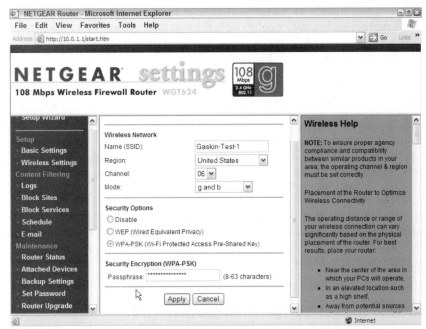

Figure 16-16: New and Improved! Security tightens for the home and small business market.

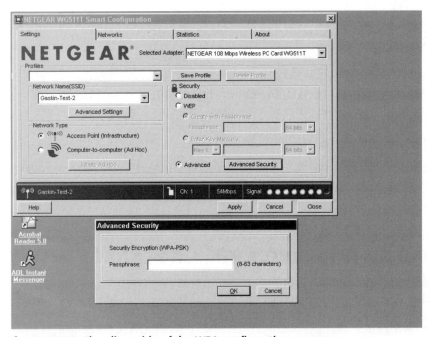

Figure 16-17: The client side of the WPA configuration process.

I reached the small Advanced Security window at the bottom of Figure 16-17 by clicking the Advanced Security command button in the bottom-right area of the main configuration window. This client had no security to start with, as will be the case when installing equipment.

It would be a cruel joke for vendors to ship products with security enabled and force you to guess the 8–63 character passphrase. It's aggravating enough when routers have usernames and passwords configured automatically and I have to search through the paperwork to find them during setup.

Again, the passphrase must be *exactly* the same on the client as on the router. If anything is different, such as a lower case letter rather than an upper case letter, you will get no connection. That's not meant to torment you, because it shows the security process works properly, but it will be aggravating.

Copy your passphrase down clearly and keep it somewhere safe. A sticky note on your monitor is not safe, and it's an old joke. After you configure the passphrase, you don't need it for normal operations.

One WPA security hole to avoid

No good deed goes unpunished, and WPA is no exception. There's a glaring security hole in the WPA message initiation process: a hacker can force your WPA router to renegotiate a connection and grab the key information sent by the server during that process. If your key is less than 20 characters long and uses common words, a dictionary attack can find your key.

Let me repeat: Short, "real" word passphrases can be hacked. This WPA hole is actually less secure than WEP at the very beginning if you use a short passphrase with real words.

Solution: Use a longer passphrase without any "real" words involved. Remember when I turned "Gaskin-Test-1" into "Ga5k1n-T3st-1" with a simple number-for-letter substitution? Some other smart person may take a phrase, like "to err is human, to forgive diving" and turn that into 2Eih-24giD. Do the same, or similar, on your WPA passphrase and you'll be okay.

Actually, you should make your passphrase longer so you'll be even more okay. But you only need type this phrase once at your router and once at every client. That's not too much of a burden for solid security, is it?

Security Improvement Checklist

One thing many vendors and informational Web sites provide is a security checklist. These are good reminders to implement security and do it properly.

You think it's funny that people today have to be reminded to implement security? A recent survey of London businesses found that 67 percent (two out of three) businesses with a wireless network did *not* have security enabled. No security of any kind protected two-thirds of London businesses during the survey in 2003.

Vendors ship WPA turned off, as all earlier security options have been turned off for installation. You'll see in Chapters 17 and 19 that security functions can interfere with wireless connections or limit the range of your network. That's why one troubleshooting technique is to turn security off. But you must remember to turn it back on.

So here is a long list of security reminders, prompts, prods, and nags collected from various places:

✦ Turn some type of security on. A little security is better than none.

✦ Update the firmware for all routers and client hardware components. Security improvements are one of the big reasons for updates from vendors.

✦ Change the default SSID value. Hackers know all the standard ones, so don't leave this glaring hole open in your network.

✦ Change your SSID every week if your wireless network doesn't use VPNs or WPA.

✦ Turn of SSID broadcasts. Don't yell "here's my network, come get me" to the world at large. Wardriving works because people are lazy with security.

✦ Do not provide Dynamic Host Control Protocol (DHCP) service to wireless connections. Put a specific IP address on every wireless client. Giving out DHCP addresses makes it easier for hackers to join your network.

✦ Set your network to "Infrastructure Mode" rather than "Ad Hoc Mode" so your network will not allow peer-to-peer connections to a laptop out in the parking lot.

✦ Use MAC address filtering.

✦ Place routers and access points out of reach. If someone resets the device, it reverts to the manufacturer's default security configuration and leaves a hole in your security wall.

✦ Use a VPN for all wireless connections.

✦ Upgrade your equipment to WPA compliance, or buy only equipment with WPA support.

✦ Enable WPA for every device. Not just some devices, but every device.

✦ Set out a trap for wardrivers: leave on old WEP-only router turned on by a window for increased broadcast range out of your building, but don't connect it to the network. Hackers will spend their time trying to find your network through that device and won't look elsewhere.

✦ Use security yourself, so everyone else in your family or business understands you strongly support the use of security procedures.

Summary

Protecting your data takes some time and effort, but your data is worth it. If you use a computer, you have a security hole in your life. Close that security hole with your wireless network and sleep easier.

One security "tool" will not protect you. WPA is the best wireless security option available so far, but you have to turn it on and you have to use it on every device.

Do you leave the keys in your car's ignition when you park at the mall? Then why would you leave the keys to your network data hanging out in the air for anyone passing by to grab and use?

Enable the security tools you have, and monitor all the routers and clients on a regular basis to make sure they are all still configured securely.

Avoiding Wireless Eavesdropping and Hacking

✦ ✦ ✦ ✦

CHAPTER 17

In This Chapter

Eavesdropping hurts

Wardriving

Sniffing your packets

Hiding from eavesdroppers

Connecting in public

Coming security improvements

✦ ✦ ✦ ✦

Eavesdropping became popular as wireless networks became popular. After all, wired networks don't broadcast their data packets to the world and hope only the destination nodes are paying attention.

So just like you can't help but eavesdrop on a cell phone caller beside you at the movies, you can't always help being an eavesdropper in the world of wireless networking. But polite members of a technical society never consciously eavesdrop, and their proper response when an outside signal intrudes is to inform the network owner of the security leak.

You may never be able to stop wireless network signals from leaking out of your home or small office. People tend to put their desks around the walls and their computers on their desks. So if you have wireless connections that have a clear signal at the outside wall, the signal almost certainly goes through your walls and out into the world. Some companies are working on this, but the equipment has yet to be affordable for any but the largest companies. It will be interesting to see if the signal control tools do become inexpensive enough for home use.

Polite isn't the term for those who intentionally eavesdrop on networks. The correct term, in almost every case, is criminal. And with preparation, you can avoid being the victim of the eavesdropping criminal.

Why You Care About Eavesdropping

Some people seem not to care about eavesdroppers. You see them all the time, chatting on their cell phones in the bathroom and laying their papers all over the table in the break room.

If you don't care about people eavesdropping on your cell phone calls, that's up to you. No one gets hurt in situations like that, although plenty of people get annoyed. But if you don't care about people eavesdropping on your wireless network, you can find yourself in serious hot water.

Here are a few things those eavesdroppers can do:

✦ Steal your broadband service bandwidth, leaving you less than you need.

✦ Read your e-mail.

✦ Find your bank account numbers.

✦ Download child pornography through your network.

✦ Deliver child pornography to others through your network.

✦ Delete your files.

✦ Store stolen software files on your server.

✦ Send spam to millions of users with your return address.

Anything intruders could do while sitting at your computer using your password, they can do from outside your home or office if your network isn't properly secured. In other words, anything you can possibly do on your computer, hackers and wardrivers can potentially do.

I know few people who would willingly broadcast every e-mail message to the world at large. Are you one of those? If you're wireless network isn't secure, you are whether you know it or not.

You know all that spam you get every day? Many of those messages come from hijacked computers under control of an outsider. You may have a great firewall in place on your broadband router between your network and your service provider, and that's wonderful. Many hackers enter through insecure broadband connections. But they can also enter through your wireless router as well.

Modern spam robot utilities don't need to communicate often with their control remote sites. The software can be "planted" in fairly small applications that come through e-mail attachments or from outsiders via your wireless network. You may never know your systems are infected and part of a spam network until you notice your computers churning like crazy at 3:22 A.M. while filling your broadband connection with outbound spam.

You put lock on your doors. You put a firewall on your broadband connection. Take the next step and invest in appropriate wireless security tools when you start your wireless network.

Note   Unlike other pornography, child pornography is illegal to buy, sell, or own. And if some wardriver puts child pornography on your system, you own it and the trouble that comes with it.

Why do you care about eavesdroppers? Because they can steal your bandwidth, your money, your good name, and your freedom if police follow child pornography trails back to your system. You may be able to prove you didn't put the child pornography on your server, but just the fact you have it makes you a felon.

How They Eavesdrop

Let me quote a hacker from an online forum run for, and by, eavesdroppers:

> "More than 75 percent of the networks you'll find will have the default SSID, and more than likely, the default router login. Just about all (name withheld) routers can be connected through via http://192.168.1.1/, leaving the username blank, and using "admin" as the password. Also, any hacker can do his dirty work from the street using poor Mr. Schmoe's network as his connection. So who do they trace the deed back to? Not Mr. Hacker, but Mr. Schmoe...poor poor Mr. Schmoe. If somebody is computer savvy, they'll most likely have WEP encryption on their network, which requires a mere key to connect. AirSnort (a tool for Linux) actually will break these keys."

All the grammar, spelling, and punctuation comes straight from Mr. Hacker, not me. For the record, I always spell Mr. Schmoe as Mr. Shmoo, but I remember reading Al Capp. (I was young, very young.)

Eavesdropping is not illegal, but using someone else's bandwidth is considered theft of services by most law enforcement groups. One Web site document I found on a wardriving says plainly, right up front: "It's illegal to connect to a nonpublic AP without permission. Period." Then the paper goes on to detail exactly which tools will help you find and connect to nonpublic Access Points (AP) without permission.

Wardriving

Don't misunderstand the intention of those mobile hackers called wardrivers. Yes, hackers like to protest they are only curious and do not cause a problem. Maybe. Certainly wardrivers can't be considered illegal, because they are in a public space when they catch leaked wireless signals. The law clearly allows photographers to capture whatever they want when standing in a public space, so wardrivers are likely allowed to receive signals while also standing in a public space. But photographers can't climb a private fence for a better shot, and wardrivers can't transmit through someone else's broadband connection.

But just because they're in public doesn't mean they aren't looking. Take a gander at the Web site and this product kit they've put together in Figure 17-1.

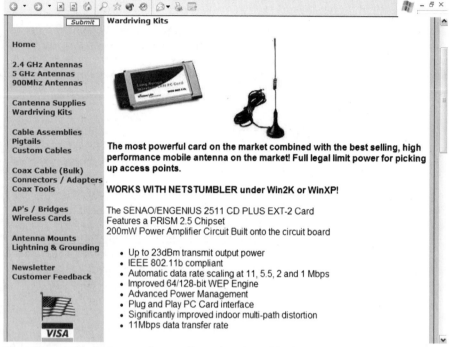

Figure 17-1: Wardriving products collected and modified.

You can't see but they describe the antenna as follows:

✦ Discrete! Low Profile Antenna

✦ Portable! Magnet Mount Antenna Base

✦ Effective! Gets the antenna outside and on top of the vehicle where it can pick up more access points.

And I do think the American flag is a nice, patriotic touch. You don't want to buy your hacking tools from someone who doesn't believe in the rule of law, do you?

Of course, carrying lock picks and safecracking tools is legal. Using them is a different story. The same goes with wardriving tools. Although I wonder whether a court has declared whether special antennas are allowable tools or burglary equipment, like lock picks, and get wardrivers in trouble when used.

Powered interface cards and external antennas have multiple legitimate uses. With the right equipment, you can stretch a wireless network connection from the standard hundreds of feet to miles.

When your network is tagged by a wardriver, one of two (legal) things can happen. First, the eavesdroppers can leave their mark on your building. This process is called warchalking and will be covered in the next section.

The second thing that can happen is your location will be entered in a global database of wireless networks. Figure 17-2 shows the main page of www.wiggle.net.

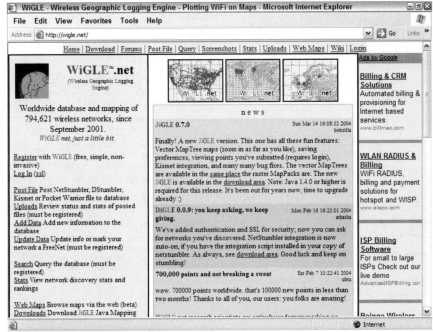

Figure 17-2: Have your wireless network security leaks advertised to the world.

It may be interesting to see where all the wireless networks are in the world, but the precision of some of these listings can be disturbing. The official toolkit for wardrivers includes a GPS device connected to the laptop scanning the air for leaky wireless networks. So if your network gets tagged, it more often than not is listed as precisely as civilian GPS equipment can pinpoint your location.

Of course, knowing where all the drug dealers are doesn't mean you will automatically go and buy drugs. But if your neighborhood has a budding wardriver looking for a network to start eavesdropping, GPS equipment can reveal the exact coordinates at which your signals leak most strongly out of your home or office.

Of course, if freeloaders just want wireless Internet access, they can go to thousands of coffee shops and even fast food restaurants. Would wardrivers be doing something illegal if they accessed a free Wi-Fi access point from out in their cars rather than while sitting in the coffee shop?

What can the budding eavesdropper do when he finds your corner and your wireless signal? He (or she) can use one of the 33 software programs gathered at `www.wardrive.net/wardriving/tool` and shown in Figure 17-3.

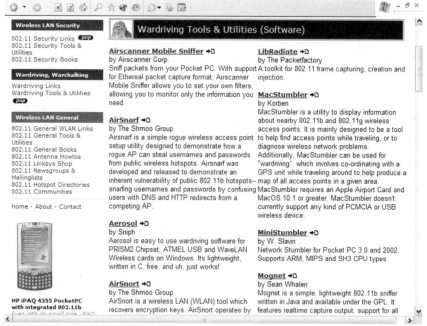

Figure 17-3: Wardriving software for every operating system.
By Jacco Tunnissen. Used with permission.

The most popular wardriving application for Windows PCs and laptops is called NetStumbler at `www.netstumbler.com`. The software download is free, and they offer a variety of toolkits for easy wardriving on their site.

Want to gauge how worried you should be? When I checked the site, there had been 1,186,752 downloads of the NetStumbler software. Yes, nearly 1.2 million downloads.

For those who prefer to travel light, there is even a lite version of this application that provides all the wardriving and net-finding software necessary and is written for the Pocket PC. There had been 235,879 downloads when I checked the site.

I can't leave without showing the primary site for this movement, `www .wardriving.com`. Figure 17-4 shows their disclaimer page.

There it is, folks, in black (or maybe dark brownish) and white: THIS INFORMATION IS FOR EDUCATIONAL PURPOSES ONLY! I feel better, don't you? And if you do feel better, you must believe every politician during campaign season.

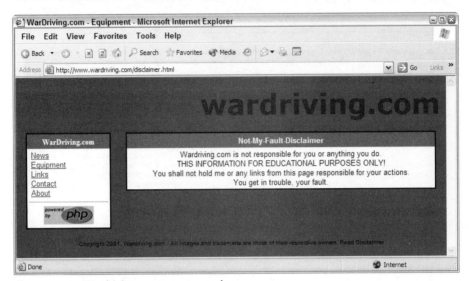

Figure 17-4: Wardriving.com warns readers.

The critical point you should take away from this somewhat disturbing section is that using wireless network connections without proper security in place is effectively broadcasting to the world. Some wardrivers are merely curious, and some just want free Internet access. But increased public Wi-Fi access satisfies those who need a wireless connection, leaving the wardrivers who are curious or worse. Security experts now warn that wardriving has become a corporate espionage activity, enabling competitors to learn company secrets while sitting comfortably in a car across the street.

Warchalking

Once a wardriver finds an open network, he or she often marks the location with specific chalk diagrams to tell others about the free Internet access. The fact that your network may be open to access as well, including your personal and business information, is (to the warchalkers) your problem.

With the Web the way it is lately, going to anything dot com often leads you to exactly what you're looking for. Unfortunately, that doesn't always work, and it didn't with www.warchalk.com (a metal band from Philadelphia—hear their music at www.garageband.com/artist/warchalk). So I tried the dot net extension, always a good second choice. Figure 17-5 shows the site awaiting me when I tried www.warchalking.net.

Warchalkers have a code of ethics, and advocate the use of symbols to advertise publicly available Wi-Fi HotSpots. Not all warchalkers follow such noble endeavors, however, so if you see the symbols near your home or business, they are telling you something. That something is that your security is worthless, your network is wide open, and only blind luck has protected you to this point.

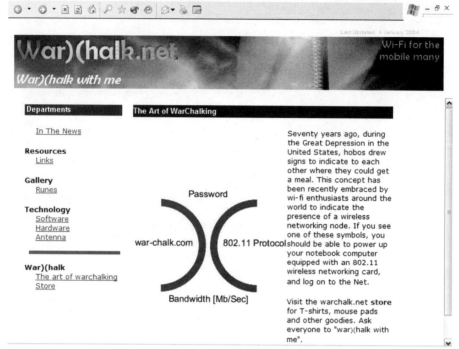

Figure 17-5: The origins of warchalking.

Notice the image in the middle of the Web page in Figure 17-5. The backward parentheses come from engineering diagrams for radio receivers if my research is correct. If your password is detected, it will be written at the top of the diagram. The bandwidth of the Internet connection will be on the bottom.

Sniffers

The official sales mark for Sniffer originated in the mid-1980s from a company named Network General based in Silicon Valley. I know this because I sold Sniffers, in their hardware incantation, in 1987 and 1988.

Based in the only real portable computer at the time, a Compaq Portable, the Sniffer used the Compaq's Intel 286 processor and whopping 20MB hard drive to grab packets from Ethernet networks for real time performance monitoring and analysis later.

Sold long ago and now owned by the McAfee company, the original Sniffer opened a window into networks that few people had ever seen before. This was back when Ethernet ran only over coax, Microsoft Windows barely existed, and a Sniffer, hardware and all, cost around $30,000.

The reason "sniffers" (the lower case must be used unless you're talking about the Network General product owned by McAfee for years and now spun out to a new Network General company) work is because of how Ethernet works. And they work whether the network runs over wires or wirelessly.

If you remember back to the networking explanations back in Chapters 11 and 12, Ethernet is (at least electrically) a bus network. Every network adapter sees every packet, because all the packets go all the way up and down the network cabling system. Adapters watch the packets go by and grab only the ones addressed to them.

The developers at Network General (led by chairman Harry Saal) wrote an application that turned on "promiscuous mode" in certain Ethernet network adapters. This was the term used to describe a node that captured every packet no matter which destination address was on the packet. I should probably say "copied" rather than "captured" because the original packet remained on the network and was not disturbed by the Sniffer.

 Of course there's a promiscuous mode, because the original Ethernet thin coax couplers came with male and female connections.

Over the years network analysis software became separated from the hardware and inexpensive versions became available. The demand for network "sniffers" remains high, especially for companies developing software and hardware products. Figure 17-6 shows the Web site of a company that makes an excellent product I've used myself many times.

Figure 17-6: A well-established company making legitimate, high-quality network analyzer software.

Various protocol analysis tools like the Sniffer and Triticom have two great customer bases: network troubleshooters and network software developers. Troubleshooters need to see when requests for services go out, when they are received (if they are received) and what the response is to the request. You might be amazed at how many packets go back and forth two systems just to type in a username.

Network software developers use these tools to see inside each protocol packet on the network involved with their software. Applications rely on standard programming hooks for network functions, but not all equipment vendors and operating system developers read the specifications in exactly the same way. The ability to see inside each packet on the network, down to the software code included in the data portion of the packet, gives modern developers a huge advantage over their predecessors.

Wireless sniffer tools have turned network monitoring into another tool of wardrivers and hackers. Although wired Ethernet hubs, switches, and routers have changed the "every adapter sees every packet" scheme of earlier days, wireless network adapters must still examine each packet as it flies by. So wireless analysis tools became tools of wardrivers.

How do "sniffers" work? Quite well, thank you. And they have worked well for two decades and will continue to do so. That means, if your network leaks and has no encryption, the contents of every data packet on your network can be captured, analyzed, and decoded into plain English with almost no effort on the part of the wardriver.

Legal issues abound

There seems to be a bit of confusion about whether all of this stuff is legal, any of this stuff is legal, or if it's all illegal. On one hand, standing in a public place like the sidewalk, and receiving "free" Internet access through a leaky wireless network doesn't seem illegal to many people. If it is, does that mean finding a dollar on the sidewalk and picking it up is stealing?

The worldwide reach of the Internet confuses things even more. Many countries have few if any restrictions about intellectual property, or at least vastly different notions than the American justice system. Most laws protect property, and the taking of property is depriving the victim of the use of the property. But if I have a digital song file and you copy it, I still have my file, so I haven't been deprived. This is an argument the record companies have been fighting for years.

Chapter 4 talked at length about community wireless broadband access. I personally think community wireless is wonderful, especially when people get together to extend broadband Internet access to areas underserved by commercial service providers.

But community access networks buy their own Internet access and provide it to their group. Wardrivers don't, they piggyback on your Internet access. And your contract with your broadband service provider may very well not allow more than one computer connection to the Internet at a time. This means that not only can a wardriver not use your connection, your spouse or children can't either (what the salesperson says doesn't matter, only the contract terms matter). Read your service provider's contract and see what you're really allowed to use.

Wardrivers claim that any open network is an invitation to access the Internet. In other works, you are offering a gesture of friendliness and goodwill, as you would offer a traveler a drink. But is it your water to offer? Read your contract to see if that's a noble offer or violation.

And if all the wardrivers and warchalkers were noble and honorable, what a wonderful world it would be. But the world contains con artists, identity thieves, burglars, muggers, swindlers, and others who often make modern life painful.

Leave the legal arguments to lawyers sipping brandy and discoursing at their club. If you want to protect your home and business, you better protect your wireless network. Perhaps it's a cold way to look at the world, but the number of noble and trustworthy fellow travelers seems to be dwindling.

Like President Reagan said: "Trust, but verify." Use verification and security on your network, so you can trust those who are using it in your home and business.

Common Wireless Hack Attacks

There are well-known weaknesses in wireless network hardware and software products, particularly products shipped with security disabled or ports open for outsiders to access. Even worse, the Wired Equivalency Protocol limitations exist and a standard 64-bit security scheme can usually be broken within two hours, depending on the traffic volume on the network.

Let me go through a list of standard wireless attacks, and show how you can defend yourself. Of course, the best defense today is Wi-Fi Protected Access (WPA) or a Virtual Private Network connection between all wireless clients and your network resources.

Wired equivalency protocol cracking

1999 was the year Wired Equivalency Protocol (WEP) became part of the 802.11 standard. The joy of an encryption scheme lasted only a short while once the vulnerabilities became known.

Because it uses a static key, WEP encryption can be broken by a variety of available tools. The trick for the hacker is to passively capture enough packets to gather enough of the Initialization Vector (IV) packets to isolate the random number used by the WEP encryption scheme. These packets are sent unencrypted, making their capture and decoding even easier.

How available are the tools needed to crack your WEP encryption? At one Web site, the software page lists almost 40 applications. The following operating systems can be used to host such cracking tools:

- ✦ Linux
- ✦ Windows
- ✦ BSD Unix
- ✦ Macintosh (OS 9 and OSX)
- ✦ Java
- ✦ PalmOS
- ✦ PocketPC
- ✦ DOS (yes, that DOS)

Want to read a real-life exploit of a WEP network? The O'Reilly Web site page for the book *Wireless Hacks* at www.oreilly.com/catalog/wirelesshks/ includes a link to an article called "Dispelling the Myth of Wireless Security." Written in mid-2003 about Macintosh systems, the article outlines how the author cracked his WEP-protected network in about 90 minutes.

One of the most popular WEP cracking tools, AirSnort, advertises that after the software captures enough packets, it breaks the security key in less than one second. While gathering the packets, AirSnort is completely invisible to the network, because it captures packets passively.

Defense: Use Wi-Fi Protected Access (WPA) or a VPN for wireless traffic.

 Cross-Reference Read Chapter 16 again for WPA details, and upgrade your wireless equipment if your network data is worth keeping private.

Man-in-the-middle attacks

All wireless Ethernet traffic can be captured by any eavesdropper stationed within range of the network transmissions. The man-in-the-middle hacker captures and decodes packets sent between the client and the access point during initial association. All manner of information, including the IP addresses and the network SSID, are exchanged during the initial handshaking.

After the information is gathered and decrypted, the hacker can emulate another access point on a different channel. This assumes the hacker even has to decrypt the information. Hackers know that the majority of wireless network managers never turn on security protections (don't be one of them). When done sitting close to a client, the hacker can persuade the client's network adapter to reassociate to the new faux access point. Then the client and the server/router believe they both are still connected to each other, but they aren't. The intervening hacker now can see all the data packets flowing between the two nodes, including all network resource login sequences.

Defense: VPN connections or strong authentication processes such those as included with WPA can stop a bogus access point from being accepted.

The VPN discussion in Chapter 16 included ways that modern Windows operating systems and VPN providers start the encryption immediately. In addition, authentication controls on the wireless access point refuse communication if the client device isn't listed in the user database. Two excellent protective measures, and both are free with the wireless products.

Media access control attacks

Media Access Control (MAC) addresses can be cracked just like WEP encryption keys. That assumes the network being attacked even uses security at all, of course. After the MAC address has been gathered, hackers can "spoof" a valid user by presenting the authentic MAC address. They can replace the MAC address (the hardware serial number of sorts) for their network interface adapter with the MAC address from an authorized user on the network. The wireless router/access point believes the spoofed packets are coming from the authenticated device, and grants access.

Defense: VPN connections (Chapter 16) or strong authentication processes like 802.1x (coming up).

Dictionary attacks

Although Blanche DuBois may rely on the kindness of strangers, hackers trying dictionary attacks rely on the stupidity of network users. Every router or access point issues a challenge to which clients must respond to before being authenticated. The most common method is the demand by the access point for a username and a password from the client seeking access. When the user types the name and password, hackers can intercept them on their trip to the access point.

When hackers capture that exchange, they assume the password is either really lame (like password) or that standard words are used for the password. Working offline, an application replays that challenge and response while electronically substituting every common word in a huge database.

After the application hits on the right word or combination of words, the hacker need only supply the newly found password when challenged by the router. With a simple login, the hackers have full access to the same network resources as the original client they monitored.

Defense: Longer passwords that include letters and numbers (but no real words) defeat the dictionary attack. Authentication schemes, such as VPNs (Chapter 16) and the new 802.1x mechanisms (coming up), also defeat these attacks.

Session hijacking

If hackers have enough information about your network, they can insert their own bogus access point into your network scheme. This is particularly easy if you have no security enabled, or just the weakest security options turned on. Clients can be fooled into connecting to this new fake access point by sending their authentication information. Then the hackers have the information needed to login to the network directly.

Defense: Strong authentication procedures, such as for VPNs described in Chapter 16, won't fall for this hijacking scheme.

Thwarting Eavesdropping and Attacks

Notice the common thread of all the defense options listed in the previous sections? Strong authentication like you get with VPNs, Wi-Fi Protected Access, and other new security enhancements. If this doesn't convince you to upgrade your wireless network security, I guess you'll have to keep reading.

I said before that turning off the SSID broadcasts, changing the SSID, and using WEP will discourage casual hackers and nosy neighbors from reading your network transmissions. If your home or office sits in the middle of a densely populated area and near many other wireless networks, just discouraging the casual snoopers may not be enough. That's when you need a more active defense.

Unfortunately, after you get beyond the security tools available with products such as WEP and WPA, things stop being free. If your wireless network supports commercial transactions, you must protect those because of banking and credit laws. If your wireless network transmits medical information, you must protect them because of federal regulations concerning patient privacy.

The following list contains four companies and one dealer that provide wireless network defense tools and/or services. They are not free, but they may be far less than the cost of losing some or all of your commercial business to wireless hackers.

I have not used these services and therefore cannot endorse any of them. These are references from others who are active in this area and these names came up more often than other product names.

✦ Wibhu Technologies (www.wibhu.com) provides several Wi-Fi enhancement products. These include tools to increase security and reliability of wireless networks. Figure 17-7 shows the home page with its three main products.

✦ AirMagnet Inc., (www.airmagnet.com) also offers wireless intrusion detection products and ways to detect "rogue" access points (the ones you didn't install but someone else did). They sell products for laptops and handhelds to make your testing as mobile as the wardriver's testing. (See Figure 17-8.)

Figure 17-7: Wireless planning, protection, and reliability tools.

Figure 17-8: More wireless security tools, including portable options.
By AirMagnet. Used with permission.

✦ Fortress Technologies (www.fortresstech.com) is big in government circles. If you or your business plays in that sandbox, this could be the supplier you need. (See Figure 17-9.)

Figure 17-9: Government certified with multiple authentication layers.

✦ Fluke Networks (www.flukenetworks.com) has been making test tools for the electronics, communications, and telephone industries seemingly forever. If you need any tools to check, verify, and maintain your wireless network, the Fluke Networks product list is a great place to start. I haven't used their wireless tools, but I have used other tools from them in the past and never had a problem. (See Figure 17-10.)

✦ Berkeley Varitronics Systems, Inc., (www.bvsystems.com) is a good collection point for a variety of training, tools, and services. (See Figure 17-11.)

One thing you may have figured out by now is that protecting yourself and your wireless network from attackers requires action, not hope. Implementing tight security takes effort. Even weak security installations require effort, so you might as well take a little extra time and do it right.

One company developed a wireless security program using an ingenious solution to a common problem. Because the SSID (the wireless network name) can't be hidden from wardrivers with the right equipment, why not hide it in plain sight, but in the middle of thousands of other SSIDs.

If a wardriver sees one or two SSIDs, your network security disappears quickly. If wardriver sees 12,448 SSIDs, what do they do? Trying them all would take days, and the hackers like action. They will, if all goes according to plan, drive on and

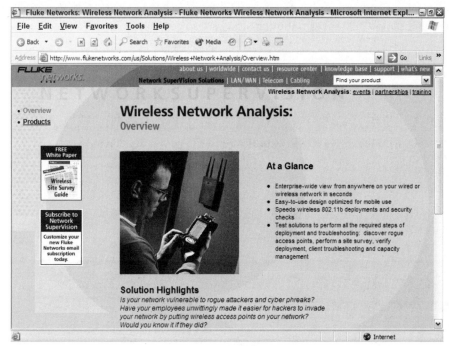

Figure 17-10: A long-time company making legitimate, high-quality test tools.
Reproduced with permission.

Figure 17-11: Many things under one Web site roof.

bother someone else's network. And that's about as good a security as you can get, if something influences potential attackers to go away.

Check out the Fake AP (Access Point) program at *www.blackalchemy.to*. It requires a Linux server to run, so a local dealer or consultant may be able to set it all up for you.

A good site for more information is the Wardrive.net folks at, guess where, *www.wardrive.net*. They include plenty of tutorials, advice, suggestions, feedback, product reviews, and experience to the problems of wireless networking in general and security options in particular. Check them out in Figure 17-12.

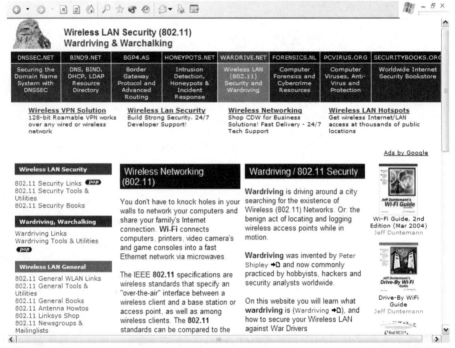

Figure 17-12: One of the many Web sites offering help on security and other wireless topics.

There's no lack of information out there on the Web on wireless network security, but much of it covers the same basic information I just covered. But that should give you a clue: when every writer and consultant says you should implement some type of security, and they have to say it over and over again, it indicates people aren't following these directions.

But you're smarter than the average bear, right? If you're reading this chapter, you're serious about keeping your business on the inside of your home or office, not on the outside where anyone driving by with a laptop can read your e-mail. But your neighbor, statistically, is not that smart.

802.1x

802.1x defines a way to authenticate a user to a network. This can be a wired or wireless network, as long as ports (software locations) are used. The basic idea is that connections require port number access, and if authentication isn't granted, the port can be shut off. Thus the user can't get access to the network. There are three parties to this process:

✦ **Authentication server**: The server that verifies the user has access to the network.

✦ **Authenticator**: The device that accepts the authentication request, formats it properly for the authentication server, and relays the information to the server and back to the user.

✦ **Supplicant**: The client application making the authentication request.

Personally, I would have used a different term than "supplicant" but nobody asked me. But that term sounds so powerless. Hmm, that may be the idea.

Large companies use a Remote Authentication Dial-in User Service (RADIUS) server for authentication. This device keeps a central database of all authorized users and their access rights to network resources. Servers of this type are more complicated and expensive than the server appliances discussed in earlier chapters.

This means the 802.1x process automatically means more money than any of the wireless options discussed to this point. But a RADIUS server provides excellent security and encryption for remote users, which is why almost all the large companies use it.

You will need familiarity with the following terms when working with 802.1x:

✦ **Extensible Authentication Protocol (EAP)**: Software to allow users to add security features.

✦ **Message Integrity Checks (MIC)**: Also used by WAP.

✦ **Public Key Infrastructure (PKI)**: The security method using one public key to make it easy for others to contact you, but the messages must include a private key for decryption.

✦ **Protected Extensible Authentication Protocol (PEAP)**: A proposed (by Microsoft, Cisco, and RSA Security) extension to EAP and LEAP.

✦ **Lightweight Extensible Authentication Protocol (LEAP)**: Cisco's proprietary version of EAP.

✦ **Remote Authentication Dial-in User Service (RADIUS)**: Authentication server software used to verify remote connections against a predefined database of users and allowed devices.

✦ **Pre-Shared Key (PSK)**: For those WPA users who don't have a RADIUS server.

✦ **Temporal Key Integrity Protocol (TKIP)**: An enhancement to 128-bit encryption.

✦ **Secure Sockets Layer (SSL)**: Most often used to encrypt traffic to and from Web sites.

✦ **Transport Layer Security (TLS)**: The upgrade to SSL.

✦ **Tunneled Transport Layer Security (TTLS)**: A proposed enhancement to TLS that requires network-based security certificates and another type of authentication such as passwords. Does the same work as LEAP, so many experts feel TTLS is enough by itself.

✦ **EAP-TTLS**: Another name for TTLS.

✦ **Advanced Encryption Standard (AES)**: Secret key cryptography using 128-bit, 192-bit, or 256-bit encryption keys. Replacement for Data Encryption Standard (DES) and the upgraded Triple-DES security standards.

Too many acronyms, right? Diving into serious security topics will require large bottles of headache remedies close by.

This list should emphasize that 802.1x isn't a magic security bullet, but a process and framework on which to hang a variety of other security and authentication services. The size and complexity of this list should drive home the point that the simple security measures you read about for wireless networks, mainly SSID changing and WEP, are far down the ladder of security products.

Here's a breakdown of the security steps in a typical 802.1x-compliant system:

1. A user requests a network connection.

2. The router or access point takes the user information but blocks the user from network access.

3. The access point forwards the user information to an authentication server of some kind.

4. The authentication server approves the user and specifies what network rights the user is granted.

5. The access point opens a port for the user. Encrypted and dynamic WEP keys are assigned to the client to use during the network session.

6. The user can access the allowed network resources over a secure connection.

Pretty complicated, isn't it? This reminds me of the old movies where a person knocks on the door of a speakeasy during Prohibition and gives a password to the guard through the small sliding door. If the boss says the visitor is cool, the door opens. If the boss says the visitor is not cool, the guard kills him. Well, maybe not. But at least the visitor does not gain entry unless authorized.

Prices are still high for implementing full-blown 802.1x authentication, and will remain so for several years because of the need for a secure RADIUS implementation. The wireless vendors are beginning to add support for 802.1x, but you need both ends. When you upgrade, 802.1x should be ready and priced low enough to be worthwhile.

Public Wi-Fi Access

The lure of the open road traveled with laptop in hand (or slung over shoulder) proves irresistible to many. If you are one of those I'm happy for you. And if you want to be as happy when you return as you are when you start your journey, you must take some extra precautions.

You don't really expect the coffee shop to include serious Wi-Fi security for your latte over laptop, do you? The whole idea of public wireless access is easy access.

This works great if you want to read the news over the Web with your coffee. This works terribly if you want to read your e-mail, order something online, or enter business information into your customer database back at the office

Secure your laptop

Chapter 12 goes into details about firewalls and their importance to your network. Yet at a coffee shop, you have no protection from any firewalls. So your only choice is a personal firewall for your laptop.

Remember ZoneAlarm, from Zone Labs, Inc., (www.zonelabs.com)? They have a free personal firewall available for download. This may be enough, or you may want a full security suite. The more business you do while traveling with your laptop, the more protection you need. Zone Labs offers upgraded products for your laptop, as do McAfee and Norton. All three products include as much or as little security as you want depending on your budget.

You may get personal firewall protection from another product you have. Vendors of products like spam blockers and virus protectors often include firewall functions as well.

If all this seems to be too much trouble, good luck. At least turn it on the by clicking Windows XP Internet Connection Firewall (My Network Places ➪ My Network Connections ➪ Local Area Connection ➪ Properties ➪ Advanced). See Figure 17-13 for a quick reminder.

Notice in Figure 17-13 I opened the Help screen. If you're curious about setting up ICF, click the "Learn more about Internet Connection Firewall" text in blue to summon the Help screen shown.

You're not really protecting yourself from your fellow coffee drinkers, but all the hackers and criminals on the Internet at large. After you connect past the coffee shop, all security bets are off. Actually, all security bets are against you unless you have specific protections like a VPN to connect back to your destination.

Figure 17-13: The least you can do is turn on Internet connection firewall.

Verify that your laptop wireless configuration profile says you're in Infrastructure mode rather than ad hoc mode. Ad hoc allows peer-to-peer connections between clients rather than going to a router or access point. That option can be helpful at times, but in a public place it allows another user to ride along on your wireless Internet connection. If you're happy with your speed and believe this is neighborly, you may not mind. If you're never happy with your surfing speed and are more cautious, turn off ad hoc mode. You can do this on the primary configuration screen of your laptop's wireless adapter, as shown in Figure 16-5. This is a major setting, so it's always easy to find.

Be mindful of physical laptop security as well. Losing your laptop may be more expensive than losing your wallet and credit cards. Get one of the security suites that block access to your laptop hard drive and operating system until you provide the password. Then please, please don't put that password on a note stuck in your laptop case.

Connect home safely

The safest way to collect your e-mail or connect back to your office is through a Virtual Private Network. Chapter 16 shows how to set one up using Windows XP inside your wireless network to protect against eavesdroppers. Calling one up from a coffee shop in another city requires more configuration.

All the authentication barriers discussed earlier this chapter come into play here. If you just want to read your e-mail online, this may seem burdensome.

I recommend that people host their e-mail servers, along with their Web servers, outside their home or small business. Your broadband service provider may be your primary e-mail vendor, and that usually works great. If you have another e-mail service or want to get one, make sure they have secure Web mail support.

Just like e-commerce sites that encrypt your communications with their Web sites using Secure Sockets Layer (SSL), e-mail servers can do the same thing. Figure 17-14 shows the Webmail login screen for www.BroadbandBible.com.

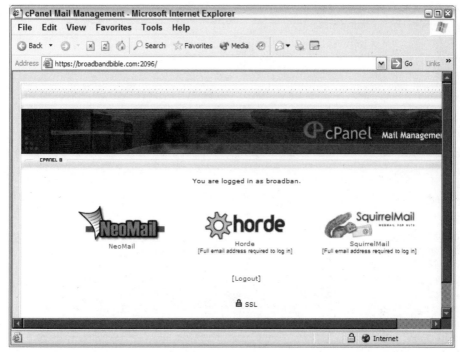

Figure 17-14: Notice the lock symbol indicating a secure, encrypted connection.

This Web site offers three different Web e-mail applications. The only thing I don't like about it is the need to select Secure Site to engage SSL. Many sites do that automatically, so check if yours does or if you need to take an extra step to gain a little peace of mind.

Watch for shoulder surfers when entering your e-mail service username and password. Strange as it seems, some people like to read other people's e-mail. And once they get your e-mail username and password, they can send anything to anybody using your name and account. That could turn out badly for you.

Probably the best option when doing any real communications from a public Wi-Fi access point is to use a Virtual Private Network from the beginning. If your company supplies a VPN, you can make the connection back there, then surf back out to the Web from that point.

If your home or small business broadband router is visible on the Internet, you can establish a VPN back to your home network. Then you can get your e-mail securely or traverse the Internet safely.

Several third-party VPN options for travelers now exist. One company seems created exactly to answer this situation. How do I know that? They call themselves HotSpotVPN (www.hotspotvpn.com). Figure 17-15 shows their opening page.

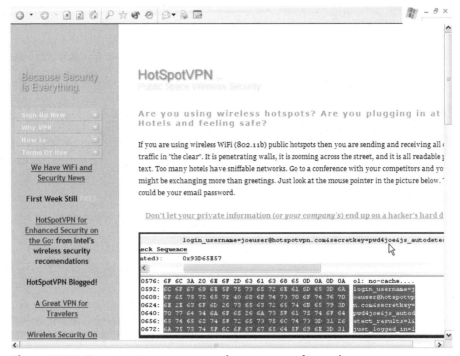

Figure 17-15: Remote yet secure connections are yours for a price.

I haven't had the occasion to use this product, but friends have recommended it to me. They offer a week trial period, so you can decide for yourself. All major operating systems are supported, along with all major browsers.

If you're an Earthlink customer, you may be happy to discover they have an agreement in place with Boingo to provide VPN service from thousands of HotSpots. If you're not an Earthlink customer but travel quite a bit, it may be worth the extra dollars.

Regardless of how you make your connections from public access HotSpots, you do need to consider security. Just popping on for a quickie will still cause your problems if you're unlucky at all. And connecting back to your home network remotely without strong security in place just leaves the door open to your network and all the resources therein.

Summary

Wireless security isn't an oxymoron anymore, but it's not without its challenges. Luckily, the tools you may be buying for your home or small office wireless network will likely ship with Wi-Fi Protected Access support. If not, the vendors probably offer a firmware upgrade to add WPA.

There are many people out there who believe it is fun to find open wireless networks. Some of those people are benign and honest. But if I were you, I wouldn't trust my security to the hope that the next wardriver who discovers my network is benign and honest. I would trust my security to at least two layers of enabled security procedures.

Troubleshooting

Life changes, and your computer or network will change as well. So don't think of this change as trouble, but rather a chance to reconfigure and improve your network.

Sometimes things on your side of the broadband connection must be improved, and I'll show you how to find and fix those details. Sometimes, your broadband service provider needs to improve their end of the connection. I'll tell you how to isolate the issue as much as possible, and how to deal with service providers who forget that their first name is *service*.

Troubleshooting Internet Access Problems

✦ ✦ ✦ ✦

In This Chapter

Following the support rules

Ignoring the support rules

Fixing problems yourself

Tracking continued problems

✦ ✦ ✦ ✦

Everything technically endowed eventually develops problems. Because you have a computer before you get broadband service, you should understand this situation. Most people realize that things sometimes go wrong, and they accept that. But making things right again doesn't have to be as painful as it often is today.

You learn in this chapter how to solve many of your own broadband service problems. True, you pay for the service and support, and you shouldn't have to learn how to do their jobs. But if you want more uptime and fewer breakdowns, even when the problems aren't your fault, pay attention in this chapter.

Learning to solve your own access problems will get you back online faster. Even more important, this chapter will teach you how not to go ballistic when dealing with two industries (cable and phone companies) who lead the ineptitude parade when it comes to solving their own customer service problems.

This chapter will cover the type of problems that fall under the responsibility of your service provider. Many of these issues you can't resolve yourself. What you will learn includes how to:

✦ Document your system when things are working well

✦ Determine when the problem is caused by something in your home or office, or by the service provider

✦ Verify whether things are bad (slow service) or worse (no service)

✦ Troubleshoot e-mail service interruptions

✦ Deal constructively with your service provider's technical support lines and personnel

✦ Possibly isolate the troubled piece of hardware or software (sometimes this is much tougher than just determining if it's your problem or the service provider's problem)

 Cross-Reference Chapter 19 covers problems that occur on your side of the broadband connection.

This chapter focuses on how to determine if the problem is on your side or not, and how to work with your service provider to get the service up and running again.

Common Problems and Fixes

Most people use their broadband Internet connection for the same types of things: view Web pages, get e-mail, stream Internet radio, and IM friends. So who's to blame if Web pages are slow, your e-mail server refuses to deliver your e-mail, your Internet radio station ignores you, and your Instant Messages aren't returned?

 Note Wires only make good connections when they're plugged in. And a monitor with the brightness turned all the way down makes a computer look dead when it's not. I learned that the hard way.

Here are a few common areas of complaint for everyone, home and business alike, and how you can determine if the problem is on your end or not. Knowing the location of the problem will direct your next steps.

Viruses and other malware

Customer service organizations from major hardware and software vendors will tell you a large number of support problems (from 12 percent to nearly half depending on the source of the numbers) are caused by viruses and other malware. Chapter 7 includes information you may want to review if your computer suddenly starts acting weirder than it usually does.

New to the trouble-causing mix lately are increasing numbers of system-resident applications called *spyware* that monitor actions and report back to some remote site. Sometimes these are relatively benign, such as applications verifying correct licensing remains in place (although privacy advocates claim this goes too far). Sometimes the spyware is from spammers delivered as a Trojan or worm and are tracking your system's profile to see if it will make a good *zombie* (machine taken over by spammers to send spam without the machine's owner knowing or approving).

If your browser suddenly starts popping up sites you don't want to see, resets your home page, or redirects you to Web sites you don't request, check quickly for spyware and viruses. If you security software doesn't include spyware removal, check out these sites for help:

✦ www.safer-networking.org

✦ www.firewallguide.com/spyware.htm

✦ www.javacoolsoftware.com

✦ www.download.com and search for "online privacy"

You may have to run two or more different spyware eliminators to get all the spyware.

Slow or dead Web pages

The first thing to check is whether the problem exists on the one Web site you want to view or all Web sites. If the remote Web server is having problems, you won't get good service no matter how fast your broadband connection delivers packets.

Sometimes you get the equivalent of a bad phone connection to a Web page. If the page creeps slowly to your computer, hit the Stop icon or the Escape key. Then hit the Refresh icon or highlight the URL and press Enter. It seems silly that reconnecting like this could deliver much faster service, but it happens regularly.

If the reconnect fails, try another Web site. I tend to use major sites with short names for tests, like www.cnn.com, www.msn.com, and www.aol.com. These sites generate lots of traffic, so your service provider may have them cached (held in memory for faster service) and you'll get immediate response. Then you know the problem is not with your computer or your service provider, but that Web site.

Sometimes entire sections of the Internet go down because of a router failure (rare, but it has happened). You may then be able to see Web sites in California but not Seattle. Major Internet problems like this generally get fixed in a few hours, but there's nothing any client can do about the situation.

E-mail disruptions

There are several ways your e-mail service may be disrupted, depending on your e-mail server location.

Disruptions at your provider

If your service provider or a hosting company hosts your e-mail services:

✦ The provider's e-mail server may be down

✦ Routing or DNS errors may isolate your e-mail server and make it invisible to other e-mail servers

In the first case, you won't get any response from your e-mail server at all. Your client will appear to work, but will time out waiting for a response from the server.

In the second case, you can login and get e-mail from your server, but there is none to get. With the amount of spam most people get today, not getting any messages for an hour means there's a problem. Two hours of no spam, blessing though that may be, definitely means something broke and needs repair.

You may be able to send e-mail out because that's often handled by a different server. The ability to send e-mail and receive e-mail rely on two different servers, and those servers may be in different physical locations, believe it or not. This is often the case when your broadband service provider handles your e-mail service.

You can't fix those problems. All you can do is wait until they get it back up again, or call technical support. If my Web or e-mail servers aren't up within 2 hours, I call the service provider and report the outage. This creates a trouble ticket or incidence report (different companies call them different things) tied to your particular e-mail server or account.

If all or a large part of the e-mail server is down, it will be restored as quickly as your hosting provider can make it happen. Believe me, other people miss their mail just as much as you miss yours, and they have filed their own trouble tickets.

It's important to call after a couple of hours to force them to examine your particular e-mail server or addresses. Sometimes not all addresses get restored properly and the hosting provider doesn't know that unless you tell them your e-mail remains out. Sometimes a server outage may have affected relatively few e-mail clients, and technical support only knows to look for your address when you tell them to look.

One thing to check, if you have this option, is to try to read your e-mail via a Web browser interface. Many providers offer a Web mail option. If you can connect to your e-mail through your Web browser, that means the problem may be in your e-mail client software or the POP3 software portion of your hosting provider's server. And if this works, at least you can check your e-mail while waiting for your e-mail client problems to get fixed.

Disruption at your site

There are two ways in ways in which an e-mail problem will be your responsibility:

✦ You host your own e-mail server

✦ Your computer or e-mail client software has a problem

The first case will only be an issue if you host your own e-mail server at your home or office. Many server appliances discussed in Chapter 10 include e-mail server software, and many programs are available to run an e-mail server on a personal computer or small server.

If you have your own e-mail server, you can check it for proper operation. Reboot the server, and verify all the parameters for communication between your e-mail server and the rest of the Internet are set properly. Your service provider may have entries in their router to handle part of that connection, so check with technical support if your side looks functional but you still have no joy.

Most homes or home offices (and many small businesses) don't host their own servers, so the first option won't be cause for concern. There are still plenty of details to check on e-mail clients, however.

The most important check when a problem arises is to discover what has changed since the system worked correctly. This statement will be repeated in later sections because it's critical to troubleshooting.

You probably didn't change a setting in your e-mail client manually, but that doesn't mean a setting didn't change. Installed software, especially downloaded modules for Microsoft's Internet Explorer, sometimes makes changes to the network configuration files relied upon by your e-mail client software. If you use Microsoft's Outlook or Outlook Express, macros or Visual Basic applications can execute within the e-mail environment and change settings.

First step is to verify your e-mail client settings are correct. Important settings for an e-mail client include:

- ✦ User name (may be just james or `james@GaskinGuides.com`)
- ✦ User password
- ✦ Mail server port number (default is 110)
- ✦ Authentication setting (can be on but is usually off)
- ✦ Mail server name for incoming messages
- ✦ Mail server name for outgoing messages

Check each of these settings against the information provided by your service provider. You will learn in Chapter 19 that documentation of such information saves you time and trouble when something breaks, but this information should be part of your signup package.

The second step is to close your e-mail client, and if you run Outlook or Outlook Express, also close Internet Explorer. These programs interrelate in a variety of ways you can't see on the surface, so just closing one may not clear up the problem.

If the e-mail client doesn't work after restarting, you must reboot your computer. Network connection problems in the computer will not reset when the e-mail program restarts, so if the problem is in your network settings only a reboot will reset those.

Cross-Reference Network settings on your computer can stop your e-mail or Web browser from functioning properly. Details on checking these settings are in Chapter 19 under the *Common TCP/IP Problems* heading.

Working with Your Provider's Customer Service

At the end of October in 2003, the Yankee Group reported that 77 percent of U.S. broadband customers were satisfied with their service provider. That's a nice statistic, until you turn it upside down. Looked at that way, nearly one in four people were unhappy enough to report that in their survey.

Some of you are unhappy with your service from time to time. That's the way life goes. Unfortunately, vicissitudes of life seem to infect customer service organizations as well, adding another potential annoyance. Some might say that annoyance with customer service is a guarantee, not a potential. If you're one of those people, this chapter will help, I promise.

The first thing every computer support technician asks when a computer stops working is, "what changed." When a computer stops working, statistics and common sense say something on that computer changed.

Complicating this problem is Microsoft's new push for automated updates. Yes, this helps get security fixes out to the public more quickly than any other method. However, any change to your computer, no matter how small, has the potential to mess up your computer in amazing ways.

All you can do is track the changes you know have been made to your computer. But that helps only about half the time, because many service problems are caused by or because of your service provider. The trick is to know which side of your cable/DSL modem has the problem.

The first time you deal with customer service, start a folder. Put every note they send you, and every thing they tell you (transcribed by you after the call) into this folder. Keep this folder close at hand every time you deal with your broadband service provider. Referring to the folder will illustrate their service habits, and eventually your folder will contain all the information you need to fix your problems without calling customer service.

Before you call for support

Calm down. Don't call when you're angry.

Calm yet? Then wait a little longer. If you're mad when you start, the time spent listening to bad music on hold will only make you madder.

Got control? OK, good. Now let me show you a variety of things you can do before you call customer service. After all, if you don't have to call, you don't have to wait on hold, and you'll be back enjoying your broadband service sooner.

Here's what you need to do before you call:

1. Reboot everything.
2. Update your drivers and firmware on devices.
3. Reboot everything again.
4. Check your settings.
5. Reboot everything again.
6. Gather all information provided by your service provider.

If the first five steps listed above don't work, perform the last step. Then get a book or magazine and prepare yourself for dealing with customer service.

But the first five steps solve more problems than you might imagine. So there's always hope.

Reboot everything

Electronic devices have a wonderful habit of waking up fresh and clean and with a blank slate. No matter how badly an electronic device gets screwed up while working, rebooting gives you a chance to start over.

Configuration files and saved settings on electronic devices, particularly your computer, take over when the system "wakes up." Those settings are almost always more reliable than the state of the system when it got so bad you turned it off.

How to reboot one device

A *reboot* is more than just turning something off and turning it on again immediately. To let your electronic device wake up fresh and ready to work again, you must purge all remnants of the problem hiding inside the device.

Here's how to reboot something properly:

1. Turn the system off (if you have a power switch).
2. Unplug the system from the power source (if you don't have a power switch, and even if you do).
3. Wait one full minute.
4. Plug the system in to the power source.
5. Turn the system on.

Seems like a lot of extra work, doesn't it? Trust me, there are reasons for everything here.

Why unplug the system? Two reasons. First, many cable/DSL modems and associated routers don't have a power switch. So your only choice is to remove the device from power by unplugging it.

Unplug your device from the wall, not from the little power connector on the back of the device. Why? When you slide the connector back on, you create voltage spikes as the connector makes better and worse contact with the metal inside the device power plug. Those spikes, small though they may be, can cause a problem.

The second reason to completely unplug the device is to make sure no power stays on inside the internal power supply if you have one. Even if you don't have a complete internal power supply, there are power control circuits inside your device.

You can tell if you have an internal power supply or an external one on your device by looking at the power cord. If it's a normal power cord, you have an internal power supply. If it's a wall wart or mid-cable brick, your power supply is the brick part and is therefore outside.

When you leave the device unplugged for a full minute, you give the device capacitors enough time to lose all their current as it bleeds away. You also give time for any electronic gates and latches to lose power and return to their normal state.

Wait a full minute. Patience is hard when you're in a hurry to get the system working again, but it can make a difference. Go get a drink or something so you won't be tempted to plug things in too quickly.

Do this for each and every device you reboot. Do it every time.

When you reboot a cable/DSL modem, you may receive a different IP address. Most broadband providers assign IP addresses to their modems dynamically when they join the network from a pool of available addresses. The chances of getting the same IP address after rebooting is very small. Of course, if your service providers assign you a specific IP address, that address will be used after rebooting.

Rebooting connected devices

Now that you know how to reboot a single device (even if you don't believe me yet), let me tell you how to reboot all devices. This is your best troubleshooting step with your service provider, especially when you do it correctly.

Here's the sequence:

1. Turn off your computer(s).
2. Turn off your router.
3. Turn off your cable/DSL modem.

4. Disconnect all the cables between the devices.

5. Wait one minute.

6. Reconnect all the cables between all devices.

7. Return the power to your cable/DSL modem.

8. Return power to your router.

9. Return power to your computer(s).

Some of this seems stupid and redundant. I know. But it can make a difference. And your customer support person will demand you do this anyway. If you do this right, you may avoid a call to that customer service person.

Update firmware and drivers

Why update drivers and firmware when things have been working? Because your service provider may have updated drivers somewhere in its network chain, and your old drivers start causing a conflict.

Tech Bits

Drivers are the software modules that fit between the operating system and hardware components such as the driver for your network adapter. Stand-alone devices have *firmware,* which is a combination of hardware drivers and the operating system all in one. You install a firmware upgrade much like you install a driver.

No, this shouldn't be necessary, but it often is. Vendors swear they test drivers with existing equipment and older drivers and the type of devices they connect to, but that's hard to do. It's nearly impossible for vendors to check every combination of every software permutation on every device that may be affected by their changes.

Security enhancements and updates drive many firmware updates today. Sometimes what happens is a security parameter update on a network device requires updates on connected devices. Many users update devices on a regular basis to include the latest security enhancements. For an example, let me update a Network Attached Storage device.

Figure 18-1 shows the screen to update the SnapAppliance 1100 storage appliance. Notice they expect you to have the update file already downloaded. Many devices expect this, but some are able to update themselves over the Internet.

Of course, if you can't get connected to the Internet, neither upgrade option will be available to you (lucky this unit isn't a router with a problem, so I still have Internet access). So put "update devices" into your monthly to-do list so you'll be ready next time.

Router DHCP settings

Your router connected to your cable/DSL modem most likely uses either Dynamic Host Control Protocol (DHCP) or a set of IP address (see the next

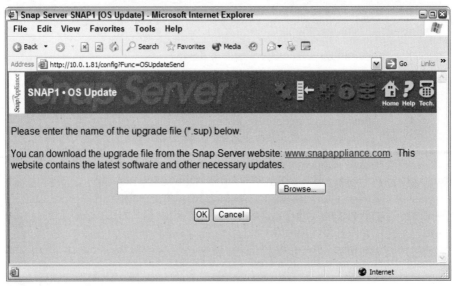

Figure 18-1: Updating a device from a previously downloaded file.

section). You have no control over the DHCP settings, because your router gets them from your cable/DSL modem, which gets them from your service provider.

Although you can't change these numbers, it will help your troubleshooting to know what they look like when things are working. At least you'll be able to reboot your router and see if things change after doing so.

Figure 18-2 shows the Kanguru iNAS-100 combination storage device and router's DHCP settings. This device looks like others in that it can connect to your cable/DSL modem using a variety of addressing options.

The important part of this page is that the Status shows Connected. There is an IP address from the cable/DSL modem (24.0.103.139 in this case) and there is at least one DNS Server IP address (204.127.202.4 and 216.148.227.68 in this case).

See the Gateway address? That's the gateway on your service provider's side of the connection. That's how your connection reaches out to the Internet.

It's important for your router to have DNS information. If your router lacks a DNS Server IP address provided by your service provider, the ask/receive handshaking between your router and your cable/DSL modem didn't work.

If you don't have DNS server IP addresses, you will get error messages when you try and find Web sites. But if you're able to reach them when you put in the IP address rather than their name (66.161.11.20 rather than Linksys.com) that's a good clue about a network problem indicating the URL name isn't being translated into an IP address. That will lead you to look at DNS settings, which refer you to the DNS server to provide that translation.

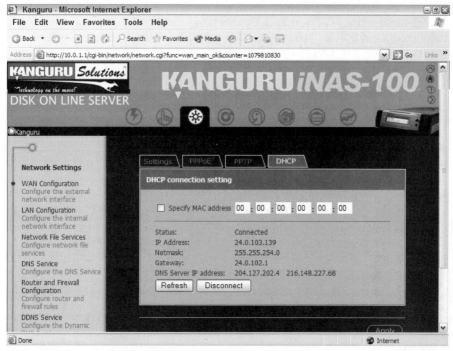

Figure 18-2: How a working DHCP page looks to my service provider.

 Cross-Reference Chapters 11 and 19 show several ways to find the IP address of your computer and ping other systems on the Internet for troubleshooting.

Router Point-to-Point Protocol over Ethernet settings

You have more to do if your cable/DSL modem requires your router to use Point-to-Point Protocol over Ethernet (PPPoE). Chapter 10 showed initial router configuration with PPPoE if that's what your service provider requires, and here you want to make sure those initial settings haven't changed. You don't have to do too much more than with a DHCP client setting for your router, but you do have to give a username and password.

Your Internet service provider will give you the username and password you must provide. Essentially, you're setting up a connection via name and password authentication (nice segue from the last chapter, right?). So your broadband service provider will not accept your connection unless your name and password (and the serial number of your cable/DSL modem, but they don't tell you that) matches their authentication database.

Figure 18-3 shows the Netgear WGT625 PPPoE screen for Yahoo! SBC DSL service. It's in the middle section toward the bottom.

Notice there are no DNS servers set. Yahoo! SBC provides those IP addresses when I log in, so my router passes those addresses along to my clients with the other DHCP information. To check them out using this router, I have to click My Network Connections ⇨ Local Area Connection ⇨ Status ⇨ Support tab ⇨ Details command button. I then see either my DNS server IP address, or the address of my router if it provides that information acting as a proxy for a remote DNS name server.

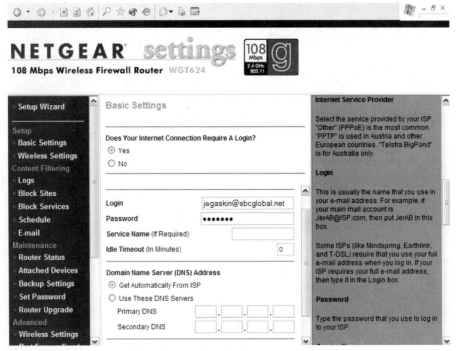

Figure 18-3: How a working PPPoE page looks to my service provider.

The critical information in this screen is your username and password. If they aren't there, or are incorrect, put them right and see what happens to your network problems (they may go away).

Ready for a new problem? If you just received your SBC service, read what Netgear has to say about one of its new DSL modems:

> The SBC DSL modem SpeedStream 5100b, used on new DSL and Yahoo SBC DSL installations since Feb. 2004, causes the NETGEAR router Setup Wizards to fail, and prevents routers from connecting to the Internet. This problem affects many router brands.

> The modem can be distinguished from the earlier 5100 by a 5th light labeled "Internet."

If you fall into this situation, check out Netgear's instructions at kbserver .netgear.com/kb_web_files/n101306.asp. Make sure you pay attention to the next section about what you need to tell your customer service representative, because the representative can only help you with this type of problem if he or she knows exactly what you have at your end.

What you need to know when you call

First thing, and most important: focus on exactly what you want to achieve through your conversation with customer service. If you can't tell the person answering the phone what you need in one sentence, keep thinking. Call when you can boil it down to something like the following:

✦ When will my service be restored?

✦ Why is the network slow?

✦ Who can authorize a refund for my service outage last week?

✦ Why can't I reach my mailbox using Webmail any more?

See those questions? Short, to the point, and the answers should be as short and as focused. You may not get the answer you want, but a clear, short question stands a better chance of eliciting a clear answer than some rambling question hidden within a complaint or three.

Other things you must know when you call include *every* single number of any kind your server provider gave you at your service installation. Any missing number may lead to a delay in customer service help.

Take a look now at all the paperwork delivered by the installation technician or mailed to you at the beginning of your service contract. Take a look at the equipment you're using. Customer service may want to know any or all of the following:

✦ Your name

✦ Your address

✦ Your phone number

✦ Your billing address

✦ Your service address (if different)

All these make sense for any type of service call. They need to know who you are, and where you're calling from. Those questions won't take any preparation on your part.

Next come the service specific questions. Be prepared to offer the following:

✦ Your account number

✦ You registration code

✦ Your username (for this service)

✦ Your service password (you called them, so it's okay to answer a question about your password)

✦ Your cable/DSL modem brand and model number

✦ Your cable/DSL modem serial number

✦ Your client operating system and other system details

✦ Any work order numbers still open

✦ Any trouble report numbers still open

Will every customer service person ask you for these numbers? No. But if the service representative can't get a necessary number from you, he or she can close the call and blame you for not having the information. Is that fair? No, but that type of thing happens now and then. Customer service reps in some companies are judged on the number of calls they close per hour, and cutting you off for lack of a number helps their average.

I put everything a service provider ever gives me in a folder. Every new piece of paper goes into that folder. E-mails sometimes get printed so I can put the paper into the folder with the other paper.

This is a lot of trouble, but this information can be important. Your service representative on the phone will have a troubleshooting script to follow. That script will vary depending on the type of equipment you have. If you can't provide the information, reps can legitimately throw up their hands and tell you they can't help you until you can tell them.

They usually will try to help if you let them. This is where being polite makes a big difference. If the service representative asks you about your cable/DSL modem type and you can't answer, ask if they can check it from their end. Usually they can.

When facing a question I don't know how to answer, I often turn it back to the service representative. "Don't you have that in your records?" That often works, because they should have the information in their records. And if you are positive nothing has changed, such as your cable/DSL modem or service location, their information should be up-to-date enough to start working on the problem.

What they won't tell you

One thing that aggravates me is a company that pretends nothing is ever wrong with its service or product, and I'm the first person in 12 years who mentioned that, say, its toilet paper umbrella melted in the rain. I know company representatives feel they must "protect their brand" and look successful, but hearing the truth now and then would be nice.

So don't expect the service representative to volunteer much about service and current problems. At least the decent ones will answer you more or less honestly if you ask them a direct question.

Don't expect them to tell you where they are. If you suspect your service call has been routed to the Lower East Side of an Asian subcontinent, you're probably right. But some companies adamantly refuse to admit this. Phone reps are provided with tips and information about the United States so they can try and answer general questions. This problem isn't serious, but it does get aggravating.

If you are connected to a service representative you can't understand because of a language problem, ask for a different representative. Rather than struggle through trying to understand someone speaking a language (technical networking) you don't understand in an accent your can't understand, bail out and call back. The time on hold will be worth the aggravation, unless you've waited an hour or more already. Then tough it out, but make the service representative repeat everything until you understand.

You probably won't get anywhere asking how much experience the service representative has. That may sound important, but the smart service reps move up fast. The ones who have been there a long time are the ones who can't get promoted or get a better job. Based on this, you should hope for someone smart who's on the way up.

Here are some other things they probably won't tell you:

✦ How large an area the current problem covers

✦ How many other users are affected by the same problem

✦ How long the problem has been going on

✦ How long they expect to take to fix the problem on their end

✦ How localized is this problem is: one central office? More? National?

What they won't tell you doesn't matter if they tell you the right answers quickly. But the more they try to hide, the more suspicious I always get. If they can't tell me how widespread the problem is, I figure they're clueless. That's not a good thing in your service provider. Knowing what's going on is the kind of good things I want to hear from my broadband customer service reps.

Dealing with Lousy Customer Service

A little empathy, please. Would you like a job where people called you up all day and whined about things you didn't cause and couldn't personally fix? Why do you think they will be in a better mood than you would be in their seat and telephone headset?

More than that, first level technical support personnel (the ones who answer the main toll-free support number calls) are generally the new hires and trainees. Anyone answering the phones may be out of training that very day and you won't know it. They could also be stuck in an entry-level job without the smarts to move up and get off the first level support desk.

So have a little understanding for the poor girl or guy who answers your phone call. Even if you've had to wait a while, they're stuck there for the rest of their shift. At least you get to hang up and go do something else. They have to pick up another call, then another, then another, then another . . . all the rest of their time.

But all that is their problem, not yours. You have a problem or you wouldn't be calling. So let me outline ways to get better service.

Just remember the voice on the other end of the phone belongs to a person. That person can help you or not help you with almost no worry of getting in trouble if they give little effort and no help. But if you work with that person, make them feel the two of you are partners in solving your problem, you'll get more help than you ever imagined.

How to complain effectively

First off, vent to your friends about how horrible your service is and how you'd like to fire everyone at your service provider for incompetence. Don't vent when you get on the phone, because you'll only make matters worse.

Second (and repeated), know what you want to get done in your call, and focus on that goal and only that goal. Do not bring up the problems you had last month unless they are directly related. Do not bring up a news report you read on the Internet about the service provider and their troubles. Do not complain about the amount of spam in your e-mail box. This is not the time.

Focus on your goal for this call, and bring up nothing else.

If you rant and emulate a crazy person, you will be tagged as a weirdo by the support staff and your complaints become the ravings of a lunatic rather than a legit problem. Don't give them an excuse to dismiss you as a nut.

Know what you want and say it clearly. Decide before you start if you:

- ✦ Want your money back
- ✦ Want a service charge to be erased
- ✦ Want a policy changed because of the problems it causes you
- ✦ Need a new cable/DSL modem
- ✦ Want to cancel the service without a penalty

If you can't put your compliant into a short, quick sentence like those above, don't call yet. Figure out exactly what you want and ask for that. Ask again if you must. Ask a third time if you must, but don't start adding related or unrelated issues. Focus on what you want and say it clearly.

Be prepared to invest the time necessary to see your problem solved. If you have a service problem, that should be solved relatively quickly. If you are looking for a refund or other hard cash, you may need to fill out forms, fill out other forms, then fill out even more forms. If you want your money back, be persistent.

Figure 18-4 shows an example of your tax dollars at work: www.consumeraction .gov.

Figure 18-4: The Federal Citizen Information Center.

Here are some other suggestions and cautions you should follow if you're going to pursue something serious:

✦ Be prepared for some BS and/or the runaround. Some companies do this as a matter of course in a short-sighted effort to save money.

✦ Be polite. Even if you're aggravated inside, don't rant, rave, or abuse the service representative on the phone.

✦ Get the service representative's name. Sometimes it helps to go back to the same person in a continuing problem. Sometimes it's good to have a name to tell people when a second service representative asks who told you some information.

✦ Keep notes, as closely and accurately as you can. Jot things down as you talk and amplify those and fill in the blanks as soon as you hang up.

These will help you through the initial customer service contacts. Most of the time, one contact will solve your problem. Unfortunately, however, things don't always work out so neatly.

When problems become more serious or drag on longer, additional steps are necessary:

✦ Ask to speak to a supervisor. Ask for some type of assurance that the "supervisor" isn't the first level customer representative sitting beside your first contact.

✦ Ask the supervisor straight out if they have the authority to resolve your issues.

✦ If the answer to the above question is no, ask for the next level of supervisor.

✦ Do not fall for the old speech about "there's nothing anyone else can do for you." Executives can always put things right when they get involved. Tell the person you're trying to escalate from you would like to hear the executives tell you themselves your problem can't be solved to your satisfaction.

Local or regional consumer advocates, often associated with an area newspaper, radio, or television station, may be able to help. Figure 18-5 shows the Web site of Benjamin Dover, a long-time consumer avenger in the Dallas and Houston area.

Figure 18-5: Yes, the name really is Ben Dover, and there's much to learn on this site.

Going past this point when demanding service or recompense for lack of service from your broadband provider doesn't happen often. There are two interesting options presented by various consumer advocates. Luckily, I've never had to resort to either one, and you probably haven't (and won't) either. But in case the worst happens, there are the two escalated options.

✦ Send certified letters, with cc: (copies) to the company's PR director, the local media, and the state attorney general. If the first batch doesn't work, send another message, via certified mail, and include all the local newspapers, radio stations, and television consumer reporters.

✦ File a charge for the lost money in Small Claims court. The companies have to appear or lose the judgment, and big companies hate to have a long line of small court judgments make them look bad. State laws vary, but you can't argue about more than $5,000 in most states Small Claims court.

Some people believe one or the other of these last two suggestions always work. I can't imagine you having to escalate a problem with a service provider to this level, but stranger things have happened. At least now you know two more options for complaint resolution of any kind.

Figure 18-6 shows "How to Complain" from the AARP (it used to be the American Association of Retired Persons but they just go by AARP now). Not all of this fits service providers, but every bit helps.

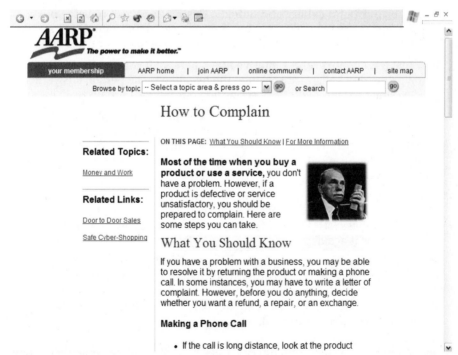

Figure 18-6: How to complain if you're over 50 or want to tap the experience of millions of members.

The AARP also has information on buying safely over the Internet and helpful forums for discussions. You don't have to be a member to view their Web site or follow their advice.

Working through their system

Every industry has "ways to do things" and the Internet service provider business certainly falls into that category. But the business structure varies greatly depending on who provides your broadband service.

Federal and city regulations play a great part in the control over telephone companies (DSL) and cable franchises (cable). There are few technical restrictions and no regulatory oversight for wireless and satellite service providers.

Some advice works for all service providers. For instance:

✦ **Be reasonable:** You can't expect a free month of service just because they dropped your connection for a few hours, even if your child was doing research for a paper due the next day.

✦ **Give them time to solve your problem:** Large companies can't drop everything and handle your complaint. To you it's critical but to them it's another in a constant flood of complaints, all listed as Top Priority. Give them a week or so before escalating your complaint process.

✦ **Make your point calmly and quickly:** Customer service reps are busy (perhaps overwhelmed would be a better term). Don't rant. Don't spew. Boil your problem and expected resolution down to one or two sentences.

✦ **Treat the support** representative **like a person:** If you want the person to help you, don't aggravate them at the beginning. The person answering the phone did not personally screw up your billing, I promise.

✦ **Stick with the same** representative **for complicated problems:** Send correspondence to one person if you can get them to agree to receive it. This eliminates the learning curve a new representative to your case must undergo, and helps commit the representative to personally solving your problem.

✦ **Personalize your situation:** One ex-service representative reports a funny or attention grabbing subject line in e-mails always helped her mood. "Vanessa, HELP!" got her more personally involved than "You idiots blew it again!"

✦ **Assure them you want to remain a customer:** The cost of keeping a customer happy is almost always less than the cost of replacing that customer. If you're not under a contract, reminding the representative you really want to remain a customer may make a difference in the resolution options at their disposal.

All companies have systems and internal rules regarding customer service. They will not change their system to accommodate your complaint. If you work with their system rather than fighting it at every turn, you will spend less mental effort and get better results.

DSL

The laws and oversight responsibilities for the telephone industry are changing and twisting and trying to understand which new services to regulate and which new services to not regulate. But the normal consumer rules of "sending copies of all letters to the CEO" for public companies may not always work in a regulated environment.

Rather than just a CEO as final arbiter, regulated monopolies answer to federal, state, and local boards and commissions. If things get bad, you can always send copies to the telephone company's CEO, and also the city Utility Board, the state Public Utilities Commission, and even the FCC (Federal Communications Commission).

If you're dealing with an Independent Local Exchange Carrier (ILEC), they have different regulatory burdens than the Regional Bell Operating Company (RBOC) for your region. Making things worse, your ILEC and every other one in the area must rely on the RBOC for all service installations, repairs, and modifications.

You can threaten to move your business from one ILECT to another. DSL service in most cities includes multiple operators. Unfortunately, if the problem really exists in "The Phone Company" in the region, no other DSL provider may be able to make your situation much better.

Some ILECs have better service integration support with the RBOC than others. Finding that information out before signing a contract is pretty much impossible. Check personal references from others in your area (see the next major section in this chapter for details).

Cable

Unlike the mess of regulatory oversight in the telephone company arena, cable companies have a clear monopoly in each served area. Of course, now that they're starting to sell telephone service over their cable lines, they may start being lumped into the telephone provider category one day.

Sending copies of problem documentation to the cable company CEO won't help much, because that person is in New York or Philadelphia and the like. These are all huge companies and the chance of getting a positive response to a problem from the Office of the CEO rates as slim to none.

However, the local franchise must renew its contract with the city on a regular basis. Customer service results and problem resolution ranks fairly high in the criteria used by cities to award these contracts.

Look at your city's Web site or phone book listings to find the appropriate office overseeing the cable franchise. Copy all your problem documentation to that city office as well as to the cable company service department. Figure 18-7 shows an excellent example of this found by my friend Rima.

Notice the contact information for the city department overseeing cable service for Foster City, CA, at the bottom of the screen. Your city has a department like this as well. Get them involved, if necessary.

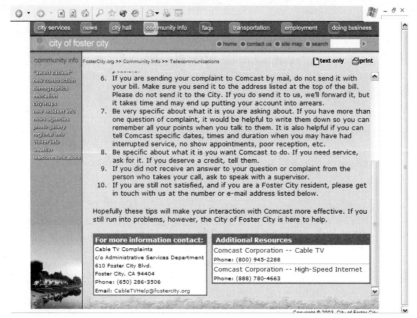

Figure 18-7: The page is titled "Tips for Getting Good Customer Service from Comcast Corporation."

Alternative suppliers

If your alternative supplier is broadband wireless, you're probably served by a small company owned and operated in your region. When you call their customer service line, the person you talk to may well be the person who installed your service or even the owner of the company.

Small companies with small customer bases understand that keeping a happy customer costs them far less in real dollars and goodwill than finding a replacement customer. You can almost always solve your problems with a local broadband wireless operator in a phone call or two and some reasonable conversation.

If your broadband wireless carrier believes they are too important to fix your problem and that they have you as a captive customer, they won't survive for long. The push for national firms to buy regional wireless operators has yet to get rolling well, so you probably have a local company to deal with. If they won't deal with you, check out satellite.

The satellite vendors are huge, national (even global) companies. Their customer service departments are just as large, and potentially inept, as the cable and telephone companies. But their response to customer service requests tend to be better according to anecdotal evidence. Your mileage may vary.

Be your own customer service representative

Want to be your own customer service rep? Talk to yourself with a bored voice, don't listen to your explanations of the problem, and put yourself on hold.

Now that you have that out of your system, start thinking like the service reps you will call. After calling for help once or twice, you should know the drill by.

✦ Reboot everything.

✦ Update your drivers.

✦ Check your system for a virus.

✦ Reboot everything.

✦ Wait for an hour for the service to find the problem and fix it.

✦ Verify that your connection configuration remains accurate.

✦ Reboot everything.

✦ Read a book.

✦ Reboot everything.

When your service drops out or slows way down, there's little you can do at your end. For problems on your side of the cable/DSL modem, look at the next chapter. But for problems under the control of your broadband service provider, there's only so much you can do.

Most of my aggravations with my cable service (AT&T taken over by Comcast) has been due to some configuration change on their side or lack of service. The good news is that rebooting (properly) my cable modem usually catches up to the configuration changes.

Every time I've called about a complete lack of service they already know there's a problem (usually caused by them). I've never had a situation where my service only was affected by a cable problem. So if you want to wait for a bit, your service provider will likely fix the problem themselves.

If you lease your cable modem from your service provider, see if you can get it updated. I got an old model when my service was installed and any configuration change on their end confused the cable modem into paralysis. After the old unit was replaced with a modern one, my connection speed increased and outages decreased.

Be your own customer service representative and order a new cable/DSL modem from your service provider. That may provide a surprising amount of problem relief.

Power in numbers: Enlist other subscribers

You are not the first user on your broadband service to have the problem you're having. Other users solved the problem vexing you, and some of them are happy to help you solve your problem. In addition, when a large group of users has a problem with a service provider, the service provider pays much more attention.

Almost every service provider (and all the large ones for sure) include forums where users can get together and discuss "issues" with their service and other problems. It's amazing how much support you can get from a group of customers using the same service you use.

On Comcast.net Broadband forums, for example, you can read dozens of complaints about promised speed upgrades that have yet to happen. Will the speeds increase? Probably so, but the schedule remains under control of Comcast. Can you get good info reported by other users who have talked to technical support people and others in the know? Absolutely.

Quick hit: Example sites

I believe the most unbiased reports (but take them under advertisement rather believing them automatically) come from third-party sites who have no affiliation with the services being discussed. One of the best of these is www.BroadbandReports.com in a wide variety of areas.

Figure 18-8 shows the BroadbandReports forum page for Comcast High Speed Internet service. The Forums page listing is on the left-hand menu of their home page.

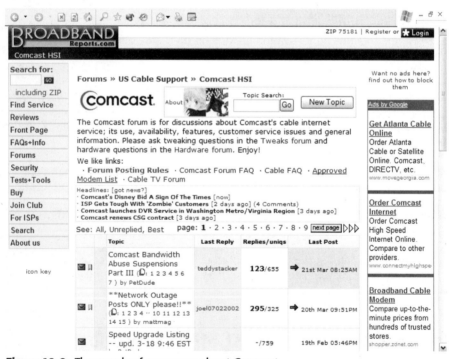

Figure 18-8: Thousands of messages about Comcast.

Figure 18-9 shows a similar forum, this time about Yahoo!-SBC DSL service. I get both this and Comcast High Speed Internet for testing purposes, so I want to be fair to each of them. Well, at least give them equal time.

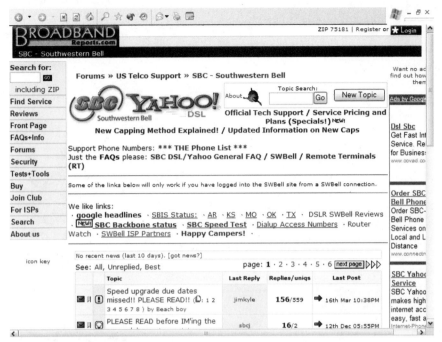

Figure 18-9: Thousands of messages about Yahoo!-SBC DSL service.

Here are a few other sites you may check for help and information about your service provider and ongoing issues, or advice on how to complain effectively:

✦ www.opentechsupport.net

✦ www.howtocomplain.com

✦ www.verizonpathetic.com

✦ www.sunflowerbroadband.com/internet/config/troubleshooting .html

✦ www.complaints.com

Don't forget your vendor pages. Most of the major vendors offer multiple pages of information on their Web sites, if only so you don't call their technical support lines for simple questions. Take advantage of this information.

Note If your broadband service won't function, you can't reach vendor Web sites to get the information. That's a classic Catch-22 (thank you, Joseph Heller). But most service providers also offer dialup for emergencies. Look at your documentation, or call their help lines and listen for an option to get dialup numbers in your area. It will be slow, but it will work. Or, you can go to a neighbor and borrow their computer. This is more sociable and more fun than waiting for dialup.

Figure 18-10 shows the Linksys Educate Me page. The menu on the left leads you directly to the page that may solve your problem or answer your question.

Figure 18-10: The Linksys Educate Me link from their home page leads here.

If you have specific product questions, check with the Knowledge Base on your vendor's Web site. Just about every vendor has one to help you search through solutions for product problems and configuration questions.

Documenting Your Problems

It may be boring and it may remind you of homework, but spending a little time tracking details and writing them down for later use will help you pass the pop quiz later. Excuse me, I mean help to prove to your customer service representative there may be a problem with your network on their end of the line.

Track normal performance

You must know what normal performance is so you know when you receive abnormal performance. The only way to know what type of performance you have is to keep track now and then.

The first thing you should do is look at your cable/DSL modem and see which lights are on. You should have labels on your lights saying some or all of the following:

✦ Power

✦ Ethernet

✦ DSL

✦ Activity

✦ Sync

✦ Ready

✦ Send

✦ USB

✦ Receive

Not all cable/DSL modems will have all the lights. My DSL modem, for example, has only four (Power, Ethernet, DSL, and Activity). Normally the first three lights stay on solid and the Activity light blinks as traffic goes through the DSL connection. There's not a power light.

My cable modem has a power light, as well as six more: USB, Ethernet, Send, Receive, Sync, and Ready. Either the USB or Ethernet lights are on, depending on how you connect to the modem, but not both. The Power light stays on if the modem is connected to a power supply (there's no on/off switch). The Ethernet light blinks when there's traffic on the local network. The Send light blinks with traffic going out through the cable modem, and the Receive light blinks with traffic coming back. The Sync and Ready lights stay on solid when I have a good connection to the Comcast network.

Basic? Yes, but if my cable modem doesn't show both Sync and Ready, I reboot it. Same for my DSL modem with the DSL light—if that's missing I know I don't have a good connection to Yahoo! SBC.

A small program called *ping* does a great job loosely tracking network performance. This isn't the tool you want to rely on for high-end throughput analysis, but it can tell you how quickly your network responds under normal conditions.

Figure 18-11 shows a DOS window or Command Prompt in Windows XP parlance with the results of a ping test on my Comcast network. I'm on a Comcast network, so there should be nothing to delay packets or interfere with my network connection.

To run this program, click Start ⇨ Run and type **cmd** in the text field that appears. That opens the DOS window.

At the command prompt, type **ping** and the name of your service provider. In my case, on this network, it is Comcast.net. So I type "ping comcast.net" and press Enter.

You can vary a number of ping parameters. I used a configuration switch to tell the ping command to send a total of 10 pings rather than the default four pings.

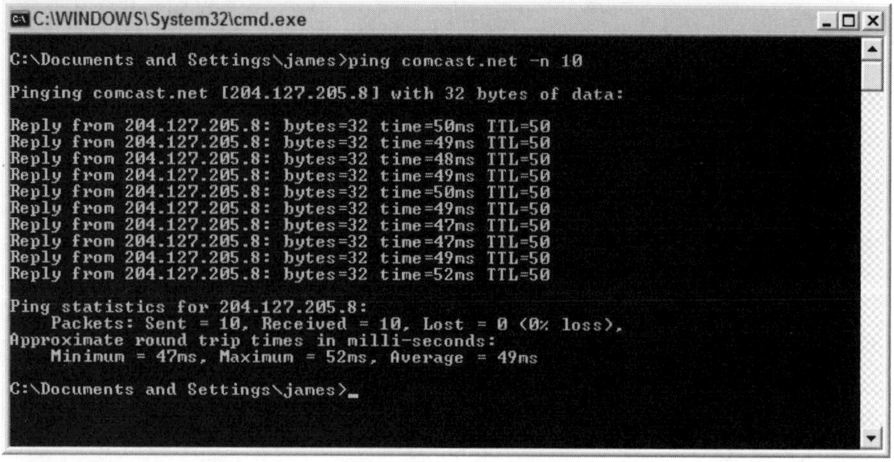

C:\WINDOWS\System32\cmd.exe
C:\Documents and Settings\james>ping comcast.net -n 10
Pinging comcast.net [204.127.205.8] with 32 bytes of data:
Reply from 204.127.205.8: bytes=32 time=50ms TTL=50
Reply from 204.127.205.8: bytes=32 time=49ms TTL=50
Reply from 204.127.205.8: bytes=32 time=48ms TTL=50
Reply from 204.127.205.8: bytes=32 time=49ms TTL=50
Reply from 204.127.205.8: bytes=32 time=50ms TTL=50
Reply from 204.127.205.8: bytes=32 time=49ms TTL=50
Reply from 204.127.205.8: bytes=32 time=47ms TTL=50
Reply from 204.127.205.8: bytes=32 time=47ms TTL=50
Reply from 204.127.205.8: bytes=32 time=49ms TTL=50
Reply from 204.127.205.8: bytes=32 time=52ms TTL=50
Ping statistics for 204.127.205.8:
Packets: Sent = 10, Received = 10, Lost = 0 (0% loss),
Approximate round trip times in milli-seconds:
Minimum = 47ms, Maximum = 52ms, Average = 49ms
C:\Documents and Settings\james>_

Figure 18-11: Checking a service provider's response time.

If you prefer to avoid dropping down to a DOS window, you should download Ping-O-Meter from Obese Armadillo Software at `www.obesearmadillo.com`. You can also find it at `www.download.com`, along with other graphical ping utilities. Figure 18-12 shows the Ping-O-Meter at work.

Ping-O-Meter - by Obese Armadillo Software
File
Actions
Options
Help
800
1200
400
1600
0
Ms
50
2000
Current Round Trip Time
800
1200
400
1600
0
Ms
51
2000
Average Round Trip Time
Min. 50
Max. 71
Bad 0
Requests: 55
Responses: 55
Host Name: comcast.net
Begin
Stop
Reset
Exit
PONG

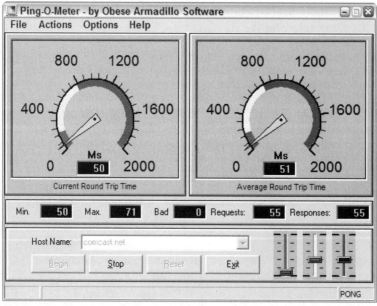

Figure 18-12: Checking a service provider's response time graphically.

The ping application relies on Internet Control Management Protocol (ICMP), which some sites turn off to outsiders. Even some of the router appliances used for this book allow you to run off requests to pings.

If the host being pinged doesn't respond to the ping by replying in the proper way to the ping request, the ping request fails. There's no difference in the ping results of a hidden site than from a host that doesn't exist, at least until the ping application reports that the domain name lookup system failed to find the domain name you typed.

Do a ping test now and then and keep an idea of the normal ping delay. It doesn't matter if your number is 30 milliseconds or 50 or 150, as long as they stay in the same range (Okay, 150 ms is too long if you're connected to that network.)

When you feel the network is slow, run a ping test. That will tell you a general state of Internet health, or at least the heath of the stations you ping.

If you don't have a domain name for a site, you can use the IP address. This is a great tool for checking the response of your wireless clients around your own network as well.

The other tool many network administrators use to check whether a problem is located in their network or somewhere on the Internet is Trace Route, shortened by Microsoft to tracert. This also uses a DOS window and provides even less visual excitement and more confusion than ping, so let's skip right to a graphical trace route utility.

Note Unusual for a computer tool name, this program actually traces the route a packet takes through the Internet to reach the defined destination. If a Web site you really want to see disappears one day, a trace may tell you where the trail ends, although as an end user you can't do much. Network administrators at a service provider can do plenty with trace route, however.

Figure 18-13 shows HyperTrace from AnalogX (www.analogx.com), a site with networking and programming tools and music (appropriate for a broadband book, don't you think?). This utility is about as fast as the DOS command-line version and easier to use.

No packet loss in our sample, which is good. Notice the longest response time came from what look to be routers past the West coast traffic hub (SJC.gblx .net) into what is probably the Phoenix AZ area (PHX1.bglx.net).

Checking on your provider's performance

People loooooove speed. NASCAR's big, the 100 Yard Dash (okay, 100 Meter Dash) fascinates us at track meets, and Andy Roddick hit a serve 150 mph (241.4 kmph) at the 2004 Davis Cup First Round in Connecticut on February 6. And broadband users love their speed, too, which is why they want to test it and verify it all the time.

The largest collection of speed tests I can find on the Internet is at BroadbandReports (www.broadbandreports.com). They have collected over 220 speed tests available for free, and have other tests and monitoring services available for a small fee.

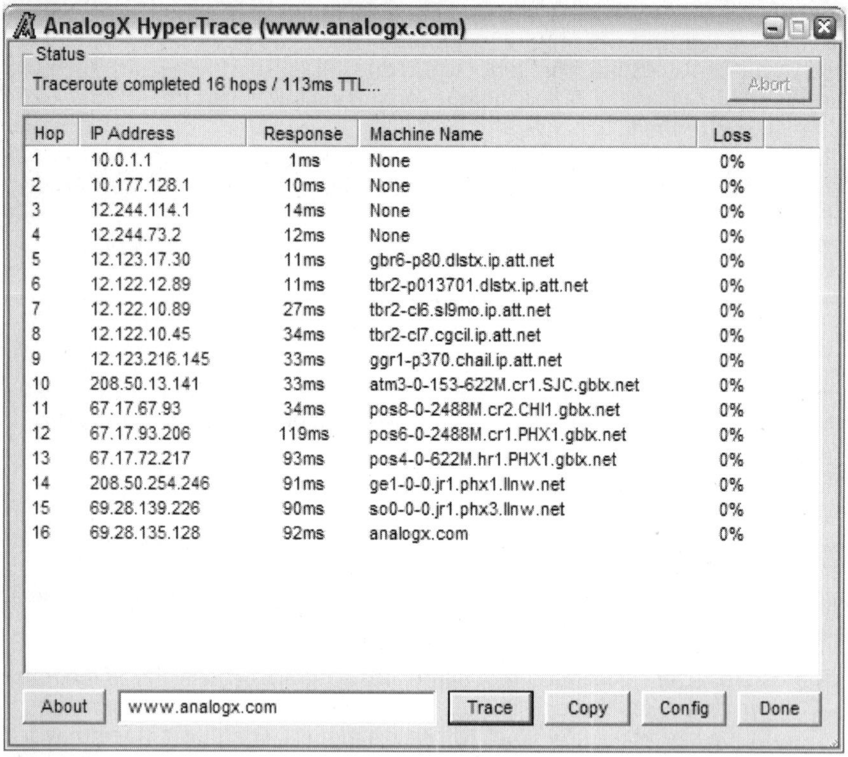

Figure 18-13: Identifying all the hops and skips between your computer and a remote host.

Of course, there's always a disclaimer. Speeds from much distance across the Internet are more a test of the bottleneck situation than of true speed. That's why I picked a speed test fairly close to me. Take a look at Figure 18-14 to see my speed test on a Sunday afternoon.

I found this test site by going to Broadband Reports, and clicking the Tests and Tools left menu. The resulting screen has a button at the top labeled Speed Tests.

One of the major Internet portals, CNet, also offers a speed test. They aren't near me so I figured the speed would show up slower than the closer test site. See Figure 18-15 to see how much slower.

Not quite as fast, is it? Conditions on the Internet change quickly, but most important, the more hops you go through the more chance for delay. Just like when you drive across town and catch traffic lights, isn't it? Except in the real world our delays are measured in quarters of an hour, not hundreds of a second.

Quick hit: Example sites

Here are a few speed test sites you might check out:

✦ www.testmyspeed.com

✦ www.cable-modem.net

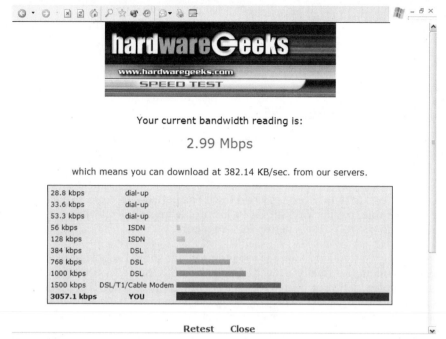

Figure 18-14: The test results from www.hardwaregeeks.com.

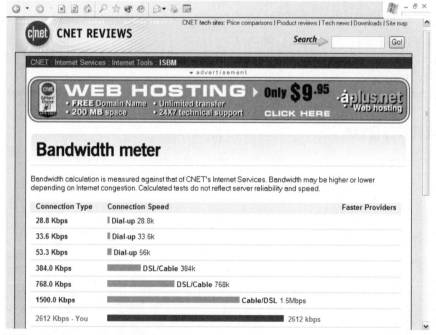

Figure 18-15: A remote test from Cnet.

✦ www.access-broadband-internet.com/broadband-speed-test.html

✦ 99 more tests: www.aerus.net/Bandwidth.htm

When All Else Fails

What happens when you know your broadband service provider has a problem and can't (or won't) fix it? You don't have too many other options, but you do have some.

Get local experts to help. Every city and town has networking experts available. They may be able to offer ways around your problem, or they may know of other service providers who have a better service record.

Start replacing equipment. Your broadband provider should supply your cable/DSL modem (for free or a few dollars per month) and suspect devices should be replaced. If your router seems to fight with your cable/DSL modem, you can try another router. That's the kind of service that a local consultant or network expert can provide using a test router so you don't have to buy one.

If worst comes to worst, you can change your broadband service provider. This isn't fun, but you have little choice. If you're using DSL, another independent DSL reseller may have better luck getting the local phone company to do its job. Or you may need to contract with the phone company directly.

Don't pay for bad service. If you can't get what you need from your current provider, switch and don't feel bad. They didn't feel bad messing you around, so you shouldn't feel bad waving goodbye.

Summary

Bad service makes everyone mad. Bad customer service makes everyone even madder. But mad, angry customers don't get good customer service from anyone.

Before calling customer service, go through the reboot procedures for all devices. Check your settings. Understand that the Internet sometimes clogs up, like any other highway, and give things a few minutes to settle down before calling technical support.

Make sure the problem is not on your side of the broadband connection before calling technical support. And even when the tech asks you to do things you've already done, do them anyway because for some reason that often helps.

When you're having a problem with your service provider, take it easy, focus on what you really want, and keep that goal in mind. Customer service ineptitude should not deter you from your goal. When you start to lose your temper, remember that although that's a natural reaction, it won't help you get your problem solved.

Eventually, you will learn to solve your own problems. That's the best customer service of all.

Troubleshooting Your Side of the Connection

◆ ◆ ◆ ◆

CHAPTER 19

In This Chapter

Chasing problems

Checking common mistakes

Looking at TCP/IP

Working with Windows9x/ME

Working with Windows 2000 and XP

◆ ◆ ◆ ◆

All the things that go wrong are not on the far side of your cable/DSL modem. Unfortunately, things go wrong on your side of the demarcation point, and you are the customer service representative for your network.

Luckily, when things jump the track a few common problems seem to be the culprits in many cases (changes due to newly-installed software, network configuration changes, and misbehaving applications). Once you learn how to deal with some of the common issues, you'll be able to solve the majority of your network problems.

These are the types of issues you will soon learn to troubleshoot and conquer:

◆ Physical connections

◆ Identifying out-of-control applications

◆ Network settings that changed

◆ Network link status

◆ Wireless connection weirdness

Troubleshooting goes much easier if you remember what I consider the most important rule: change *one* thing at a time. If that doesn't help, change it back and change something (one something only) and try again. The trying again part may be the second most important rule, because the best troubleshooters understand they may have to check a dozen settings before finding a resolution.

Common Computer and Network Problems

The first question to ask when a computer stops working is, what changed? Many times a software change of some type made a mess of something else, and your lovely computer is now an object of scorn.

Software changes can be as large and noticeable as installing a new application or as small as a minor upgrade to a utility program. Microsoft Windows updates fall into this blame bucket. Automatic updates are great, but when they clobber something else it's tough to uncover the cause of the problem and even tougher to fix.

> **Note** If you aren't sure if your Windows XP system is updating automatically, open Start ⇨ Control Panel ⇨ System and click the Automatic Updates tab. Here you can tell the system to not update at all, update automatically every day, or download updates and ask your permission to install those updates. The last option is the one I use, so I know when an update causes a problem.

Anytime you're surfing on the Internet and you accidentally download some application and things stop, you know what happened. Fixing that mistake takes more effort. Unfortunately, the relationship between loading something you shouldn't and seeing the effects are rarely that obviously linked.

System Restore Before You Need It

Windows XP Home and Professional include System Restore in an easy-to-use and reliable form. None of the system restore functions available through various methods in earlier Windows versions worked easily or all that reliably.

System Restore has a variety of options. Some are automatic, and some you can set. Make a habit of saving a system restore point before you install new software and you'll curse much less when an application doesn't work the way it should and clobbers your personal settings or network configuration.

Reach System Restore by going through Start ⇨ Programs ⇨ Accessories ⇨ System Tools and choosing System Restore. From the main screen you can restore your system back to an earlier restore point, or set a new restore point. Remember this step and do it before installing new software or making major configuration setting changes.

The only bad news is that System Restore requires hard disk space. If you're running low, be careful. You may have to turn off System Restore if it keeps reinstalling a system file that has been contaminated by a worm or virus. And please don't use this as a backup tool, or you'll be crying. Chapter 13 has the backup information, so use System Restore for installation recovery but not file protection.

Add anything to your computer? Even a new mouse with special drivers and programmable buttons can interfere with other software.

Did your antivirus application perform a live update? Turn the antivirus software off (but don't download anything when it's off) and see if your problem clears up. You may have to reboot your computer and leave the antivirus software off to make the ultimate test.

Tools for system examination

You might want to take a look at the Task Manager application. Shown in Figure 19-1, the Task Manager can be accessed by right-clicking the task bar at the bottom and choosing Task Manager from the context menu. You can also press Ctrl+Alt+Delete to summon Task Manager (with Windows 2000 you had to press Ctrl+Alt+Delete and choose Task Manager from that context menu, but now the shutdown options are in the Task Manager).

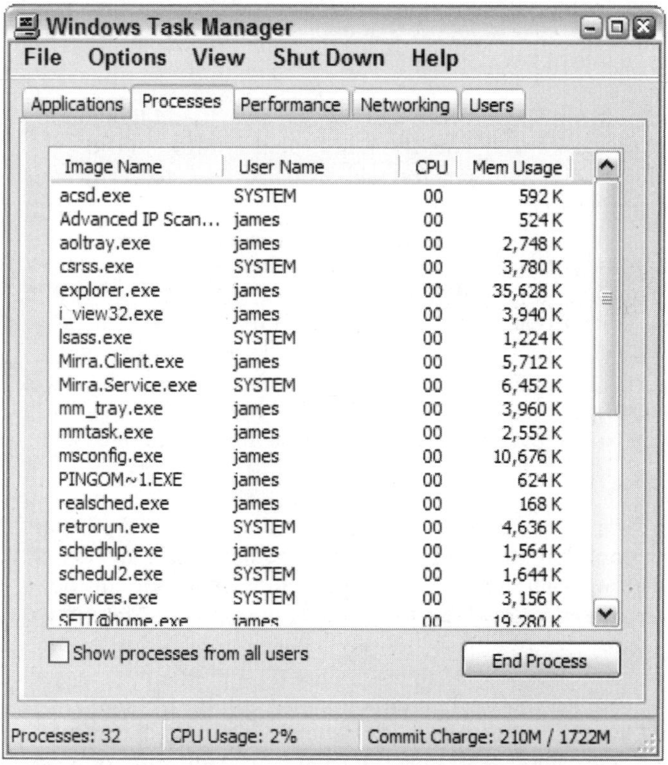

Image Name	User Name	CPU	Mem Usage
acsd.exe	SYSTEM	00	592 K
Advanced IP Scan...	james	00	524 K
aoltray.exe	james	00	2,748 K
csrss.exe	SYSTEM	00	3,780 K
explorer.exe	james	00	35,628 K
i_view32.exe	james	00	3,940 K
lsass.exe	SYSTEM	00	1,224 K
Mirra.Client.exe	james	00	5,712 K
Mirra.Service.exe	SYSTEM	00	6,452 K
mm_tray.exe	james	00	3,960 K
mmtask.exe	james	00	2,552 K
msconfig.exe	james	00	10,676 K
PINGOM~1.EXE	james	00	624 K
realsched.exe	james	00	168 K
retrorun.exe	SYSTEM	00	4,636 K
schedhlp.exe	james	00	1,564 K
schedul2.exe	SYSTEM	00	1,644 K
services.exe	SYSTEM	00	3,156 K
SETI@home.exe	james	00	19,280 K

Processes: 32   CPU Usage: 2%   Commit Charge: 210M / 1722M

Figure 19-1: The tasks running on my Windows XP Home PC.

The other pages in Task Manager are useful, but I find myself looking at this screen, Processes, most of all. All software modules from Windows and third parties show up here, along with applications and their helper files.

These processes are programs executing on the computer. Some of these you can recognize easily, such as the well-labeled `Mirra.Client.exe` and `Mirra.Service.exe` programs about halfway down the list. Those are the memory-resident programs used by the Mirra Personal Server discussed in Chapter 13. These two applications keep an eye on all your files and copy the changed files to the server automatically.

The list in Figure 19-1 is sorted by application name, although Microsoft calls it Image Name at the top of the list. When you click any of those headings (Image Name, User Name, CPU, or Mem Usage), the list sorts according to the information in that column.

Whenever something seems to be eating all my CPU cycles, I open Task Manager and click the CPU heading. This puts the highest CPU hog at the top of the list. When things are going well, that item should be the System Idle Process at around 90 percent. If a program is hung, monopolizing the CPU, it will appear at the top of the list.

Tech Bits Think of this as target practice: highlight the memory hog by clicking its name. This makes it easy to follow that application as it bounced around because the highlight bar stays on the name.

When you find the program sucking all your CPU cycles away and highlight it, you can then stop that process by clicking the End Process button in the bottom-right corner of the Task Manager. You will probably have to verify you really want to kill that process.

If you check the Applications tab for the Task Manager, you will see the names of primary applications running on your Windows system. If you know one of the applications is causing your problem, it may show up in that list as nonresponsive. If so, you can end that task using the End Task button.

Most often, however, a subprocess of an application will be causing your problems. The only way to find that process is to use the Processes page as shown in Figure 19-1.

Drilling down to more details for the services requires using a second program called MSConfig. A program that Microsoft doesn't advertise, MSConfig, helps you control all the startup parameters and show you more details about the processes for your computer. Figure 19-2 shows the main screen of MSConfig on Windows XP Home.

Booting problems and troubleshooting is tough. If your computer boots completely but doesn't act right afterwards, you can use MSConfig to try a diagnostic startup, or select which system services and configuration profiles are run during startup.

If you check the Services tab, MSConfig will show you manufacturer of all the services on your system. One handy option is to check the box labeled Hide All Microsoft Services so you can see just the third party services installed on your system.

If you check the Startup tab, MSConfig will show you the location of the files that launch the services during the boot process. Applications you never heard of may be spyware or virus related, and you can uncheck the listing for those services and boot without them to see if that solves any aggravating problems.

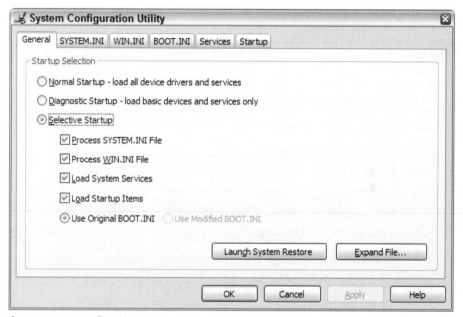

Figure 19-2: Configuring startup options on Windows XP Home PC.

Start MSConfig, which is officially the System Configuration Utility, by clicking Start ➪ Run and type **msconfig**. Alternately, you can go to the File menu on Task Manager and choose New Task (Run) to open the same text field in which you type **msconfig** to start the application.

The default is for the Normal Startup radio button to be clicked, but I clicked the Selective Startup to make the five listings underneath that option active. That made them dark enough to read in the screenshot.

This utility makes it possible to turn off a new driver or service (or driver launched by a serverice) you suspect of causing problems. You can also use this utility to launch System Restore from the command button in the bottom-middle of the page.

Bottom-up network troubleshooting

Some advocate the bottom-up method of network troubleshooting. There's a lot to recommend this, particularly because some of these items are easy to check.

Essentially, you want to start at the lowest, most basic part of the computer or network process and verify the easy things are done correctly. Whatever you think is the beginning level, go down more.

The "bottom" of this method is the bottom of the seven-layer protocol stack. Guess what's at the bottom: the physical layer. You want to make sure everything is connected to the appropriate device. Every plug goes somewhere, and taking the time at the start of your troubleshooting session to verify a plug didn't fall somewhere will save you time in the long run, I promise. This approach is like making sure you car has gas before calling the garage to get your engine repaired.

Go through the following checklist when a computer refuses to cooperate at all, or doesn't want to play on the network anymore:

- ❏ Is the computer plugged in?
- ❏ Is the monitor plugged in?
- ❏ Is the monitor brightness turned up?
- ❏ Is the monitor plugged into the computer?
- ❏ Are the keyboard and mouse plugged into the computer?
- ❏ Is the network patch cable plugged into the computer?
- ❏ Are all the hubs, routers, or switches still turned on?
- ❏ Is the network patch cable plugged into the wiring hub, switch, or router?
- ❏ Are the rest of the network cables plugged in on both ends?
- ❏ Are some computers working but not others?
- ❏ Are all the computers showing the same symptoms?
- ❏ Can the problem computer see any of the other network devices through My Network Places?
- ❏ Did your cat step on the keyboard?
- ❏ Have you replaced the cable in question with one you know works?
- ❏ Have you rebooted the computer in question? Completely cold-booted, where you turn it off for a full minute before restarting?

These things sound stupid, don't they? Every one has roots in real situations. I once drove across town in a snowstorm (granted, Dallas snowstorms aren't exactly Rocky Mountain blizzards, but still...) to turn the monitor brightness back up on a system. It took more time to slide across town than it did to figure out the problem by using the bottom-up method. That's when I became a convert to this process.

Cables must be plugged in to work properly, and mysterious forces will pull cables out at the strangest times. You may think it's demeaning to make sure a power cord still connects properly to the wall socket, but that's only because you haven't kicked a power cord out accidentally, then spent hours wondering what went wrong.

Look at the 10/100Base-T plugs on the computers. The connector should light up when signals are seen on the network (most plugs include at least one light). Corresponding light(s) should be active on the port of the connected hub or router. If one side is not lit, that side has a problem. If neither side is lit, try a new, known-working 10/100Base-T cable.

One thing you need to agree to right now: if you can find an easy workaround to a problem, you'll accept it. That sounds weird, but trust me this will make more sense after you read through this chapter.

Consultants sometimes quote two prices: one to get the system working again, and a second higher price to explain exactly what happened to cause the problem. Trying to understand why Windows or the network went screwy after it worked fine for weeks will only lead you to start pulling your hair out. When you can use Plan B to make things work again, don't let Plan A haunt you. Accept it and move on.

Common TCP/IP Problems

Once you're fairly sure the physical layer network details are under control (everything's plugged in and turned on), you can start up the protocol layers in TCP/IP. There are two critical things to check for TCP/IP at a client:

✦ TCP/IP is enabled and functioning in the client itself

✦ TCP/IP packets can get out of the clients onto the network.

Yes, TCP/IP can be working on the client although the network adapter (wired or wireless) isn't working. So there are several places to verify how TCP/IP is doing inside your computer and out to the world.

The first place to check is the Local Area Connection icon in My Network Places (Network Neighborhood in Windows 9x/ME). If things are working there, as they are in Figure 19-3, you're in good shape.

Reach this screen by clicking My Network Places ➪ View Network Connections ➪ Local Area Connection ➪ Status ➪ Support tab ➪ Details.

Some people may stop at the Local Area Connections Status screen, but that's not going far enough. Figure 19-4 shows the Status screen General page from within the linked windows shown in the previous figure.

It's nice to see that the network connection in Figure 19-4 is working and sending and receiving packets. But that doesn't tell me that those packets can get out to the Internet.

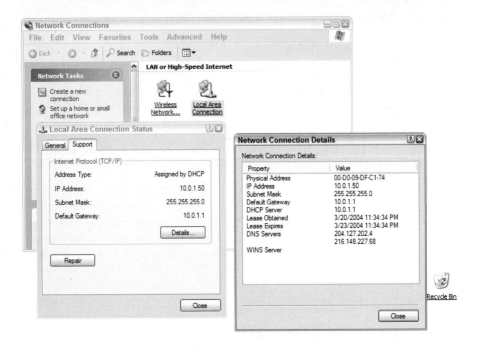

Figure 19-3: Complete network connection details.

Figure 19-4: The general status page for a local area connection.

The important details in Figure 19-3 in the Details window show the following:

✦ The connection has a valid IP address in the correct address range (from your DHCP server)

✦ The Subnet mask matches the rest of the systems on the network (from the DHCP server)

✦ The Default Gateway is the right address (the router connected to your cable/DSL modem)

✦ The DHCP server provided an address lease covering the time this display was checked

✦ DNS server IP addresses are listed

Your service provider's modem will send the Domain Name System (DNS) server IP address to your router, which should pass it on to your network clients along with an available IP address for your client. The IP address shown in Figure 19-3 must be within the range for your internal network, and will be assigned by your router/DHCP server. The time for the lease will be provided by your DHCP server at the same time.

If all these details are correct for a client your network should be working properly.

Checking inside your computer

First verify that your computer has an IP address assigned permanently to it, or has the correct instructions to receive an IP address from a Dynamic Host Configuration Protocol (DHCP) server. Figure 19-5 shows the Internet Protocol (TCP/IP) Properties window where you set that IP address choice. I suggest you use your router to supply internal IP addresses and hide the public address using Network Address Translation (NAT), so you should verify the setting here requests and IP address.

Reach this screen by going to My Network Places ⇨ View Network Connections ⇨ Local Area Connection ⇨ Properties. Highlight the Internet Protocol (TCP/IP) item in the middle section of the screen and then click Properties. When you click the Obtain An IP Address Automatically radio button you have a choice to set the DNS server address automatically (top radio button) or set a particular DNS server address (bottom radio button).

If you choose to supply an IP address in the top part, you must supply the DNS server address. You may use only a single DNS server address, but using two provides redundancy in case one goes down or slows down so much it might as well be dead. Requests for DNS support from the first server that go unanswered after about 3 seconds will fail over to the second choice without your knowledge or involvement

There are two more things to check in general for your client's TCP/IP health. Both of these require going to a DOS window (or CMD program) to run the ping

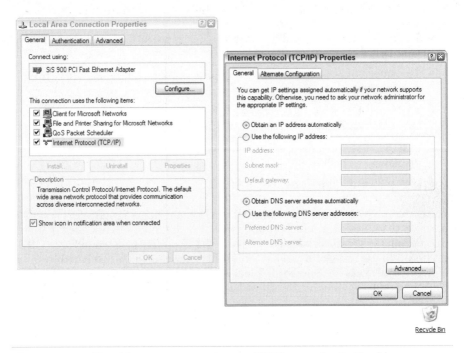

Figure 19-5: Telling this computer to rely on a DHCP server for its IP address.

program. Ping is a diagnostic utility that relies on the Internet Control Management Protocol (ICMP) standard that provides a way to sort of knock on the door of a network device and see if it's home. In other words, an easy tool to tell you that your computer's TCP/IP software is working correctly, that the remote device is alive, and the network connects the two of you. Figure 19-6 shows them both in two connected operations.

To open a DOS window, click Start ⇨ Run. Type **cmd** and then pressEnter.

Type **ping 127.0.0.1** first. The address 127.0.0.1 is known as the localhost and is the assigned IP address for the computer's internal network. You see, in the first part of the information in the DOS window that the 127.0.0.1 address responded to each ping.

The second task is to check the IP address of the network interface card used in the computer. Earlier I saw that this address was 10.0.1.50 (assigned by a DHCP server and shown in Figure 19-5). I pinged that address, and it told me the network interface board was operational.

Note Some Web sites turn off their response to pings as part of their security controls against hackers. Several of the diagnostic tools related to ping can be used to disrupt devices. If you don't get a ping back from a big company (www.ibm.com, for one example), that's the reason.

When things are going badly, and the computer's internal network or the connection to the rest of the world (and the DHCP server) is broken, Microsoft

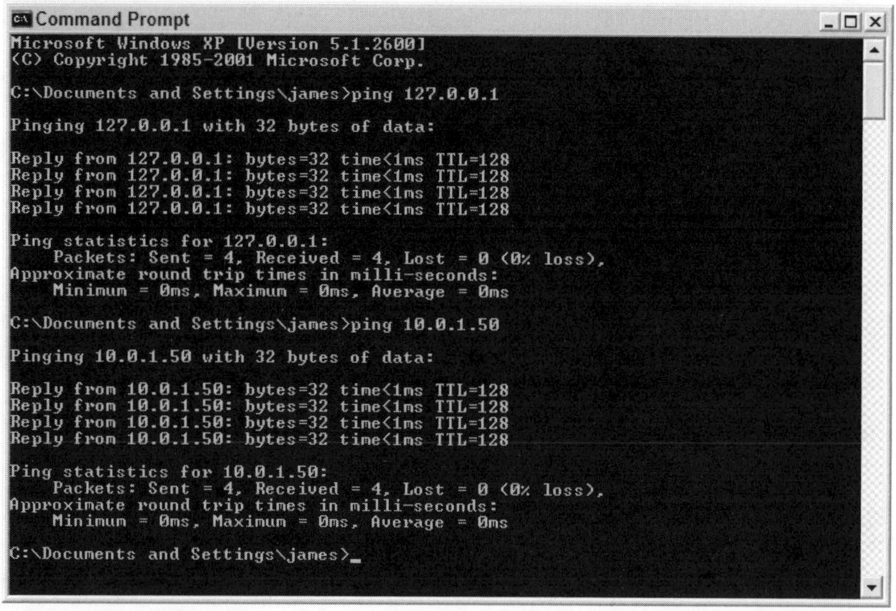

```
Command Prompt                                                    _□×
Microsoft Windows XP [Version 5.1.2600]
(C) Copyright 1985-2001 Microsoft Corp.

C:\Documents and Settings\james>ping 127.0.0.1

Pinging 127.0.0.1 with 32 bytes of data:

Reply from 127.0.0.1: bytes=32 time<1ms TTL=128
Reply from 127.0.0.1: bytes=32 time<1ms TTL=128
Reply from 127.0.0.1: bytes=32 time<1ms TTL=128
Reply from 127.0.0.1: bytes=32 time<1ms TTL=128

Ping statistics for 127.0.0.1:
    Packets: Sent = 4, Received = 4, Lost = 0 (0% loss),
Approximate round trip times in milli-seconds:
    Minimum = 0ms, Maximum = 0ms, Average = 0ms

C:\Documents and Settings\james>ping 10.0.1.50

Pinging 10.0.1.50 with 32 bytes of data:

Reply from 10.0.1.50: bytes=32 time<1ms TTL=128
Reply from 10.0.1.50: bytes=32 time<1ms TTL=128
Reply from 10.0.1.50: bytes=32 time<1ms TTL=128
Reply from 10.0.1.50: bytes=32 time<1ms TTL=128

Ping statistics for 10.0.1.50:
    Packets: Sent = 4, Received = 4, Lost = 0 (0% loss),
Approximate round trip times in milli-seconds:
    Minimum = 0ms, Maximum = 0ms, Average = 0ms

C:\Documents and Settings\james>_
```

Figure 19-6: This shows the results of pinging the internal IP address and then pinging the network adapter.

assigns an IP address to the computer for you. You will find this out when you can't reach anything else on your network or the Internet, and ping doesn't work out to other devices although it works internally to the local host address.

Unfortunately, the IP address makes no sense with any other network and is hard to reset. Figure 19-7 shows what happens if you start your network when a cable is missing.

Yes, that's the sign of network failure. When you see this, you will curse and sigh and start troubleshooting.

So far (ignoring the last figure), everything in this computer used as an example works fine. I'll show you options in the next few sections to pursue when things don't look this nice.

Checking outside your computer

The same ping command used to check your internal network available works outside as well. Figure 19-8 shows a ping of the network router (10.0.1.1) and an Internet site (www.BroadbandBible.com).

10.0.1.1 is the router on all my networks. Putting the router for the network at the first address number is a long network tradition that's hard to break. And because it provides an excellent starting place and locates the router on all networks, it's a good tradition to keep.

Figure 19-7: When you see the
Microsoft-assigned address, you have troubles.

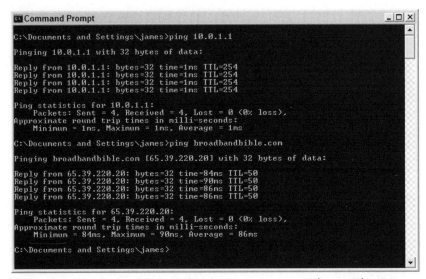

Figure 19-8: Another set of pings, this time to my router and out to the Internet.

Notice the response time for this connection: 1ms. That's the displayed time for
Windows XP, but the time is actually less than that on a small local network like
this one.

The second ping is out to the Internet. Notice that the ping command returned
the IP address of the Web site named in the ping. That can be handy as you'll see
in a bit.

Notice the response times for this connection: 84ms-90ms. Those numbers aren't too bad, and they're fairly consistent, which shows the traffic is flowing smoothly.

Going to the DOS prompt bothers some people, and the basic ping also lacks a discovery mechanism. That's why I searched for and found two third-party tools that make ping much more useful.

The first tool, Ping-O-Meter is from Obese Amadillo Software. Take a look at it in Figure 19-9.

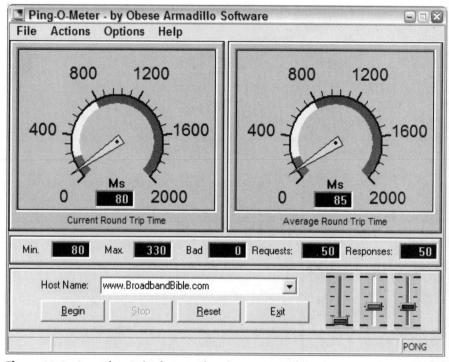

Figure 19-9: A much prettier face on the ping command.

Go to www.ObeseArmadillo.com or www.Download.com to download this free utility. This version offers multiple upgrades over the original, and even the earliest version makes ping more fun than ever before.

Take a look at the Min. and Max. numbers under the dials. Notice the Maximum dial is 330ms. You can see I ran Ping-O-Meter for 50 requests, and at least one round trip had a router hiccup somewhere that slowed down a packet by a factor of four. That happens, and doesn't indicate a problem for just a few packets. And because it's out somewhere on the Internet, you can't do anything about it anyway.

Because the ping command lacks a discovery mechanism, if you have a large network, or even a handful of network devices, tracking their IP addresses can be a pain. Do you write them down on a piece of paper you can lose? How do you find the ones assigned by your DHCP server until you ping each possible address individually?

You get Advanced IP Scanner from Famatech, LLC. (www.Famatech.com). Figure 19-10 shows the scanner at work on one of the test networks.

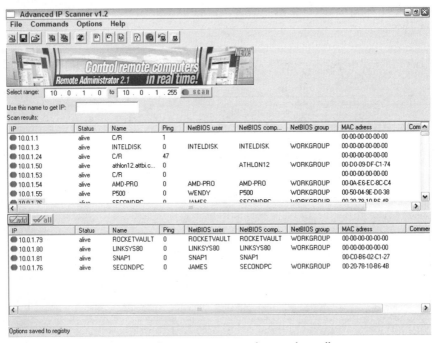

Figure 19-10: Finally, a ping discovery program that works well.

This application pings every address within the range you set (see the range setting just under the advertisement for Famatech's Remote Administrator package). Responses are further interrogated for details such as name, workgroup, Media Access Control (MAC) address, and comments listed on the system. You can right-click any live device and drill down for more details.

I don't need to do that in this situation. I'm only looking for computers that should be up and running and connected to the network. If I don't see a device I expect to see, I can go to that one unit and start troubleshooting.

DNS hiccups

When Domain Name System (DNS) service is not available to a client computer or it can't make connection to the DNS server at your service provider, you can do many things on the network, but you can't resolve names. DNS changes 64.68.6.131 (hard to remember) to www.SoundClick.com (easy to remember).

If you can't get to Web sites with a URL, but everything else looks good, try putting in just the IP address. If you make connection then, you know one of the following is true: You can find the IP address for a host by typing ping and the host name in a DOC command box as shown in Figure 19-8.

✦ Your listed DNS servers are unreachable.

✦ DNS isn't configured correctly on your client.

Of the two options, the latter one turns out to be correct more often than not because your service provider keeps their DNS servers available at all times. In this case, disable your network connection in the My Network Connections page (right-click on the Local Area Connection then choose Disable in the context menu). Then enable the device after about 30 seconds of delay by clicking the Local Area Connection icon.

Your computer should then make contact and get new information from the DHCP server on your network. If that doesn't work, your DHCP server is having a problem, which almost always means your router to cable/DSL modem connection is having a problem as well. That means it's time to read a book until your broadband service provider gets its part of the connection working again.

DHCP timeouts

Check your DHCP server for the default lease time if stations start doing weird things every few hours, or at the same time every day. Some applications and/or update levels of Windows don't do well when their DHCP lease expires and they must reclaim their IP address. Figure 19-11 shows an example of setting the DHCP lease time.

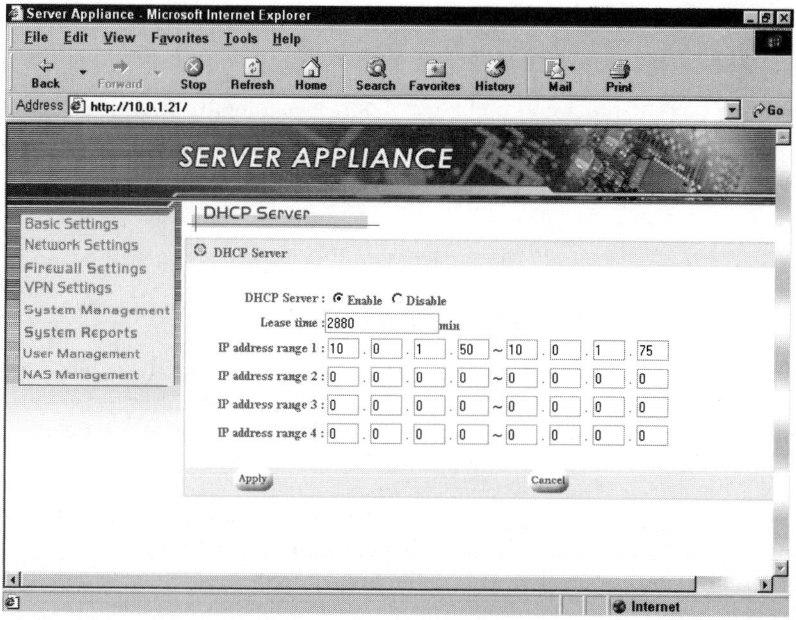

Figure 19-11: Setting DHCP lease time on the Tritton ASAP storage device/router.

This Tritton device sets the lease time in minutes rather than hours or days. An unfortunate trend today in many DHCP server devices is to set the default lease time to one day and not let you change that default. The way you find that disturbingly short lease time information is to check the client properties as in Figure 19-3.

If your DHCP server stops and a station tries to reclaim its lease, it will fail. Then the Microsoft IP default address will be applied and you'll know the DHCP service is the culprit.

Game playing and connection help

Vendors making networking products for home use understand that game players require some special treatment. Each vendor has some information about games and other applications that need a way through your firewall through specific port assignments. Some vendors, however, tend to give a bit more than others.

Netgear has a wealth of information. Go to `http://kbserver.netgear` `.com/main.asp` and Search for "games" for a complete listing. However, the Knowledge Base article n11495 may answer all your gaming questions: `kbserver.netgear.com/kb_web_files/n100495.asp`.

Just like Netgear, Linksys and SMC have information available. Follow these links:

✦ `http://kb.linksys.com/cgi-bin/om_isapi.dll?clientID=1358622` and search for "games"

✦ `http://www.smc.com/index.cfm?sec=Support&pg=Knowledge-Base&site=c` and search for "games"

The game maker has the most complete list of port assignments and other arrangements that must be made for gaming. But these few places are good ones to start with if you're having trouble. The Netgear link has the most complete listing of games and requested ports of all the major vendors I checked, so start there.

Common Wireless Problems

These can be aggravating, because your problem may be completely outside your network, and even outside your home or office. If your neighbor gets a new cordless phone and puts it on the wall nearest your office, your wireless network can head downhill fast. And how will you find that?

Only by the results of your worsening network situation. If you see a ham radio tower going up in your neighbor's back yard, you will know to look for interference. If not, you can only guess by the intermittent problems. Or get sneaky and test your network although you call your neighbor and see if the interference appears when he or she picks up their new cordless phone.

Let me go through a few of the common problems and provide some options for you to check to eliminate or work around the problem:

✦ **Problem (Interference):** Changing local conditions can disrupt a working network. A new phone or a microwave can wreak havoc on an 802.11b network.

- **Solution:** Change channels, move the router/access point (Chapter 15), and look for new electrical equipment of any kind.

✦ **Problem (Range):** Wireless troubleshooters, especially when adding or moving devices, must take range into account. Range in this case also includes walls or other obstructions, because they shorten range. Even moving the furniture in an office can change the wave patterns through the space and shorten range.

- **Solution:** Move the router/access station around, reorient antennas on clients and access points, and even look into adding external antennas to devices. Verify that all removable antennas remain well attached to their boxes, because a loose antenna doesn't cover as much range.

✦ **Problem (Encryption):** Changing encryptions keys can be trouble if there's a typo or missed setting in any one unit.

- **Solution:** When installing wireless networks, start with encryption off. Add encryption in phases and verify all wireless devices work properly before moving to stricter encryption methods.

✦ **Problem (Vendor incompatibility):** Yes, standards are supposed to eliminate vendor incompatibilities, but your network must function in the real world. Even name brand equipment using well-established standards may not work together. You can go crazy trying to figure out why.

- **Solution:** Easier to try another unit, and then the same brand on both ends of the connection, before you start redoing your entire network.

This short section just worries about the wireless-only connections. Protocol and other networking issues can affect wired and wireless performance equally.

When changing the wireless channels to try and avoid conflicts, here's a little good news: you only need to change the router/access point channels (if you're using Infrastructure mode). When in Infrastructure mode (the better choice over ad hoc mode as shown in Figure 16-5), the clients take their channel cue from their access point.

Don't trust Windows XP to manage the wireless adapter in your PC. XP keeps trying to show how it will be more efficient for Windows to run the client operating system and the client wireless device, but resist. XP doesn't show everything it knows about your local wireless network, and especially hides the details when multiple wireless network access points get involved. That's why I say use the wireless card's utility rather than trust Microsoft.

After traveling with a laptop, make sure you have reconfigured anything in your wireless connection profile you changed to connect while on the road. If you forget to change your wireless profile, you'll wonder why you can't connect back at home. Then you discover you're still trying to connect through the Bronx Zoo access point, and you're a long way from the Bronx.

Microsoft published a little tip that may be critical for your laptop configuration routine. If you use your Internet Connection Firewall (ICF) in Windows XP while traveling, check it when you return home. If you have ICF on for an adapter, that adapter will ignore all local network devices. In other words, your My Network Places will be empty. Another reason to use a different personal firewall on your laptop rather than trust the Microsoft included utility.

Windows 9x/ME Family

Microsoft added plenty of networking functionality to the Windows 9x family, but it's hard to appreciate that now that Windows 95 is long dead and Windows 98 is on life support.

One report from AssetMetrix Research Labs at the end of 2003 showed that more than 80 percent of all U.S. companies were still using at least one PC with Windows 9x/ME. Estimates in the range of 21 million Windows 95 users and 58 million Windows 98 users seem to be the consensus. In other words, about 20 percent of all desktop systems remain in the Windows 9x/ME family.

Yes, Microsoft has continued support for the Windows 9x/ME family longer than most software companies continue their support. But even Microsoft, rich as they are, don't really want to cut their ties for around 70 million users. And Microsoft has tried everything to get these people to upgrade yet hasn't been able to do so.

You will find that wireless products do not always come with Windows 9x/ME drivers anymore. If they do include those drivers, check the dates on the files. I bet they're the oldest drivers included with the wireless product.

Why you should upgrade

Much technological water has gone under the bridge since Windows 98 appeared. Your network can use many of those advances, so seriously consider upgrading.

 Refer to Chapter 11 to remind yourself why you should upgrade. Then do so and save yourself some aggravation.

I installed Windows 2000 Professional on an old Dell laptop with a Pentium 166 MHz (the original Pentium, not Pentium II or Pentium III) and only 32MB of RAM. If I can get Windows 2000 Professional running on that machine, you can almost certainly upgrade any Windows 98 systems you have to at least Windows 2000.

Do you enjoy rebooting your computer? With Windows 98, you must reboot every time you make a change to any of the network configuration options. Every time. Not only that, you almost always have to supply the original Windows 98 files from the CD to finish the configuration. You can have the files on a network drive so you don't have to have the actual CD on hand, but the process remains slow and aggravating.

One of the nice advantages of Windows XP Home and Professional is the System Restore utility. Windows XP takes a system "snapshot" now and then of your working system and saves that. If you add a program that messes up your configuration, you can rollback to a known good point.

Even better, you can specify when to make a snapshot. Going to try something risky? Then take your snapshot before you start the installation process. If anything goes wrong, rollback and start again. Very handy.

The standard Windows 9x/ME DHCP client support (Get an IP address automatically) does not always support getting your DNS server addresses from the DHCP server. If those server addresses change, your client will work fine inside your network but will be unable to connect to Web sites across the Internet. You may well forget this, because all other DHCP clients (Windows 2000/XP, Linux, and Macintosh) properly grab the DNS servers from the DHCP servers. Lagging behind in the Windows 9x world will complicate your troubleshooting.

Haven't you done something worth celebrating lately? If so, buy yourself a new computer as a reward. It will make life easier in a variety of broadband ways.

Check Your Patch Levels

If you're not going to upgrade, at least get the latest patches and updates from Microsoft. They won't be nearly as current as those for later operating systems, but get the latest ones you can.

A few critical security updates will no doubt continue to be released, although Microsoft regularly threatens to stop patching the Windows 9x/ME family. Whenever you have a problem, cross your fingers and check the Microsoft support pages for updates.

Checking processes

In another example of progressing by stepping sideways, Microsoft changed the way you check processes considerably between Windows 98 and Windows 2000. You can stop processes easier in Windows 2000/XP, but you can see more details about them in Windows 98.

Figure 19-12 shows the Windows 98 version of the Processes display. Here it's called Running Tasks, and you can't stop a process from this screen.

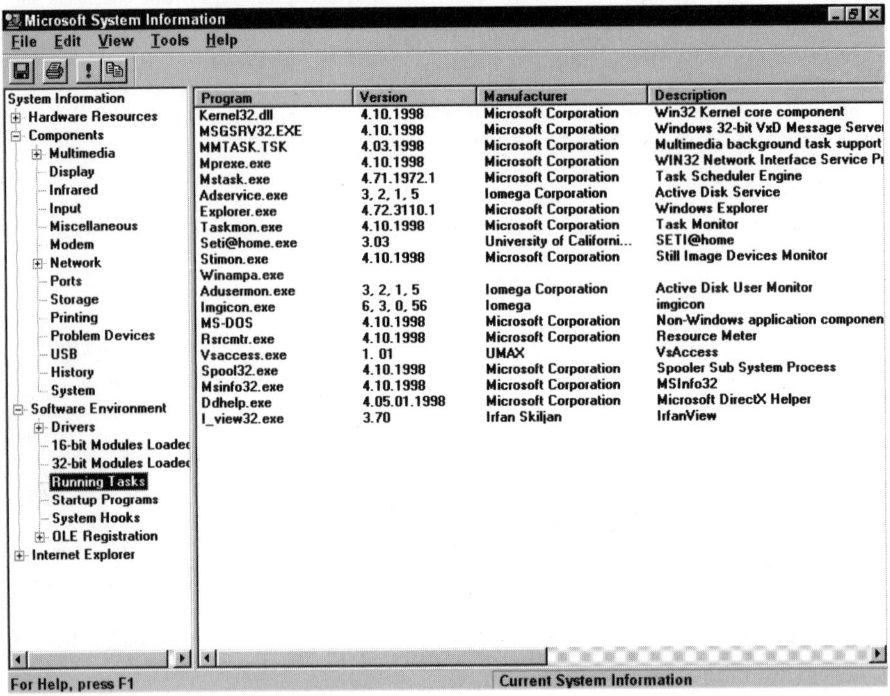
Microsoft System Information
File Edit View Tools Help
System Information
Hardware Resources
Components
Multimedia
Display
Infrared
Input
Miscellaneous
Modem
Network
Ports
Storage
Printing
Problem Devices
USB
History
System
Software Environment
Drivers
16-bit Modules Loaded
32-bit Modules Loaded
Running Tasks
Startup Programs
System Hooks
OLE Registration
Internet Explorer
Program Version Manufacturer Description
Kernel32.dll 4.10.1998 Microsoft Corporation Win32 Kernel core component
MSGSRV32.EXE 4.10.1998 Microsoft Corporation Windows 32-bit VxD Message Server
MMTASK.TSK 4.03.1998 Microsoft Corporation Multimedia background task support
Mprexe.exe 4.10.1998 Microsoft Corporation WIN32 Network Interface Service Pr
Mstask.exe 4.71.1972.1 Microsoft Corporation Task Scheduler Engine
Adservice.exe 3, 2, 1, 5 Iomega Corporation Active Disk Service
Explorer.exe 4.72.3110.1 Microsoft Corporation Windows Explorer
Taskmon.exe 4.10.1998 Microsoft Corporation Task Monitor
Seti@home.exe 3.03 University of Californi... SETI@home
Stimon.exe 4.10.1998 Microsoft Corporation Still Image Devices Monitor
Winampa.exe
Adusermon.exe 3, 2, 1, 5 Iomega Corporation Active Disk User Monitor
Imgicon.exe 6, 3, 0, 56 Iomega imgicon
MS-DOS 4.10.1998 Microsoft Corporation Non-Windows application componen
Rsrcmtr.exe 4.10.1998 Microsoft Corporation Resource Meter
Vsaccess.exe 1. 01 UMAX VsAccess
Spool32.exe 4.10.1998 Microsoft Corporation Spooler Sub System Process
Msinfo32.exe 4.10.1998 Microsoft Corporation MSInfo32
Ddhelp.exe 4.05.01.1998 Microsoft Corporation Microsoft DirectX Helper
I_view32.exe 3.70 Irfan Skiljan IrfanView
For Help, press F1
Current System Information

Figure 19-12: Quite a bit more information here, but less control than in Windows XP.

Check out the normal processes listing when your Windows 9x/ME system is running correctly (hurry before you have to reboot). When something goes wrong that you can't find elsewhere, see if a rogue process has appeared in here. Viruses show up here, as do memory-resident programs like spyware. Neither are fun, and you didn't ask for them. Do delete them.

Reach this spot by going through Start ➪ Programs ➪ Accessories ➪ System Tools ➪ System Information. This page shown is the Software Environment, Running Tasks display.

Under the Tools heading in this screen you can find System Configuration. That's MSConfig. Click there to open the MSConfig application (or run msconfig from a DOS prompt).

Figure 19-13 shows the Windows 98 MSConfig. Once again I clicked the radio button for Selective Startup so more of the options would be active and viewable.

Your only option to control the running processes is to go to the Startup tab on MSConfig and choose what to start or not start. That's one good way to make sure something weird with the network is bothering the PC, rather than the other way around. Stop various programs from loading and compare what starts then with what starts when all the modules are rolled into the startup. This

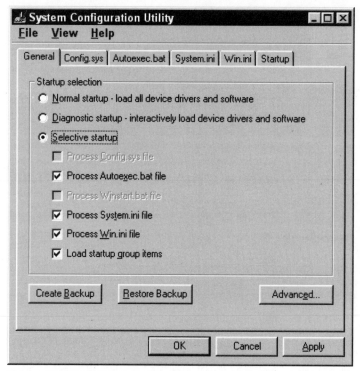

Figure 19-13: MSConfig in Windows 98.

method doesn't work all that often, honestly, but you can try loading everything interactively with the Diagnostic Startup option and see what kills the booting process. When the computer hangs again, the last thing you loaded is the problem.

Many people suggest you check out error messages at Microsoft Support's Web site. Feel free, and start here: http://support.microsoft.com/ default.aspx. However, Microsoft doesn't update the Windows 98 section with new troubleshooting messages anymore, so your chances of success are even lower than they usually are. In other words, if you go searching around Microsoft's Knowledge Base you're one step away from reinstalling your operating system or trying a restoration from the backup tricks you learned back in Chapter 13.

WinIPConfig

Another example of Microsoft progressing to the rear is the lack of WinIP Config (winipcfg) past Windows 9x/ME. Would be nice to have this in Windows XP, even if you have to reach it through the DOS command line as you do in Windows 9x/ME. WinIPConfig provides a quick look at all the network protocol information that Windows XP provides through the six or seven clicks through various menus to reach the display shown in Figure 19-3.

Figure 19-14 shows the TCP/IP networking protocol information through the WinIP Configuration program. Start this by going to Start⇨Run. Type **winipcfg** on the DOS command line that appears and press Enter.

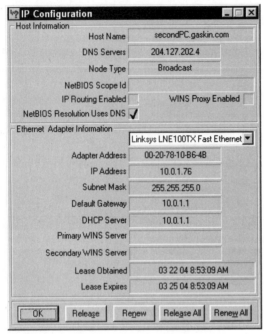

Figure 19-14: A nice graphical display of Windows 9x/ME network information.

You can choose any of a number of network-enabled connections from the drop-down list in the Ethernet Adapter Information field. AOL adds some, other network applications add some, and the TCP/IP adapter list can get pretty full.

Notice Microsoft provides some NetBIOS details, such as the computer name. It would be nice if it showed the workgroup here as well, but them's the breaks.

Use WinIPcfg to verify your IP address has been assigned properly and your gateway and DHCP lease is in decent order. If the gateway listing is wrong, for instance, you won't have any luck getting to the Internet, even though you can use your browser within your own network.

Windows 2000 and XP

Windows 2000 may look more like Windows 9x/ME than it does Windows XP, but there are enough advantages over Windows 9x/ME that I consider Windows 2000 the minimum acceptable modern Windows operating system. If you have Windows 2000, don't feel the need to rush out and upgrade.

The added bonus of complete vendor support for Windows 2000 and XP helps, as well. All the developers now focus on Windows XP, which is backwardly compatible (for the most part) with Windows 2000. If your application calls for Windows 2000, it will almost always work on Windows XP. If it calls for Windows XP, it will probably work on Windows 2000.

Check your patch levels

Microsoft has announced (Spring 2004) that the successor to Windows XP, Longhorn, will be out, absolutely, in 2005. Oops, make that 2006. Absolutely guaranteed, says Microsoft. Of course, everyone in the technology business knows that a date announced this far in advance for a major upgrade from Microsoft will slip at least one year past their absolutely guaranteed date. That means Windows XP will be the main application for us all until at least 2007.

Get used to patching and repatching your operating system. I'm torn about the automatic update process and can't say yea or nay with enthusiasm either way. The convenience is great, until an upgrade clobbers an application. Then the time you saved through automatic updates, and much more besides, goes into repairing your system.

On balance, I recommend automatic updates for nontechnical people. Why? Because they are less likely to remember to upgrade themselves. So unless you (honestly) remember to check with Microsoft on a set date every month for updates, you should turn on the automatic update process in Windows XP as shown at the beginning of this chapter, or go to `http://v4.windowsupdate` `.microsoft.com/en/default.asp` on any Windows version to scan your computer and get the necessary updates.

When something goes even a little screwy, check for updates again. Microsoft wants to ration the updates to once a week, but that doesn't always work. In addition, Microsoft has a habit of pulling updates, adding different features to the updates, then putting them back out there and claiming they never touched them. Sometimes all this is the best possible advertisement for consultants on retainer or Linux. Or maybe both.

Get your operating system up to date whenever you have a minor problem and you may keep it from becoming major. Then you can argue with your vendors about patches messing you up rather than begging for patches that haven't been supplied.

Checking processes

The processes list in Windows 2000/XP are less descriptive but more manageable than in Windows 9x/ME. To open the display, right-click the Taskbar and choose Task Manager. Then click the Processes tab to see a display much like the one in Figure 19-15.

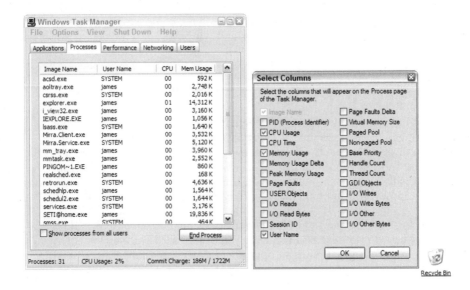

Figure 19-15: The Processes display for Windows XP.

You can choose how to display the processes by clicking the column heading. I use either the alphabetical option (as shown) to better find processes, or arrange them by memory usage.

The second window, Select Columns, opens when you click View ➪ Select Columns. The defaults work most of the time, but if a help desk person asks you to search for one of these numbers, you know where they are.

Take a look and see if anything in your systems screams virus or spyware. Sort on the CPU percentage used and see which process is stealing all your cycles. That may be the virus, or at least it will be the screwed-up program you need to stop. Unlike Windows 9x/ME, the Windows XP version of Processes doesn't offer a way to print out the list or otherwise track the details.

IPCONFIG

There are two ways to see the information about your IP protocol in Windows 2000/XP: run ipconfig from a DOS command line or check out the details in your Local Area Network connection. If you prefer the graphical approach, refer to Figure 19-3. If you still remember (and like) a DOS prompt, open a DOS window and type **ipconfig/all** to show the information in Figure 19-16.

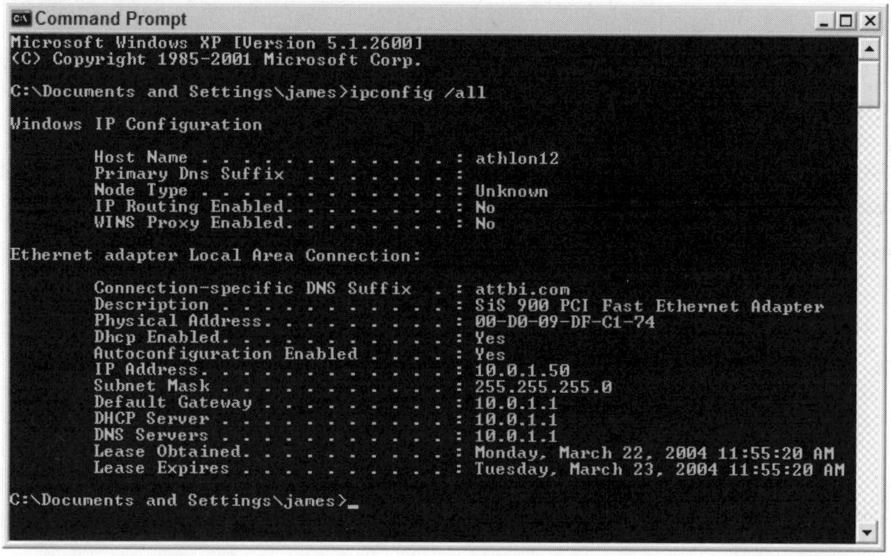

Figure 19-16: Complete ipconfig information for Windows XP.

Notice the information looks quite a bit like that from the Windows 9x/ME listing. But instead of a graphical utility, Microsoft retreated to a DOS window. Oh well, who can fathom the unfathomable mind of Microsoft?

This shows the DHCP lease time, which helps if you're having some odd disconnect problems. It shows that the DNS server is the gateway. Some routers like to do that, and cache some of the DNS information for the local network. As long as your clients can get to the Web and refer to sites by their names, you're in good shape.

Checking Your Router Settings

Problems on your part of the network include the router connected to your cable/DSL modem. Different routers obviously have different administration screens, but let me show you a few places where I've had to do some troubleshooting while researching this book.

For security, always check the level of firewall settings you have available on your router. Figure 19-17 shows the default settings for the Linksys WRV54G router.

Some network hardware, particularly wireless routers and access points from Microsoft, want to configure the network for you. The process for this is network Universal Plug and Play. I turn this off the first time I configure a piece of network equipment, because if there's a problem with a router or other device after another device changed the settings without telling anyone, how will I ever find and fix that problem?

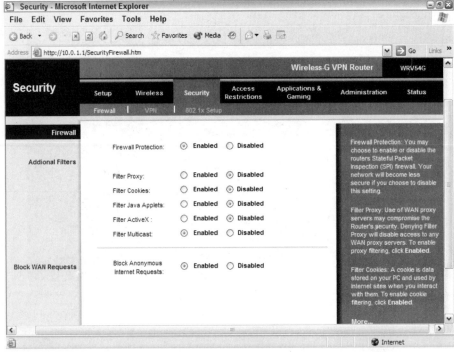

Figure 19-17: Turn on the firewall, and block anonymous requests (pings).

Universal Plug and Pray Not Usually an Uplifting Experience

Perhaps Universal Plug and Play will improve. Perhaps all vendors will coordinate every UPnP command so there's never a mistake on my network. Perhaps my hair will stop turning gray and start growing back.

UPnP will get better (before my hair grows back in, at least). However, the idea that any vendor of any hardware or software device on my network can change configurations on other devices makes me nervous. When UPnP works, with Microsoft operating system and Microsoft routers in a small network, it doesn't save much time at all. And when it doesn't work, you waste an enormous amount of time tracking down what went wrong.

That's why I call this Plug and Pray. It's more alliterative than Plug and Curse.

Figure 19-18 shows the UPnP disable setting for the Linksys router shown in the previous figure. The UPnP settings locations vary depending on the manufacturer, but check out the security or advanced settings first in your search.

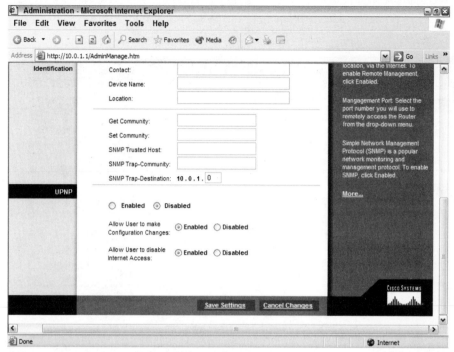

Figure 19-18: UPnP is disabled using the radio button so network devices can't shut down Internet access without my knowledge.

The router status is a good screen to keep an eye on. If you don't see your DNS server addresses (at the bottom of Figure 19-19) or there is no IP address in the Default Gateway on the broadband service provider portion of the network, you know the problem is outside your network.

The router software version may be worth keeping an eye on as well. Upgrades to the router firmware (the internal software that runs the router) add new features and fix old bugs. Upgrading the router software on a regular basis may help keep some of the potential network problems at bay. And if you're talking about network problems, keeping them somewhere besides your network is always a good goal.

Summary

Things will go wrong on your network. No network or network manager, is immune from this sad fact of life.

Remember bottom-up troubleshooting and make sure the easy things are right. Plugs are in, devices are turned on, and the monitor is turned up. Remember to make sure your network protocol software is running by using internal computer

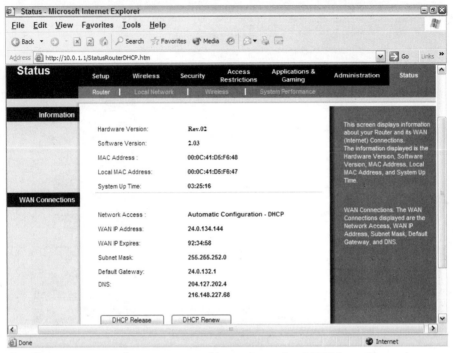

Figure 19-19: Status of a router to a cable modem using DHCP from the service provider to gather the information on this screen.

tests, local network tests, and then Internet tests. Most of all, remember what software or hardware changes you made that could have caused the problem.

Remember to check only one thing at a time. Nothing wastes more time than adding to your problems during troubleshooting, so change only one thing at a time.

Remember you can dial up when your broadband connection is down. Remember to update your operating system.

Remember that Windows XP System Restore really will help your computer recover if you mess up an installation or the new application messes up your configuration. Everyone deserves a second chance, and System Restore gives that to you.

At least now you'll have an idea where some of the information you must check and modify is hidden on your computer and the router. I just hope you don't see all this very often. You look like a nice reader who deserves smooth sailing through the world of networking.

Quick Hits Roundup

Music Sites: Listen and Download

GarageBand: Discovering the best independent music

www.GarageBand.com

GarageBand.com does a good job showing the most popular tracks in each main genre with their Charts pages. Many of the songs allow you to download an MP3 file for personal use. GarageBand also makes it easy to find CDs for sale by groups, it shows whether they have live gigs planned (although those don't seem to be up to date), and you can leave messages for the artist or group. The site also helps you find groups who "sound like" another band.

SoundClick: What a click!

www.SoundClick.com

Perhaps the most popular of the music sites after the unfortunate demise of MP3.com, SoundClick appears to be chasing that market full tilt. They promise to create playlists so people can string together their favorite tunes, like MP3.com did, and they now show the number of plays a tune has gotten.

CDBaby: A little CD store full of independent music

www.CDBaby.com

Built by a working musician trying to market his own music, CD Baby now showcases nearly 55,000 CDs, all straight from the artist. You can listen to tracks CDs, search genres you like, and crank up your PC speakers.

Internet Underground Music Archives

www.IUMA.com

The Internet Underground Music Archive (IUMA) started in 1993, one of the first music sites on the infant WWW. Also includes a streaming radio station, and a strong focus on offering multiple tracks from every artist. Free MP3 downloads, streams in MP3 or Real format, links to CD sales and the like.

Vita-minic: download all the free music you want

www.VitaminiC.com

Connected to IUMA, VitaminiC offers much more international exposure and song protection by using Windows Media format files.

Ampcast: another site to try to fill the hole from MP3.com

www.Ampcast.com

Another artist-oriented site, Ampcast started in 1998 and already includes playlists to gather favorites together. They stream plenty of tracks, provide downloads, and sell CDs directly or direct you to other sites.

Acid Planet: your world of music (especially if you use Acid music software)

www.AcidPlanet.com

One of many sites sponsored by music tool vendors, this Sony-owned site to showcase artists using their products. In this case, Sony now owns Acid Pro and Sound Forge, among others.

BeSonic (English and German)

www.BeSonic.com

Not only another music product vendor (TerraTec sound hardware), BeSonic offers a ton of European groups (TerraTec is a German company). Their excellent Mood Radio screenshot is at the beginning of this section. They also provide a visually cool artists "cube" to help locate groups playing the type of music you want. Many artists provide a playlist of their favorite BeSonic artists, offering another way to get some interesting connections to different artists.

ArtistLaunch: The sound of independents

www.ArtistLaunch.com

Pretty self-explanatory, but this site adds some nice touches with a CD catalog listing CDs for sale by genre. The graphics are large enough to actually see the CD cover, an unusual idea for many sites.

DMusic: Your digital music oasis

www.DMusic.com

Yet another artist promotion site, with an icon by songs to let you send a friend a link to that song. Clever marketing.

Streaming radio sites:

> www.Shoutcast.com
>
> www.GrooveRadio.com
>
> www.RantRadio.com
>
> www.ThePavedEarth.com
>
> www.SomaFM.com
>
> www.DI.fm
>
> www.AccuRadio.com
>
> www.RadioIO.com
>
> www.NetRadio.com

Video Sites: Stream or Download

Although the computer has yet to supplant the TV as a great place to view films, there are plenty of sites offering video that works just fine on your computer. In a few more years with a bit more hardware, you will be able to stream broadband video directly to your TV, but not yet. However, many companies use computer-based training, which includes video and audio clips. More fun than training films, however, are the Web sites filled with interesting video stories you won't see on your TV anytime soon, so enjoy them on your computer now.

Mainstream and advertising supported

Atom Films: Instant entertainment

www.AtomFilms.com

Originally independent and pushing the Internet bubble, AtomFilms.com is now owned by Macromedia, the people who make Shockwave and Flash. Still edgy, since Macromedia appeals to many creative people, AtomFilms.com is a fun place to visit.

IFilms, including Instant iFilm

www.iFilm.com

Another edgy entry, iFilm.com includes more adult short films than you may want your children to view. But the Rated R ones are still funny or thought provoking, or both. Some of the famous short films that have been e-mailed around the Internet started here.

Guide to new and upcoming movies and DVD releases

www.Movies.com

Not edgy, unless you think movie trailers for R movies push the boundaries of good taste. But when you hear about a new movie through the grapevine, the trailer is usually here waiting for you.

Music TV

www.MTV.com

Used to be edgy, now alternately mainstream, corporate, tired, greedy, or historical. But there are a ton of music videos here, and few things on the Web benefit more from a broadband connection than music videos.

All major network television Web sites

ABC, CBS, NBC, CNN, and even Fox offer plenty of streaming video, although most from the "TV rerun" closet. The news sides of the major networks often include video from other parts of the world not shown on network television often.

Corporate

Apple: See the new iPod ads

www.Apple.com/Quicktime

Apple computers didn't invent multimedia computing, but don't say that to a Macintosh fan unless you want to fight. The QuickTime player is a must-have, even when you already have Windows Media Player and Real Player on your system.

A broadband test drive

www.Edmunds.com

Yes, a car magazine site. Look to the bottom of the home page for the Video section, and enjoy car videos almost never seen on TV or anywhere except a dealership. Enjoy them at home without a salesperson bugging you to sign on the line.

Odd and thrilling (and funny) independent

Award winning sites from all over

www.WebbyAwards.com

This group picks the best of the Web each year and shows the winners and runner's up. Not all of these are videos, obviously, but the ones they have will amaze you. They are all actual award-winning sites and you will agree the level of quality rises far above any site collection you've seen before.

Music videos, film, music, anime and others

www.Sputnik7.com

Music videos you won't see on MTV.com, and short films you won't see on the other film sites.

Laugh at some strange things

www.Spongi.com

Cable access meets the Web. No clue who is behind this, or what the site hosts are thinking (or smoking). That's a joke, because some of these videos are hysterical.

Laugh a little more, eh

www.alldaybreakfast.ca/

Sketch humor translated successfully to the Internet. Canadian humor loosed upon the world.

Webcam Sites

A Webcam network

www.earthcam.com

Shows some of the most interesting webcam sites I've ever seen, including an office in Tehran and www.antcam.com.

Watch the rain in Spain

www.tvweather.com/tv_cams.htm

Weather cams galore.

High-end Webcams

www.axis.com/

This is the company who made the cameras for the check cashing monitoring project. They also sell many of the traffic cameras and other used in public places.

Broadband telephones

www.vonage.com

One of the first companies to offer VoIP products to the consumer and small business market.

Game Sites

everquest.station.sony.com/

www.blizzard.com/

www.unrealtournament.com/

www.ubi.com/US/

www.gamespot.com/index.html?reflash=1

games.yahoo.com/

General Support Sites

Clearing house for broadband information and rumors

www.broadbandreports.com

www.opentechsupport.net

www.howtocomplain.com

www.verizonpathetic.com

www.sunflowerbroadband.com/internet/config/troubleshooting.html

www.complaints.com

Speed Test Sites

www.testmyspeed.comwww.cable-modem.net

www.access-broadband-internet.com/broadband-speed-test.html

Compendium

www.aerus.net/Bandwidth.htm

Additional Web Directory Listings

There needs to be some place where Web sites that don't fit easily into the flow of a chapter can be listed, so this is it. Many times, a site is slightly off the track of the chapter narrative, so putting it in the chapter doesn't fit well. Other times a site may have some valuable information on the topic, but the site itself focuses on a different topic.

Sometimes, I find sites doing my research that don't exactly fit, but are too cool to forget and ignore. So here they are, organized by topic.

Reference Sites

The Web encyclopedia for technology

www.webopedia.com

Obviously slanted toward technical areas, but the host (www.Internet.com) includes a wealth of other content, including a Small Business Computing Essentials area.

The TechEncyclopedia

www.techweb.com/encyclopedia

Presented by competing magazine publisher CMP, this encyclopedia site often includes diagrams and other linked information.

The standard for real-world encyclopedias now online

www.britannica.com/

Anyone not regard the Britannica as one of the leading real world reference sources for the past 50 years or more? Now they're online.

Institute of Electrical and Electronic Engineers

`ieee.org`

If you want the detailed scope and the product is electrical or electronic, you can find it here. Or, at least find the standards the product is supposed to follow.

Broadband everything (almost) here

`www.broadbandreports.com`

This site has more information about more broadband providers than any other I found. If you have a question and this site doesn't have the answer, you have a tough question.

DSL-Related Sites

The "official" DSL site

`dslforum.org`

The DSL Forum would like you to believe they are the official site, but I think there are many other definitive DSL site options out there. At least this is a good place to catch up on global information.

DSL for consumers

`www.dsllife.com`

The DSL Forum's view of the world of DSL for consumers.

More DSL specifics in depth

`www.dsl-services.info`

Another site with plenty of information about various flavors of DSL and working with your provider.

Cable-Related Sites

National Cable & Telecommunications Association

`www.ncta.com`

Read what the cable industry says about itself.

Cable modems galore

www.cable-modems.org

More information about cable modem innards than I ever thought existed.

Cable modems galore again, and more

www.cable-modem.net

Another site full of information about cable modems and other home networking help.

Entertainment Sites

Customize your streaming radio

www.epitonic.com/radio.jsp

An interesting site with a different presentation model.

Modern alternative rock

www.wazee.org/

Lots of undiscovered artists, some undiscovered talent, and forums to talk about both.

More independent music

www.musicianmp3.com/

This site offers streaming radio and plenty of information about the bands, including a 1–10 rating system for tunes.

Music lists deep and cheap

www.musicrebellion.com

An interesting approach to selling online music. This site varies the price based on music popularity. Popular music is 90 cents, or even a little more, per song for download. Some music, especially independent artists, can be had for a nickel or dime per song. I found the Greatest Hits of the Chad Mitchell Trio for a dime a song.

Linux Desktop Information Sites

Run Linux on your PC

www.desktoplinux.com

Collection of information, software, reviews, advice, arguments, and fascinating advancements in the world of running Linux on your desktop. I guarantee that a Linux desktop package for less than $100 will give you everything that Windows XP Professional and Microsoft Office System will give you, and you'll have fewer problems.

Linux questions answered

www.linuxquestions.org

More people in the Linux community take time helping new users than in any computer community I've ever seen. If you have questions, they will help you.

A small business guide for Linux on the desktop

www.reallylinux.com/docs/desktop.shtml

Good overview article about moving your small business to Linux. Save money, save time, work smarter. A good combination.

Wireless Sites

WiMax subscribers in NY, Boston, Chicago, and other cities

www.towerstream.com

This company has working WiMax installations in multiple northeast cities. I interviewed the cofounder for a story in Network World's NWFusion Small Business Technology site (see my link at www.gaskinguides.com).

WiMax news and information

www.wimaxforum.org/home

Expect many more WiMax information sites to appear as 2004 turns into 2005.

The European world of wireless standards

www.etsi.org/

News of wireless implementation in Europe, where many countries are more conducive to wireless advances than is the U.S.

Get in touch with the universe (they say)

www.wi-lan.com/

A dealer site, but full of interesting links, products, and information about broadband wireless.

Personal Area Network wireless

www.wimedia.org/

This group wants your pants pocket devices to talk to your shirt pocket devices without wires. Any maybe your shoe phone, too.

Wireless LAN security

www.drizzle.com/~aboba/IEEE/

The official title is "The Unofficial 802.11b Security Web Page." How's that for irony? But there are more security tips here than in most places.

Security Config

www.securityconfig.com

More tools for the paranoid. I just hope they aren't tools for the stalkers as well.

Steve Gibson's products

www.grc.com

Outstanding products, including free security checking software. Well worth a regular visit.

Security options for businesses

www.criticalsecurity.com

Plenty of information and products for companies working to improve their security profile.

Security Sites

The Government's site

cybercrime.gov

Your tax dollars at work helping to fight cybercrime.

The encyclopedia of computer security

www.itsecurity.com

More security information than you want to read at any one time, or the nightmares will keep you up as they kept me from sleeping.

Maximum security for a connected world

www.antionline.com

Less establishment and more street, this security information strips away any veneer of safety you may think you have when computing.

Political Sites of all Persuasions

The recording industry

www.riaa.com

Amazingly clueless group who should stop suing their customers and figure out a way to harness the demand for online music for the good of their artists and the fans.

Defending freedom in the digital world

www.eff.org

The antidote to groups like the RIAA who are trying to force obsolete intellectual property ideas onto new technology.

Political commercials

www.bushin30seconds.org/

A Web site created for the MoveOn.org contest to find a commercial that CBS refused to air during the 2004 Super Bowl. Maybe if CBS had put this on the air, people would have had something to talk about beside Janet Jackson.

Challenging the status quo

www.moveon.org

The group that sponsored the contest for the Bush in 30 Seconds commercials. Too bad they got less exposure at the 2004 Super Bowl than Janet.

Miscellaneous Sites

Advocates for Fiber to the home

www.ftthcouncil.org/

They want more fiber in our broadband diet. Good for them.

The many paradoxes of broadband

www.firstmonday.org/issues/issue89/odlyzko

Scholarly article with questions, answers, and though-provoking arguments.

Broadband, Internet, and Networking Definitions

◆　　◆　　◆　　◆

In This Appendix

Broadband acroynyms

Glossary of
broadband terms

◆　　◆　　◆　　◆

Acronyms

ADSL: Asynchronous Digital Subscriber Line

AOL: America OnLine

BLEC: Building Local Exchange Carrier

BWA: Broadband Wireless Access

CLEC: Competitive Local Exchange Carrier

CO: Central Office

CPE: Customer Premises Equipment

CPU: Central Processing Unit

CSMA/CA: Carrier Sense Multiple Access/Collision
Avoidance

DDNS: Dynamic Domain Name System

DHCP: Dynamic Host Configuration Protocol

DLC: Digital Loop Carrier

DOCSIS: Data Over Cable Service Interface Specification

DMT: Discreet Multi Tone

DMZ: Demilitarized Zone

DNS: Domain Name Service

DSL: Digital Subscriber Line

DSSS: Direct-Sequence Spread-Spectrum

EFF: Electronic Frontier Foundation

FCC: Federal Communications Commission

FTC: Federal Trace Commission

FTP: File Transfer Protocol

FTTP: Fiber to the Premises

FWB: Fixed Wireless Broadband

GHz: Gigahertz

HDSL: High Speed Digital Subscriber Line

HDTV: High Definition Television

HTML: HyperText Markup Language

HTTP: HyperText Transport Protocol

ICF: Internet Connection Firewall

ICS: Internet Connection Sharing

IDSL: ISDN Digital Subscriber Line

IEEE: Institute of Electrical and Electronic Engineers

ILEC: Incumbent Local Exchange Carrier

IP: Internet Protocol

ISDN: Integrated Services Digital Network

IEEE: The Institute of Electrical and Electronics Engineers

IP: Internet Protocol

IPSec: Internet Protocol Security

ISP: Internet Service Provider

LAN: Local Area Network

LOS: Line of Sight

MAC Address: Media Access Control Address

MB: Megabyte (one million bytes)

Mbps: Megabits per second

MHz: Megahertz

MSN: Microsoft Network

NAS: Network Attached Storage

NAT: Network Address Translation

NLOS: Non Line of Sight

OFDM: Orthogonal Frequency Division Multiplexing

Ping: Packet INternet Groper

PON: Passive Optical Networking

POP3: Post Office Protocol version 3

POTS: Plain Old Telephone Service

PPPoE: Point-to-Point Protocol over Ethernet

PPTP: Point-to-Point Tunneling Protocol

RADIUS: Remote Authentication Dial-in User Service

RBOC: Regional Bell Operating Company

RIAA: Recording Industry Association of America

RJ11: Registered Jack-11

RJ45: Registered Jack-45

RTF: Rich Text Format

SDSL: Synchronous Digital Subscriber Line

SLA: Service Level Agreement

SMTP: Simple Mail Transfer Protocol

SNMP: Simple Network Management Protocol

SSID: Service Set Identifier

T1: A digital data line of 1.5 Mbps

TCP/IP: Transmission Control Protocol/Internet Protocol

TOS: Terms of Service

UDP: User Datagram Protocol

UTP: Unshielded Twisted Pair

URL: Uniform Resource Locator

VPN: Virtual Private Network

WAN: Wide Area Network

WEP: Wired Equivalent Privacy

WISP: Wireless Internet Service Provider

WLAN: Wireless Local Area Network

WPA: Wi-Fi Protected Access

WWW: World Wide Web

Glossary

10Base-T, 100Base-T, 1000Base-T: Wiring standards to support Ethernet over twisted pair wiring in increasing speeds from 10 Mbps, 100 Mbps, and now 1 Gbps for 1000Base-T

802.11a: Wireless standard for 54 Mbps bandwidth in the 5 GHz frequency range

802.11b: Wireless standard for 11 Mbps bandwidth in the 2.4 GHz frequency range

802.11g: Wireless standard for 54 Mbps bandwidth in the 2.4 GHz frequency range

802.1x: Standard detailing methods of authenticating a users at the edge of a network

address: A unique identifier on the network, most often the number assigned to the network card by the manufacturer. It may also refer to memory location in an operating system. IP addresses (such as 204.251.122.48) are identifiers for systems on the Internet or other TCP/IP (Transmission Control Protocol/Internet Protocol) networks

analog: A signal that is continuous, and normally represented in a form that emphasizes a range of settings

application: A software program, which may or may not use the available network resources

backup: A copy of hard disk information made to a tape system, optical disk, or another hard disk. A backup is used more often to recover from accidents than from catastrophes

bandwidth: The amount of data that can be sent or received in a set amount of time

broadband: High speed data access of at least 200 Kbps downstream

buffer: Memory area set aside to hold temporary data until the data can be accepted by either the workstation or network

cache buffer: A server memory buffer that improves performance by keeping recently used files in server memory. Often used in Web servers or by service providers to cache information from popular Web servers

central office: Telephone company switching station

communication protocol: Rules governing the sending and receiving of data between two machines

configuration: Details concerning the physical or software components of a system and how each is instructed to work with the other pieces of the system

demarcation point: The physical point in the link from a service provider where responsibility for maintenance passes from one party to the other

device driver: Software that connects a system's operating system to the system's hardware, such as a disk or network controller

Digital Subscribe Line (DSL): A technology providing high-bandwidth over ordinary copper telephone lines. Aimed primarily at residential and mall-business customers, DSL offers a wide range of speeds (144 Kbps to 6 1Mbps) depending on distance and line quality

digital: Distinct measurements of values but not the points in between

disk partition: A hard disk section treated by the operating system as if it were a separate drive

Domain Name Service (DNS): A service developed in the early 1980s to automate the previously manual editing of host files on Internet-connected systems. DNS allowed the number of hosts to double each year, and it is still the directory service in use on the Internet and the World Wide Web

Dynamic Host Configuration Protocol (DHCP): A protocol used to provide IP address and other configuration details from available IP addresses. DHCP is an update of the Bootstrap Protocol (BOOTP)

Ethernet: Bus-based network standard used by the majority of homes and businesses today

firewall: Hardware and/or software sitting between a private network and a public network

File Transfer Protocol (FTP): An Internet protocol that permits transfer of files between dissimilar clients

FTP server: Server software that allows remote clients to place and retrieve files from the server, generally over the Internet

HomePlug: The standard for running Ethernet over electrical wires within a home or business

HomePNA: Home Phoneline Network Association, a group of vendors coordinating standards to ensure their products work together

HyperText Markup Language (HTML): A standard set of "markup" symbols or codes inserted in a file so that when it is displayed by a Web browser, it appears formatted properly regardless of the client operating system

HyperText Transfer Protocol (HTTP): An Internet protocol designed to allow the exchange of text, graphics, and multimedia information between an HTTP Web server and a Web browser client

Institute of Electrical and Electronic Engineers (IEEE): A professional society of engineers and scientists. This society has numerous standards committees that control and promote network standards such as 10BaseT, Ethernet, and the 802.11 family of wireless standards

Integrated Services Digital Network (ISDN): A set of standards for providing digital data service over ordinary telephone copper wiring. A Basic Rate ISDN line provides data rates from 64 to 138 Kbps. The ISDN channels can be used for data, voice, video, or link management

Internet backbone: The highest level of connection network between all the other large networks that make up the Internet

Internet Control Management Protocol (ICMP): The standard that defines diagnostic utilities and tools for TCP/IP networks

Internet Protocol (IP): Part of the TCP/IP (Transmission Control Protocol/Internet Protocol) protocol suite. IP makes a best-effort attempt to deliver packets but does not guarantee delivery. TCP is required for that guarantee

Internet service provider (ISP): An organization that provides connectivity to the Internet as well as other Internet services, such as mail and Web server hosting

IP address: The four-byte address, which must be unique in the entire Internet if connected, that identifies host network connections. Normally seen in the dotted-decimal format, such as 204.251.122.12. Internet committees oversee IP address coordination and distribution

latency: Delay over a data transmission line for a signal's round trip

Linux: A Unix-like operating system created by a worldwide group of volunteers and packaged for convenience by some software companies but also available free in most cases if you download it from the Internet

Local Area Network (LAN): A network connected by physical cables, such as within a floor or building. Wireless networks are usually called WLANs, but the mixing of connection options is blurring that distinction and now many people call the network a LAN no matter what types of connections are used

localhost: Standard IP address, 127.0.0.1, used as an internal address for each network device for troubleshooting and references for software on that device

malware: Generic term for malicious software, including viruses, worms, and Trojans

modem: Originally short form for MOdulator-DEModulator, to turn digital computer signals into analog sounds for transport over a voice telephone link. Now it refers to any box connecting computers to a communications link

msconfig: Microsoft System Configuration utility

Network Attached Storage (NAS): A specialized server providing access to storage separate from any file server. Includes a cut-down operating system that just controls file access through common protocols like Windows networking, TCP/IP, SMB, and AppleTalk

Open Systems Interconnection (OSI) **model**: A reference model for the layering of common functions in a telecommunications system. This model consists of seven layers that define how an ideal network operates. These layers include Application, Presentation, Session, Transport, Network, Data Link, and Physical

open systems: Technically, a goal of guaranteed interoperability between disparate operating systems. Marketing has recast this term to mean any system that can be coerced to communicate with TCP/IP (Transmission Control Protocol/Internet Protocol). Realistically, open systems utilize Internet and Web technologies to support any client connecting to any server

packet: A block of data sent across the network; the basic unit of information used in network communications. Service requests, service responses, and data are all formed into packets by the network interface card driver software before the information is transmitted. Packets may be of fixed or variable length. Large blocks of information will automatically be broken into appropriately sized packets for the network and reassembled by the receiving system

password: The most common security measure used in networks to identify a specific, authorized user of the system. Each user should have a unique password, and each network resource should require a password

peer-to-peer: Communications from one station directly to another station without a server of any kind in the middle

ping: Diagnostic utility to check network connections between devices and that a remote device is awake and functioning

port: Address location in software

Post Office Protocol v3 (POP3): An Internet protocol for retrieving e-mail from a mailbox located on a server

Powerline: Another name for HomePlug Ethernet over electrical wiring

Program: A software program, which may or may not use the available network resources. Also referred to as an *application*

proxy server: A server that acts on behalf of others, such as for caching Web content

Public Key Infrastructure Services (PKIS): A service that allows developers to take advantage of a public/private key infrastructure rather than writing their own public/private key systems

public key/private key security: An encryption mechanism that employs two unique keys for encrypting data. The publicly available key is used to encrypt the data, and the private key is used to decrypt the data. The public key cannot be used to decrypt data that it has previously encrypted

restore: To replace a file or files from the backup media onto the server hard disk. This is done when the file or files on the server hard disk have been erased or corrupted by accident (most commonly) or when an entire disk's worth of files needs to be replaced after a disk failure

router: A hardware and/or software device that links two or more networks and sends data packets to the correct network based on the packet's destination address. The router maintains tables of available routes and forwards the data packet on toward the destination based on the optimal route. Routers function at the third layer of the OSI model

Secure Sockets Layer (SSL): Program extensions created by Netscape that manage the security of data crossing a network by encrypting the data. SSL can be implemented between many different types of clients and servers, including Web browser and mail clients

Simple Mail Transfer Protocol (SMTP): An Internet protocol standard used for transporting e-mail messages across the Internet from SMTP clients to SMTP servers

spam: Commercial not requested by the receiver, and often obnoxious, indecent, fraudulent, or all three

subnet mask: An IP address technique used to differentiate between different TCP/IP (Transmission Control Protocol/Internet Protocol) networks. Each client must have a subnet mask, so it will know the exact network address range. The format is in dotted decimal. The most common subnet mask is 255.255.255.0

switch: A hardware device connecting multiple networks that separates traffic based on packet addresses

Transmission Control Protocol/Internet Protocol (TCP/IP): The primary, industry-standard suite of networking protocols, and the only protocol allowed on the Internet since 1983. TCP/IP is built upon four layers that roughly correspond to the seven-layer OSI model. The TCP/IP layers are process/application, host-to-host, Internet, and network access.

Transmission Control Protocol (TCP): The Internet protocol that provides reliable, connection-oriented delivery of data between a client and a server. TCP requires that a connection be negotiated with the client and the server first; then it requires acknowledgments of data transmitted

Trojan: A malicious program hidden inside a benign program

virtual circuit: A communications connection that creates a complete, unbroken link between endpoints

virus: An application that reaches your computer surreptitiously and causes some problem there

warchalking: Marking a public space to indicate access to a private wireless network

wardriving: Traveling through a public area with equipment used to find and connect to other people's private wireless networks

Web server: A software system based on HyperText Transfer Protocol (HTTP) communications to send HyperText Markup Language-enabled (HTML) documents to Web client systems

wide area network (WAN): A network that communicates long distance across nonphysical media, such as public or private telephone lines, satellites, or microwaves. Traditionally, a WAN includes modems connecting different LANs (local area networks) across leased data lines

Wi-Fi: Wireless Fidelity

WiMax: Wireless Broadband, and the 802.16 standard

winipcfg: A graphical protocol display utility in Windows 9x/ME

winipcfg: DOS-based TCP/IP information utility

Index

Index

Continued